Solaris™ Solutions for System Administrators

Solaris™ Solutions for System Administrators

Time-Saving Tips, Techniques, and Workarounds

Sandra Henry-Stocker

Evan R. Marks

Wiley Computer Publishing

John Wiley & Sons, Inc.

NEW YORK · CHICHESTER · WEINHEIM · BRISBANE · SINGAPORE · TORONTO

Publisher: Robert Ipsen

Editor: Robert M. Elliott

Managing Editor: Micheline Frederick

Associate New Media Editor: Brian Snapp

Text Design & Composition: North Market Street Graphics

Library of Congress Cataloging-in-Publication Data:

Henry-Stocker, Sandra, 1949–
    Solaris solutions for system administrators : time-saving tips, techniques, and
  workarounds / Sandra Henry-Stocker, Evan R. Marks
      p. cm.
    "Wiley Computer Publishing."
    ISBN 0-471-34810-4 (pbk. : alk. paper)
    1. Operating systems (Computers)   2. Solaris (Computer file)   I. Marks, Evan R., 1964–
  II. Title.

QA76.76.063 H476 2000
005.4'4769—dc21

                                                            99-055645

Printed in the United States of America.

10 9 8 7 6 5 4 3

To the Boogie Man and the Possum for having the courage to pull me from the recycle bin.

—SANDRA HENRY-STOCKER

To my wife Jodi, without whom I could never have accomplished this task, and in memory of my sister Darci, who taught me that positive thinking is a way of life.

—EVAN R. MARKS

CONTENTS

Sandra Henry-Stocker is the author of *Solaris 2.x: System Administrator's Guide* and wrote a column on systems administration for *SunExpert* magazine for eight years. She was on the Board of Directors of the Sun User Group for six years and has been administering Sun systems for fifteen years. She also speaks at conferences and teaches classes on Unix systems administration and network security. Sandra is currently Lead Systems Engineer at Confluent, Inc.—a wholly owned subsidiary of E*Trade (E*Group).

Evan R. Marks was on the Board of Directors for the Sun User Group for three years and served as Vice President for two. He has over ten years experience in systems administration in manufacturing, electric utility, financial services, and health care. He has written articles and spoken at Unix conferences. Evan is currently in charge of the Web Engineering group at Aetna in Hartford, CT.

About the Contributors

Bob Damato has worked as a Sun system administrator since 1988 when he was responsible for what was then one of the largest Sun Networks on the East Coast at Southern New England Telephone. Since then, he has been involved in network design (WAN and LAN) and Unix administration. Eventually he moved to the ISP side and became their Webmaster. In April 1998 he started working at Advo Systems as their Senior Unix Administration person and also the corporate Unix security person.

Jeff Ruggeri is currently employed as a Solaris system administrator at Aetna in Middletown, CT. He has been hacking Unix in one form or another since he was about 13. His interests include randomness and searching for enlightenment.

Basic Strategies

The network is the computer. More than a catchy phrase, this slogan (which Sun coined back more than a decade ago) describes a fundamental reality of computing today: The location of data, processing, and services are not as important as how and when these resources are used. With advances in the Web, we might even say, "The Internet is the computer". The systems we manage have evolved into portholes to a universe of information and tools. Basic software applications are increasingly Internet-, intranet-, and Web-centric.

But how do we manage our systems and networks to best effect this reality? How do we effect this reality and keep our systems and networks manageable? What kind of foundation do we need to lay locally so that the layers of complication wrought by services provided internally and externally go down smoothly and reliably? Our users are sending e-mail around the globe. Our networks are comprised of ever-changing configurations of new and aging systems. Our responsibilities as systems administrators now often incorporate network configuration, security, Webmastering, performance monitoring and debugging in addition to the standard fare of software installation, account and printer management, and backups.

Everything in this book is intended to move you in the direction of the manageable network—to introduce you to tools and provide you with strategies that will help you manage your systems.

No one can manage infinite complexity. And, if anyone could, that person would likely be smart enough or "interesting" enough that he or she wouldn't want to. Those of us who have been in the business of managing large networks for a while understand that it is far easier to manage several hundred systems that are all the same than half a dozen that are all different. These two scenarios represent opposite ends of the spectrum with respect to homogeneity and heterogeneity. However, most of us are managing networks of systems that are somewhere in between these all-the-same and all-different models. Regardless of where you sit on the spectrum, you will find that your job will be easier and your life more pleasant in direct proportion to the degree of uniformity you can introduce into the environment that you manage. The more you can configure systems and services more or less identically, the easier a time you will have in every phase of managing them—from installation to backups.

At the same time, there are a number of services that you will provide on your network that will exist on only one or a small number of systems. The servers on which they run provide unique or near-unique services to your network as a whole. Though you will want to provide some redundancy for any service that is critical to your organization's operations (e.g., name services and e-mail), you will undoubtedly prefer to have these services run centrally on systems that are well under your control.

You may, at times, find yourself participating in the debate over whether it is better to install critical network services on the most powerful and reliable computer system on your network or to run each critical service on a separate computer system. Though there are no clear winners in this argument, we discuss each approach and give you our recommendations on how to build reliability and availability into your network while keeping it manageable.

Of all the strategies that we suggest to you within the pages of this book, the best is one that we've borrowed from the Boy Scouts:—Be Prepared. Regardless of how carefully and wisely you lay out your network and configure your systems and services, something will break. Adopting a policy of planning for disaster, of thinking through all the what-if scenarios that you can imagine, will help reduce your stress as well as your down time when one of these disasters actually happens.

How to Read This Book

If you are familiar with systems administration but new to Solaris, we recommend that you read this book from cover to cover to give yourself a solid framework. Even if you're a seasoned Solaris sysadmin you should still skim all chapters, since we've crammed this book full of tricks and strategies that we've learned in our roughly 30 years on the job that we think will help simplify and streamline your work. If you're new to the topics of DNS or security——the chapters in this book should give you a strong foundation. Very few chapters in this book, however, are not themselves the topics of entire books. We encourage you to pick up other texts to reinforce and expand upon what you learn here. Take a look at our bibliography and visit our Web site for recommendations

Above all else, remember that there is no substitute for doing. To the extent possible, put what you learn to immediate use. This is the only way to fully understand any complex topic. Through the challenges that you encounter, you will earn your stripes and become confident of your skills and insights.

What's in This Book

This book is organized as a series of chapters divided into four major technical areas.

Part One: Setting Up Your Solaris Infrastructure

Part One covers basic network services as well as installation issues. Our goal in Part One is to help you make decisions on the basis of your overall network so that your systems will be easy to manage—whether you have several systems or several thousand. Chapter 1 covers file systems from the ground up. One of the most important assets of today's organizations, file systems can become the source of your most severe performance problems and your most nagging maintenance nightmares. Chapter 2 discusses backup and restore operations. Chapters 3 and 4 cover booting, system diagnostics, and run states. In these chapters, we describe the environment and commands available to you on a system that is halted. We go on to describe how you can modify the processes that start up and shut down as the system moves from one run state to the next. Chapters 5 and 6 discuss installation and patching. For sites with numerous systems of the same basic architecture, the material on JumpStart should give you a solid understanding of what you need to do to take advantage of this tool. After investing some time in setting up your systems to support JumpStart installation, you can install system after system with minimal effort. Chapters 7 and 8 cover naming services—DNS, NIS, and NIS+. These chapters provide overviews of how these services work, their configuration, and troubleshooting.

Part Two: Managing Your Systems

Part Two takes you to the next step—what do you do when your systems are up and running? Chapter 9 describes monitoring tools and approaches to keeping track of the health of your systems. It discusses network management software and what you can expect it to do for you. It logically addresses each step in the process of setting up your own monitoring—deciding what needs to be monitored, deciding how you want to be alerted when something goes awry and setting up monitoring tasks. Chapter 10 identifies file systems, system daemons, and configuration and log files that play an important role on a Solaris system. Chapter 11 suggests that you automate as much as is reasonably possible. On a busy network, something is always breaking and some never-seen-before problem is around every corner. To the extent that you automate the repetitive tasks, you'll have time for the intriguing ones. Chapter 12 covers basic system security. It describes the services provided by inetd and the process of turning services on and off. It includes many suggestions on services that we think you should turn off and why. Chapter 13 describes approaches you can take to ensure that your systems are up and usable most of the time.

Part Three: Looking After Your Hardware

Part Three provides information on Sun hardware. Chapter 14 covers hardware maintenance. It addresses some of the things that you should know regardless of whether or not you are responsible for hardware maintenance. Chapter 15 explains the setup and configuration of printers and modems. Chapter 16 describes the E10000 system. Also called Starfire or abbreviated E10k, the Starfire is Sun's most amazing server yet. It's like other Sun systems—and it's very different. If you're blessed with one or wondering if you'd like to be, this chapter will tell you a lot that we've learned about this awesome box.

Part Four: Surviving in the Real World

Part Four addresses two critical issues in today's networks—managing the threats and opportunities presented by connecting to the Internet and coping with heterogeneity. Chapter 17 describes the concerns that the Internet presents. It describes network services as well as Internet security issues. Chapter 18 describes tools and techniques for coexisting with the Evil Empire—and some smaller, less-dark empires, as well.

Appendixes

Last, but not least, the appendixes in this book should not be overlooked. Appendix A includes some of our favorite Web sites, many with tools and links of their own. Appendix B lists some additional resources on NIS+. There is also a glossary of terms relating to Solaris systems administration, and a Bibliography and recommended reading list.

What's on the Web Site

We also welcome you to visit our Web site at www.wiley.com/henry. We will periodically update it with corrections, additional tips and tools, suggestions, and scripts.

## PART ONE

Setting Up Your Solaris Infrastructure

No matter what anyone tells you (even us!), systems administration is as much an art as it is a science. Were you to systematically gather all the relevant facts before embarking on the task of setting up your systems, you would *still* encounter problems. Some systems would be overused, and some underused. Some disks would fill to the brim while others would be rarely used. Small projects would end up taking enormous amounts of time while major ones would come to run themselves. The problem is simple—things change. The needs of the users change, the software on the system changes, hardware breaks, upgrades arrive, people come and go, people change their minds, and estimates are only estimates. The best you can do is to configure your systems so that you can work in spite of the flux. In spite of all this, we still cling to the Boy Scout motto: Be Prepared!

Let us assume that the goal is not to avoid problems, but rather to have processes and procedures in place that force them to approach you in single file (no pun intended). The manageable network is not one that runs flawlessly, but one in which there is time and capacity enough to resolve each problem without major disruption.

In this initial part of the book, we provide our thoughts and suggestions to help you accomplish this goal. We make suggestions about automating your system installation and patching by using JumpStart. We encourage you to plan file systems with reliability, security, performance and manageability in mind. We provide insights into naming services such as DNS and Sun's NIS and NIS+. We detail the Solaris boot process as it moves from cold hardware to fully operational. We describe Solaris run states and provide instructions on modifying the processes that start or shut down automatically. We discuss PROM level diagnostics that you can use to isolate problems.

We don't live in the world of infinite budgets and patient users, waiting for every problem to occur like the Maytag repair man. We assume you don't either. We're not sitting in front of a pile of brand new systems in an office space not yet filled with people and activity. We assume you're not either. Our networks are not comprised entirely of Solaris servers and Solaris clients. We assume yours are not either. We want leisure hours, happy families, and personal down time. We assume you do too. Our vantage point is that of system administrators with too much to do, working in an environment where change is the only thing that remains a constant. We hope you will find something in this section to make setup and management of your systems less chaotic.

## CHAPTER 1

Making Smart Decisions about File Systems

L aying out file systems on your servers and clients is one of the most important steps you will take in building a manageable network. How you arrange file systems on individual hosts and across a network can dramatically affect the performance of your systems and network, the reliability of your systems, security, cost, your backup strategy, and the amount of work that you have to do to maintain these file systems and the software and data they house. In fact, your file systems can easily be the single most significant factor in the overall performance and reliability of your network.

In this chapter, we will look at how file systems are organized and how this organization affects performance. We will offer suggestions on how you might arrange file systems on a network basis to make your network more manageable.

File Systems from the Roots Up

The file system that Unix uses to store everything from device drivers to users' data is undoubtedly familiar to you. With a single root from which all branches of the treelike structure derive, the file system provides a degree of consistency across the most divergent variations of Unix. Yet the simplicity of this hierarchical file system (playfully depicted in Figure 1.1) hides an increasing degree of complexity with every major release of Solaris. Early versions of Unix systems employed a single disk-based file system. The current version of Solaris supports many different types of file systems—the customary disk-based fast file system; network-based file systems; compact-disc read-only memory (CD-ROM) file systems; redundant array of inexpensive disk (RAID) systems, in which many disks combine into one logical file system; file systems on disk operating system (DOS) diskettes; and even pseudo or *virtual* file systems, which are comprised not of files at all but of processes, network sockets, character device drivers, and the like. Even so, the convenient abstraction of the familiar treelike structure persists, and most Unix users are oblivious to the complex structures upon which this abstraction is built.

To begin our examination of Solaris file systems and how you can optimize the performance and utility of file systems across your network, let's first examine a traditional Unix file system (UFS) from the ground up. A single file is, first and foremost, a collection of data—whether ASCII or binary—that is stored in contiguous and/or noncontiguous chunks on a disk. These chunks are sized according to a storage unit called a *block* (for UFS, the default block size is 8192 bytes). You have probably also noticed that directory files are always some multiple of 512 bytes. When you first create a directory with mkdir, you will notice that it looks something like this:

```
solaris% mkdir mydir; ls -ld mydir
drwxr-xr-x   2 sdraven      staff          512 Nov 11 11:15 mydir
```

and, later, as you add files, it jumps in size:

```
solaris% mkdir mydir; ls -ld mydir
drwxr-xr-x   2 sdraven      staff         1024 Nov 22 16:05 mydir
```

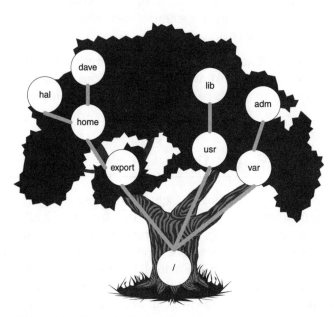

Figure 1.1   The Unix file system tree.

This is because space for directory growth is allocated in 512-byte units. By pre-allocating space in directories, they can grow without as much overhead as if space had to be added each time the contents of a directory changed.

Files, of course, don't grow in units of blocks, but by the amount of data they contain. The space allocated for them, however, does grow in units of blocks, which allows them to grow up to the next increment of a block before additional disk space must be allocated. In general, all but the last block of a file is full. Figure 1.2 illustrates disk space allocation for a regular file.

Some file systems milk this efficiency even further by allocating more than a single additional block when a file grows. These are referred to as *extent-based*, as opposed to *block-based*, file systems. By allocating a larger amount of disk space, the files can grow more contiguously. On the other hand, an extent-based file system runs a greater risk of wasting space that is allocated and not used.

The separate blocks of data comprising a single file are linked to each other by on-disk record structures, which store the location of each of the blocks. This structure is sometimes referred to as a *block map*. In a similar manner, the available disk space on a file system is maintained in a free-block list. A more complex record structure is used to store the descriptive data concerning each file, sometimes referred to as *metadata* (a common term for data that describes data). This metadata includes the file's owner (i.e., the user ID [UID]); the file's associated group (the group ID [GID]); the permissions matrix; the file creation, modification and access times; the size and type of the file; and so on. In fact, the only items not stored in this structure are the contents of the file (as mentioned, this is stored on disk) and the file's name and location within the file system.

A file's name is stored within another file called the *directory file*. The inclusion of the filename within a particular directory also determines where it "lives" within the tree structure. This location has almost nothing to do with the location of the data itself. In fact, the same file can exist in any number of locations, even in the same directory more than once if it has more than one name. If a single collection of data blocks comprising a single file has more than one file system identity, this duplication is only expressed through the separate directory entries and in the number of links indicated within the inode. Directory files, as you might suspect, also contain the inode numbers of the files they contain.

Figure 1.2 Blocks of data comprising a single file.

This provides a way for the file system to easily retrieve the metadata when a long file listing is requested with the ls -l command. Figure 1.3 illustrates the components of a single file in a traditional Unix file system.

File Systems: Short Cuts to Data

A file system can be said to be an interface to files—a way to address files and access their contents. When a user issues an ls command, for example, the file system receives a request for the contents of a directory file. If the user has execute permission, the contents of the directory will be displayed. If the user issues an ls -l command, additional resources must be tapped. Information stored in the associated inode must also be read and displayed. In addition, some of this information must first be resolved; the UID and GID fields will be looked up in the password and group files (or maps) and the textual name will be displayed in place of the numeric identifiers.

Adding a single line to a file can cause it to extend beyond its current last block and require allocation of another block. The new block must be added to the block map. The length of the file as noted in the inode must be changed and the modification time updated to reflect the change, as well.

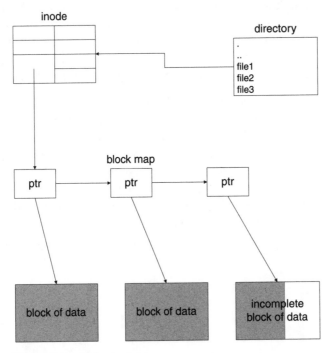

Figure 1.3 Disk structures.

If a hard link is created to an existing file, the number of links field in the inode must be incremented. If a hard link is removed, the field must be decremented. If the number of links field drops to 0 (i.e., all instances of the file have been removed), the file space can then be reclaimed and the blocks can be restored to the free list. Figure 1.4 displays the file structures associated with two hard-linked files.

Adding or deleting a file involves a similar sequence of operations. When a file is added to a directory, an inode is reserved, space is allocated, the directory file is updated with the name and inode number of the new file, and the block map is updated. When a file is removed, its blocks are added to the free-block list, the directory file is updated as the file's entry is removed, and the inode is made available (provided there are no other links to the file).

When a user is reading a file, the directory identifies the inode—used to determine file access privileges and locate the file on disk. In fact, a file's access permissions are used in any file operation to determine if the individual performing the operation has the proper privilege to do so. The file's content is then retrieved from disk.

If a file is moved, one or more directory files must be updated. If it is moved within a directory, a single directory file is modified. If it is moved from one directory to another, two directory files must be modified. Neither the block

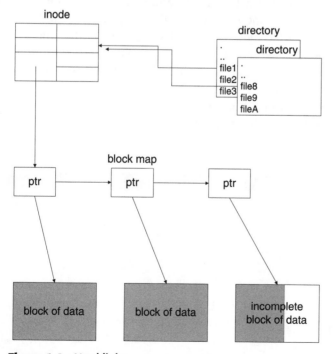

Figure 1.4   Hard links.

map nor the inode associated with the file is affected. If a file is moved from one file system to another, however, the process of establishing it on the new file system is like creating a new file. The existing inode can no longer be used because it belongs to the initial file system.

File Types

The classification of files in Solaris can confuse neophytes. The first breakdown they often hear about is that of regular versus special files. The classification of *regular files* encompasses a wide range of file types as users think about them—binaries, scripts, data files, configuration files, and so on. The organizing element is this: The kernel doesn't make any distinction between any of these file types. Differences between them exist only at the user level (e.g., the content, whether they are executable, and so on). File types that don't fall into the regular category are links, pipes, sockets, and so on. These files are recognized as being different and are treated differently by the kernel. Table 1.1 lists file types and the characters used to designate them in a long listing (i.e., ls -l).

Although the Solaris kernel does not differentiate between different types of regular files, users do. So do windowing systems. For this purpose, there is an underlying classing structure that identifies files by type. This structure enables the expected thing to happen when a user double-clicks on an icon within the file manager tool or drops it into another window (e.g., a print tool). In addition, the /etc/magic file is used to identify file types using embedded magic numbers. Not all file types have magic numbers, of course. For those that do, the offset (generally 0), type (length), and the identifying pattern are specified in the /etc/magic file. The entry `0 string %PDF-1.2 Adobe Portable Document Format (PDF)` specifies that version 1.2 of the PDF format is identified by virtue of the fact that its files begin with the string `%PDF-1.2`. A user can determine the file

Table 1.1   File Type Designators

FILE TYPE	DESIGNATOR
Regular file	-
Directory file	d
Block special device	b
Character special device	c
Name pipe (FIFO)	p
Symbolic link	l
Door (Solaris 2.6 and later)	D
Socket	s

type of a specific file by issuing the *file* command. This command will look at the first several bytes of the file and reference the /etc/magic file to determine the file type.

```
file *
subdir:                directory
dumpxfer:              executable /opt/LWperl/bin/perl script
log.out:               ascii text
logmon:                executable /bin/ksh script
mailman:               executable /bin/ksh script
processlog:            executable shell script
watcher:               executable /bin/ksh script
nightlyreport:         executable c-shell script
killit: whois:         ELF 32-bit MSB executable SPARC Version
                       1, dynamically linked,stripped
```

You can add file types to /etc/magic by editing the /etc/magic file and placing the offset, string, and type in the file. For example, if you have a type of file called a *testfile*, which always starts with the string test, the following /etc/magic entry would be coded:

```
#offset     type      value     File Type
0           string    test      testfile
```

With this entry, if you have a file called *myfile* with contents *testing 1 2 3*, the file command would identify the file type as shown here:

```
# file myfile
myfile:   testfile
```

Taking advantage of /etc/magic is a great way to help your users identify their files. Consider defining file types for any major applications that your users access.

If you have never browsed through the wide range of file bindings available in your windowing system's binder tool, you will probably be impressed by the variety of file types that the windowing system can recognize and treat differently, although most of these you will probably never see. The kernel knows only the eight types listed in Table 1.1. Figure 1.5 illustrates a breakdown of files by type, from a user's point of view. The file types recognized by the kernel are circled. You can see from this incomplete breakdown that differentiating files by type can get to be quite arbitrary. The important thing to remember is that as far as the kernel is concerned, a regular file is a regular file. It will not try to stop you from making a file of C source code executable and running it any more than it would try to prevent you from printing a binary; you'll simply get some very odd results.

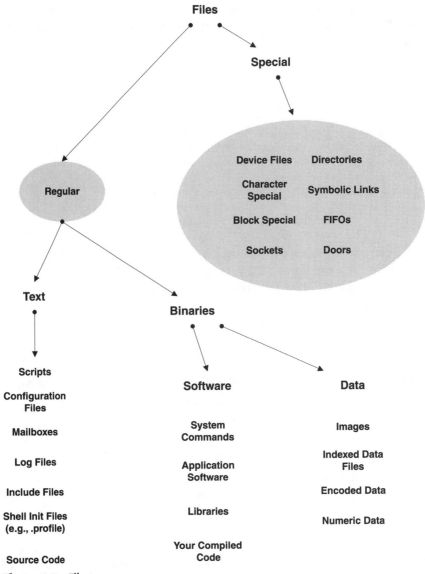

Figure 1.5 File types.

Directory files, as we've mentioned earlier, are special files that contain the names and inode numbers of the files they "contain." We put that word in quotes for a good reason. The relationship between directories and files exists only because of these entries. Directory entries, by the way (you might want to look at the include file dirent.h), also contain a file name length for each entry.

Block special device and *character special device files* are unusual in that they do not contain data. Meant solely as access points for physical devices, such as disks and tapes, these files provide the means to access the related device drivers. The main difference between the two is how they handle input/output (I/O). Block special device files operate on blocks, while character special device drivers work on a character-by-character basis.

Sockets are special files used for communications between processes, generally between systems. Client/server applications, as well as many network services, use sockets.

Named pipes—also called *FIFOs* for "first in, first out"—are special files used for communications between processes, generally on the same system.

Symbolic links are pointers to other files. They are similar but not identical to shortcuts in Windows. Symbolic links—sometimes called *symlinks* or *soft links*—have as their contents the names of the files they point to.

Hard links, as you probably recognize, are not special files at all. As mentioned earlier in this chapter, a hard link is indistinguishable from the file it links to—not true with symbolic links—except for their locations within the file system. In fact, either could be called the link or the file. There is no difference.

Controlling File Access with Access Control Lists

Recent versions of Solaris extend the common file access permissions with optional access control lists (ACLs). For example, if you want to associate a file with more than one group of individuals without having to go through the bother of creating a single group containing all of them or running the risk of making the file accessible to the world, ACLs will come in very handy. ACLs do not require any up-front preparation at the file system or directory level. This puts some of the responsibility for maintaining groups onto users, who can now, essentially, create their own groups. Before ACLs, it was nearly impossible to exclude a particular user from having access to your files or one of your files; now it's both possible and easy. Before ACLs, you could not associate more than one group with a file; now you can.

Each file in Solaris (or any version of Unix, for that matter) has a set of owner, group, and world permissions detailing what each of these entities can do with the files. This access control structure is stored in the inode and consulted each time a file access is attempted. We describe this traditional access control in Chapter 12. The subsidiary ACL is stored on disk and read into an *in-core* memory structure as needed. ACLs define accesses in excess of those provided by the traditional structure.

The content of an ACL entry can be described as three colon-separated fields, for example, user:mfs:–, where the first of the fields identifies the type of entry; the second holds the UID or GID for the entry type chosen; and the third holds the permissions to be set for that user or group. In our example, user:mfs:–, the user mfs is given no permission to the file in question. Even if the file permissions are set to rwxr-xr-x, mfs cannot read or execute it because the ACL specifically denies mfs this access.

The entry type field can be any of the values user, group, other, or mask. ACLs provide the user with the ability to define a mask that applies to all accesses to a set of files for all users—except the owner—and takes precedence over other settings.

The two commands that are used to set and report on ACLs are setfacl and getfacl. The *getfacl* command displays the owner, group, and ACLs established for a particular file. With the -a option, the command displays the owner, group, and access control list for a file. With a -d option, the command displays the owner, group, and default ACLs established for the file. Examples of the command and responses follow:

```
spoon% getacl regfile
# file: regfile
# owner: em
# group: staff
user::rw-
group::r--
mask::rw-
other::---
spoon% getacl extfile
# file: extfile
# owner: em
# group: staff
user::rw-
user:shs:rw-
user:mfs:---
group::r-
mask::---
other::---
```

Not all file system types support ACLs, but they are supported in UFS, NFS, cachefs, and LOFS.

The *setfacl* command sets, modifies, or removes the permissions for a file or group of files. It can be used to replace the ACL or to modify particular entries. It has a number of options.

-s	Sets the permissions specified on the command line
-f	Uses the specified file for file settings to be set
-d	Deletes entries from the file's ACL
-m	Modifies one or more ACL entries
-r	Resets the mask permissions

Keep in mind that the setfacl command doesn't create an ACL if it isn't needed. If the user isn't specifying permissions beyond those provided in the normal permissions fields of the inode, the command simply alters those values. In other words, the setfacl command can be used to modify the normal permissions for the normal users (owner, group, and world)—just like a chmod or chgrp command—or it can be used to add permissions for specific other users or additional groups, something that chmod and chgrp cannot do.

Where a setfacl command is similar to a chmod or chgrp command, a getfacl is similar to an ls -l. They do similar things, but use a different format both for the command and for the output.

UFS Logging

Beginning with Solaris 7, the standard Solaris UFS file system incorporates a logging function that, while transparent to users, makes the file system considerably more reliable. Those of us who remember sitting through painfully long fscks will probably be delighted by the "File system is stable" messages that we now usually see when rebooting a system that has crashed. The reason for the change is logging. Because UFS file systems now maintain a log detailing updates to files, they have the means for recovering the state of a file system without an extensive analysis and rebuilding by fsck.

Fsck makes five passes over a file system, checking different file system structures in each pass, as follows:

1. Blocks and sizes.
2. Pathnames.
3. Connectivity.
4. Reference counts.
5. Cylinder groups.

By examining the file system from each of these perspectives, it is able to repair damages resulting in a file system that is, once again, consistent.

Most file system inconsistencies in the past were due to the constant state of fluctuation that file systems are in and the fact that changes to file systems usually require several operations, as shown in the previous section. Modified data blocks must be written back to disk; additional blocks must be allocated and represented in the block map; inodes must be created, removed, and updated; and directory structures must be updated to reflect new files, deleted files, and moved files. If a crash occurs when some, but not all, of these changes have taken place, an inconsistency is created. The fsck tool attempts to resolve this kind of inconsistency by examining the various structures and determining how to complete the interrupted file system changes. It examines inodes, the block map, and directory files in an effort to piece together a consistent file system by adding, removing, or modifying file system structures. For example, if a directory contains the name and inode number of a file that no longer exists, fsck can remove the reference. When fsck knows nothing about the state of a file system that it is asked to check, it is extremely thorough and time-consuming while examining and repairing it.

The way that logging works in Solaris today is as follows. First, there is a logging file structure in the same partition as the file system. Before any change is made to the file system, a record is written to this log that documents the intended change. The file system change is then made. Afterward, the log is once again modified—this time to reflect the completion of the intended change. The log file, in other words, maintains enough information about the status of the file system to determine whether it is intact. If there are outstanding changes at mount time, the file structures associated with those changes are checked and adjusted as needed, and an examination of the entire file system is avoided.

Types of File Systems

There are a number of file systems that Solaris can support, out of the box or with some additional software. Before we get into all of the file systems, we will briefly describe the major categories of file systems: disk-based, memory-based, network-based, and so on. The framework within which these different file system types are supported simultaneously has come to be known as the *virtual file system*. The generalization of the inode structure into the vnode makes allowances for the non-UFS types.

The basic difference between different disk-based file systems is how they store and access data. Earlier in this chapter, we describe how UFS structures such as inodes, block maps, and directories are used to organize data and make it available. It's easy to imagine a file system without directory files; it would simply have a "flat" file space, though it might still use inodes and lists to keep track of files and free and used space. UFS, along with probably every other file system available today, however, is hierarchical. It's fairly accurate to picture each file system as a structure between you and the data on disk that allows you to find and use portions you think of as files.

Regular file systems include the types shown in Table 1.2.

Table 1.2 Regular File Systems

FILE SYSTEM TYPE	MEDIUM	DESCRIPTION
UFS	Disk-based	The Berkeley fat fast file system; Solaris default
VxFS	Disk-based	VERITAS file system
QFS	Disk-based	LSC Inc.'s file system
pcfs	Disk-based	MS-DOS fat file system; floppies
hsfs	Disk-based	High Sierra file system; CD-ROM
tmpfs	Memory/disk	Temporary file system; swapping

UFS is the standard Berkeley fat fast file system (FFFS) and the one we have been discussing. UFS is the file system you will most commonly encounter on Solaris systems. Others in this list are third-party file systems with features similar to those of UFS. VxFS is a product from VERITAS Corporation and QFS is from LSC. These two file systems provide some advantages over UFS, primarily by providing for extremely large files and file systems.

For UFS, the maximum for both is a terabyte; for the others the maximum is, more or less, a petabyte (actually 2^{63} bytes). Another difference is whether the file system is block- or extent-based; the difference here is whether files are extended a block at a time or some number of blocks. A third is whether there is support for hierarchical storage management (HSM), in which data transparently flows from faster to slower media on the basis on infrequent use; HSM is not available in UFS, but is available in VxFS and QFS. Some of the major differences between these and the UFS file systems are shown in Table 1.3.

Table 1.3 File System Comparison

	UFS	VXFS	QFS
Maximum file size	1Tb	2^{63} bytes	2^{63} bytes
Maximum file system size	1Tb	2^{63} bytes	2^{63} bytes
Allocation method	Block-based	Extent-based	Extent-based
ACL support	Yes	Yes	No
HSM support	No	Yes	Yes
Logging (type)	Yes (meta)	Yes (meta/data)	No
Direct I/O	Yes (2.6+)	Yes	Yes
Quotas	Yes	Yes	No
Page cache	Yes	No	No

If you have particular need for file systems larger than 1Tb or for some of the other features shown in Table 1.3, the article by McDougall cited in The Recommended Readings will provide further insights into the trade-offs of using these products.

In addition to Unix file systems, Solaris supports pcfs and hsfs. These file system types are most commonly encountered when dealing with diskettes and CD-ROMs, but we are not necessarily restricted to these media types.

The *pcfs*-type file system implements the DOS fat file system. Once mounted, standard Unix commands such as ls and cd can be used with these files. One should be careful, however, in managing the differing line termination conventions between DOS and Unix files. Whereas DOS files end lines with both a carriage return and a line feed, Unix files end lines with only a line feed. The unix2dos and dos2unix commands overcome this minor inconsistency quite handily.

The *hsfs* is the High Sierra file system, also referred to by the name *ISO 9660*. The Solaris implementation also supports the Rock Ridge extensions. While mounted, standard Unix commands can be used to access files and move around in directories. However, the underlying geometry and structure of an hsfs file systems is dramatically different from that of UFS—and, of course, you cannot write to files on a CD-ROM.

File systems of type *tmpfs* may look and act like disk-based file systems, but actually reside in memory more than on disk. The primary use of /tmp is for swapping. Data is not written to disk unless physical memory is exhausted. The contents of tmpfs file systems are, therefore, temporary. In fact, the /tmp file system, the only file system of this type on most Solaris systems, is emptied out on a system reboot. We briefly describe swapping a little later in this chapter.

The *Network File System* (NFS), now available on virtually every operating system, ties systems together by providing an intuitive file-sharing mechanism across a network and divergent platforms. Happily, differences in the underlying system's processing (e.g., whether the processor orders bytes into words using the big-endian or little-endian method) are transparent. With automount support, NFS performance can be greatly improved.

Pseudo File Systems

Pseudo file systems, though they may appear as file systems to users, are actually abstractions through which various system and process data can be accessed. Pseudo file systems are used to represent such things as processes,

Table 1.4 Pseudo File Systems

FILE SYSTEM	DESCRIPTION
NFS	Network File System (generally remote UFS)
cachefs	Local disk-based cache for NFS file systems
autofs	Used for automatic mounting via NFS
specfs	Access for device drivers in /dev
procfs	Access to running processes and kernel structures
sockfs	Access to network sockets
fifofs	Access to FIFO structures
lofs	Loopback file system, used to create alternate paths to existing files

network sockets, device drivers, and FIFOs. In our discussion of the /proc file system, we will clearly show the benefits of accessing information about running processes through pseudo file system abstraction.

Pseudo file systems include those listed in Table 1.4.

Cachefs

Cachefs is a file system type that inserts itself into the interaction between an NFS server and a client. Blocks of data obtained by the client are stored (or cached) in the cachefs portion of the local disk. Cachefs improves access to slow or heavily used file systems. The local copies of files are accessed after the initial fetch, making subsequent fetches unnecessary and reducing traffic on the network. Cachefs is optional and not used by default. File systems are not cached in this way unless you create a cachefs file system and specify it in your mount of the remote file system, either in your /etc/vfstab file or automount maps.

Cachefs uses the concepts of back and front file systems—*back* being the authoritative actual file system and *front* being the local copy. The back file system is unaware of the way the files are being cached locally. The front file system is used predominantly. Whenever you access a file on the back file system, it is cached on the front file system.

The contents of the local cache can become outdated if the original file on the server is modified after the file has been cached. The system, therefore, keeps track of each cached file's attributes and checks these periodically against the copy on the server to determine whether modification has happened. If it has, the local copy is purged and the next access results in a new load of the file from the server. The time interval between checks of file attributes can be modified.

The *cfsadmin* command is used to build and manage caches. The command options are listed following:

c   Creates a cache within the specified directory

d   Removes the specified file system from cache

l   Lists file systems stored in the cache specified

s   Requests a consistency check with the back file system

u   Updates the resource parameters of the specified cache directory (all file systems in the cache must be unmounted at the time you issue this command)

See the man page for the cfsadmin command for additional details.

In the following example, a cache is being created and used with NFS file system /usr/local.

```
spoon# cfsadmin -c /vol/cache/cache1
spoon# mount -F cachefs -o backfstype=nfs,backpath=/usr/local,\
cachedir=/vol/cache/cache1 server:/usr/local /usr/local
```

Automount entries using cachefs might look like one of the following:

```
/homeauto.home -fstype=cachefs,backfstype=nfs
* -fstype=cachefs,backfstype=nfs,cachedir=/vol/cache/cache1 \
server1:/export/home/&
```

In these examples, the arguments specify the following:

backfstype. The type of the file system being backed.

backpath. Where the back file system is currently mounted.

cachedir. The name of the local (front) directory created to be used as cache.

As specified in the example, the mount sits on top of the same file system that it is backing. In other words, the mount of the cache becomes transparent as far as the user is concerned. The file system mounted as /usr/local is still referred to as /usr/local. This is not necessary, but is a good convention to adopt.

It is important to understand that, as much as cachefs can provide a dramatic improvement in NFS performance, it can also degrade performance quite dramatically. The overall effect hinges on the balance between local and remote file accesses. The more cached files can be used, the greater savings will result from not having to go back to the server to fetch them again. If, on the other hand, most every file access requires an update of the file from the server, little is gained. Further, when a cached file is updated on the client, the local copy is marked invalid and the file is written back to the server. When the file is needed again, it is fetched from the server. This behavior results in more NFS overhead than were the file system not cached.

In general, file systems that change frequently are not good candidates for cachefs because of the possible performance hits. File systems that change infrequently, such as /usr/local (usually a repository of site-specific tools), *are* good candidates.

Cachefs options can be specified in automounter maps. In the master map entry shown here, we're using cachefs for an entire indirect map:

```
*    -fstype=cachefs,backfstype=nfs,cachedir=/vol/cache/cache1 \
     server:/export/home/&
```

Swapping

Swapping should not be confused with paging. These are related but different system activities. A Solaris system replaces pages (chunks of data comprising processes and their data) in memory as needed to give all running processes opportunities to execute. This is *paging*. While this is happening, the page daemon is keeping track of memory requests. When the demand for memory is excessive and the system is having difficulty maintaining the free-memory list, entire processes—rather than just pages—are replaced in memory. This is *swapping*.

When swapping occurs, anonymous memory (basically, the process's data) is moved to the swap area while other pages are flushed to disk. In time, so that a process moved out of memory can continue, the page in swap is returned to memory and page faults (i.e., messages indicating that desired pages are not in memory) result in the pages corresponding to executable code being reloaded from disk.

Though /tmp looks like a normal file system to users and has open permissions so that anyone can store files there, you don't want users to do so, both because these files will not survive a reboot and because an excessive use of the space in /tmp could affect performance if swapping were required. In older versions of Solaris, files were removed from /tmp on reboot, but not directories and their contents. This behavior has since changed and now a recursive operation cleans out everything.

A Solaris system with sufficient memory to hold all processes and data wouldn't actually need disk-based swap space at all. Few, if any, of our systems are ever this well endowed. On the other end of the spectrum, systems that use swap on a regular basis will be obviously suffering; their performance will be unacceptable. On an adequately endowed file system, the swap -l command will often show results such as these, showing that available swap (the disk-based portion) is only lightly used (i.e., most of it is free).

```
myhost% swap -l
swapfile              dev  swaplo blocks   free
/dev/dsk/c0t3d0s1    32,25      8 524392 417400
```

Making Use of /proc

The /proc file system is an interesting and very useful file system. Though its contents do not correspond to files on disk, its appears to the user as a regular file system. Users can cd into /proc as with any directory for which they have execute permission. They can list its contents with ls or ls -l.

What the contents of the /proc file system represent, however, are not files but interfaces to kernel structures and running processes. By providing an interface which looks like a file system, /proc simplifies the work involved in accessing information available about these processes. For example, before the advent of /proc, programs that use information about kernel structures (e.g., the ps command, which reads and displays the process table) had to read kernel memory. With the /proc file system, these structures are more readily available. This is useful not only to the OS developers, but to any programmers or sysadmins needing access to this type of information.

Although /proc may not be every sysadmin's favorite place to poke around, it offers advantages in debugging. With images of running processes as readily available as files, they are much easier to analyze. Solaris provides a set of tools to facilitate access even further—the commands in /usr/proc/bin, discussed in the next section.

When you examine the contents of /proc, the first thing you'll likely notice is that the directory names correspond to the process IDs of running processes. The init process, for example, will show up as a directory named 1. Within each process directory are a number of files or subdirectories which represent different aspects of the corresponding process.

```
spoon% cd /proc
spoon% ls
0       1129    1281    167     2       22416   23334   27148   28524   3532    382
1       11352   13400   17018   20201   22882   23508   27153   28535   362     436
10382   11353   13403   17065   20281   230     23509   27159   28572   363     467
1039    11354   136     174     20318   23073   23514   28070   29141   366     468
1040    1136    14091   181     20319   23076   23520   28071   3       367     484
1042    1143    14092   18437   20378   23261   238     28072   309     369     5191
1058    1144    158     18494   20418   23264   23898   28437   311     374     5194
1060    11569   1608    187     208     23286   23901   28498   316     375     5705
1068    11570   1615    19024   21357   23289   24431   28508   322     376     5722
```

```
1107    11571   16279   19028   217     23308   248     28509   327     377     5725
1110    11591   16280   19570   22247   23311   254     28510   328     378     9562
1125    124     16338   19574   22252   23312   25463   28515   332     379     9877
1126    126     16376   19881   22362   23315   265     28517   349     380
1127    1277    166     19884   22364   23331   27147   28522   3529    381
```

If you were to compare this list with a ps -ef command, you would notice the matching process IDs.

```
spoon% ps -ef | head -11
     UID    PID   PPID  C     STIME TTY       TIME CMD
    root      0      0  0     Mar 11 ?        0:02 sched
    root      1      0  0     Mar 11 ?       76:54 /etc/init -
    root      2      0  0     Mar 11 ?        4:55 pageout
    root      3      0  0     Mar 11 ?      247:55 fsflush
  nobody   3529    349  0 15:18:44 ?         0:01 /usr/sbin/httpd-apache -f
/etc/httpd-apache.conf
    root    362      1  0     Mar 11 ?        0:11 /usr/lib/saf/sac -t 300
    root    124      1  0     Mar 11 ?       90:48 /usr/sbin/rpcbind
    root    126      1  0     Mar 11 ?        0:06 /usr/sbin/keyserv
    root    187      1  0     Mar 11 ?        3:05 /usr/sbin/cron
  daemon    166      1  0     Mar 11 ?        0:09 /usr/lib/nfs/statd
```

Each process is actually represented by a directory that holds a number of files and other directories corresponding to different portions and attributes of the process. Note the various structures associated with a single process in the following example. The owner and group reflect those of the person running the process. Read the man page on /proc for additional information.

```
spoon% ls "1 23308
-rw-------   1 nici     staff    1323008 May 31 12:02 as
-r--------   1 nici     staff        152 May 31 12:02 auxv
-r--------   1 nici     staff         40 May 31 12:02 cred
--w-------   1 nici     staff          0 May 31 12:02 ctl
lr-x------   1 nici     staff          0 May 31 12:02 cwd ->
dr-x------   2 nici     staff       1184 May 31 12:02 fd
-r--r--r--   1 nici     staff        120 May 31 12:02 lpsinfo
-r--------   1 nici     staff        912 May 31 12:02 lstatus
-r--r--r--   1 nici     staff        536 May 31 12:02 lusage
dr-xr-xr-x   3 nici     staff         48 May 31 12:02 lwp
-r--------   1 nici     staff       1536 May 31 12:02 map
dr-x------   2 nici     staff        288 May 31 12:02 object
-r--------   1 nici     staff       1952 May 31 12:02 pagedata
-r--r--r--   1 nici     staff        336 May 31 12:02 psinfo
-r--------   1 nici     staff       1536 May 31 12:02 rmap
lr-x------   1 nici     staff          0 May 31 12:02 root ->
-r--------   1 nici     staff       1440 May 31 12:02 sigact
-r--------   1 nici     staff       1232 May 31 12:02 status
-r--r--r--   1 nici     staff        256 May 31 12:02 usage
-r--------   1 nici     staff          0 May 31 12:02 watch
-r--------   1 nici     staff       2432 May 31 12:02 xmap
```

The /proc Commands

The set of commands that facilitate use of the information stored in a /proc file system, sometime referred to as the *proc tools*, includes the following: pcred, pfiles, pflags, pldd, pmap, prun, psig, pstack, pstop, ptime, ptree, pwait, and pwdx.

pcred

The command pcred prints the effective, real, and saved UID and GID of a running process. The command pcred 1234, as shown here, shows that process 1234 has UID of 111 and GID of 11:

```
solaris% pcred 1234
1234:   e/r/suid=111  e/r/sgid=11
```

pfiles

The pfiles command lists open files associated with the specified process along with any file limits the process may have imposed. Each open file is described by a number of values, including the inode number, major and minor device numbers of the partition in which the file is stored, UID, GID, and permissions. Although the identity of each file may not be easily apparent from the display, any particular file can be identified by using a combination of the device numbers and inode number, as we shall explain shortly:

```
spoon% pfiles 28555
28555:   -csh
  Current rlimit: 64 file descriptors
   0: S_IFCHR mode:0666 dev:32,24 ino:127001 uid:0 gid:3 rdev:13,2
      O_RDONLY|O_LARGEFILE
   1: S_IFCHR mode:0666 dev:32,24 ino:127001 uid:0 gid:3 rdev:13,2
      O_RDONLY|O_LARGEFILE
   2: S_IFCHR mode:0666 dev:32,24 ino:127001 uid:0 gid:3 rdev:13,2
      O_RDONLY|O_LARGEFILE
   3: S_IFDOOR mode:0444 dev:163,0 ino:59379 uid:0 gid:0 size:0
      O_RDONLY|O_LARGEFILE FD_CLOEXEC  door to nscd[208]
  15: S_IFCHR mode:0620 dev:32,24 ino:127110 uid:131 gid:7 rdev:24,6
      O_RDWR FD_CLOEXEC
  16: S_IFCHR mode:0620 dev:32,24 ino:127110 uid:131 gid:7 rdev:24,6
      O_RDWR FD_CLOEXEC
  17: S_IFCHR mode:0620 dev:32,24 ino:127110 uid:131 gid:7 rdev:24,6
      O_RDWR FD_CLOEXEC
  18: S_IFCHR mode:0620 dev:32,24 ino:127110 uid:131 gid:7 rdev:24,6
      O_RDWR FD_CLOEXEC
  19: S_IFCHR mode:0620 dev:32,24 ino:127110 uid:131 gid:7 rdev:24,6
      O_RDWR FD_CLOEXEC
```

In the example shown, the process is using nine file handles, but only three actual files. This is evident from looking at a combination of the device numbers (e.g., 32,24) and the inode number (e.g., 127001). Since the same inode number can be used in different file systems for different files, only the combination of these values is sufficient.

pflags

The pflags command displays the status of the process, as shown in the following example:

```
spoon% pflags 28555
28555:  -csh
        data model = _ILP32  flags = PR_ORPHAN
  /1:   flags = PR_PCINVAL|PR_ASLEEP [ sigsuspend(0xeffff878) ]
  sigmask = 0x00000002,0x00000000
```

pgrep

The pgrep command searches for processes by name using the /proc interface. Many sysadmins used to using commands like `ps -ef | grep sendmail` will come to appreciate the simplification of `pgrep sendmail`.

pkill

The pkill command sends a signal to the process. Like the pgrep command, pkill sends signals to the process named on the command line. Sysadmins familiar with the killbyname script will find the operation of this command familiar. Replacing command sequences of `ps -ef | grep inetd; kill -HUP 101`, pkill (e.g., `pkill -HUP inetd`) saves time and simplifies scripting as well.

pldd

The pldd command lists the dynamic libraries used with the process.

pmap

The pmap command displays the process's address space with memory segment sizes, as shown in the following example output:

```
spoon% pmap 28555
28555:  -csh
00010000    140K read/exec        /usr/bin/csh
00042000     12K read/write/exec  /usr/bin/csh
00045000     68K read/write/exec   [ heap ]
EF600000    648K read/exec        /usr/lib/libc.so.1
EF6B1000     32K read/write/exec  /usr/lib/libc.so.1
```

```
EF6B9000      4K read/write/exec      [ anon ]
EF6C0000      8K read/exec            /usr/lib/libmapmalloc.so.1
EF6D1000      4K read/write/exec      /usr/lib/libmapmalloc.so.1
EF700000    168K read/exec            /usr/lib/libcurses.so.1
EF739000     32K read/write/exec      /usr/lib/libcurses.so.1
EF741000     12K read/write/exec      [ anon ]
EF780000      4K read/exec            /usr/lib/libdl.so.1
EF7B0000      4K read/write/exec      [ anon ]
EF7C0000    116K read/exec            /usr/lib/ld.so.1
EF7EC000      8K read/write/exec      /usr/lib/ld.so.1
EFFF6000     40K read/write           [ stack ]
 total     1300K
```

prun

The prun command sets processes running and is the opposite of the pstop command.

psig

The psig command lists the signal actions of the process.

pstack

The pstack command shows the stack trace for each process thread.

pstop

The pstop command stops processes in similar manner to the default kill command (i.e., the kill command without an argument). It is the opposite of the prun command.

ptime

The ptime command displays timing information for processes—real, user, and system. The following sample output illustrates:

```
spoon% ptime 28555
real       0.024
user       0.001
sys        0.017
```

ptree

The ptree command prints the process's tree containing the process IDs or users:

```
spoon% ptree 28555
158   /usr/sbin/inetd -s
  28553 in.telnetd
    28555 -csh
      28586 ptree 28555
```

pwait

The command pwait waits for the process to terminate.

pwdx

The pwdx command prints the current working directory of the specified process, as shown in the following example:

```
spoon% pwdx 28555
28555:  /home/nici
```

Building and Maintaining File Systems

With respect to function, there is little that is more fundamental to systems maintenance than your users' access to their files. Maintenance of file systems—ensuring their availability and integrity—is, therefore, one of the most important aspects of any sysadmin's job.

For many sysadmins, the task of building file systems is simply something that happens during installation. Whether you use the automatic layout feature or profiles in JumpStart, the building of file systems is automated. If you are adding a new disk to a system, on the other hand, you may need to repartition it and manually construct file systems to your own specifications. Once the disk has been physically attached to the system, you want to be sure that the system recognizes it. For Small Computer System Interface (SCSI) disks, you should be sure that the SCSI target is unique for the intended bus. On a system which already has a /dev/dsk/c0t3d0 and a /dev/dsk/c0t0d0 disk, the most common next choice is /dev/dsk/c0t1d0 - SCSI target 1. We recommend attaching new drives when the system is halted.

When you first power up a system after adding a drive, you should stop at the boot monitor (i.e., hit **L1-A** or **Stop-A** before it gets too far along in the boot process) and type **probe-scsi** at the ok prompt. With OpenBoot 3.0, the recommended procedure is to setenv autoboot? false, and then do a reset. This interaction should look something like this:

```
Type 'go' to resume
Type help for more information
ok probe-scsi
...
Target 1
  Unit 0  Disk Seagate   ST1523ON  1234
```

showing you that the new disk is recognized. If you don't see your disk at this point, you probably have a problem with your SCSI cabling or with the disk itself. It's pointless to proceed without resolving this problem.

In order to build support for a new disk, you need to reboot with the command `boot -r`. This command instructs the system to rebuild, and it will configure the device support needed for the new disk. If for some reason you cannot easily boot the system at the console, you can effect this command indirectly by touching the file /reconfigure and then rebooting the system. (Yes, you can do this remotely.) The boot sequence will then include the rebuild and remove the file, preventing the rebuild from occurring during every subsequent reboot. The correct device nodes for the disk are automatically added. If you cannot reboot, or if you have rebooted, but forgot the *-r*, you can simulate the reconfigure boot with the following set of commands:

drvconfig. Reconfigures the drivers

disks. Looks for new disks and adds the correct /dev links

Once you're booting, you should notice references to the new disk that will look roughly like what follows:

```
sd1 at esp0: target 1 lun 0
sd1 is
/iommu@f,e0000000/sbus@f,e0001000/espdma@f,400000/esp@f,800000/sd@3,0
  <SEAGATE-ST15230N-0638 cyl 3974 alt 2 hd 19 sec 111>
```

This is a second indication that the disk is recognized and you will be able to access it when the system is fully booted. Most disks that you are likely to purchase will be preformatted and already partitioned. The question is, of course, whether they are partitioned to your liking. Usually, new disks are partitioned as if they are going to contain all the ordinary file systems for a Unix host. If you want to use a disk as one big file system, you don't need to change anything. Simply use *slice 2* (once known as *partition c*), which represents the entire disk. Given the size and price of disks today, you might easily wind up with a 9- or 18Gb file system! You should consider the intended content and how you intend to back up file systems of this size before you choose to go this way. A decision to build a huge file system that might be filled to capacity should be partnered with a commitment to a digital linear tape (DLT) or other high-capacity backup device.

Formatting and Partitioning

Partitioning disks into usable chunks prevents one file system from spilling over into another. This can be a good thing if you're interested in protecting one file system from others. It's also a good thing if your backup strategies are different—some file systems you will want to back up much more frequently than others. On the other hand, breaking your disk into separate buckets costs you some amount of flexibility. You might easily wind up with excess space in one file system while another fills up.

In Solaris, there are strong conventions about which slice is used for what, but no hard and fast rules. Unless there is an overriding reason, we always recommend following the conventions. Being obvious is a time saver in the long run. Should someone else at some point try to recover data from one of the disks that you set up using another system, they will be more confident working with a disk that is laid out in a familiar way.

```
0    root (bootable)
1    swap (/tmp)
2    the entire disk
3    /var
4    /usr/local (could be /usr/openwin)
5    /opt
6    /usr
7    /export/home
```

Physically, disks are composed of platters and heads that hover over the spinning platters in order to read and write. Accessing any particular file, therefore, depends on how much one of these heads has to move and how much disk I/O is backed up. Access time is composed of several things: how fast the disk is spinning, how far the head moves on the average, and so on.

Partitioning drives is done with the format command. You must be root to run it. Be careful if you are working on a live system. One of the authors once mistyped a disk address—the intended drive was one character different from the one she wound up using—and blew a file system out from underneath a dozen or more busy users. Along with the privilege of being root goes the possibility of making the Big Mistake. Double-check every choice before you hit **return.**

The format command is usually invoked simply with the command `format`, but it can also include the disk device as an argument (e.g., `format /dev/rdsk/c0t1d0s2`). Note that it is the raw device that is specified:

```
# format /dev/rdsk/c0t1d0s2
    selecting /dev/rdsk/c0t1d0s2
    [disk formatted]
```

```
FORMAT MENU:
        disk       - select a disk
        type       - select (define) a disk type
        partition  - select (define) a partition table
        current    - describe the current disk
        format     - format and analyze the disk
        repair     - repair a defective sector
        label      - write label to the disk
        analyze    - surface analysis
        defect     - defect list management
        backup     - search for backup labels
        verify     - read and display labels
        save       - save new disk/partition definitions
        inquiry    - show vendor, product and revision
        volname    - set 8-character volume name
        quit
```

If you enter **format** at this point, you'll wind up doing a low-level format on the disk. This will take a lot of time and is almost never needed. Only if you are using a drive that you suspect may have problems should you bother with the formatting, analysis, and repair options provided with the format command.

The next step is to repartition the drive. Type **partition** at the prompt. The following menu will appear:

```
format> partition

PARTITION MENU:
        0      - change `0' partition
        1      - change `1' partition
        2      - change `2' partition
        3      - change `3' partition
        4      - change `4' partition
        5      - change `5' partition
        6      - change `6' partition
        7      - change `7' partition
        select - select a predefined table
        modify - modify a predefined partition table
        name   - name the current table
        print  - display the current table
        label  - write partition map and label to the disk
        quit
```

To view the existing partition, enter **print**.

```
        partition> print
Current partition table (original):
Total disk cylinders available: 8152 + 2 (reserved cylinders)
```

Part	Tag	Flag	Cylinders	Size	Blocks	
0	root	wm	0 - 59	128.32MB	(60/0/0)	262800
1	swap	wu	60 - 179	256.64MB	(120/0/0)	525600
2	backup	wu	0 - 8151	17.03GB	(8152/0/0)	35705760

```
3       stand    wm     180 - 6975      14.19GB   (6796/0/0) 29766480
4        home    wm    6976 - 7487       1.07GB    (512/0/0)  2242560
5  unassigned    wm    7488 - 7743     547.50MB    (256/0/0)  1121280
6         usr    wm    7744 - 7999     547.50MB    (256/0/0)  1121280
7         var    wm    8000 - 8031      68.44MB     (32/0/0)   140160
```

If you want to change the partitioning on this drive, you should be careful to preserve the continuity of the cylinders. Note how the ranges follow in sequence: 0–59, 60–179, 180–6975, and so on. If you alter the size of one partition, adjust the adjoining partitions accordingly and print the partition table again to be sure that the partitions still line up. To adjust a partition, enter its partition number and respond to the prompts. Here, we're combining two partitions into one and assigning the space to partition 6:

```
partition> 5
Enter partition id tag[unassigned]:
Enter partition permission flags[wm]:
Enter new starting cyl[7488]:
Enter partition size[1121280b, 256c, 547.50mb]: 0c
partition> 6
Enter partition id tag[usr]:
Enter partition permission flags[wm]:
Enter new starting cyl[0]: 7488
Enter partition size[1121280b, 256c, 547.50mb]: 512c
```

Note that the space can be allocated in blocks, cylinders, or megabytes. We prefer to work in cylinders. When you've finished partitioning the disk and are sure your partition map makes sense, write the label back to the disk:

```
partition> label
Ready to label disk, continue? y
```

You don't have to be using the format command to view the partition table. You can also list it with the *prtvtoc* command (at the normal Unix prompt), as shown here:

```
spoon# prtvtoc /dev/dsk/c0t0d0s2
* /dev/dsk/c0t0d0s2 partition map
*
* Dimensions:
*     512 bytes/sector
*     219 sectors/track
*      20 tracks/cylinder
*    4380 sectors/cylinder
*    8154 cylinders
*    8152 accessible cylinders
*
* Flags:
*   1: unmountable
*  10: read-only
*
```

```
* Unallocated space:
*       First     Sector    Last
*       Sector    Count     Sector
*      35180160   521220   35701379
*
*                          First     Sector    Last
* Partition  Tag  Flags    Sector     Count    Sector    Mount
Directory
         0     2   00           0    262800    262799
         1     3   01      262800    525600    788399
         2     5   01           0  35705760  35705759
         3     6   00      788400  29766480  30554879
         4     8   00    30554880   2242560  32797439
         5     0   00    32797440   1121280  33918719
         6     4   00    33918720   1121280  35039999
         7     7   00    35040000    140160  35180159
```

TIP

You can use the fmthard command to put a partition table on a disk and avoid the
format command. If you have several disks with the same layout, this can save you
time. Try using prtvtoc to get the vtoc that you want to copy.

Creating New File Systems

After you've partitioned your new disk to your liking, it's time to build new file
systems. You need to build a file system before you can use a partition (unless
it's to be used as a raw partition). A certain percentage of the overall space will
be used for overhead—the inodes, free-block lists, block maps, superblocks,
and space reserved for file system elbow room (free space), as an absolutely
full disk would be impossible to work with. As file systems become too full,
they slow down. Space becomes harder to allocate, fragmentation increases,
and file activity is likely to be higher. See the material on monitoring your environment in Chapter 9.

When preparing to create a file system, there are a number of decisions that you
can make that might significantly influence its performance. These include the
block size, ratio of disk space to inodes, and free space—all of which are parameters that can be specified with the *newfs* command. The newfs command
is, in effect, a front end to mkfs that supplies values for many of the command's
options.

At a minimum, you have to tell newfs where to build the file system. A command like `newfs /dev/rdsk/c0t2d0s2` would create a file system using all the
space on the specified disk. For values for parameters different from the
default, use the options shown here:

-a   Alternate blocks per cylinder (default is 0).

-b   Block size, in bytes (default is 8192).

-c   Cylinders per cylinder group (default is 16).

-i   Amount of disk space to reserve, in bytes, for each inode created (default is 2048).

-f   Size of a fragment, in bytes (default is 1024).

-m   Percentage of free space (10 percent on small disks, less on larger disks).

-o   Optimization method, space or time (default is time).

-r   Rotational speed of the disk, in revolutions per minute (default is 5).

-s   Size of the file system, in blocks (default is 2880).

-t   Tracks per cylinder (default is 2).

-v   Verbose—displays parameters passed to mkfs (not used by default).

-N   No change—don't create file system, but provide parameters that would be used (not used by default).

Here is an example of a newfs command that specifies one inode for each 8K of disk space and reserves 1 percent of the overall space for free space:

```
newfs -i 8192 -m 1 /dev/rdsk/c0t2d0s2
```

The ratio of disk space reserved for inodes to disk space reserved for files in this case is 1 to 16. This is because inodes are roughly, if not precisely, 512 bytes in size. Since the default is 1 to 4, this shows the user is expecting larger files than is usually the case.

If you specify the -N and -v options with newfs, you'll see output that details the resulting mkfs command and the parameters that would be used in creating a file system *without* creating it. Similarly, the mkfs command with a -m parameter reveals the parameters of an existing file system, as shown here:

```
# mkfs -m /dev/rdsk/c0t2d0s2
mkfs -F ufs -o nsect=80,ntrack=19,bsize=8192,fragsize=1024,
cgsize=32,free=4,rps=90,nbpi=4136,opt=t,apc=0,gap=0,nrpos=8,
maxcontig=16 /dev/rdsk/c0t2d0s2 4023460
```

Note that the mkfs command includes a parameter for the type of file system. The newfs command defaults to UFS.

UFS supports block sizes up to 64K. The block size is specified when a file system is created. In addition, a smaller unit of space—the fragment—is created to allow for more efficient data storage within the last block of a file. Each block can hold a number of segments (1,2,4,8) fragments. Transfer is still done in blocks. Superblock replication makes the file system more resistant to failure. Also, placement of superblocks and inodes is such that it is unlikely that damage to the file system would destroy so much data that the file system would not be largely recoverable.

A raw partition does not contain a file system at all. Instead, the application using it (often a data base) keeps track of where the data is on the disk. This kind of access can be faster, since updates to metadata and block-mapping structures are not required. On the other hand, it is not general purpose; only the controlling application knows how to access the data it contains.

The newfs command provides a simplified interface to the mkfs command. In the following command, we're building a file system on partition 5, specifying less than the normal percentage of free space. There are numerous other parameters that you can specify (especially if you deal directly with mkfs) to tune your file systems, but you should not use these options without considerable knowledge of how the file system will be used and the implications of each parameter.

```
spoon# newfs -m 4 /dev/rdsk/c0t0d0s5
setting optimization for space with minfree less than 10%
newfs: construct a new file system /dev/rdsk/c0t0d0s5: (y/n)? y
/dev/rdsk/c0t0d0s5:     1121280 sectors in 256 cylinders of 20 tracks, 219
sectors
        547.5MB in 16 cyl groups (16 c/g, 34.22MB/g, 16448 i/g)
super-block backups (for fsck -F ufs -o b=#) at:
 32, 70336, 140640, 210944, 281248, 351552, 421856, 492160, 562464, 632768,
 703072, 773376, 843680, 913984, 984288, 1054592,
```

Some file system tuning parameters can be adjusted at any time, but only a few. The best source of advice on file system and general performance tuning is, of course, Adrian Cockcroft, who writes for Sun and for *SunWorld* magazine. The second edition of his *Sun Performance and Tuning* book (with Richard Pettit) is included in the bibliography and recommended reading list.

Mounting and Unmounting

Sysadminis used to do a lot of mounting and unmounting of file systems; the mount and unmount commands are, after all, privileged. Only the superuser can issue them to mount or unmount a file system. Then automounter and vold came along, relieving sysadmins of having to be present and involved in every mount and, in the case of automounter, bringing considerable improvement in NFS performance at the same time.

With *automounter*, reference to a mountable file system results in its being mounted. A cd to a directory or an ls of its contents causes a file system to mount—provided the user issuing the command has proper permissions for the mount point, and the client has permission to mount the file system in question. A mount point is simply a directory. However, those that automount uses are reserved; you cannot, for example, mount a file system on /home when automounter is running and the mounting of home directories is within its purview. *Vold* automatically mounts file systems on diskette or CD-ROM when they are inserted into the drive—provided, of course, that it is running. It is by default. The file systems unmount and eject the media if the eject command is issued—provided that no one is using the mounted files; simply having cd'ed into a mounted directory occupies it.

The Life Cycle of Mount Operations

Whenever a system is booted, file systems are mounted. Certain of these file systems are mounted early in the boot process; the system would not be able to boot without them. You might have noticed in the /etc/vfstab file shown earlier in this chapter that neither the root nor the /usr file system was specified to mount at boot time. These file systems house the files that direct the process of booting (described in Chapter 4) and must be available soon after the basic hardware checks. Other file systems are mounted later in the boot process, as configured in the /etc/vfstab file. Still others are mounted only as requested via a mount command or, as previously mentioned, in response to requests via automounter.

The /etc/vfstab file specifies file systems to be mounted along with locations and options. It is read during the boot process by the start script /etc/rc2.d/mountall.

The file itself is a white space delimited list of files with columns specifying the following:

- The file system to be mounted
- The corresponding raw device
- The mount point
- The file system type
- The fsck order
- Whether to mount at boot and with the mountall command
- Options—other mounting options (e.g., readonly)

Here is a sample /etc/vfstab file:

```
#device               device              mount   FS      fsck   mount    mount
#to mount             to fsck             point   type    pass   at boot  options
/proc                 -                   /proc   procfs  -      no       -
fd                    -                   /dev/fd fd      -      no       -
swap                  -                   /tmp    tmpfs   -      yes      -
/dev/dsk/c0t3d0s0     /dev/rdsk/c0t3d0s0  /       ufs     1      no       -
/dev/dsk/c0t3d0s6     /dev/rdsk/c0t3d0s6  /usr    ufs     2      no       -
/dev/dsk/c0t3d0s5     /dev/rdsk/c0t3d0s5  /opt    ufs     5      yes      -
/dev/dsk/c0t3d0s1     -                   -       swapfs  -      no       -
```

NFS server support is not provided (by default) until run state 3 (discussed in Chapter 4). This means that systems do not export their files systems until they have moved into this run state, commonly referred to as *multiuser with NFS*. Refer to the file /etc/rc3.d/S15nfs.server to see how the NFS processes are started for an NFS server. The client script, /etc/rc2.d/S73nfs.client, allows mounting of remote file systems in run state 2 (this is also effective in run state 3 as we shall explain in Chapter 4).

The file that controls what file systems are shared by a host is /etc/dfs/dfstab. In the following sample dfstab file, we're using a netgroup rather than a string of host names. Refer to the man page for more information on netgroups.

```
#     place share (1M) commands here for automatic execution
#     on entering init state 3.
#
#     share [-F fstype] [ -o options] [-d "<text>"] <pathname> [resource]
#     .e.g.,
#     share  -F nfs  -o rw=engineering  -d "home dirs"  /export/home2
share -F nfs -o rw=utensils -d "apps" /apps
share -F nfs -o rw=utensils -d "archives" /archives
share -F nfs -o rw=utensils -d "home" /raid/home
share -F nfs -o ro=utensils -d "cdrom" /cdrom/cdrom0
```

File systems of type UFS repeat superblock information at various intervals within a file system. These structures contain file system statistics (e.g., the number of files, the label, the overall size, etc.). If the initial superblock is damaged, fsck gives you an opportunity to provide another reboot -n after an fsck; avoid the sync so you don't overwrite your fixes by flushing the output buffers.

The Automounter

Automounter is a standard Solaris feature that streamlines the management of shared file systems and reduces network traffic. Automounter also helps avoid file system problems in environments with many servers and many more clients by timing out on file system mounts instead of freezing one system's resources when a server from which it has mounted a file system becomes unavailable. In addition to the material presented here, we suggest that you refer to anything written by Hal Stern (see bibliography and recommended reading) regarding NFS and automounter to get a more thorough picture than we can present here.

Automounter uses centrally managed configuration information to specify the file systems and mount points for a network. By doing so, it helps to enforce a consistency in the overall naming and arrangement of file systems. It reduces the overhead of NFS mounts by dismounting file systems after a period of nonuse (the default is 5 minutes). Automounter is one of the busy sysadmin's best friends—it provides what a user needs, when a user needs it, and it goes away by itself. It dramatically reduces NFS hangs and is fairly easy to administer. File systems that are automounted don't need to be specified in each potential client's /etc/vfstab file. In fact, all the client system needs is the mount point (created by automountd), and a reference to the file system will cause it to be mounted. The rest is accomplished through NIS maps or NIS+ tables—or their file equivalents, but this is rarely the case.

The services provided by automount are actually brought about through the efforts of several components—the automount maps (detailing what gets mounted, where and how), the user-level process that acts like an NFS daemon, and the kernel module, autofs, that invokes mounts and dismounts.

The daemon process, automountd, runs on clients. RPC requests are generated in response to requests for file systems as routine as a user changing directory (i.e., using cd) into a directory managed by automounter. Once automountd intercepts a request for data, it passes the request to the NFS server and steps aside (there would be a performance hit if automounter got involved in every transfer of data). After 5 minutes of inactivity, however, automounter sends an NFS request for a dismount.

On large and frequently changing networks, there are few tools that will save you as much headache as the automounter. The days of hand editing files on numerous hosts (e.g., the /etc/vfstab files) are over with the centralized management possible with automounter. Not only does automounter make it possible for users to log in virtually anywhere on your net and have their familiar home environment available to them, it ensures that file systems unmount when not in use and reduces the network traffic related to NFS. A third advantage is that automounter keeps a system from hanging if the server from which it is automounting file systems is not available.

Although automounter provides users with automatic mounting, there is some setup required on the part of the sysadmin—a proper configuration of the automount maps and sharing entries on the systems from which these file systems derive.

Security and Automounter

Automounter is subject to the same security considerations as NFS. Even though the tool provides a convenient way to automate mounts, it still requires basic access privilege. Regardless of what automount maps may dictate, a remote file system cannot be mounted if it is not shared and cannot be mounted if access to the mount point is not available.

Configuration Files

Automounter uses one or more files—usually two or three—to control what file systems are mounted and when. The /etc/auto_master file details the other files and maps that are used. The other two maps that you'll generally find in use are */etc/auto_home* and */etc/auto_direct*. The existence and configuration of these files depends on how automounter is used at a particular site.

```
# Master map for automounter
#
#+auto_master
/net        -hosts              -nosuid
/home       auto_home
/-          auto_direct
```

In this particular /etc/auto_master file, the /net entry tells automounter (i.e., automountd) that it is to manage the mounting of file systems in the /net directory. Any file systems exported and available to the local system can be access via the /net directory. The /home entry instructs automounter to manage home directories using the information found in the /etc/auto_home file. The third entry, starting with /-, calls the /etc/auto_direct map into use. We'll discuss direct maps in just a moment.

```
# Home directory map for automounter
#
#+auto_home
*     -rw  Rwanda:/raid/home/&
```

Entries in /etc/auto_home of the type `user -nosuid host:/home/user` cause an individual's home directory to mount when requested. An entry of the form `* -nosuid server:/home/&`, on the other hand, causes any home not previously specified to be mounted from the system server. The nosuid option prevents suid program execution from the mounted file system.

The third commonly used automounter file that you will encounter is auto_direct. This file is used for direct maps. Let's briefly examine the difference between direct and indirect maps and the implications of these differences on your network.

Direct and Indirect Maps

Automounter uses two types of maps to describe the mounting of file systems and directories onto mount points. They are called direct and indirect. For file systems using *direct maps*, the mounts occur on a directory (e.g., /export/home is mounted on /home). For file systems using *indirect maps*, the mounts occur within a directory (e.g., /export/home/sandra is mounted on /home/sandra). Figure 1.6 displays the result of both direct and indirect maps. Automounter knows what file systems it is required to watch. It can be said to own certain mount points and to intercept requests when they are made.

Here is an example of a direct map. The lines in this particular map direct automounter to use webserver:/usr/WWW whenever anyone refers to the directory /WWW, the intranet:/usr/intranet directory when anyone refers to /intranet, and mailserver:/var/mail when anyone refers to /var/mail.

```
# direct directory map for NFS mounts
#
/WWW       webserver:/usr/WWW
/intranet intranet:/usr/intranet
/var/mail -actimeo=0 mailserver:/var/mail
^          ^
|          |
key        value
```

An indirect map might look like this:

```
evan       server:/export/home/evan
sandra     server:/export/home/sandra
```

It would mount the file systems/export/home/evan and /export/home/sandra on /home/evan and /home/sandra (these entries appear in the auto_home map). A more general solution is to use an entry such as the following one. It would cause the home directory for any user from the file server `server` to be mounted as /home/username.

```
server:/export/home/&
```

This causes each user's home directory to mount on /home/user, and so on.

Direct maps are a lot like indirect maps, but are more explicit. Each direct map entry provides a one-to-one mapping of source and mount point, much like a traditional mount. Whereas with indirect maps, more general-purpose associations between mount points and directories are managed by the automounter using the entries both literal and wild-carded from the /etc/auto-* files, direct maps specify direct relationships.

Direct maps can also be of the form `/filesystem host1,host2,host3:/filesystem`. When this is the case, any of the hosts listed can supply the file system

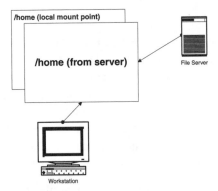

(a) Mount with Direct Map

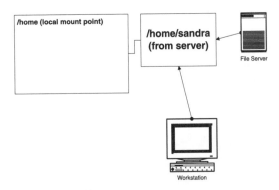

(b) Mount with Indirect Map

Figure 1.6 Direct and indirect maps: (*a*) mount with direct map, and (*b*) mount with indirect map.

when a request for an automount is made. Whichever system responds first provides the mount—an easy way to load balance and reduce reliance on any single server, without a lot of extra effort. You can also add weighting factors in parentheses (the higher the better) to influence this process. An auto_direct entry of /apps server1(50),server2,server3(10):/apps would encourage your systems to mount the /apps directory from server1.

As stated earlier, automounter is more useful the more systems you manage and the more your users move from one system to another, whether physically or using remote login commands. To simplify maintenance of your automount maps, the automounter provides a number of variables that take the place of literal entries. The variable ARCH, for example, represents the architecture of a particular machine. OSREL, on the other hand, specifies the OS release. If you were mounting /usr/lib from a remote system, you could more easily and more

Table 1.5 Automounter Variables

VARIABLE	DESCRIPTION	AS DERIVED FROM	EXAMPLE
ARCH	Application architecture	uname -m	sun4m
CPU	Processor type	uname -p	sparc
HOST	Host name	uname -n	spoon
OSNAME	Operating system name	uname -s	SunOS
OSREL	Operating system release	uname -r	5.7
OSVERS	Operating system version	uname -v	Generic
NATISA	Native instruction set	isainfo -n	sparc

generically specify file systems to be mounted by using these variables. They are listed and briefly explained in Table 1.5.

File Systems and Performance

With respect to system performance, file systems are often the most significant factor—whether we're looking at performance on a single host or across a network. Because disk I/O is generally slower than any other system operation, it tends to be the weak link in the performance chain; faster central processing units (CPUs), increases in network bandwidth, and more efficient applications are easily lost in the shadow of disk I/O.

In general, the single improvement that will have the greatest impact on a system's performance, however, is additional memory. A large amount of random access memory (RAM) reduces disk operations since data can be kept in memory for longer periods of time.

Other factors that affect file system performance include the disks themselves (i.e., seek time, latency, etc.), the block size, whether disk accesses are random or sequential, the degree to which caching is used to speed up disk I/O, the location of disks (local or remote), and so on.

Usage patterns differ depending on the operations a disk performs. Sequential reads, for example, are generally much more efficient than random-access reads. File systems can be configured to optimize a particular usage pattern—and this is a good idea if they are used in one particular way most of the time. In general, however, file system defaults provide a good general-purpose configuration.

If you know that a file system will be used primarily for sequential reads, a larger block size and a higher value for maxcontig (read-ahead cluster size) will improve performance. File systems such as UFS adjust themselves to some degree to observed access patterns. If the file system detects that reads are happening sequentially, it will use a read-ahead algorithm and initiate reads for the following blocks as it reads a requested block. Different types of file systems use different algorithms. The UFS file system requires that the previous and current reads be sequential; there is only one reader of the file at the time, the blocks of the file must be sequential on the disk, and the file I/O must be accomplished with read and write system calls. These precautions keep the file system from going into read-ahead mode when it might not be appropriate.

The default values for the read-ahead algorithm might not be optimal. For the best performance on highly sequential reads, an increase in the read-ahead cluster size is suggested. The read-ahead cluster size is set using the maxcontig parameter. A maxcontig of 8 means 8 blocks. With the default block size of 8192 bytes, this represents 64K.

Where applicable, the use of raw partitions can provide a significant speedup in system performance. Increasingly, applications such as database software bypass the conveniences and the performance costs of file systems and access data on disks directly.

If a system has more than one disk, it's a good idea to spread file systems across the disks in such a way that disk I/O is likely to be balanced. This will prevent the situation where one disk has a long queue of pending requests while the other is basically idle, giving you more balanced I/O and overall better throughput. The iostat command will help you evaluate disk activity.

Local disks will almost always perform better than disks that must be accessed over a network, but this is not always the case. Trade-offs are made between convenience and performance. A good rule of thumb is expressed in the use of dataless clients in which root and swap are local file systems and less frequently accessed file systems are accessed over the network. Though we are not particularly advocating the use of dataless clients, the design principle is a good one. By centralizing infrequently used systems and keeping the most basic file systems locally, you buy yourself some efficiencies of scale while maintaining reasonable performance on your clients.

There are other techniques to increase the speed or the reliability of file systems (both are important). *Disk mirroring*, for example, provides two copies of everything and is the greatest boon to reliability, but at the cost of doubling your disks. *Disk striping*, in which data file systems span disks, increases performance significantly but increases the risk of data loss; the greater the number of disks involved in a striping operation, the greater the chance that one will fail. *RAID* offers many configurations for increased reliability, including the ability in RAID Level 5 to recreate data, when one disk in a set is lost, from data on the other disks, but is generally expensive.

Like many aspects of running a network, choices of disk technology boil down to trade-offs. As Adrian Cockroft (see references) says in his book, *Sun Performance Tuning*, the choices are "fast, cheap, safe; pick any two."

Laying Out File Systems

The location of file systems across your network is an issue that you should consider critical to your system management strategy. The use of central servers for home directories, e-mail, and applications adds a level of serviceability that doesn't exist if your networked clients are all fully independent standalone hosts. At the same time, it introduces a certain complexity and raises some security concerns.

When making decisions about where to locate file systems, you should consider both the complexity of your network and its performance and reliability. The authors, in fact, suggest trading off performance in favor of an easier-to-manage overall file system arrangement across your network.

One way to look at the issue of file system layout is to consider that, on a network where each host's file systems are local, the work load of installing, managing, and backing up these file systems is on your shoulders or is dispersed throughout the network onto the shoulders of your users. If, on the other hand, file systems are primarily hosted on file servers, the effort is condensed onto your file servers and traffic is added to your network. On a network where file systems are dispersed but their use is primarily managed through client/server applications, the complexity and load are often on the applications themselves. In a typical network, there is often a mix of these layout strategies. Still, there is benefit in considering the pros and cons of each approach before making decisions regarding how you will distribute files and applications across a network.

There are two seemingly opposing goals that you should keep in mind when deciding how to lay out file systems on a network basis. One goal is to aggregate functions so that your network is easier to manage. The other is to isolate functions (minimizing the dependencies between systems) so that each system is easier to manage. Obviously, these two opposing goals require you to make some very thoughtful choices. You also need to consider performance. At the same time that there is an advantage to having smaller file systems and optimizing each for its particular role, there is a flexibility benefit in joining smaller file systems into larger ones so that available space is not reserved for anything in particular but for whatever need presents itself.

Related functions should be colocated whenever possible. If you use the same tools or even the same occasions to manage a certain function, it makes sense to have them on the same system. At the same time, a single-purpose file server will be much easier to support and will provide more overall reliability. Whenever two or more critical services are provided by a single system, there will be occasions when a failure of one service takes out the other.

A name server that is also a print server or a mail server introduces a certain risk—though we're sure there is considerable debate over whether a single extremely powerful system well equipped with disk and memory is a better choice than a number of less well endowed systems, each providing a single service. Unless you can afford a system with virtually unlimited resources and set it up with high availability in mind (see Chapter 13), the authors consider the separation of functions among a group of modest systems a better choice than providing all services on a single box.

Clients and File Systems

Before we get into the layout of client file systems, it makes sense to consider the various types of clients likely to be present on a network and, accordingly, the file systems likely to be resident on them. Solaris clients fall into three general classes—diskless, dataless, and standalone. *Diskless clients* have no disks; all file activity occurs over the network—even swapping. Due to the burden that diskless clients put on a network, they are seldom used today. Their one-time popularity in highly security-conscious environments was short-lived.

Dataless clients have disks, but use them only for swapping and to hold the root file system. All system, application, and user files are accessed over the network. This keeps the more I/O-intense operations off the network while providing for centralized system administration of the other file systems.

Standalone clients have a full complement of file systems on their local disks. Capable of running without the network, these clients seldom actually run this way for fairly obvious reasons. They generally use services available over the network—such as naming services, printing services, e-mail, and access to the Internet.

Most networks today are heterogeneous. In addition to Solaris servers (and Solaris clients), they have other Unix systems and a mix of Intel and Macintosh systems running variations of Microsoft Windows, MacOS, and Linux. These clients get certain types of support from the network—for example, home directories, applications, mail, and sometimes data directories and other shared directories to facilitate working together when the application itself doesn't run in a client/server mode.

Sizing Partitions

The layout of an individual system should involve adequately sized partitions. Before you can make intelligent decisions about how much space to allocate to each partition, you need to know how the system is to be used. You can probably get by with a fairly standard configuration for your Solaris clients. We recommend this, especially if you have a lot of them, as this will make it possible for you to use JumpStart to install and upgrade them (see Chapter 6). It's generally a different story where your file servers are concerned. The default partitioning cannot anticipate the applications you'll install, the number of users you'll be supporting, or how often you purge directories.

Here are some general guidelines about space on server and client systems. Clearly, the amount of disk space available will impact how large your partitions should be. The values in the following listing are suggested ranges.

```
File System          Server          Client
/                    32-128          32-64
swap                 100-200         50-100
/usr                 400             400
/opt                 150-500         150-200
/var                 100-300         50-100
/usr/local           100-500         --
/home                100 * users     --
/export/install      500             --
/opt                 100-1500        100-300
```

Things you should consider when planning partition sizes include:

- How often you clean out log files
- If you're running a Web site, how long your access logs sit online and how busy your site is
- What kind of work your users do and whether they clean up after themselves (not very likely!)
- Whether you enforce a quota system on disk space
- Whether your users have disk space in addition to their home directories on the server

Centralizing Services

For most networks, centralizing mail services makes a lot of sense—you only have to configure one server sendmail file and you can keep mail files in a single place where they are easy to manage. The central location also facilitates removal of lock files or pop files. You probably will want to provide a single mail server that corresponds to MX record in DNS; individual hosts can get mail by mounting /var/mail, or by using services such as POP3 or IMAP4.

With the low price and large disks often available on PC and Macintosh systems, it might make sense to limit the use they make of network resources. Some server resources, on the other hand, can facilitate file sharing without requiring users to use ftp or fetch to transfer files back and forth, an extra step.

How do you decide what to mount and what to automount? One of the clear advantages of automounting is that it's all driven from maps that you create and administer centrally. This is in line with what we've been saying all along about the ideal configuration for sysadmins who want to go home at night. Avoid complexity—and when you can't, keep it where you can closely watch it. More important, the network load is considerably decreased with automount and you won't suffer from system hangs when systems or file systems are unavailable— (see Figure 1.7).

As a general rule, it is best to avoid hard mounting remote file systems on NFS servers. To do so is complicated and somewhat risky (it could lead to a deadlock situation in which each of two servers is waiting on the other). However, it isn't necessarily obvious how to avoid mounts if users telnet to your file servers, because their home directories will be automounted. One of the authors, in fact, recently saw a file server run out of swap space while trying to mount home directories from another server that had crashed. Though no one was logged in at the time, the server with the mount problem was a mail server, and it was attempting to automount a home directory each time a piece of mail arrived. The necessity to check for .forward files in the users' home directories required this. As the number of hung sendmail processes skyrocketed, swap space was soon exhausted. Codependency problems of this sort can be avoided, but only with careful assignment of server roles and an understanding of the processes involved.

TIP

A tidy solution to the problems mentioned in the previous paragraph is to configure sendmail to look somewhere else for .forward files. This feature is available in current releases of sendmail (look for the ForwardPath variable). Another option is to run mail and home directory services on the same machine, avoiding the requirement for cross-mounting and its potential consequences.

NFS starts up only when a system boots or enters run state 3—if and only if there are file systems to be shared. How does the system know? Easy—it looks at the file /etc/dfs/dfstab. If there are file systems listed in the file, NFS will share them. The /etc/rc3.d/nfs.server script starts NFS.

NFS file systems should always be shared using host lists—and should never be available to the world in general. To share file systems with no access restrictions introduces a security risk. File systems can be shared read-only (as should always be the case with CD-ROMs unless you want to encounter a lot of errors). The most common mode of sharing file systems is to include a list of hosts and give them read/write access, like this:

```
share -o rw=congo,rwanda,malawi
```

Only under extreme circumstances should you allow another host to have the same authority on a file system as the local root. To allow this, use the following syntax:

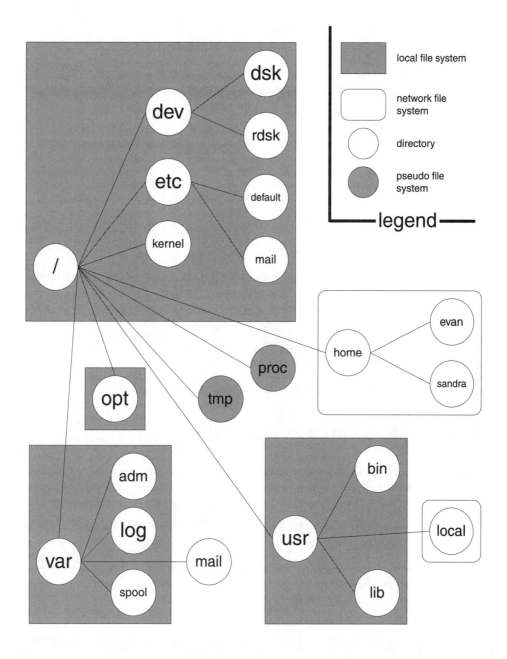

Figure 1.7 File systems of a typical Solaris client.

```
share -o rw=congo,rwanda,malawi root=zimbabwe
```

If you are supporting netgroups (available only with NIS or NIS+), you can often save yourself a lot of trouble by using them in place of lists of hosts. Consider, for example, the following /etc/dfs/dfstab file:

```
#this is the dfstab file
share /home -o
rw=congo,rwanda,malawi,chad,zaire,sudan,burundi,kenya,zimbabwe
share /usr/local -o
rw=congo,rwanda,malawi,chad,zaire,sudan,burundi,kenya,zimbabwe
```

This file could be reduced to the following more approachable file:

```
#this is the dfstab file
share /home -o rw=africa
share /usr/local -o rw=africa
```

You would define the netgroup africa in the /etc/netgroup file. To view the file systems that are shared by any system, simply use the share command, as shown here:

```
congo% share
- /usr/man  ro=africa    "man pages"
- /usr/WWW  rw=tonga:botswana:malawi:gabon:zaire:burundi "WWW"
```

The NFS mount options are described in Table 1.6.

Securing NFS versus Secure NFS

There are a number of measures that you can take to improve the security of your NFS services. If your security concerns warrant, you should probably go to the trouble of running Secure NFS. However, you should be prepared to deal with the added complexity and be prepared for the lack of Secure NFS products for non-Solaris clients.

Here are some guidelines for running NFS. Refer to Chapter 12 for more information on NFS and security:

Table 1.6 NFS Mount Options

OPTION	DESCRIPTION
rw	Read-write
ro	Read only
root	Root access enabled
suid	setuid permitted
nosuid	setuid not permitted

- Don't run NFS on any secure gateway.
- Share files only with known hosts or netgroups of hosts.
- Share file systems with the least privilege possible. If file systems can be exported read-only, do so. Use nosuid. Don't use root= unless you absolutely must.
- Don't forget automount maps.

Administering Secure NFS

Authentication is the process of validating a username and password entered at login. For Secure NFS, the authentication system is more rigid. You have a choice of the Diffie-Hellman and/or the Kerberos authentication, each of which uses complex encryption to provide the validation information that supports the authentication process. Authentication services work because the public and private keys are established ahead of time. Public and private keys, the user elements of asymmetric authentication systems, can be thought of as reverse operations—one undoes what the other does. Keeping one private while openly disclosing the other sets the stage for both private messaging (public key used for encryption, private key used for decryption) and nonrepudiation (private key used for encryption, public key used for description).

The commands to establish key sets for the *Diffie-Hellman authentication* are the newkey and nisaddcred commands. Your users will have to establish their own secure RPC passwords. Once created, these keys are stored in the publickey database.

Verify that the name service is running. If you are using NIS+, the command to do this is nisping -u. This command will tell you if the service is up and when the last updates were made. It also will tell you about replica servers. For NIS, use ypwhich. It will tell you if ypbind is running and which NIS server the system is bound to.

The process that manages authentication keys is the keyserv process (/usr/sbin/keyserv). This needs to be running for secure NFS to work. Use keylogin to decrypt and store the secret key. If the login password is the same as the network password, you don't have to do this.

Add the option -o sec=dh to the share options. For example:

```
share -F nfs -o sec=dh /export/home
```

Add the entry to the auto_master map as well. For example:

```
/home auto_home -nosuid,sec=dh
```

NFS refuses access if the security modes do not match, unless -sec=none is on the command line.

The file /etc/.rootkey should be preserved across system upgrades and changes to ensure that the authentication continues to work. If you inadvertently destroy this file, you can create another with the keylogin -r command.

The process for *Kerberos authentication* involves updating the dfstab file and the auto_master map, as shown here:

```
# share -F nfs -o sec=krb4 /export/home
/home auto_home -nosuid,sec=krb4
```

Again, NFS refuses the mount if the security modes do not match.

Summary

The decisions that you make regarding the layout of file systems on a single host and, even more so, across a network will determine, to a large degree, how easy your site is to manage and how well it runs. Solaris supports a plethora of file system types, many of which are not file systems in the traditional sense, but interfaces to the system. Become familiar with the tools and options at your disposal—it will be a good investment of your time.

In this chapter, we explained that:

- File systems provide a convenient way for users to manage their data, but do not accurately reflect the way data are stored on disk.

- The Unix kernel distinguishes only a few types of files, while users think of their files as source code, compiled programs, scripts, lists, e-mail, and so on.

- Most of the information describing files (other than the contents and the file names) is stored in a file system structure called an inode.

- Logging file systems (like UFS in Solaris 7 and later) provide a degree of resistance to corruption and are, therefore, more reliable.

- Pseudo file systems provide access to system resources—for example, devices and running processes—by *appearing* to be regular file systems.

- Caching can be used to improve file system performance, but does not do so in every situation.

- The layout of file systems across a network can be the single most important factor with respect to performance and manageability.

- Automounter provides a tremendously useful way to automate mounting and unmounting of file systems—without requiring superuser intervention.

Planning Backups and Restores

N o task in systems administration has a poorer balance of work and reward than that of backing up our systems. Many of us back up file systems every night and rarely, if ever, use the backups. Instead, we eject them, label them, store them, eventually reuse or replace the media on which they are written, and clean the heads on the tape drives used to write them. Any script we write stands a good chance of being used a dozen times or more. Any backup we create has maybe 1 chance in 100 of ever being used.

Still, the data on our systems is somehow worth the effort. Loss of a day's worth of scientific data or a script or program intrinsic to supporting operations can have an impact on our work that is way out of proportion to its seeming size and significance before the loss. For this reason, we accept the task of creating backups we are likely never to use and protecting them from loss and harm as one of our primary responsibilities and carry it out with boring persistence.

File Systems and Backups

As mentioned in Chapter 1, one of the factors that you should consider when laying out file systems is how and how often you will back them up. Some file systems are updated constantly and house data that is critical to your organization. The loss of data of this sort might result in lost revenue or worse. For file systems of this type, even frequent backup might not be adequate protection. Simple disk mirroring or some other level of RAID technology might be required before the risk of data loss is acceptable.

For most file systems, daily backup is generally sufficient protection against the unlikely risk of disk failure or the accidental destruction of data resulting from human error. Reproducing a day's worth of work might strain the patience of your users, but is probably within the limits of acceptable loss, especially for losses resulting from "fat fingering" or other forms of user error. Recovering yesterday's versions of files since mangled or deleted will probably not set your users back too much in their work. (At least the work that your users will need to reproduce will likely still be in *their* memory banks!)

Some file systems need only be backed up on the rare occasions when they have been significantly modified. Daily backup of file systems containing only binaries and configuration files that never change is probably a waste of time as well as backup media.

Keep basically static file systems separate (i.e., make sure they are separate file systems), and you will rarely have to back them up.

Housing files that change throughout the day and those that never change in the same file system is not a good strategy from the point of view of backup and restore operations. For this reason, most Unix sysadmins have, for decades, separated basically static file systems such as /usr from those more frequently updated such as /home and /usr/local. Keeping /usr "pure" (i.e., operating system files only) makes the file system stable, requiring little attention in terms of backups.

Full versus Incremental Backups

Full backups are backups in which everything in a file system is backed up. Contrasted with this, *incremental backups* include only those files that have been modified since the last backup at the same or a lower level.

Backup levels, except for level 0 (representing the full backup), are arbitrary. They mean nothing in and of themselves. Their only significance is with respect to other backups. If a backup at level 5 is made on a Tuesday night, a backup at level 6 on Wednesday would include only files that have changed since Tuesday night. If another backup at level 5 is made on Thursday night, it would also include all files that have changed since Tuesday night.

Don't use more than two or three dump levels. It's too much work to keep track of more than that.

Most sysadmins back up their file systems at only two or three different backup levels. Anything more complicated will probably make it too much trouble to manage the backups and keep track of which tapes cover what files for what periods of time. When you're staring at a pile of backup tapes and listening to a user desperately pleading with you to recover a file inadvertently overwritten, you'll need to determine which tape in the pile contains the most recent copy of the file before its unfortunate demise. A simple, reliable backup scheme can reduce the effort and stress at these moments.

Backup Scheduling

The traditional backup strategy calls for weekly full backups and in-between incremental backups. This strategy strikes a balance between the period for which you can still recover files and the number of backups you need to load to restore a file or a file system. With today's high-capacity tape drives, it is possible to dramatically reduce the frequency with which you need to change and label tapes. To the extent possible, backups should be automated. The corresponding restore option should be automated to the same degree.

Figure 2.1 illustrates a backup schedule in which five tapes are used to provide backups over a four-week period. Note how tapes 1 through 4 are each used once every four weeks, while tape 5 is used five days a week. In this backup scenario, files can be restored from as far back as four weeks, but a file created and deleted in the same week (but not the current week) is no longer recoverable.

Many sites, in addition to a standard weekly schedule, save one full backup each month so that it is possible to restore files as much as a year later. Whether this is a good idea for you depends on the files you use and how you use them. The cost of an extra dozen tapes may be a very small price to pay for this added protection.

S	M	T	W	Th	F	Sa
	1 5	2 5	3 5	4 5	5 5	6 1
	8 5	9 5	10 5	11 5	12 5	13 2
	15 5	16 5	17 5	18 5	19 5	20 3
	22 5	23 5	24 5	25 5	26 5	27 4
	29 5	30 5				

Figure 2.1 Sample backup schedule.

TIP

Back up file systems when they are not in use if at all possible.

The best backup insurance is to back up all files every night, but this can be expensive insurance, not so much because of the cost of the backup media as because of the processing time of the backup operation. If backups start after midnight and do not complete until the next morning, they might start interfering with other tasks or slowing network performance. Pay attention to the time your backups take to run.

If you back up a file system every night, you can fully restore it (as needed) using a single tape. Contrast this with the possibility of requiring a full backup and three incremental backups to accomplish the same thing. Most backup strategies attempt to find a compromise between the time and expense of backups and the time and expense of recovery.

Backups versus Archives

Strictly speaking, backups and archives are not the same thing. *Backups* are routine operations intended to preserve the integrity of entire file systems from mistakes and acts of God. *Archives*, on the other hand, are snapshots of files taken at some point appropriate for their preservation—for example, when a development project is ready for beta testing or when the data for scientific analysis have been assembled in one place. Backups are generally kept for some period of time and then overwritten with newer backups. Archives are generally kept indefinitely or until the contents are no longer relevant.

TIP

Encourage your users to make their own backup copies of important files. Teach them to use tar and gzip to create personal archives.

Some of the same commands are used for backups and archives, but, for the most part, file systems are backed up with dump commands (e.g., ufsdump) and archives are created with commands such as tar (tape archive).

Backup Software

The commands most frequently used for backups include *ufsdump*, *ufsrestore*, and *tar*. Other commands that can be used, but which are not discussed here, are dd and cpio. Most backups are initiated through cron and run in the middle of the night when their impact on performance is minimal and file systems are not likely to be in use. It is considered best practice for file systems to be made inaccessible when they are being backed up so that there is no chance of files changing during the backup operation, possibly corrupting the backups. For some sites, file systems must be available around the clock, and this cannot be done. Some backup software provides options for freezing file systems in ways that allow file systems to remain in use while a stable image is written to the backup media.

Commercial backup software sometimes provides significant advantages over home-brew solutions. The most significant of these is a front end that makes it possible for naïve users to retrieve backups of files without expert help. This feature is sometimes complemented with a choice of several versions of the same file (in case the most recently backed up version is *not* the one required). Another important advantage that commercial backup software often provides is electronic labeling and label verification. With this feature, you don't have to label tapes manually or be concerned that you might overwrite a backup you need.

Backup systems with tape robots may make it possible for you to have completely unattended backups and restores. A week's worth or more of tapes can be loaded at once and used in succession. An alternative to robot systems is a high-capacity DLT drive on which a number of backups can be written (excuse the pun) back to back. When backups are done in this way, you'll need to keep track of the number of dump images on the tape to know where to position the tape for a particular restore. The ufsdump utility includes a record of the file system backed up and the date and time of the backup, so it isn't difficult to examine this information and move forward and backward on the media if you find yourself using the wrong day's backup in a restore operation.

Other backup options include recently emerging Internet services that allow you to send you backup data in encrypted form over the Internet to a physically remote location where your file systems are then securely stored. Although options such as these require that you trust your backups to a remote service organization, the off-site location can be a security advantage. Services such as these should be evaluated with consideration to the security level and subsequent availability of data for recovery. As a security-conscious sysadmin, you will want to be confident that you and only you (or you and one or two trusted colleagues) can invoke a restore operation and that you will be able to gain access to your backups in a timely manner; we suggest an hour or less.

It is rare these days for systems to back up to local tape drives. Most systems, except for heavy-duty file servers, back up to remote drives. If you've followed our advice in setting up your file systems, there may be little on each client that you'd want to back up. If user's home directories, applications and data, and network services are all housed on file servers, there may be little on a client system that cannot be easily rebuilt from installation media and printouts of configuration files.

If you have important data on client systems and a central backup server, keep in mind that sending file systems over the network to back them up can seriously degrade network performance. Execute your backups during the night if at all possible.

Backup Security

Backups should be secured in a manner that reflects the sensitivity of the data they contain. It makes little sense to enforce good security practices on your network while leaving your backups unprotected. Consider how much data could walk out your door on one tape alone—and its value in the hands of a competitor or a malicious hacker.

Whether stored in a locked, restricted access computer room or in a safe, backups should be kept out of reach of the general population of your work space. If client systems are backed up to local drives, it may be very hard to ensure that those tapes are not accessible during normal business hours and by casual visitors.

Do not consider standard office file cabinets to represent safe storage. One of the authors was taught how to pick the lock on many such file cabinets with a common X-Acto knife.

Part of the short-lived popularity of diskless clients was that they provided no local access to data other than through the normal login process. There were no tapes hanging out of drives or external disks to be whisked away under any circumstances.

Backup Commands

The backup commands—ufsdump, ufsrestore, and tar—are fairly easy to use, but the arguments vary with the media used. Tape device drivers on Solaris systems are stored in the /dev/rmt directory. The device /dev/rmt/0 may represent an 8-mm drive or a DLT on your server. You'll need to know its characteristics to select the proper parameters in your backup commands.

The ufsdump Command

The ufsdump command is best at dumping an entire file system. As mentioned earlier in this chapter, its operation is affected by a parameter—the dump level—which determines whether it is doing a full or incremental backup and, if incremental, how far back it should go in picking up changed files.

The format of the ufsdump command is:

```
ufsdump [options] [arguments] file-system
```

The options and arguments part of the command is a little unusual. Instead of using a format where each option and argument is presented together (e.g., -s 31120 -f /dev/rmt/0), the command groups options together and looks for arguments to follow in the same order (e.g., sf 31120 /dev/rmt/0). A common ufsdump command might look like this:

```
ufsdump 0ubsf 126 31120 /dev/rmt/0 /home
```

In this example, the first three arguments (126, 31120 and /dev/rmt/0) align with the third, fourth, and fifth options (bsf). The first two options (0 for full backup and u for requesting an update of the /etc/dumpdates file) do not require arguments. The last argument listed is the file system being dumped.

Options for the ufsdump command include:

0–9	Sets the dump level
u	Updates the /etc/dumpdates file
b	Sets the blocking factor (default is 20 blocks per write with a 512-byte block size)
c	Indicates that a cartridge tape is being used and sets density to 1000 bits per inch and blocking factor to 126
d	Sets the density (default is 6250 bits per inch)
D	Indicates that a floppy diskette is being used
f	Selects the device to write to (stands for *file*, but this is almost always a device instead)
s	Sets the size (length)
v	Verifies content of the dump command after completion

You will often see a device with an *n* at the end of the name—for example, /dev/rmt/0n. This represents the *no-rewind option* of the device, which is useful, for example, if you are stacking backups one after the other on a high-capacity drive.

The ufsdump command can be invoked by hand, but it is predominantly used in crontab files or backup scripts called by cron, as shown in the following examples:

```
11 1 * * 0-5 /usr/sbin/ufsdump 0ubsf 126 31120 /dev/rmt/0n /home
59 23 * * 0,1,2,3,4,5 /etc/daily_backup 2>&1 | mailx -s daily_backup
sysadmin
```

The following script creates full backups of some local and some remote file systems. Note that it uses the .rhosts facility to permit the remote dumps. If the /.rhosts file exists only during the backup operation, the risk is limited. Note also that it waits 2 hours before starting the dumps. It picks up the proper date for the backup when invoked at 11:59 P.M. (see the second of the two cron entries in the example) and then waits for a less busy time (many scripts are invoked right after midnight) to start the backups.

```
#! /bin/csh -f
#
# script to do daily backup of active partitions

set me = 'basename $0'
set rm = /bin/rm
set mt = /usr/bin/mt
set day = "'date +%a'"
set date = "'date +%Y.%m.%d'"
set bserver = "spoon"        # backup server
set device = "/dev/rmt/0n"
set echo = "/usr/bin/echo"

(date ; echo "${me}: sleeping for two (2) hours" ; sleep 7200 ; date ;
echo "")

######################################################################
##
## local - no need to use rsh
set i = spoon
ufsdump 0usf 311220 $device /home

######################################################################
##
## remote
set i = www
rsh $i ufsdump 0usf 311220 ${bserver}:${device} /WWW

######################################################################
##
## remote
set i = remhost2
rsh $i ufsdump 0usf 311220 ${bserver}:${device} /var
rsh $i ufsdump 0usf 311220 ${bserver}:${device} /etc

######################################################################
##
```

```
## cleanup
$mt -f $device rew
$mt -f $device offline
$echo "Please switch tape in DLT drive" | mailx -s "Backup Complete"
$sysadmin
```

TIP

━━━━ **Set up a backup user that is a member of the sys group. If you look at the disk devices, you will notice that sys has read permission. Therefore, backups do not have to run as root, yet you can still secure the backup account.**

You'll note that the backup script also rewinds and ejects the tape, and then sends an e-mail reminder to the sysadmin to put the next backup tape in the drive. There could be a problem if the backup does not complete successfully—for example, if it runs out of tape before dumping all the files. The script will hang waiting for someone to insert another tape, the e-mail will never arrive, and it may take the sysadmin a while to notice that anything is wrong. One of the authors once ran into a case where a system being backed up to the same cartridge tape every night had been running out of tape every night for more than three months. By the time the disk crashed, the backup was practically useless, and several months of grad student data went with it. Verifying the successful completion of backups is as critical a step as initiating them.

The ufsrestore Command

The ufsrestore command is similar in syntax to its counterpart, ufsdump. Because it works with an existing dump file, however, the arguments you need to supply are reduced. Note the following command:

```
ufsrestore rvf /dev/rmt/0
```

This restores the backup from the specified device into the current directory. If you're restoring the /home file system, you'll want to do this:

```
spoon# cd /home
spoon# ufsrestore rvf /dev/rmt/0
```

The arguments rvf specify a complete restore, verbose operation (displays the names and inode numbers of the files as they are restored), and the specified tape device.

The restore operation can be run interactively, giving you the opportunity to move around in the contents of the backup and select files that you want restored. This is the easiest way to retrieve the backup copy of a single file or directory that may have been clobbered on disk. The following command initiates an interactive restore:

```
spoon# ufsrestore ivf /dev/rmt/0
```

You will see in the output of the ufsrestore command the date and time of the backup as well as the identity of the file system backed up. If you notice that you have the wrong tape in the drive, you can rewind and eject it and start over again with a new tape. Here's an example:

```
ufsrestore> quit
spoon# mt -f /dev/rmt/0 rew
spoon# mt -f /dev/rmt/0 offline
```

To continue with the restore, use the following commands:

cd	Changes directories
add	Selects files and directories to restore
ls	Lists files (files already selected will have their names prepended with an asterisk)
extract	Begins extracting the files after they have been selected
quit	Exits ufsrestore

If you are restoring select files, it is a good idea to extract them to temporary space, examine them, and then move them into place if they are the proper files and are intact. Starting up your restore operation in the /var/tmp directory, you will note that the extracted files will be stored into a directory structure corresponding to their original pathname appended to /var/tmp. For example, restoring /home/nici/Mail/projects in this way would result in a file named /var/tmp /home/nici/Mail/projects. After examining the file, you should copy it to its original location.

The tar Command

The tape archive (tar) command is generally used to create tar files from groups of related files for archival purposes, to transfer them to different locations, or to make them available to others. Most of the software archives on the Internet, for example, are in a compressed tar format. The file extension .tar is used to designate tar files, and either tar.Z, .tar.gz or .tgz is used to designate compressed tar files using Unix or gunzip compression.

The command options for tar are as follows:

-c	Create
-x	Extract

-v   Verbose

-t   Table of contents

Note, for example, the following command:

```
spoon% tar cvf spectro.tar spectro
```

This backs up the directory spectro in the current directory to a file called spectro.tar.

The tar command works from the directory in which it is invoked and incorporates the directory structure from that point of view in the archives it creates. For example, the archive created with the preceding command would contain files with the following structure:

```
spectro/1999-09/nw
spectro/1999-09/sw
```

If this archive were extracted in the directory /var/tmp, it would create these files:

```
/var/tmp/spectro/1999-09/nw
/var/tmp/spectro/1999-09/sw
```

This is important to know when extracting files from an archive. If the archive was created from the root file system, for example, the embedded files will contain pathnames starting with a slash (/), and ufsrestore will attempt to restore the files to the full pathname specified. This might mean that they will end up in your root file system. If this isn't what you intended and you don't have room for the files there, this could present you with a problem. One workaround is to create a symbolic link that will move the target directory somewhere else.

The *tar tvf* command will list the files included in a tar file. This is useful in determining what the resultant file names will be and in determining whether the archives includes what you are looking for without having to extract it.

Examine tar files with the tar -t command before extracting their contents so that you can anticipate where the extracted files will be stored.

Summary

Backups are a vital part of systems administration. Though seldom used, they are nevertheless important when they are needed. The smart sysadmin will minimize the work involved by automating the backup tasks and preparing a restore script that facilitates the retrieval of files.

Even if backups run attended, you should make some efforts to ensure that they are running smoothly and completing successfully. If your backup script sends e-mail to you at the completion of each backup, you can be confident that your file systems are backed up. If you fail to notice, however, when this e-mail does not arrive, you may be lulling yourself into a false sense of security.

The best advice that we can offer about backups is this:

- Keep the manual effort to a minimum.

- Be as familiar with the process of restoring files as you are with the process of backing them up. If you back up your file systems with a script, have a script for restoring them, as well.

- Make sure someone else knows the routine. If you change tapes every night, someone else must know how and when this is done.

- If it is at all possible for users to retrieve their own files from backup (obviously without affecting the proper functioning of the service or introducing security risks), encourage this. All other things being equal, it is generally reasonable to provide the most motivated individuals with the means for accomplishing a task.

Booting and Hardware Diagnostics

With Solaris, the process of starting with cold hardware and winding up with a system ready for users to login is flexible and elegant. Understanding how this process works when all is well will help you know what to do on the rare occasions when you have trouble. There are numerous options at boot time that involve not only the boot process but also hardware settings and diagnostics. The tests that you can run before booting will help you understand and fix problems. Commands available to you at this point also provide a lot of information about a system's layout—the attached devices, the PROM version, and so on—that is useful in making decisions about installations and upgrades.

The boot process involves the processes that start up between the time you turn on the power or enter **boot** to the time that the system is ready for logins. These processes include everything from core operating systems services to application software that is specific to your site or to a single system.

This chapter describes commands available at the OpenBoot prompt. It explains the boot process, the boot command, configuration parameters, and troubleshooting. It also provides commands for setting up an alternate boot disk.

The PROM Monitor and OpenBoot Firmware

The firmware in a Sun system's programmable read-only memory (PROM) is executed whenever you turn a system on. After a short sequence of hardware tests, it loads the bootblock from the boot disk. This, in turn, loads the secondary bootblock (created during system installation or with the installboot command). At this point, you have barely withdrawn your fingers from the system's power button. The secondary bootblock then loads a standalone program into the system's memory and starts running it. When booting off a local disk, the standalone program is *ufsboot*. When booting off a network, *inetboot* is loaded.

The standalone program loads the system kernel and starts the init process, which then takes over control of the booting process. Init first reads the file /etc/default/init to set up environment variables and determine which run state to assume. Figure 3.1 illustrates the boot process up to this point. The remainder of the boot process is described in Chapter 4.

If you interrupt a system during normal booting (i.e., by entering the Stop-A or L1-A sequence), you will find yourself communicating with one of two programs. The most basic of these, which offers you a > prompt, is a very limited monitor program that listens to the keyboard and offers you the command choices shown here:

```
Type b (boot), c (continue), or n (new command mode)
>
```

You can restart the boot at this point by entering **b**. If you enter **n** (which, as you can see from the preceding output, stands for *new command mode*), you'll see the prompt change to ok, telling you that you are now interacting with a more sophisticated Forth program instead. The ok prompt is the Forth language's normal prompt. The particular Forth program that you are running, called the *OpenBoot* program, does several things. It supplies hardware diagnostics, provides you with access to a number of parameters that influence the boot process as well as the operations of the system when fully booted, and allows you to boot the system from one of a number of devices. In the OpenBoot environment you can, for example, specify a different disk as the default boot disk or modify the amount of memory that is tested on bootup.

You may never have heard of the Forth language. It is an interpreted language, long popular among companies developing embedded systems because it is so compact that the controlling software can easily be resident on a single chip.

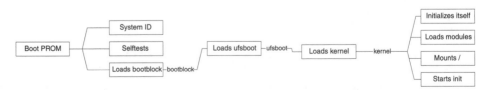

Figure 3.1 The boot process.

Unlike Jini, it's a language that has been around for a long time. For applications where the entire computer may be on a single board inside some small device—for example, on a spacecraft or in your next car—this language has much to offer.

For you, while booting your Sun system, Forth offers a way to start the process that, in turn, starts all the other processes associated with an up-and-running Unix environment. In fact, this single strategy works across a family of systems (with quite diverse hardware) through the loading of the appropriate device drivers into the nonvolatile random access memory (NVRAM).

Though neophyte Sun users may think that the only thing they can type at the ok prompt is **boot** or **boot cdrom,** this is far from true. Forth is a small but complete programming language, and it is sitting there under your fingertips. There are two major versions of the OpenBoot firmware that you are likely to encounter, depending on the particular Sun hardware you are using—version 2.x (e.g., 2.2) and version 3.x (e.g., 3.1). Each offers a collection of commands that you can use to interact with your hardware.

In fact, there is a *device tree* available to you through the OpenBoot firmware. It corresponds, in a less than completely obvious way, to the file system tree that resides under the /devices directory of a running system. You can move around within this tree, probe devices or list their attributes, and run diagnostic tests.

If you want to convince yourself that you're actually interacting with an interpreted language, try giving it some commands to execute. We have to warn you, however, that Forth is a language that uses *postfix* (i.e., operator last) notation. If you want it to add two numbers, you have to put the + sign at the end. You should type, for example, **1 2 +.** Forth will give you the answer and then prompt with another ok. To define a simple procedure, try the following (typing in the bold entries). These commands create, run, and then display the code for a procedure that multiplies a number by 10:

```
ok : times10 ( n1 ) 10 * ;
ok 3 times10 .
30
ok see times10
: times10
    10 *
;
```

All the commands shown in Table 3.1 are available to you at the ok prompt. This list is not exhaustive. It contains most of the commands that you are likely to need when interacting with the OpenBoot firmware. Refer to the release notes for your particular hardware for a complete listing of available commands.

Table 3.1   OpenBoot Commands

COMMAND	ACTION
.attributes	Displays attributes for the device node (2.x)
.properties	Displays attributes for the device node (3.x)
.fregisters	Displays values in registers %f0 through %f31
.locals	Displays values in the input, local, and output registers
.registers	Displays values in registers %g0 through %g7, plus %pc, %npc, %psr, %y, %wim, and %tbr
banner	Displays power-on banner
boot	Boots the system
cd	Changes the directory in the device tree (2.x)
cd..	Chooses the device node that is parent of the current node (2.x)
cd/	Chooses the root node of the device tree (2.x)
dev	Changes the directory in the device tree (3.x)
dev..	Chooses the device node that is parent of the current node (3.x)
dev/	Chooses the root node of the device tree (3.x)
devalias	Displays the real device associated with a device alias (such as disk0)
firmware-version	Shows version of OpenProm firmware (e.g., 0x00030001 represents 3.1)
help	Lists categories of help available
help diag	Lists help available under a given category; in this case, under the *diag* category
go	Continues executing
ls	Lists the nodes under the current nodes
nvalias alias device-path	Stores a device alias in NVRAM
nvunalias alias	Deletes the named alias from NVRAMRC
password	Sets a PROM password that will be required for boot
printenv	Displays all current configuration parameter values
printenv boot-device	Displays value of the default boot device
printenv bootfile	Displays value of the default boot file
printenv parameter	Displays value of the specified parameter
probe-scsi	Identifies SCSI devices attached to only the built-in SCSI bus
probe-scsi-all	Identifies all SCSI devices attached to the system

Table 3.1 (Continued)

COMMAND	ACTION
pwd	Displays the pathname of the current node
reset	Resets the complete system, similar to a power cycle
set-default parameter	Resets the specified parameter to factory default
set-defaults	Resets all parameters to factory default
setenv parameter value	Sets the named parameter to the given value
unsetenv parameter value	Unsets the named parameter
show-devs	Displays the entire device tree
show-sbus	Displays all the installed and probed Sbus devices
sync	Synchronizes all mounted file systems and flushes out all dirty pages to the disks before reboot
test disk	Executes the named device's method selftest, if available
test-all	Tests all the devices in the system
watch-clock	Tests the clock function
watch-net	Monitors the network traffic; displays a dot (.) each time it receives an error-free packet
words	Displays the values for the current node

The Boot Command

The easiest way to boot a system from the powered-down state is, of course, simply to turn it on. When you turn a system on, the system locates the boot device using information stored in its NVRAM and starts loading various boot software, as described earlier. If you interrupt this process with a Stop-A or by setting the auto-boot? parameter (discussed later in this chapter) to false, you can choose to boot from a different device or explore the OpenBoot environment.

The full syntax of the boot command is as follows:

```
boot [device-specifier] [filename] [options]
```

Here [device-specifier] is one of a number of devices that can supply the boot software, [filename] is the name of the program to be booted (e.g., stand/diag), and [options] can be either -a, so that you are prompted for the name of boot file; -h, which will halt the boot process after the program specified as filename has been loaded; or -r, which rebuilds device drivers on bootup (needed if you add a disk or other SCSI device to the system). You can also specify the run state that you want to assume, if you want to assume a run state that is different from the default.

To boot off a device other than the default (boot disk), there must be a bootblock available on the device in question. If, for example, you want to boot off disk1, which corresponds to /sbus/esp/sd@1,0 (the default disk is /sbus/esp/ sd@3,0), you must have at some point used the installboot command to create a bootblock on this disk (see the section "Setting Up an Alternate Boot Disk" later in this chapter). To boot off the network, you must have prepared a boot server to accommodate this system as a boot client.

NOTE
The drive designators used at this point resemble the Solaris 1 naming conventions more than those used in Solaris 2. Regardless, they refer to the same devices as those you'll see on a booted system as /dev/dsk/c0t1d0s0, and so on.

You can, alternately, boot from other devices (if they are set up for this) including, but not limited to the following:

cdrom	If the installation CD is in your drive
disk2 (the second disk)	If this disk has a bootblock
floppy	If a boot floppy disk is in your drive
net (Ethernet)	If you have a boot server prepared to support the local system
tape	If you have a boot tape in your drive

These labels (e.g., cdrom) are not the actual addresses of the devices, but are device *aliases* that make it easier to refer to any of these devices. The defined device aliases will differ from one system to the next. You can obtain a complete listing of the device aliases on a system with the OpenBoot firmware's *devalias* command. A typical list of aliases is displayed in Table 3.2. The relationship between device aliases and boot paths is probably familiar to you if you've been working on Sun systems for a while.

To establish a new alias, use the *nvalias* command (nvalias alias device-path). For example, if you want to refer to your alternate boot disk as *altdisk*, you can create an alias with the following command, provided you have a bootblock installed on this disk:

```
nvalias altdisk /sbus/esp/sd@2,0
```

The *nvunalias* command deletes an alias.

Table 3.2 Typical Device Aliases

ALIAS	BOOT PATH	DESCRIPTION
disk	/sbus/esp/sd@3,0	Default disk
disk0	/sbus/esp/sd@3,0	Same as above
disk1	/sbus/esp/sd@1,0	Second internal disk
disk2	/sbus/esp/sd@2,0	First external disk
disk3	/sbus/esp/sd@0,0	Second external disk
tape	/sbus/esp/st@4,0	First tape drive
tape0	/sbus/esp/st@5,0	Second tape drive
cdrom	/sbus/esp/sd@6,0:c	CD-ROM, partition c
cdroma	/sbus/esp/sd@6,0:a	CD-ROM, partition a
net	/sbus/le	Ethernet
floppy	/fd	Diskette drive

TIP

A useful convention might be to create an *altdisk* alias on all systems that have an alternate boot disk available. Then, regardless of which of the attached disks is serving as the alternate boot disk on a particular system, you can use the same command for booting from it.

Boot Options

The familiar automatic booting on power-up is, surprisingly, not mandatory. Even this setting can be modified within the OpenBoot environment. If you set the auto-boot? parameter to false, the system will not boot when you power it on, but will, instead, wait at the > or the ok prompt for you to enter the next command. This can be a useful feature if you plan to run diagnostics before you fully boot a system and don't want to have to enter a Stop-A sequence at the right moment to interrupt a normal boot.

You can change the boot disk as well as the boot file that is normally used in the boot process. If you have an alternate boot disk and need to boot off of it rather than the default (which may have been damaged), you can specify this information at the ok prompt. To change the disk that is used for booting, use the *setenv boot-device* command. To change which file is used as the boot file, use the *setenv boot-file* command.

Table 3.3 Boot-Time Abort Commands

COMMAND	DESCRIPTION
Stop-A	Aborts boot
Stop-D	Enters diagnostics mode
Stop-F	Enters Forth (OpenBoot) environment
Stop-N	Resets NVRAM contents to default values

TIP

If only a few of your systems have alternate boot disks set up, it is a good idea to label them with instructions for its use—for example, "Alternate Boot Disk. To use, type boot disk2 at the ok prompt".

The Stop-A (same as L1-A) sequence is a fairly drastic operation if run on an operational system. Proper shutdown of a system with the init 0 command is *far* preferable. On bootup, however, before file systems have been mounted, there is little, if any, consequence to running this command. Alternatives to the Stop-A command available in the later revisions of the OpenBoot firmware are listed along with Stop-A in Table 3.3. The *Stop-F* command is the same as doing a Stop-A, n sequence of commands; it aborts the boot process and leaves you at the ok prompt. The *Stop-N* command resets all the factory defaults, similar to the set-defaults command at the ok prompt. The *Stop-D* command aborts the boot and leaves your system in diagnostics mode. Diagnostics mode loads a special diagnostic program that allows you to run a collection of hardware tests. System administrators who have been working on Sun systems awhile are probably familiar with the *boot diag* command and the interface provided for running tests ranging from monitor testing to port checks.

Configuration Parameters

One of the commands you will use often with the OpenBoot firmware is *printenv*. In similar manner to the same-named /bin/csh command, printenv displays the names and values of parameters. As far as the OpenBoot firmware is concerned, these are the hardware configuration parameters that reflect the settings of your system hardware and influence the boot process. The printenv command displays the values of all current parameter settings, along with the default values. Sample output from this command follows:

```
ok printenv
Parameter Name          Value        Default Value

Selftest-#megs          1
oem logo                5a 5a 5a 5a   5a 5a 5a 5a
```

oem-logo?	false	false
oem-banner		
oem-banner?	false	false
output-device	screen	screen
input-device	keyboard	keyboard
sbus-probe-list	0123	0123
keyboard-click?	false	false
keymap		
ttyb-rts-dtr-off	false	false
ttyb-ignore-cd	true	true
ttya-rts-dtr-off	false	false
ttya-ignore-cd	true	true
ttyb-mode	9600,8,n,1,-	9600,8,n,1,-
ttya-mode	9600,8,n,1,-	9600,8,n,1,-
diag-file	vmunix	
diag-device	net	net
boot-file	vmunix	
boot-device	disk	disk
auto-boot?	true	true
watchdog-reboot	false	false
fcode-debug	false	false
local-mac-address?	false	false
use-nvramrc?	false	false
nvramrc		
screen-#columns	80	80
screen-#rows	34	34
sunmon-compat?	true	true\
security-mode	none	none
security-password		
security-#badlogins	0	
scsi-initiator-id	7	7
hardware-version	xxxxx	
last-hardware-update		
testarea	85	0
mfg-switch?	false	false
diag-switch?	false	false

You can change defaults, including, for example, where the output displays when you're booting. This can be very useful information if a monitor fails and all you have on hand to replace it is a dumb terminal. In this case, you will want to send system output as well as system input to the terminal, but the only thing you will have at your disposal is your system keyboard. If you blindly issue the following commands on power-up (assuming the terminal is attached to serial port A) and reset, you should have a working terminal from which to continue your diagnostics and booting:

```
Stop-A
n
setenv output-device ttya
setenv input-device ttya
```

You can reset all of the parameters to their default (factory) settings with the *set-defaults* command or a single parameter to its default with the command *set-default [parameter]*. You can change the value of a parameter with the command *setenv [parameter] [value]*. However, most parameter changes do not take effect until the next time you power cycle the system or use the reset command (which is virtually the same as a power cycle). Table 3.4 lists the parameter display and setting commands.

When changing parameters, keep in mind that the OpenBoot firmware will not check what you enter to ensure that it is a proper setting for your hardware. An incorrect setting may keep your system from booting. Resetting all of the parameters to the default or determining the correct setting for the parameter entered in error will be necessary before such a system will boot on its own.

Perusing the Device Tree

The set of commands that you use to move around the device tree (corresponding to your system hardware) and examine features and attributes varies somewhat between the two versions of the OpenBoot firmware. Table 3.5 provides the commands and descriptions.

As mentioned earlier, the device tree corresponds to the devices on your system and provides you with the means of running tests on these devices when the system is not yet booted. This low-level access to your hardware may be the only way that you can isolate certain problems.

Depending on the particular OpenBoot firmware revision, the command that you will use to move around the device tree and run tests will be slightly different. In any case, we strongly advise that you become comfortable with working at this level sometime when you have spare time and no emergencies. Later on, when an important system is not booting and you have to use these commands to determine what is wrong, you will be much more comfortable.

Table 3.4 Parameter Display and Setting Commands

COMMAND	DESCRIPTION
printenv	Displays current configuration parameters
setenv parameter value	Sets parameter to value provided
set-default parameter	Resets specified parameter to the factory default
set-defaults	Resets all parameters to the factory defaults

Table 3.5 Device Tree Navigational Commands

COMMAND	DESCRIPTION
.attributes	Displays the names and values of the current node's properties (2.x)
.properties	Displays the names and values of the current node's properties (3.x)
cd node-name	Finds a node with the specified name, starting with current location node in the tree (2.x)
cd..	Selects the node that is parent to the current node (2.x)
dev node-name	Finds a node with the specified name, starting with current location node in the tree(3.x)
dev..	Selects the node that is parent to the current node (3.x)
device-end	Exits the tree, explains
ls	Lists the names of nodes that are children of the current node
pwd	Displays the path name that corresponds to the current node
show-devs [path]	Displays devices directly under the specified device in the device tree
words	Displays the currents node's methods

TIP

Plan for disaster. Reserve a system that you can play with. Practice alternate boots. Run diagnostics just for fun. When a real disaster strikes, you'll be ready for it.

Similarly to moving around a Unix file system, navigating within the device tree uses simple commands. For OpenBoot 2.x systems, the command is the familiar cd. For the later version, 3.x, the command is dev. In either case, you can think of the device structure that you are working within as if it were a treelike file system. Instead of directories, this structure has *nodes*. Nodes correspond to the structure of hardware devices.

To view the entire device tree, use the *show-devs* command, as shown here:

```
ok show-devs
/options
/virtual-memory@0,0
/memory@0,0
/sbus@1,f8000000
/auxiliary-io@1,f7400003
/interrupt-enable@1,f4000000
/counter-timer@1,f3000000
/eeprom@1,f2000000
```

```
/audio@1,f7201000
/fd@1,f7200000
/zs@1,f0000000
/zs@1,f1000000
/openprom
/packages
/sbus@1,f8000000/bwtwo@3,0
/sbus@1,f8000000/le@0,c00000
/sbus@1,f8000000/esp@0,800000
/sbus@1,f8000000/dma@0,400000
/sbus@1,f8000000/esp@0,800000/st
/sbus@1,f8000000/esp@0,800000/sd
/packages/ibx?-tftp
deblocker
disk-label
```

The listing you will see depends on your particular hardware, of course, but you will see something roughly resembling what we have shown here. Each line in this output represents a device. If you compare this listing to what you see under /devices on your up-and-running system, you will recognize many of the devices:

```
sunstation:/devices 9# ls
audio@1,f7201000:sound,audio       sbus@1,f8000000
audio@1,f7201000:sound,audioctl    zs@1,f1000000:a
eeprom@1,f2000000:eeprom           zs@1,f1000000:a,cu
profile:profile                    zs@1,f1000000:b
pseudo                             zs@1,f1000000:b,cu

sunstation:/devices/sbus@1,f8000000/esp@0,8000000 36# ls -a
.              sd@3,0:f      sd@6,0:d      st@4,0:bn      st@4,0:ln
..             sd@3,0:f,raw  sd@6,0:d,raw  st@4,0:c       st@4,0:m
sd@3,0:a       sd@3,0:g      sd@6,0:e      st@4,0:cb      st@4,0:mb
sd@3,0:a,raw   sd@3,0:g,raw  sd@6,0:e,raw  st@4,0:cbn     st@4,0:mbn
sd@3,0:b       sd@3,0:h      sd@6,0:f      st@4,0:cn      st@4,0:mn
sd@3,0:b,raw   sd@3,0:h,raw  sd@6,0:f,raw  st@4,0:h       st@4,0:n
sd@3,0:c       sd@6,0:a      sd@6,0:g      st@4,0:hb      st@4,0:u
sd@3,0:c,raw   sd@6,0:a,raw  sd@6,0:g,raw  st@4,0:hbn     st@4,0:ub
sd@3,0:d       sd@6,0:b      sd@6,0:h      st@4,0:hn      st@4,0:ubn
sd@3,0:d,raw   sd@6,0:b,raw  sd@6,0:h,raw  st@4,0:l       st@4,0:un
sd@3,0:e       sd@6,0:c      st@4,0:       st@4,0:lb
sd@3,0:e,raw   sd@6,0:c,raw  st@4,0:b      st@4,0:lbn
```

When located at a node corresponding to a particular device, you can determine what, if any, selftests are available for that device and run them.

Troubleshooting

If you're having trouble booting your system or aren't sure that the attached devices are working properly, you can take advantage of the diagnostic utilities available through the OpenBoot firmware. After all, there are occasions when this will be all that you have to work with. We have used the *probe-scsi* command, explained in the next paragraph, many times to determine whether an attached disk that appears to be nonfunctional on a booted system might actually be working. If a probe-scsi does not respond with an entry for a device that is attached and turned on, you can be confident that the disk is fundamentally hosed. Most likely, there is a problem with the controller hardware on the disk itself (but please be sure that you're using a known-to-be-good SCSI cable!).

The probe-scsi command provides information on each device attached to the built-in SCSI bus. If you have additional SCSI buses, use the *probe-scsi-all* command instead. Both commands will probe the attached devices and display the information that they retrieve. This usually includes information on the manufacturer and model number of each device. Importantly, the SCSI target address is also included. If you were to inadvertently press the SCSI selector of an external device while moving it, you might notice this fact by examining the probe-scsi output. Once a SCSI target no longer matches what has been defined in the system, your system will not be able to communicate with it. If you have many external devices, the likelihood of creating a SCSI target conflict is higher. The probe-scsi command will help you make this kind of determination without requiring you to climb over your desk and read the SCSI selector while hanging upside-down.

To test an installed device, use the command *test [device-specifier]*. This command will execute the selftest defined for the particular device. Here are some samples:

```
test floppy
test /memory
test net
test-net
```

Other commands include:

```
eject-floppy
watch-clock
watch-net
```

You can use the *test-all* command to test all of the devices. Tests will be run only for devices that have defined selftests, of course, but this is more the rule than the exception.

To test the system clock, use the command *watch-clock*. The response should be a tick every second until you stop the command. If you have reason to suspect problems with your system clock (e.g., complaints from cron that it is having to make adjustments), this command will help you pinpoint the problem.

The *watch-net* command both tests your Ethernet loopback connection and tells you whether packets are arriving on the Ethernet interface. If you do not see a string of dots, you are not properly connected to your network or you have a problem with your network interface. You might want to check the cable and/or transceiver that connects to the system or the port on the hub to which this cable connects. If you see *X* characters interspersed with a series of dots, your interface is receiving bad (probably malformed) packets. This probably indicates a problem elsewhere on your network.

A series of commands provides you with the ability to display information about your system. These include the following:

banner   Displays the power-on banner

show-sbus   Displays a list of installed and probed sbus devices (compare with probe-scsi)

.enet-addr   Displays the Ethernet hardware address associated with the network interface

.idprom   Displays the contents of your ID PROM

.traps   Lists trap types

.version   Shows the version and date associated with the boot PROM

Setting Up an Alternate Boot Disk

A corrupt root file system can keep a system from booting. If you'd like a quick workaround for critical systems, install a second root and make it bootable. This solution is most effective on systems that have a reasonably sized root file system—in other words, *not* one of those root file systems where everything is in root.

The ideal candidate for an alternate root is a separate drive or an unused partition on a different drive than your current root. An unused partition on the same drive is okay, but less desirable since it might be affected by whatever evil is going to befall your original root file system.

Once you've identified your partition (let's say you've salvaged a half-megabyte drive from an old client), attach it to your system and reboot (see Chapter 1). Then make sure it is formatted and prepared with a file system of the approximate size of the one that it will be backing up. You might have to partition the drive. If so, refer to Chapter 1 if you need help.

Mount the alternate root partition on /mnt (the universal mount point). You don't need or want to create an entry in your /etc/vfstab file since you won't be using it in any capacity during normal operations.

The next thing you want to do is copy your existing root file system to the new one. The easiest thing to do is to copy the entire file system. If your /var directory is in root, you may want to go through the trouble of emptying out log files; they will be outdated by the time you need to use the alternate partition, so there's little sense in preserving them. Commands such as `cat /dev/null >` `/mnt/var/adm/wtmp` will make this process fairly painless (but don't forget to include /mnt in the pathname!).

There are numerous ways to copy the root partition. Don't use the cp command! To create a duplicate of a file system, the best approach is to use a back-to-back tar command or a back-to-back dump/restore, as shown in the following examples:

```
spoon# cd /; tar cpBf - | (cd /mnt;tar x -)
spoon# ufsdump 0f - / | (cd /mnt; ufsrestore xf -)
```

Either of these commands preserves ownership and permissions of all the copied files—vital to the functioning of a root file system. Once the copy operation has completed, you need to modify the /etc/vfstab in the alternate root so that it refers to itself as the root file system. Look for a line that looks like this and change the first two arguments to reflect the new partition:

```
/dev/dsk/c0t3d0s0   /dev/rdsk/c0t3d0s0   /   ufs   1   no   -
```

Unmount /mnt and label the disk (assuming it's an external drive) with the commands needed to boot from it in any emergency. Depending on your system, the address of the alternate root will be different from what we show here. Verify this on your system with the probe-scsi command explained earlier in this chapter:

```
ok devalias disk2 /sbus/esp/sd@1,0
ok boot disk2
```

The only tricky part to this process is finding and installing the right bootblock. The following commands should do the trick. Replace the device name with your device. The command *uname -i* will put you in the correct directory for your system:

```
spoon# cd /usr/platform/`uname -I` /lib/fs/ufs
spoon# installboot bootblk /dev/rdsk/c0t1d0s0
```

For Solaris x86 systems, the installboot syntax is slightly different; there's an extra bootblock to install. Use this command instead:

```
spoon# installboot pboot bootblock /dev/rdsk/c0t1d0s0
```

Your alternate root partition is now ready to come to your rescue.

Summary

A wealth of information about the configuration and health of your systems is available behind the modest little ok prompt. The diagnostics and boot options available to you might come in extremely handy when a hardware problem arises. For example, if a new disk does not respond when a system is booted or a network interface appears inoperable, you can use probe-scsi or watch-net to gather critical information about these components.

Key things to remember during the normal boot process include:

- Systems administrators frequently add or modify the start/stop scripts in the /etc/rc*.d directories that control which processes start and stop in each of the Solaris run states.

- Careful setup and testing of these scripts is essential.

- We also provided instructions for creating an alternate, bootable, root partition. The steps involve creating an alternate root file system and then making it bootable.

## CHAPTER 4

Configuring Run States

Every Unix system has processes that must start "automagically" when the system is turned on or rebooted. Most of these configure and initialize basic operating services including mounting file systems, starting network communications, monitoring the keyboard for login activity, listening for e-mail or print requests, and invoking many other processes that provide the eventual users with the services they require.

The process through which all of these services spring to life somewhere between a cold boot and a working system is elegantly designed and is both easy to understand and easy to modify. Given a basic understanding of how the important files are organized and invoked, you can provide support for additional services, ensuring that they are started and stopped as required in the life cycle of your Solaris systems.

The first and most important thing to recognize—even before you cd over to /etc/init.d or start vi to create a new start/stop script—is that the configuration of run states "out of the box" reflects a careful orchestration of system resources. The prudent systems administrator, or *sysadmin*, as we affectionately call him or her (and as both of us have proudly called ourselves for many years), will change little or nothing of this default setup. What he or she will do, however, is add scripts for site-specific processes and use the scripts already in place to start and stop processes as needed on running systems.

Picturing Run States

Without overdoing the case for the value of images in understanding concepts related to operating systems, allow us to give you our image of what a run state represents. Most references seem to define run states by enumerating the run states that are possible and then associating each with a brief description—for example: Run Level 3, Multiuser mode with NFS support. Though we appreciate these descriptions, we prefer to stress that each run state is effectively the collection of processes that start and stop as that run state is invoked.

In *run state 0*, basically nothing is running; the system is halted. Only the monitor process or the OpenBoot environment is available. In *run state 1* or *s*, single user, limited processes are running. Run state 1, single user, is limited because the processes that support login through devices other than the console, log system messages, run cron jobs, mount remote file systems, and provide the bulk of the usual Unix environment are simply not required. In single-user mode, you will, obviously, have some local file systems mounted and be able to log in as root on the system console. Naming support and network information services, such as DNS and NIS, will not be available. This run state is used for system repair and troubleshooting (e.g., checking file systems). In *run state 2*, on the other hand, most processes are running, but file systems are not shared (exported). Users with homes on the system will find they cannot access them.

There is nothing peculiar about run states. They have nothing to do with the state of the CPU or even the kernel. The only real difference between one run state and another is, once again, what is running. It is not until we get to run state 2 that we begin to see the familiar environment we have come to identify as Unix.

Configuring run states is simply a matter of selecting which processes are to start and stop when that run state is entered and, then, setting up the proper scripts to make this happen. More precisely, it is a matter of selecting which processes *stop* and *start*. We will explain this distinction shortly.

The Init Process

You will recall from Chapter 2 that control during the boot process eventually rests with the init process. With process ID (PID) 1 and owner root, init is the single process that can be said to be parent to all other processes running on a Unix system—in any of its run states (other than halted, of course). This is why experienced (read: "been there, made that mistake") systems administrators fear the mistyped *kill -1 1* command—meant to be *kill -HUP 1*, kill 1 1 will ungraciously halt the system). When the init process gains control early in the boot process, the first thing it does is read its configuration file. This file, */etc/inittab*, is one that every senior sysadmin should know well. Though few, if any, of us will every modify this file, it is so critical to the boot process that familiarity with its format and function is part of the essential knowledge that none of us can afford to be without.

```
ap::sysinit:/sbin/autopush -f /etc/iu.ap
fs::sysinit:/sbin/rcS              >/dev/console 2>&1 </dev/console
is:3:initdefault:
p3:s1234:powerfail:/usr/sbin/shutdown -y -i5 -g0 >/dev/console 2>&1
s0:0:wait:/sbin/rc0               >/dev/console 2>&1 </dev/console
s1:1:wait:/usr/sbin/shutdown -y -iS -g0  >/dev/console 2>&1 </dev/console
s2:23:wait:/sbin/rc2              >/dev/console 2>&1 </dev/console
s3:3:wait:/sbin/rc3               >/dev/console 2>&1 </dev/console
s5:5:wait:/sbin/rc5               >/dev/console 2>&1 </dev/console
s6:6:wait:/sbin/rc6               >/dev/console 2>&1 </dev/console
fw:0:wait:/sbin/uadmin 2 0        >/dev/console 2>&1 </dev/console
of:5:wait:/sbin/uadmin 2 6        >/dev/console 2>&1 </dev/console
rb:6:wait:/sbin/uadmin 2 1        >/dev/console 2>&1 </dev/console
sc:234:respawn:/usr/lib/saf/sac -t 300
co:234:respawn:/usr/lib/saf/ttymon -g -h -p "`uname -n` console login: "
 -T sun -d /dev/console -1 console -m ldeterm,ttcompat
```

The first thing you're likely to notice as you look at this file is that it is columnar, with fields separated by colons. Look at the third line; the third field in this line reads `initdefault`. This is the run state that the system will assume when you boot, unless you specify a different run state in at the ok prompt. The other lines in /etc/inittab have the following format:

```
id:rstate:action:process
```

The first field, `id`, is simply a label identifying the entry. The second identifies the run state in which the particular entry will be used. The third details how the process will be run; we'll talk about this in a moment. The fourth specifies the process that will be run.

Although there are numerous options that can be specified in the third field— `respawn`, `wait`, `once`, `boot`, `bootwait`, `powerfail`, `powerwait`, `off`, `ondemand` **and** `initdefault--` only half are used in the out-of-the-box /etc/inittab. Let's look at these:

```
spoon% cat /etc/inittab | awk -F: '{print $3}' | uniq
sysinit
initdefault
powerfail
wait
respawn
```

Of these, the most common is *wait* (i.e., wait for the process to complete) and the next most common (other than sysinit) is *respawn*. You can read the man page on inittab for an explanation of each of the action fields or refer to Table 4.1, but the function of the respawn keyword is especially worth noting, so we'll discuss it here.

The respawn action is basically a *keep alive* directive. If any process that is started by init with this keyword specified in the action field dies, init will restart it. If you, as superuser, kill either the service access controller (/usr/lib /saf/sac) or the port monitor (/usr/lib/saf/ttymon), init will restart it. Clearly, very few processes on a system warrant this kind of electronic babysitting. However, these two services are critical to your access to the machine, so they must be started up again if they go down for any reason.

Now, let's pick up again with the process of the normal system boot. The init process reads the initdefault line to determine which run state to enter. If the field is blank, init prompts the user for this information. If the field has more than one digit, it sets the target run state to the highest of those present. It executes the sysinit entries (the first two lines in the inittab file) sometime before you see the login prompt on the console.

Table 4.1 Actions in /etc/inittab

ACTION	MEANING
boot	Executed only when /etc/inittan is read for the first time.
bootwait	Executed when changing states from single-user to multiuser; init waits for completion of process before moving to the next appropriate entry.
initdefault	Specifies the run state that init will assume if no other state is explicitly requested.
off	Process to be stopped when entering the specified run state.
once	Starts specified process without waiting for completion; executed once only.
powerfail	Specifies process to be executed if init receives a powerfail signal; read and remembered for later use.
powerwait	Works like the powerwait signal, except that init waits for the process to complete.
respawn	Starts the process on entering run state and starts again if process dies at any point.
sysinit	Run before logins are accepted.
wait	Runs process and waits for completion.

In a normal boot, init is then going to run the process specified in each line that includes a 3 in the *rstate* field. Discounting the respawn and powerfail entries (these are special cases), this leaves us with these entries:

```
/sbin/rc2                    >/dev/console 2>&1 </dev/console
/sbin/rc3                    >/dev/console 2>&1 </dev/console
```

Of these, /sbin/rc2 is the primary run script for run state 2 and /sbin/rc3 is the same for run state 3. These two scripts, therefore, drive the boot process, initiating all the processes that you are used to seeing in an up-and-running Solaris system. The way that they do this is quite clever and dictates the steps that you must take in amending the boot process with your own site-specific processing. This process is illustrated in Figure 4.1.

The information in the /etc/inittab file is used whenever a system's run state is changed, not only on initial booting. For example, if you issue the command *init 2* on a system in run state 3, init will start run state 2. It will use the s2 entry and then run the /sbin/rc2 script. This script will, in turn, execute the kill scripts in /etc/rc2.d, stopping the NFS file service, but will not execute the start scripts (because we are coming down a run state, the processes are already running and a line in the /sbin/rc2 script prevents this from happening). Subsequent calls to init specifying the *same* run level are ignored.

The rc Scripts

If you look at either of these two scripts (/sbin/rc2 and /sbin/rc3), you'll note that they do several things. First, they look at certain parameters related to the state of the system and make some basic processing decisions based on their

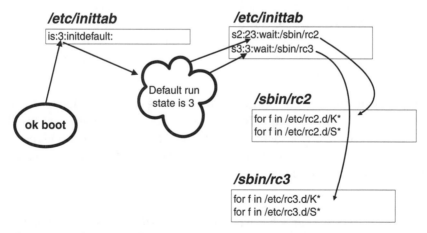

Figure 4.1   The normal boot sequence.

value. More specifically, note that each of the scripts—rc1, rc2, and rc3—uses the *who -r* command. You may be familiar with this command as the way to tell what run state your system is in. If you run this command on most systems, you'll get a response like this:

```
unixhost% who -r
       .          run-level 3  May  1 08:14      3      0  S
```

Though the man page tells us only that this command indicates the run level, it clearly does more than this, and the rc scripts make use of the additional information provided. When the rc2 script determines whether x$9 is equal to "xS", it is simply evaluating the last field in the response to the who -r command. The set part of the `set '/usr/bin/who -r'` command assigns each field in this response to a separate variable, as shown here:

```
congo% who -r
      .          run-level 3  Nov 30 19:08      3      0  S
      ^                ^        ^  ^  ^    ^          ^      ^  ^
      |                |        |  |  |    |          |      |  |
      |                |        |  |  |    |          |      |  |
     $1               $2       $3 $4 $5   $6         $7     $8 $9
```

$9 is the ninth field in this response (in this example, S), so x$9 is "xS." The x is a scripting trick to ensure that there will be some text for the comparison regardless of the response of this command. In other words, we will not wind up with invalid syntax.

These lines in the run script are essentially saying, "If previous run state was 'S' (i.e., single-user), then issue the message 'The system is coming up. Please wait.' "

```
if [ x$9 = "xS" -o x$9 = "x1" ]
then
      echo 'The system is coming up.  Please wait.'
      BOOT=yes
or if the 7th was 2, then this:
elif [ x$7 = "x2" ]
then

        echo 'Changing to state 2.'
```

The bulk of the work of the rc scripts is done in two for loops, the order of which is well worth noting. First, these scripts run through what we shall call the *kill scripts* in the associated directory—/etc/rc2.d for rc2 and /etc/rc3.d for rc3. The kill scripts are all the files in this directory starting with a capital letter *K*, picked out by the following for command:

```
for f in /etc/rc2.d/K*
```

Then, the rc scripts run what we shall call the *start scripts*, again in the associated directory. The start scripts are all the files in this directory that start with a capital letter *S*, as identified by the following line of code (executed only if you are coming from some state other than 2 or 3):

```
for f in /etc/rc2.d/S*
```

TIP

Read through one of the rc scripts—preferably /sbin/rc2 or /sbin/rc3—sometime when you're bored. Then compare the contents of /etc/init.d with /etc/rc2.d.

Kill and Start Scripts

Kill and start scripts start up or stop individual processes or groups of related processes in the order determined by their names (e.g., K02* would run before K17*).

It's important to note that the K and S scripts are actually the same files with different names. In fact, they are set up as hard links. Recall from Chapter 1 that hard links provide a way of giving a single file more than one *identity* in the file system. The overhead associated with hard links is very small. They only use the space required by the directory entry. They share inodes and disk space with the original files. If you modify one of a set of hard links, you modify them all, since they really are nothing more than multiple references to a single file.

TIP

Always use hard links when creating start/stop scripts. Put the original in /etc/init.d and the link in the appropriate /etc/rc?.d (usually /etc/rc2.d) directory.

As an aside, a number of Unix commands are actually hard links as well. Consider the mv and cp commands. They are actually the same file. The way to tell is by doing a long listing including the inode number, as shown here:

```
congo% ls -li mv
39720 -r-xr-xr-x   3 bin     bin       15992 Oct 25  1995 mv
congo% ls -li cp
39720 -r-xr-xr-x   3 bin     bin       15992 Oct 25  1995 cp
```

There is a *correct* way to implement start/stop scripts. In short, you want to follow the model that the system uses. Build each script in the /etc/init.d directory, giving it a meaningful name that relates to the service it starts and stops, (e.g., /etc/init.d/httpd-apache). Include processing for both a start and a stop argument (and maybe a usage statement as well), if it's appropriate. Then, after carefully selecting the points at which these processes should be started and stopped, add the K* and S* hard links to the rc?.d directories, as shown in this example:

```
ln /etc/init.d/httpd-apache /etc/rc3.d/S98httpd-apache
ln /etc/init.d/httpd-apache /etc/rc2.d/K56httpd-apache
```

These lines indicate that we want to start the httpd process late in the sequence of processes that start when we enter run state 3. Further, we want to kill the process when we enter run state 2.

TIP

Test your start/stop scripts by manually invoking them (as root) sometime when no one's work will be disrupted.

The kill and start scripts are not only used during bootup and with changes in the run state (as invoked with the init command). Most sysadmins who have made more than one Big Mistake will also use the scripts in the /etc/init.d directory to start and stop processes whenever the need arises. After all, these scripts are generally coded with considerable care. If more than one process needs to start, or a process id file, which identifies the process id of a process, needs to be created or removed, the scripts will include the code to make this happen. Shutting down or restarting processes with these scripts is, therefore, the *safest* way to do so. A restart of an Apache daemon might look like this:

```
www# /etc/init.d/httpd-apache stop;/etc/init.d/httpd-apache start
```

Further, if you are adding your own kill and start scripts, you should follow the coding conventions that the existing scripts use. Create parameters, enclose commands in if statements that ensure that a file exists before you try to invoke it, and use a case statement to handle start and stop parameters. The following script is a skeleton to be used for creating start/stop scripts that actually do something.

```
#!/bin/sh                               ← Identify shell
start=/usr/local/bin/start              ← Create parameters as needed
stop=/usr/local/bin/stop

case "$1" in                            ← Test the argument
'start')                                ← Set up start and stop options
        if [ -f $start ]; then
                echo "hello";
        fi
        ;;
'stop')
        if [ -f $stop ]; then
                echo "byebye";
        fi
        ;;
*)
        echo "Usage: $0 { start | stop }" ← Offer usage statement
        ;;
esac
exit 0
```

TIP

A good way to disable a script temporarily is to change its first letter from a capital to a small letter. Scripts starting with lowercase *s* or lowercase *k* will be ignored by the /sbin/rc? scripts, but will otherwise retain complete knowledge of what they were set up to accomplish and can easily be put back into service when the need arises. If you use the mv command, they will retain their hard-link relationship to their counterpart in the /etc/init.d directory.

The preferred way to disable a service that is started and stopped via start and stop scripts in the /etc/rc?.d directories is to rename the processes involved. Changing the initial *K* or *S* to a lowercase *k* or *s* will disable the script while retaining the script in such a way that it can easily be turned back on should you need the service at some later time.

WARNING

The kill/start scripts are Bourne shell scripts. Some force Bourne shell execution by specifying #!*/bin/sh* on the first line. Others do not. Be careful if you change the root's default shell or if you execute any of these scripts from a different shell environment. Better yet, insert this line into any scripts that lack it and, while you're at it, ensure that root's umask is 077 or 027 (or add *umask 077* or *umask 027* to the scripts).

Summary

The configuration of run states on Solaris systems is elegant and easy to manage—at least, it is once you get the hang of the structure. Here are the most important points to remember.

- Some processes will be restarted by init any time they die. Even the superuser cannot effectively able to kill these processes.
- When you boot a system with the default inittab configuration, it will first run the /etc/rc2 script and then /etc/rc3. Most processes are started through /sbin/rc2.
- You can change run states at any time with the init command. The init 0 command is the proper way to shut down a system, but you should warn users—local users and those who may be using shared file systems.
- You can change the default run state if you have good reason.
- You can add your own scripts to start and stop application processes during boot and shutdown operations. Proper startup and shutdown are critical to the operation of certain applications.
- Start/stop scripts should all have the same basic format. Follow the coding guidelines in this chapter to keep your scripts from abending and to allow their use during bootup or normal operations.

## CHAPTER 5

Installing and Patching Your Solaris System

I f you're going to be installing a lot of systems, the clear choice is to use Jump-Start. The investment you make up front—to understand the steps involved and set up the necessary files—will pay off quickly and repeatedly. In the next chapter, we tell you how you can get the most advantage from JumpStart. If you have only a few systems, taking them on one by one is probably just as easy.

Most new Sun systems will arrive preinstalled and ready to be configured for the roles they will play on your network. Be prepared to answer a series of questions when you first turn them on. You should have a general idea how the system is to be used so that you can lay out file systems and select software appropriate to this role. Here's a checklist of things we think you should know ahead of time:

- The hostname to be used
- The domain name
- The IP address of the system
- The IP address of the router (if there is one)
- The name and IP address of your NIS/NIS+ server
- The name and IP address of your DNS server
- Whether you are using subnets (if so, you will need to know the subnet mask)
- Remote file systems that are to be mounted
- Any unusual requirements for disk usage

- The role the system is to serve (server, client)
- The appropriate software cluster (e.g., end user, developer)
- If the system is to be a server, the number of clients and/or users to be served

Don't overlook the fact that most of this information will be readily accessible on a system *before* it is upgraded. Don't fail to double-check the host's name and address information. We suggest that you maintain logs with the vital statistics of all of the systems you'll be managing, including who the primary user is. Installation time may be the only time you touch some systems in a year or more. Use it as an opportunity to update your inventory, as well.

TIP

During installation, update a prepared form with all pertinent information about the system, including the primary user, the names of anyone with root access, the location of the system, the peripherals, and identifying information.

If you are installing Solaris on a system running an earlier release, you may have the option of doing an upgrade instead of a full installation. An upgrade will only overwrite files that have changed since the last release and will leave most, if not all, of your configuration files intact. Check your release notes, as the option to upgrade will be dependent on your system type and your current configuration.

The installer will walk you gently through the steps involved in the installation process. You will spend a short period of time answering questions and a long period of time while the files are read off the installation CD or over the network. Ideally, you would start an installation before leaving for the day and check the next morning to be sure the installation has completed properly.

Any time you are going to reinstall or upgrade a system, back it up first. You will probably never need anything off these backups, but if you do, it will be a simple matter to fetch a configuration file you don't want to recreate from memory or notes. Installation-time disasters are rare indeed, but you don't want to be the first in your company to have a system you can't return to its prior state.

The Installation

Once you collect the information that you're going to need for an installation, the rest of the process is remarkably straightforward. The authors recall the days when it was necessary to know what disk controller was resident on your system in order to install the operating system. Solaris installation has become considerably easier since then. The forms presented to you during installation are straightforward and the process is, on the whole, painless.

At any time in the question-and-answer part of the installation process, you can exit the process and pick it up later. The installation forms also provide for limited capability to back up and change your answers. Though the installation process may change from one release to the next, the steps in the process are generally the same. These involve the following activities:

- Identifying the system (name, network address, and so on)
- Laying out the file systems
- Selecting the software

We strongly suggest that you adopt a few *standard* configurations, each of which fits a particular type of user or system role. Even if you don't use Jump-Start, the job of managing these systems will be much easier.

The answers that you provide during installation are used to build system files. The /etc/hosts, /etc/defaultrouter, /etc/netmasks, /etc/vfstab files, and others will be customized from generic prototypes. New file systems are created as needed (e.g., if you change partitioning or are doing a full installation) and then populated. The process of installing a system from scratch can take many hours to complete. Most of this does not involve any interaction with you. For this reason, we generally start the process and then go off to other tasks (or home for the day).

If you make any wrong choices during installation, don't panic. You can fix almost anything without going through the process again. You can add packages you omitted and change answers you provided. In Chapter 10, we show you where the answers to various installation questions are stored so that you can find and fix any installation-time configuration mistakes—for example, in the hostname or domainname, DNS server, IP address, and so on.

Patching Your Systems

The first thing you want to do once your system installation is complete is to install the accompanying patches. Consider these part of the operating system; your job is not done until you have installed them.

On a routine basis, perhaps once or twice a month, check whether new security patches or other mandatory patches have been issued, and install them. This is a sound regimen that is well worth adopting. The best way to keep track of released patches is to subscribe to e-mail alerting systems that will send you reports when security holes are discovered and when patches for various problems are released. Subscribe to the following alerting services:

The CERT Advisory Mailing List www.cert.org/contact cert/certmaillist.html

The SANS Network Security Digest www.sans.org

TIP

Use JumpStart to automate installation of patches if you are administering a lot of systems.

If you are not sure whether a patch has been installed, use the *showrev* command; showrev -p will list the patches that are currently installed. Pipe the output to grep if you are looking for a particular patch. Use this command any time you want to see all the patches installed on a particular system. Chances are the information won't mean much to you, but it will give you an idea of what's installed.

This is a small example of the output:

```
Patch: 106193-03 Obsoletes: 106350-01 Requires:  Incompatibles: Packages:
SUNWadmap
Patch: 105421-01 Obsoletes:  Requires:  Incompatibles: Packages: SUNWapppr
Patch: 105472-01 Obsoletes:  Requires:  Incompatibles: Packages: SUNWatfsu
Patch: 105837-01 Obsoletes:  Requires:  Incompatibles: Packages: SUNWdtdte
Patch: 105566-01 Obsoletes:  Requires:  Incompatibles: Packages: SUNWdtdmn
Patch: 105497-01 Obsoletes:  Requires:  Incompatibles: Packages: SUNWoldst
Patch: 105377-03 Obsoletes:  Requires:  Incompatibles: Packages: SUNWbcp
Patch: 105492-01 Obsoletes:  Requires:  Incompatibles: Packages: SUNWcg6
Patch: 105798-02 Obsoletes:  Requires:  Incompatibles: Packages: SUNWcpr
Patch: 105558-01 Obsoletes:  Requires:  Incompatibles: Packages: SUNWdtdst
Patch: 105338-04 Obsoletes:  Requires:  Incompatibles: Packages: SUNWdtdst,
SUNWdthev, SUNWdtma
```

Why so Many Patches?

Patches are released for three reasons: bug fixes, new hardware support (which sometimes also requires new packages), and new features. As releases stay out in the field longer, more bugs are discovered. Many bugs are fixed during the development cycle and are fixed in the next release. However, for many customers, an upgrade is out of the question. As a result, more and more patches are released. Patches are fixes to software problems (generally) discovered after distribution and (generally) made available via the Web or an FTP site. Most patches are simply replacement executables; in other words, a new binary file might replace a system process such as the file transfer protocol daemon (ftpd) when a flaw or a security hole is discovered in the corresponding binary in the previously released operating system. Occasionally, but rarely, patches are distributed as file insertions used to update existing files rather than replace them. Download and install all pertinent security patches. Recheck the patch list frequently. (There are many places on the Net to find out what patches are available, such as http://sunsolve.sun.com.) Not all security patches need be installed on every machine. As a matter of fact, it would generally be extremely unwise to install any more patches than you need. Even with the extent to which patches are tested, no patch is tested in concert with every other patch. If you install patches irresponsibly, you could end up creating more problems— as a result of incompatible patches—than you were hoping to fix. But to protect machines, especially those with public access, patching should be kept up-to-date. You should always install the patches that come with a new release of Solaris. Consider these patches simply as part of the release that didn't quite make it in time to be incorporated into the files used in the primary installation. These patches *will* have been tested together with the release and will bring you up to the proper and expected operating level.

The patchdiag program that is available on the SunSolve CD and at the SunSolve Web site will automatically compare the patch level of a host against the current Sun-recommended patch set and display any differences. It is a good idea to run this every so often.

Different Types of Patches

You will hear a number of descriptors prepended to the word *patch*: jumbo patch, megapatch, mandatory patch, recommended patch, and security patch come to mind. The words *jumbo* and *mega-* indicate that a number of binaries are being replaced or modified in the same patch file. The term *mandatory* implies that the referenced patch must be installed if you want your system to work properly. *Recommended*, which is the term Sun prefers to use today, means that Sun considers the patches to be universally applicable.

It is not necessary or advisable to install every patch that is released. Read the patch descriptions before installing any patch and make sure that it pertains to your particular environment. Not every one will be relevant to your systems. Be sure to install the security patches, but, as a general rule of thumb, install only the patches that you know you require.

Obtaining Patches

You can obtain patches from your Sun warranty provider or from the SunSolve Web site. Patches can be downloaded individually or as part of larger groups called *clusters*. A cluster is a set of patches that will rectify a certain set of issues, such as making the operating system Y2K compliant. Sun also provides a tool called SUNSCAN which can be downloaded from www.sun.com/y2000 /sunscan/. This tools will scan your systems for missing Y2K patches and recommend updates. Depending on the version of Solaris you are using, there can be many patches or just a few.

By now you've most likely updated your operating system for the millennium. If you haven't, check out www.sun.com/y2000/ to find out what you need to do to make *your* system Y2K compliant.

Summary

Installation doesn't require much preparation, and, unless you've never done it before, it is a painless process, but one that takes a lot of time. Use JumpStart (see Chapter 6) if you are going to install more than a handful of systems, especially if they'll be serving the same role and are similar systems. You will be very glad you made the investment.

Patching is a necessary part of systems administration. Here are some tips:

- Periodic application of appropriate patches will keep your systems more secure and is so important that it should become a routine.

- We suggest patching your systems as needed once or twice a month. Don't install patches unless you know that you need them, however. Doing so can create new problems, as patches are not tested in conjunction with all other patches—except for those that arrive with new releases of Solaris.

- Using JumpStart to install patches will simplify the process of installing patches on numerous systems.

## CHAPTER 6

Exploiting JumpStart

The single most energy-saving strategy that any systems administrator can adopt is to enforce a uniformity in the configuration of his or her systems. By doing so, most of the work involved in managing these systems and the networks on which they reside is greatly simplified. JumpStart is a tool that was derived from Sun's internal need to install its inventory of systems. When used properly, it helps to facilitate this uniformity by automating the installation process. It reduces the time and effort involved in installing systems in proportion to the number of systems that need to be installed and automates installation of patch releases and application software. JumpStart requires an up-front investment of time and planning, but pays off each time you use it.

You observe JumpStart in its simplest form when, on initial booting of a new system, you simply accept all the defaults and allow the installation process to proceed. Once you've provided the identification information for such a system (i.e., its host name, IP address, time zone, and so on) and make a few choices regarding the configuration you want, the rest of the installation continues without intervention.

For most of us, because of site-specific requirements, this simplest form of JumpStart does not provide enough flexibility. Some modification of this process is needed to allow for our peculiar disk setups, configure services provided by remote systems (e.g., mail and printing), take advantage of larger disks, and provide for the needs of some extremely diverse user populations. For us, a modification of the JumpStart process, or *Custom JumpStart*, can provide just the right balance of automation and customization. Custom Jump-Start is the subject of this chapter.

Custom JumpStart

Custom JumpStart provides for the automated installation of systems accord-ing to directions stored in simply formatted text files called *profiles*. What Cus-tom JumpStart does for you is this: It allows you to describe the setup of systems—specifying file system layout, software packages, and other installa-tion parameters—and then use these descriptions to install, in a streamlined fashion, as many systems as fit the particular profile.

Preparing for an individual client or a group of clients to be installed with the same basic layout requires you to: (1) build a profile that describes the layout and configuration of these systems and makes it accessible to the clients being installed, (2) identify the systems for which this profile applies, (3) provide access to the installation media, and (4) provide boot support for each of the specific clients to be installed. The various roles systems play in the installation process are depicted in Figure 6.1. We explain each of these roles in detail in the next section.

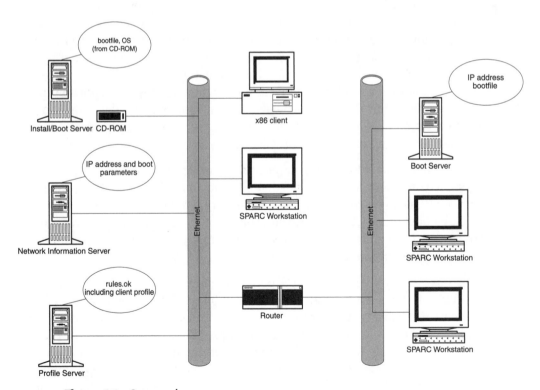

Figure 6.1   Server roles.

Server Roles

It is important to note that although each of the server roles we are about to describe is fairly distinct, a single server can be used to provide any or all of these services. The only exception to this rule is that if you have subnets, you will need to have a boot server (if not an installation server) on each.

Further, any of these roles can be served by systems that are already up and running on your network. Although we advocate a separation of major network services to the extent that this is reasonable (so that problems with one critical network service do not affect the operation of others), some doubling up of services makes a lot of sense. Your NIS/NIS+ server might, for example, be the ideal candidate to also serve as your profile server. An existing file server might conveniently serve as a boot server. Combining related services on a single server may, in fact, turn out to save you quite a bit of time and effort.

Figure 6.1 depicts the different roles that servers play during installation on a network with subnets. Note the position of the two boot servers relative to the clients and the doubling up of server roles on one system.

Install Servers

An install server provides the software and /media for the installation. Generally, this is available through a Solaris installation CD, which is mounted and exported so that the client being installed or upgraded can access it. Alternately, an install server can have the files from the Solaris installation CD copied onto its hard disks. An install server can be located anywhere on your network; however, it is generally better (because of the possible impact on network traffic) to have the install server in close proximity (with respect to network cabling) to the client being installed. Figure 6.2 depicts an install server.

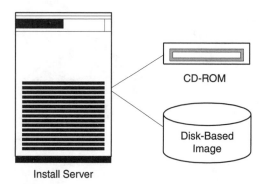

Install Server

Figure 6.2 Install server.

Boot Servers

A boot server is a system that supports the client's initial booting so that the installation process can begin. In other words, it provides the boot software to the client. The role of a boot server during a Solaris installation is much like the role a boot server plays in booting a diskless client. The client, booted with a command which diverts its attention away from its hard disk (e.g., *boot net* or *boot net—install*), needs to first establish its identity with respect to the network and then obtain the boot software that will allow it to complete the installation process.

Unless the clients you are installing are on a different subnet than your install server, you do not need to set up a separate boot server. The install server already contains the files that the client needs to boot. For clients on subnets that do not have local install servers, however, a boot server must be provided. Clients that boot from a local boot server can still obtain the installation software from a remote install server.

Profile Servers

A profile server is a server that houses the profiles for each of the various system configurations you want to install using JumpStart. Since the amount of information that it provides during installation, though critical, is minimal, a profile server can be located anywhere on your network.

To create a profile server, you create a directory, share it, and populate it with the client profiles and the rules file that determines when each profile is to be used. Figure 6.3 depicts a profile server.

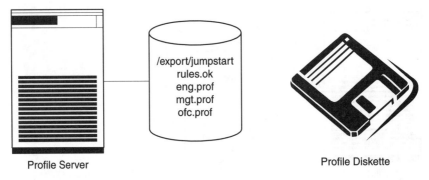

/export/jumpstart
rules.ok
eng.prof
mgt.prof
ofc.prof

Profile Server

Profile Diskette

Figure 6.3 Profile server.

An alternative to a profile server, a profile diskette, can be created in essentially the same manner. In short, you format a diskette, create a file system, and add the profiles and rules files. Profile diskettes for use with SPARC systems must contain a UFS or pcfs file system. Profile diskettes for x86 systems must be copies of the Solaris diskette that also contain the profiles and the rules.ok file.

Network Information Server

A network information server, for the purposes of a Custom JumpStart installation, provides a mapping not only of hostnames to IP addresses but also the mapping of hardware addresses to IP addresses needed for booting. It also supplies boot parameters for clients booting over the network. We're using the term *network information server* somewhat loosely here. This information can be derived from system files (such as the familiar /etc/hosts and the /etc/bootparams files) rather than supplied by a formal name/information service such as NIS or NIS+. Figure 6.4 depicts a NIS server.

Configuring Your Site for JumpStart

Setting up your site in order to maximize the utility of JumpStart involves pre-configuring a number of services so that the per-client investment at installation time is minimized. In order to make use of the JumpStart technology, you will need to have servers ready to assume the server roles that we just described. Figure 6.5 shows an approach to configuring JumpStart that starts with those services that we are assuming are already in place (and are required by JumpStart) and ends with those steps that you must take to invoke a JumpStart installation on the client.

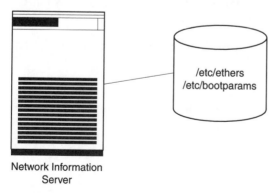

Network Information
Server

Figure 6.4 NIS Server.

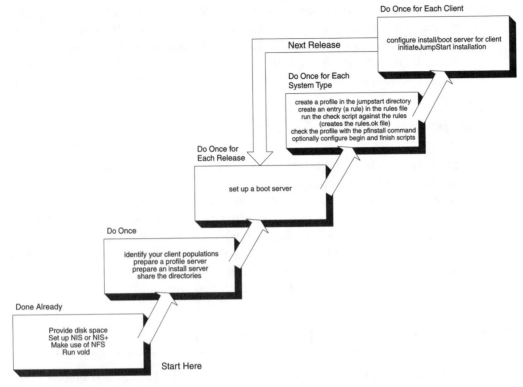

Figure 6.5   JumpStart steps.

Done Already

A certain portion of the preparation for JumpScript installation is, undoubtedly, already part of your network configuration. Most likely, for example, you already have NIS or NIS+ support and can provide boot parameters, time zones, regions, and maps in the information service or system files. We are assuming that you meet the following requirements:

- Have disk space available for profiles, client support (boot files and client root and swap), and so on
- Are running NIS or NIS+
- Are well acquainted with NFS sharing and mounting
- Are running volume manager (vold)

Do Once

The most intense effort of Custom JumpStart installation involves creating the profiles and providing them, along with the installation media, to the clients during the boot process. Most sites will set up servers to fill the roles of boot server, install server, and profile server on a more or less permanent basis, updating these systems as needed. To prepare for later steps in your JumpStart configuration, you must do the following:

- Prepare an inventory of your systems
- Identify and preconfigure a profile server
- Identify and preconfigure an install server
- Share the required directories

Preparing a Client Inventory

A good first step in preparing for Custom JumpStart is to prepare a description of the systems you will be installing. Remember that to reap the greatest benefit, you need to organize your systems into groups that can share profiles. The effort that you put into compiling an accurate system inventory will pay off later in the ease with which these systems can be managed and upgraded. Your inventory should include the type of system, model, disk size, memory, and a description of the primary user or primary role the system plays. Development systems will require a different suite of software and tools than systems that only run packaged applications.

Preparing a Profile Server

Selecting a system to server as profile server does not involve a lot of effort. Almost any system will serve the purpose quite well. The disk space and operational demands placed on a profile server are minimal. Once you've selected a system to play this role, you then create the directory that will house the profiles and other JumpStart files and share it. Later, we will populate this directory with profiles and other JumpStart files corresponding to the distinct client populations isolated in the system inventory.

```
# mkdir /export/jumpstart
# echo "share -F nfs -o ro,anon=0 /export/jumpstart" > /etc/dfs/dfstab
# shareall
```

Do for Each Release

Every time you receive a new release of Solaris, you'll need to update a number of your servers to prepare for installation upgrades. You will need to do the following:

- Provide the new installation software on your install server
- Update any boot servers with the new boot files

Roughly 16Mb of space will be required for each architecture the boot server will support. The setup_install_server -b command will copy the files specific to the client architecture to the boot server.

Update Your Install Server

To update your install server, you can simply choose to mount the new installation CD or copy the installation software onto your hard disk from the CD or from another server. In general, copying the install image onto your hard disk will provide for much faster installation; reading from disk is considerably faster than reading from a CD-ROM. Keep in mind, however, that a disk-based copy of the installation software will require as much as 200Mb of disk space and will take a considerably long time to be copied onto your hard disk. In fact, this is one of those tasks that is best started before you leave for the night and checked the following morning.

If the volume manager (vold) is running, simply loading the media is all that's required to mount it. Whether you're using a CD or a disk-based install image, the file system on which the file resides must be exported. Share a CD-ROM at the subdirectory level (not at the /cdrom level), as shown here:

```
# ls -l /cdrom
lrwxrwxrwx   1 root   nobody  13 Feb 16:29 cdrom0 -> ./sol_7_sparc
drwxr-xr-x   8 root   nobody  512 sol_7_sparc
# share -o ro /cdrom/sol_7_sparc
```

Use the setup_install_server command if you want to create a disk-based image of the installation media. Disk-based installation provides the added benefit of allowing you to effect a prompt-free installation through modification of only a few files (which, clearly, cannot be done using a CD). Once the installation files are located on your disk, site-specific information can be inserted into the appropriate files.

You will find the setup_install_server command on the installation CD in a Tools directory on slice 0, as shown here:

```
# cd /cdrom/sol_7_sparc/s0/Solaris_2.7/Tools
# ls set*
setup_install_server
```

To run the command, you need to provide the directory to be used for the disk-based installation software:

```
# ./setup_install_server /export/install
```

Once you run this command, you will have an image of the CD on your server that will contain files required for client installation. A sample directory listing is shown here:

```
installserver% pwd
/export/install/Solaris_2.7/Tools/Boot
installserver% ls -l
total 40
drwxr-xr-x    2 root       sys         512 Oct   6 13:38 a
lrwxrwxrwx    1 root       other         9 Feb   1 17:23 bin -> ./usr/bin
drwxr-xr-x    2 root       sys         512 Oct   6 13:38 cdrom
drwxrwxr-x   10 root       sys        1024 Oct   6 13:43 dev
drwxrwxr-x    3 root       sys         512 Oct   6 13:43 devices
drwxr-xr-x   24 root       sys        2560 Oct   6 13:48 etc
drwxr-xr-x    9 root       sys         512 Oct   6 13:44 kernel
lrwxrwxrwx    1 root       other         9 Feb   1 17:31 lib -> ./usr/lib
drwxrwxr-x    2 root       sys         512 Oct   6 13:31 mnt
-rw-r--r--    1 root       other        14 Feb   1 19:58 netmask
drwxrwxr-x    2 root       sys         512 Oct   6 13:31 opt
drwxr-xr-x   20 root       sys        1536 Oct   6 13:45 platform
drwxr-xr-x    2 root       sys         512 Oct   6 13:31 proc
-rw-r--r--    1 root       other         0 Oct   6 13:37 reconfigure
drwxrwxr-x    3 root       sys        1024 Oct   6 13:44 sbin
drwxrwxrwt    4 sys        sys         512 Oct   6 13:45 tmp
drwxrwxr-x   22 root       sys         512 Oct   6 13:43 usr
lrwxrwxrwx    1 root       other        14 Feb   1 19:57 var -> ./tmp/root/var
```

You can maintain more than one release of the installation software if you want to be able to install clients at different release levels. As noted in the preceding example, the setup_install_server command creates a directory specific to the release being installed. A different release of the software created with the same command (and a different CD in the drive) would create a sister directory in /export/install.

Do Once for Each System Type

For every distinct population of clients, you will need to prepare a profile describing the way these systems should be installed and make it available to the clients. The steps involve the following:

- Creating a profile for each group of similar systems (see following section)
- Checking each profile
- Adding each profile to rules file (see following section)
- Validating the rules file
- Exporting the /export/jumpstart directory (share -F nfs -o ro,anon=0 /export/jumpstart)

Creating a Profile

Creating a profile involves describing a group of the systems that you identified when you prepared your system inventory and outlining how these systems should be configured and installed.

Give your profiles names that clearly describe the type of system or its use (e.g., eng-client.prof or basic-server.prof). Store each profile as a separate file and save it in the jumpstart directory on your server (or on diskette if you are going to use a profile diskette).

Many sites will start the process of building profiles by copying the sample profiles from the installation CD. This is a good idea as long as you take the time to understand each line in the file. Figure 6.6 shows a sample profile, and the keywords available for JumpStart profiles in Solaris 7 are shown in Table 6.1.

The first two lines in Figure 6.6 are comments, helping to identify the use of this profile. The next two describe the type of installation and the type of the system. The three filesys lines specify that the system should use the 0th partition on the disk 0 for the root file system, that the system should create a 32Mb swap partition on the system disk, and that the system should build the /usr file system on any disk and allocate file space automatically. The SUNWCprog line is requesting the developer cluster. The dontuse keyword specifies that the disk listed should not be affected in any way by the installation.

The Profile Syntax

The syntax for creating profiles uses very simple keyword/value pairs. The number of options available, on the other hand, is substantial. Table 6.1 provides a description of each keyword along with examples of possible values.

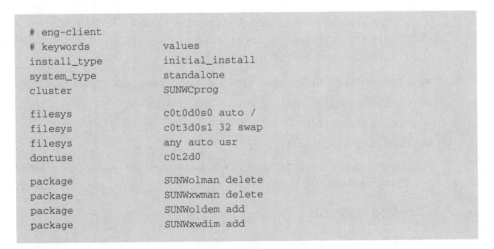

```
# eng-client
# keywords            values
install_type          initial_install
system_type           standalone
cluster               SUNWCprog

filesys               c0t0d0s0 auto /
filesys               c0t3d0s1 32 swap
filesys               any auto usr
dontuse               c0t2d0

package               SUNWolman delete
package               SUNWxwman delete
package               SUNWoldem add
package               SUNWxwdim add
```

Figure 6.6 Sample profile.

Table 6.1 Profile Keywords

KEYWORD	DESCRIPTION
backup_media	Defines media that will be used if, due to space problems, files need to bebacked up (moved aside) during the installation—keeps you from running out of room. local_tape /dev/rmt/# local_diskette /dev/rdiskette/# local_filesystem /dev/dsk/c#t#d#s# or /export/spare remote_filesystem remhost:/export/spare remote_system user@host:/directory (uses rsh)
boot_device	Specifies where the system's root file system will be. This will also be the boot device. With a third argument, specifies what to do with the current EEPROM boot disk value c#t#d#s# or (x86) c#t#d# or c#d# existing—current boot device any—installation program chooses, most likely existing boot device The EEPROM argument can be set to update (modify EEPROM entry for boot device) or preserve (leave EEPROM as is).
client_arch	Specifies the client hardware—sparc or i386. Must be used if the system is a server that will support a client architecture different from its own. Can be any of the following: sun4d, sun4c, sun4m, sun4u, or i86pc. This option can be used *only* if the system_type is set to server.
client_root	Defines the amount of space to allocate for client root file systems. This option can be used *only* if the system_type is set to server. If this value is not specified, the installation software will allocate 15Mb for each client (determined by the num_clients value). The space allocation is used to build the /export/root file system.
client_swap	Defines the amount of space to allocate for client swap space. This option can be used *only* if the system_type is set to server. If this value is not specified, the installation software will allocate 32Mb for each client (determined by the num_clients value). The space allocation is used to build the /export/swap file system.
cluster	With a single argument, specifies the software group to install on the system. The options include SUNWCreq (i.e., core, the minimal installation cluster), SUNWCuser (i.e., end user support), SUNWCprog (i.e., the developer installation), SUNWCall (i.e., the entire distribution) and SUNWCXall (i.e., the entire distribution plus OEM support, available for SPARC systems only).
cluster	With both a cluster name and an add or delete argument, specifies a particular software cluster that should be added to the software group being installed or omitted from it. This keyword/value set is required only if you want to tailor your installation more finely than the software groups. If neither add nor delete is specified, add is assumed.

continues

Table 6.1 *(Continued)*

KEYWORD	DESCRIPTION
dontuse	Specifies a disk that will not be used by the installation software. If this command is not used, all disks on a system are assumed available for use. This command, therefore, should be used to preserve a disk that you do not want the installation to affect. Applications and data files or Web sites and their log files are some examples of files that you might want to preserve with this command—if they are on a disk that you do not need for the new release. You cannot use both this keyword and the usedisk keyword in the same profile.
fdisk	Specifies how the installation will affect the fdisk partitions on an x86 system. If the intention is to have a dual-boot client, you want to be sure that existing partitions are not overwritten during the install. If this keyword is not used at all, existing partitions are overwritten. Three arguments are available with this keyword: diskname, type, and size. The disk argument lets you choose which disk to use. The most common format specifies the disk by controller, target, and disk (e.g., c0t3d0) or controller and disk (e.g., c0d0). Alternately, you can specify rootdisk (i.e., the installation software will determine the disk to use) or all (i.e., all of the selected disks). The type argument determines the type of fdisk partition to be created or deleted. Three values are available: solaris (a Solaris fdisk partition), dosprimary (a primary DOS fdisk partition), and DDD (an integer fdisk partition). To overwrite the existing fdisk partitions explicitly, use *fdisk all solaris maxfree.* One choice for preserving the existing fdisk partitions is *fdisk rootdisk solaris maxfree.*
filesys	There are two uses for the filesys keyword—to specify which file systems are mounted automatically when the system boots and to create local file systems. Both uses affect the /etc/vfstab file on the client. If the filesys keyword is used with a remote filesystem, the first type is assumed. The remaining arguments (following the server:/filesystem argument) are server IP address, local mount point, and file system options (e.g., -o ro). If the filesys keyword specifies a local filesystem, the first argument is the slice (e.g., c0t0d0s5 or any for any available slice). The remaining arguments are the size (from the following list), the file system to create, and optional parameters. Size Values for filesys Keyword number—for example, 500 existing—whatever the current size is auto—determined by software selection all—all the space on the disk free—all the available space on the disk start:size—starting cylinder and number of cylinders File System Types mount point name—for example, /apps swap—file system is to be used for swap space overlap—the entire disk unnamed—raw partition ignore—ignore the specified file system

KEYWORD	DESCRIPTION
	Optional Parameters preserve—preserve the existing file system on the specified slice mount options—for example, -o ro as with the mount command
install_type	Defines the type of installation. Possible values are initial_install or upgrade. An initial_install will recreate file systems and leave you with a rebuilt system. An upgrade will preserve most of the modifications you've made to the system and overwrite only those files that are required by the new OS.
isa_bits	Determines whether 32- or 64-bit packages are installed. The default for UltraSPARC is 64-bit while the default for all other systems is 32-bit.
layout_constraint	Specifies a constraint to be used when reallocation is required during the installation. If you do not use this keyword, all file systems requiring more space or affected by other file systems requiring more space (i.e., residing on the same disk) are considered changeable and may be rebuilt during the installation. The backup_media keyword will determine what space is used during this movement and reallocation. File systems identified with the layout_constraint command, on the other hand, will have the particular constraint enforced. These constraints include: changeable—okay to move or to resize. movable—can be moved, but not resized. available—can be sacrificed if space is required. collapse—can be merged into parent file system (i.e., file system where its mount directory is located) if necessary; this works only with file systems specified within the /etc/vfstab file (i.e., not automounted). minimum_size_value—the particular value specified is the minimum size that the file system must have following reallocation.
locale	Designates localization packages for support of non-English sites. Locale can be set to any of the following: zh—Chinese fr—French de—German it—Italian ja—Japanese ko—Korean es—Spanish sw—Swedish zh_TW—Taiwanese
num_clients	Specifies the number of diskless clients. This keyword can be used *only* when the system_type is server. It is used to allocate space for client partitions.
package	Specifies that a particular package should be added or omitted during the installation, regardless of whether it is part of the selected software group. Options are add/delete. Add is default. When upgrading a system, all packages already on the system will be upgraded unless you specify delete.

continues

Table 6.1 *(Continued)*

KEYWORD	DESCRIPTION
partitioning	defines how the disks are partitioned during installation. The options include the following: default—the installation software selects the disk and slice for each file system subject to constraints that you have specified with the filesys and layout_constraint keywords. existing—the installation software uses the existing file systems. All non-system file systems (i.e., file systems other than /, /usr, /usr/openwin, /opt, and /var) are preserved.
root_device	Specifies the system's root file system. This keyword can be used with initial installations and with upgrades. With upgrades, this keyword specifies the root file system to be upgraded.
system_type	Specifies the role the system will play. This keyword determines whether other keywords can be used (e.g., client_arch). Possible values are stand-alone, dataless, and server. Diskless systems are not installed with Jump-Start, but with the add_client_whatever command.
usedisk	Specifies a disk that will be used during the installation. If you specify one disk with this keyword, you must specify all disks. Otherwise, the specified disks are the only ones that will be used. Keep in mind that you cannot use this keyword in the same profile as the dontuse keyword, so you must select your strategy to include or omit disks.

To check a profile, use the *pfinstall* command with a *-d* or *-D* option. This command provides verification that the new profile creates the configuration you think you've specified. It does this by showing you how the system would be created using the new profile without actually installing anything anywhere. It only works for initial installations (i.e., not with upgrades). Be sure to specify the -d or -D option; these ensure that you are testing the profile rather than installing software. The -D option instructs the software to use the disk of the system you are logged into to test the profile. The -d instructs the software to use a disk configuration file instead. Use one of the formats shown here:

```
/usr/sbin/install.d/pfinstall -D [ -c Cdpath ] profile
/usr/sbin/install.d/pfinstall -d disk_config_file [ -c Cdpath ]
profile
```

You need to run profile tests on a system that is running the same version of Solaris as the clients for which the profile is intended.

To add a rule to the rules file on the profile server that describes the client and identifies the profile that should be used during installation of clients of this type, the rules file (e.g., it could be called /export/install/rules) has the following format:

```
[!]keyword value [&& [!]keyword value] begin-script profile finish-script
```

Here's an example of a rule:

```
karch sun4m - eng.prof -
```

You need to have a validated rule in the rules.ok file, including a reference to a profile set up for this particular set of systems. You need to identify the systems and describe the target configuration.

A rules files has a rule for each distinct set of systems that you intend to install. It must reside in the JumpStart directory (for our purposes, we'll refer to this as */export/jumpstart*). Profiles, on the other hand, can be used by more than one rule. This is helpful if you have several populations of systems which ought to be set up the same way—that is, you can differentiate these from the rest with a single rule.

To validate your rules file, use the check command available with the install media. The check script will create the rules.ok file.

Creating a Profile Diskette

An alternative to the profile server is the profile diskette. If you have systems that are not on your network or that you prefer to install using profiles stored on a diskette, you can take this approach instead. For SPARC clients, creating a profile diskette involves preparing a diskette with a file system. This can be either a UFS or a pcfs file system, but we use a UFS file system in the following example. The JumpStart files are then copied to the diskette.

```
# fdformat -U
# newfs /vol/dev/aliases/floppy
# eject floppy          (then reinsert)
# volcheck
# cp /export/jumpstart/rules.ok /floppy/floppy0
# cp /export/jumpstart/eng.prof /floppy/floppy0
```

For x86 clients, the process is a bit more complicated. The diskette must contain boot software as well as the JumpStart files. In the following sample, we start by inserting a Solaris x86 boot diskette into the drive..

```
# dd if=/vol/dev/aliases/floppy0 of=/export/install/x86_boot
# eject floppy          (insert a blank)
# volcheck
# fdformat -d -U
# dd if=/export/install/x86_boot
# eject floppy          (then reinsert)
```

```
# volcheck
# cp /export/jumpstart/rules.ok /floppy/floppy0
# cp /export/jumpstart/eng.prof /floppy/floppy0
```

Creating Rules

Rules allow you to specify which clients will use each of the profiles you've created. Each rule selects a single profile for a group of clients identified by one or more of the keywords listed in Table 6.2, as illustrated in Figure 6.7. In addition, once a matching rule is found, the rest of the file is not read. Each rule has the following form:

```
keyword value [&& keyword value] begin_script finish_script profile
```

A keyword can be preceded by an exclamation point (also referred to as a *not* sign) to effect its opposite. Any number of keyword/value pairs can be used if they are appended with double ampersands (also referred to as an *and* symbol). Begin and finish scripts are optional, but a hyphen must be used as a placeholder if there is no begin script.

A sample rule for a JumpStart installation on Sparcstations on the Engineering subnet might look something like this:

```
arch SPARC && disksize 1000-2000 && network 192.9.201.0 - eng.prof -
```

Note that this rule specifies the subnet and applies only to systems with 1- to 2Gb of disk. It then specifies that the profile named *eng.prof* is to be used to detail the rest of the installation parameters.

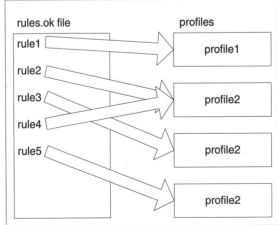

Figure 6.7 JumpStart rules and profiles.

Table 6.2 Rule Keywords

KEYWORD	DESCRIPTION	EXAMPLE
any	Matches any client	any -
arch	Specifies CPU architecture (SPARC or i386)	arch SPARC
domainname	Depends on client's existing domain	domainname nici.net
disksize	Specifies the client's disk size as a range (in megabytes)	disksize c0t3d0 500–1000
hostname	Specifies the client's host name	scotty
installed	Specifies current installed release	installed c0t3d0s0 Solaris_6
karch	Specifies the kernel architecture of the client	karch sun4m
memsize	Depends on the memory on the client (in megabytes)	memsize 32–64
model	Specifies the client model designator	model SUNW, SPARCstation-20
network	Matches on the network number of the client	network 192.9.200.0
totaldisk	Specifies a range of disk space (in megabytes)	totaldisk 1000–2000

Once the rules file is created (or any time you update it), you must run the check script to validate your rules and create the rules.ok file that will be used during installation.

```
# ./check
Checking validity of rules
Checking validity of eng.prof
Checking validity of mgt.prof
Checking validity of ofc.prof
The auto-install configuration is ok.
```

Creating Begin and Finish Scripts

Begin and finish scripts are optional customization scripts that allow you to fine-tune your installations even further than your install profiles. Specific changes that you might otherwise make before or after installation can be automated and applied to any number of systems. Examples of things that you might find convenient to do in begin and end scripts include configuring network printers, customizing your windowing environment, installing patches, or adding rc scripts (discussed in the next chapter) to automatically start site-specific services.

Begin and finish scripts are written in the Bourne shell (/bin/sh) and must be specified within the rules file. This means that for every client population you identify, you may identify a single begin and a single finish script. If you do not elect to use begin and finish scripts, you will need to put a hyphen in their positions in each rule.

All begin and finish scripts should be root-owned and have their permissions set to 644. Execute permission is not required, as these scripts will be provided as input to the /bin/sh command; this also lessens the chance that these scripts will be inadvertently run at other times.

File systems referenced in finish scripts should append /a to the beginning of any pathnames, as all the install client's file systems will be mounted within this mount point during and following the installation.

There are a number of environment variables (see Table 6.3) available within the installation environment that you can use within your begin and end scripts to facilitate your coding.

Output from the begin and finish scripts can be examined later by looking at the log files—/var/sadm/begin.log and /var/sadm/finish.log—following the client's reboot.

Starting the Installation

To start a JumpStart installation over the network, once the servers are ready and the profiles and rules are in place, you merely have to enter the boot command on the halted client (i.e., at the ok prompt). Once you enter the appropriate boot command to boot over the network, (e.g., the following command), SPARC clients will begin the preinstallation sequence.

```
ok boot net - install
```

For x86 clients, you'll need to insert the Solaris boot diskette into the drive and then select a few options first.

Since very little has to be typed on the client with a well-crafted custom Jump-Start installation, the requirement for hands-on access to the client is limited. You could have a junior systems administrator or a cooperative user start the installation for you, whereas they would probably be unable or too intimidated to perform a traditional installation. Figure 6.8 depicts booting over the network.

SPARC Clients

SPARC clients will start the preinstallation boot process by broadcasting a reverse address resolution protocol (RARP) request. Since the system ethernet

Table 6.3 Environment Variables for Begin and Finish Scripts

VARIABLE	DESCRIPTION
CHECK_INPUT	Specifies the path to the rules.ok file, mounted as /tmp/install_config/rules.ok
HOME	Home directory of root user during the installation
PATH	Search path during the installation
SI_ARCH	Hardware (CPU) architecture of the client, set by the arch keyword in the rules.ok file
SI_BEGIN	Name of the begin script, if specified; see SI_FINISH
SI_CLASS	Profile name
SI_CONFIG_DIR	Path of JumpStart directory
SI_CONFIG_FILE	Same as CHECK_INPUT?
SI_CONFIG_PROG	rules.ok file (without path)
SI_CUSTOM_PROBES_FILE	Used to define additional rule keywords
SI_DISKLIST	List of the client's disks
SI_DISKSIZES	Disk size of install client
SI_DOMAINNAME	Domain name, set when domainname keyword is used in the rules file
SI_FINISH	Name of the finish script
SI_HOSTADDRESS	IP address of the client
SI_HOSTID	Hardware address of the client
SI_HOSTNAME	Client's host name, if set in the rules file
SI_INSTALLED	Device name of disk with installed OS, set when installed keyword is used in the rules file
SI_INST_OS	Name of operating system
SI_INST_VER	Version of the operating system
SI_KARCH	Kernel architecture of the client, set in rules with karch keyword
SI_MEMSIZE	Amount of physical memory on the client, set with memsize keyword
SI_MODEL	Model name of the client, set with model keyword
SI_NETWORK	Network number of the client, set with network keyword
SI_NUMDISKS	Number of disks on the client
SI_OSNAME	Release of OS on the CD or disk-based image
SI_PROFILE	Path to profile
SI_ROOTDISK	Device name of the rootdisk
SI_ROOTDISKSIZE	Size of the rootdisk

continues

Table 6.3 *(Continued)*

VARIABLE	DESCRIPTION
SI_SYS_STATE	The /a/etc/.sysIDtool.state file
SI_TOTALDISK	Total amount of disk space on the client
SHELL	Default shell for installation, /sbin/sh
TERM	Install client terminal type
TZ	Default time zone

interface (hardware) address is stored on PROM, this information is available for use in determining the corresponding network (IP) address. Once the client has received its IP address, it can use this information to request its boot program.

If you're using a profile diskette, the client will notice. Otherwise, it will look for a rules.ok file on the profile server. The client will obtain its IP address and then its boot file. The boot parameters will specify the profile server. The client will then mount its client partitions. If you have defined a begin script, it will be run before the installation begins.

If the install client has a CD-ROM and you want to use it instead of a remote install server to supply the installation media, you must supply the JumpStart files on a diskette. The installation software will find the rules.ok file on the diskette and, from it, determine the profile to use much in the same way it would if you were installing over the network (the first rule that matches the client). If none of the rules in the rules.ok file match the system, the software will initiate an interactive installation, abandoning JumpStart.

For systems that are not connected to a network, this is the only way you can use Custom JumpStart. It is possible, however, to prepare a diskette that can be used for a group of similar systems or to override the standard profile that a particular client would use if you were booting over the net.

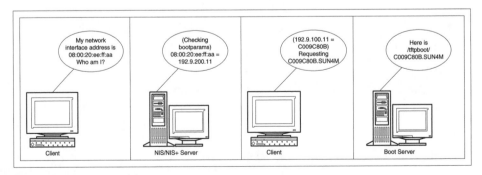

Figure 6.8 Booting over the network.

Do Once for Each Client

By using JumpStart properly, you will find that the work that needs to be done for each client being installed or upgraded is fairly minimal. Still, there are some steps that must be taken. These include the following:

- Preparing the boot server to provide boot support for this client
- Starting the installation

Just as with any installation, it is a good idea to back up systems before you reinstall or upgrade them. This is a precaution in case anything in the install should fail, but is really needed only for files beyond the OS—configuration files and the like.

Some systems may not be able to run the newer OS. If you have older systems, you should check whether they are supported in the new release before making plans to reinstall or upgrade.

Depending on the release of SunOS installed on a system, you may have the option to upgrade rather than install. This is likely to take less time, but, more important, an upgrade operation will not overwrite your configuration files.

If the system you're installing has a local CD-ROM that you want to use in place of the install server, you will have to present the client with a profile diskette.

For Intel-based systems, insert the Solaris boot diskette into the local drive and hit reset or power cycle the system. At that point, you can choose to boot from a local CD or across the network. After selecting network boot, you have to select the custom JumpStart method (versus the interactive install method in which you are prompted for all that is required).

For network use, Custom JumpStart requires that you have already provided for network recognition of the client to be installed. When it broadcasts a request for identifying information on being told to boot over the network during the initial phase of the installation, some server must be prepared to respond, and some server must have boot software that the client can use. For this to be the case, you must have provided information about the system and prepared a boot server. That is to say, the server must both be able to identify the client in question (i.e., provide an IP address corresponding to the hardware or Ethernet address of the client) and, subsequently, provide a bootfile and a root file system. Preparing a server for this role is fairly minimal work, provided it has adequate space (check to make sure this is still the case).

Add client support for each system to be installed by using the add_install_client -c command or by adding a wildcard entry to the bootparams file or map that allows any system to determine the location of the jumpstart directory (* install_config=servername:/export/jumpstart). This allows a single entry to provide a response for any client install.

```
client-name root=enterprise:/export/exec/kvm/sparc.Solaris_7
install=install-server:/export/install/Solaris_7 boottype=:in
install_config=profile_server:/export/jumpstart÷
```

Figure 6.9 Sample /etc/bootparams entry.

```
add_install_client -c profile-server:/export/jumpstart hostnamearch
```

It is useful to understand what the add_install_client command does, what files it creates, and how they are used. First, the command adds an entry to the /etc/bootparams file on the install server (see Figure 6.9). It specifies, among other things, where the profile JumpStart directory is located. It also adds files to the /tftpboot directory on the boot server (or the /rplboot directory if this is an x86 system). It enables, if necessary, the in.tftpd daemon (see the /etc/inetd.conf file). It adds the client's hardware address to the ethers file and its name and IP address to /etc/hosts. The command also ensures that the host entry in the /etc/nsswitch.conf file includes a correct entry and that the path to the CD image is shared (adds line to /etc/dfs/dfstab). If necessary, it will also start certain daemons (e.g., rpc.bootparamd, mountd, nfsd, in.rarpd, rpld, and in.tftpd).

If the client is an x86 system, the add_install_client command starts the rpld daemon and sets up the /rplboot directory with the inetboot program for x86 clients, as shown here:

```
inetboot.i86pc.Solaris_7
```

The link itself has the client's IP address as part of the name (e.g., 192.9.200.11.inetboot).

```
192.9.200.11.glue.com -> gluecode.com
192.9.200.11.hw.com -> smc.com
192.9.200.11.inetboot -> inetboot.i86pc.Solaris_7
gluecode.com
inetdboot.i86pc.Solaris_7
rm.192.9.200.11
smc.com
```

Summary

This chapter discusses JumpStart on both Sun and x86 systems and suggests the sequence of steps that you need to take to get the most benefit out of the tool. JumpStart can save you tremendous amounts of time and effort if you are responsible for installing or upgrading numerous systems. JumpStart can also be used for installation of patches.

JumpStart is particularly valuable if you:

- Are installing many systems with the same basic setup.
- Want to make it possible for junior sysadmins or users to assist with the work of upgrading systems.
- Are installing patches on numerous systems.

Should you take the wise step of using JumpStart, you'll need to prepare your install servers and a profile for each client type. The syntax is not difficult and, properly set up, reduces installations to little more than getting them started.

## CHAPTER 7

Setting Up Name Services

This chapter details the installation and configuration of the Domain Name System (DNS). The next discusses NIS and NIS+. We will provide a brief but sound picture of what the name service is and how it works. After that, we will first detail installation and configuration from the server side, and then work our way to the client configuration.

Even if you are not responsible for supporting DNS within your organization, an understanding of how DNS works and the extent to which the Internet would *not* work without it is essential to systems administration. This chapter provides a gentle but fairly thorough introduction to the services, files, and options involved in running and using DNS.

Domain Name System

The implementation of the Domain Name System or Domain Name Service (DNS) that ships with Solaris is called the *Berkeley Internet Name Daemon* (BIND). If you're interested in the technical details of DNS, the specifications can be found in the requests for comments (RFCs) listed in Table 7.1.

DNS is commonly and frequently used to resolve the alphanumeric names of systems into IP addresses. In fact, it is used by almost every computer user, but goes largely unnoticed because it works quickly and invisibly. Were it not for DNS, there would be no way that one system could arbitrarily connect to another. DNS manages the collaboration of name servers across the Internet, each of which knows about a relatively small collection of systems—usually

Table 7.1 Requests for Comments (RFCs) on the Domain Name System (DNS)

RFC NUMBER	DESCRIPTION
974	Partridge, C., "Mail Routing and the Domain Name System," STD 14, RFC 974, BBN, January 1986.
1032	Stahl, M., "Domain Administrators Guide," RFC 1032, SRI International, November 1987.
1033	Lottor, M., "Domain Administrative Operations Guide," RFC 1033, SRI International, November 1987.
1034	Mockapetris, P., "Domain Names—Concepts and Facilities," STD 13, RFC 1034, ISI, November 1987.
1340	Reynolds, J., and J. Postel, "Assigned Numbers," STD 2, RFC 1340, ISI, July 1992.
1359	ACM SIGUCCS Networking Taskforce, "Connecting to the Internet—What Connecting Institutions Should Anticipate," FYI 16, RFC 1359, August 1992.
1480	Cooper, A., and J. Postel, "The US Domain," RFC 1480, June 1993.
2065	Elz, R., and R. Bush, "Clarifications to the DNS Specification," RFC 2181, July 1997.
2136	Vixie, P., S. Thomson, Y. Rekhter, and J. Bound, "Dynamic Updates in the Domain Name System (DNS Update)," RFC 2136, April 1997.
2137	Eastlake, D., "Secure Domain Name System Dynamic Update," RFC 2137, April 1997.
2182	Elz, R., R. Bush, S. Bradner, and M. Patton, "Selection and Operation of Secondary DNS Servers (Best Current Practices)," July 1997.

those in the local organization. In fact, DNS can be said to be the most widely distributed database in existence. An example of DNS in action is the translation of www.foo.com to the IP address 224.2.130.2. Unless you just happen to work for Foo, the likelihood is that a series of lookups must be performed before your attempt to gain access to this Web site results in a page displayed within your favorite browser. DNS is also used to turn IP addresses back into alphanumeric names. This is called a *reverse lookup*.

DNS is extremely effective within a heterogeneous environment, as neither the servers nor the clients care what platform provides this information and getting almost any type of system configured to use it is straightforward. Anyone connecting to the Internet must be using a DNS client (if not a server) in order to use fully qualified names. Fully qualified domain names (FQDN's) are names such as www.foo.com or mail.adamrachel.com that spell out every level in the DNS tree.

Before we go any further, here are some quick definitions:

The DNS *tree* is the entire DNS structure starting from the root (see Figure 7.1) and descending to each and every host.

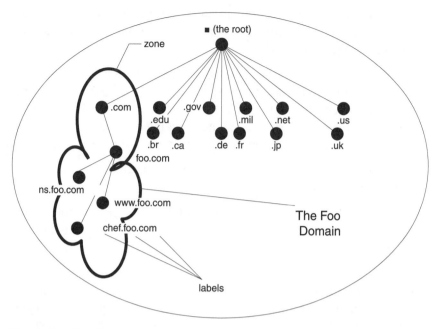

Figure 7.1 The DNS tree.

A DNS *domain* consists of the complete subtree starting from a particular node (but not just any node). It is the complete set of names within a domain. For example, foo.com is a domain name and the corresponding DNS domain contains all names within the foo.com domain space. Figure 7.1 illustrates this naming structure. It is important to understand that domains relate to the naming structure itself, not to the way systems are distributed on networks or subnetworks. Each domain can have one or more subdomains, and different name servers can be authoritative for these subdomains.

A DNS *subdomain* is a portion of a domain for which an authoritative name server exists. Subdomains are often used to identify departments or geographic locations. For example, sales.foo.com might be a subdomain in the foo.com domain.

A *zone* is a boundary for a name server's authoritativeness and relates to the way the DNS database is partitioned and distributed. While a subdomain has to be a zone, a zone does not necessarily have to be a subdomain. Examples of the latter (i.e., zones that are not subdomains) are the zones for the reverse lookups, which are IP address based, rather than name based. A *forward zone* is a zone that contains data-mapping alphanumeric names to IP addresses. A *reverse zone* does the reverse—maps addresses to names.

A *label* is one element of a domain name. Labels need only be unique at a specific point in the tree. www.foo.com and www.east.foo.com are valid fqdns, while *foo* and *east* are labels.

A *server* is a system that answers DNS queries. The answers may derive from information the server knows (i.e., for which it is authoritative) or which it obtains from another server. An *authoritative server* is one that provides answers from local information without asking other servers. A *listed server* is one for which there is a name server (NS) resource record (explained later).

A *primary (master) server* is one that is authoritative and in which information is locally configured.

A *secondary (slave) server* is an authoritative server that obtains its information from a primary using zone transfers. A *stealth server* is an authoritative server that is not listed.

A *cache-only server* is a DNS server that does not contain any local DNS information. Instead, it stores DNS information in its cache and responds to DNS queries with information it has cached from previous queries or requested from another server. Cache-only servers are a good choice for small sites not interested in maintaining their own DNS servers. The caching increases DNS performance since most queries are likely to be repeated. All DNS servers use cache, but cache-only servers use *only* cache.

A *resolver* is a client that seeks information using DNS.

The *root name servers* are responsible for the root level domain (.) of DNS. In other words, these are the servers responsible for the highest level domains— .com, .edu, .gov, .mil, .net, .org, and .us in the United States and .ca, .jp, .br, and so on for other countries. Clearly outside of our control, these servers are nevertheless critical for the proper and overall function of DNS in our daily use of it and are referenced in our DNS configuration files.

The current implementation of DNS is a *static distributed database*, with a primary DNS server defined for each domain. By *static*, we don't mean to imply that it doesn't change. We mean to emphasize that the information deposited in a huge number of DNS data stores located around the globe changes slowly with the deliberate efforts of systems administrators like ourselves. Updates to DNS files are manual and are replicated to secondary servers via *zone transfers*. RFCs 2136 and 2137 detail a dynamic version of DNS, and, starting with BIND version 8, dynamic updates are allowed. BIND version 8 ships only with Solaris 7.0 or higher.

A single server can be primary for multiple domains, but you cannot have multiple primaries for a single domain. Within each domain, there can be subdomains known as *zones*. These zones can be served by the same name server, or the server can delegate the zones to other name servers. Setting up your internal network for the first time is a task that requires careful planning. Chances are that any domain structure you set up now will be hard to change in the future.

Most companies will set up subdomains based on location or organizational structure. If you are planning on connecting to the Internet, it is imperative that you register your domain name. In the United States, domain name registration is handled by Network Solutions, Inc. (rs.internic.net).

TIP

Carefully plan your DNS configuration before you begin to create it. Consider the natural boundaries of your organization as a template for where you should construct subdomains.

There are a small number of root domain name servers that are responsible for tracking the top-level domains and the addresses for the name servers of all of the domains that are one level down

For a name server to be *authoritative* means that if a server receives a query about a system in that domain, it can look up the information directly without forwarding the request to another name server. For example, if a name server that is authoritative solely for the foo.com domain receives a query for the address of www.geof.com, it must forward that request to the machine that is authoritative for the geof.com domain, and will subsequently return a nonauthoritative answer.

A *lame server* is a name server that has been listed as authoritative for a domain, but does not seem to be performing authoritative service for that domain. That is, the name server appears to be answering out of its cache instead of out of its data. Note that even a server that is performing secondary service for a domain is still an authoritative server, and should be returning authoritative data. The information about authoritative name servers is stored in the DNS itself, and as long as you have pointers to other name servers that know about the domains you are querying about, you are in good shape.

When a change is made, it propagates slowly out through the Internet to eventually reach all name servers. Since DNS name servers utilize caching, there is the notion of the *time to live* (TTL). The TTL determines how long an address is valid before an authoritative name server needs to be asked again. Up until that TTL expires, the name server can use the cached address without a second thought.

Along with telling you what DNS is, we should add a few comments about what DNS is not. DNS does not control routing. IP addresses returned by DNS will, of course, be used in determining what routes are taken, but DNS does not make any routing choices. In addition, DNS has no implications for Internet connectivity. Failing to resolve a host name is not the same thing as failing to reach a host. Whenever there is any doubt in your mind as to the cause of a connection problem, ruling out the involvement of naming services is an important first step.

Installing the DNS

Starting with Solaris 7, the version of BIND implemented is BIND version 8.1.x. However, most companies are still running the older version, version 4.9.x. To determine the version of BIND you are running on your system, type */usr/ccs/bin/what /usr/sbin/in.named | grep named*. For more information on the latest version of BIND, you should refer to the Internet Software Consortium, which sponsors the development of BIND. Its Web site is located at www.isc.org/bind.html. In the sections that follow, we start by detailing the installation of the older version of BIND, then discuss the changes for the newer version.

The steps involved in setting up DNS are quite logical:

1. Set up the boot file that denotes the DNS primary and secondary servers, and the zones for which they are authoritative. For versions of DNS preceding version 8, this is the file /etc/named.boot. For BIND version 8, this is the named.conf file.

2. Create the forward and reverse mapping files to detail the systems within each zone. These files are the same for all releases.

3. Start the in.named daemon and start serving DNS entries.

The Boot File

The two versions of the boot file, */etc/named.boot* and */etc/named.conf*, are detailed in the following sections. We also mention the script *named-bootconf*, which creates a file with the new format (i.e., a named.conf file) from one with the old format (i.e., a named.boot file).

named.boot

The first step in setting up DNS in older versions of Solaris (before BIND 8) is to create the /etc/named.boot file. This file details the zones and the servers that are authoritative for these zones. It also points to the root.cache file that knows how to reach all of the root name servers.

When the in.named daemon is started or sent a sig-hup (kill -1) signal, it reads the named.boot file. The server's start script is /etc/init.d/inetsvc (i.e., /etc/rc2.d/S72inetsvc). For each domain, the configuration file, named.boot, directs in.named where to get its data—from local data files if it is primary, and from other servers if it is a secondary.

Here is a sample of a typical named.boot file:

```
directory /var/named
cache                   named.ca
forwarders              10.69.0.1 10.69.1.1
primary                 foo.com                 foo.com.db
primary                 0.0.127.in-addr.arpa  0.0.127.db
primary                 2.224.in-addr.arpa    69.10.db
secondary adamrachel.com              10.69.2.1     adamrachel.com.db
secondary 1.192.in-addr.arpa          10.69.2.1  1.192.db
```

The lines in the named.boot file have the following meanings:

Directory. This line identifies the root path where named will look for all of the data files. If no directory is specified, named will look for files relative to the /etc directory. If a subdirectory is desired, list it without preceding slashes (e.g., *named* would represent */etc/named*).

Cache. This line identifies the file that named uses to get back to the root name servers for domains for which it is not authoritative and doesn't know the authoritative source. It contains the name and IP addresses of the root name servers on the Internet. Make sure your cache file is up-to-date, or else queries may not be answered for domains beyond your span of control. The latest version of the cache file can always be pulled from ftp://rs.internic.net/domain/named.root.

NOTE
Don't confuse this cache file with the name server's internal cache (used to cache DNS responses).

Primary. Each of these lines specifies a zone for which this machine is authoritative. The first argument is either the domain suffix to be appended to every label in the file or, in the case of a reverse table, the reverse of the IP address that is to be prefixed to every network address in the file followed by in-addr.arpa. Reverse entries are a major source of confusion, since the IP network 10.69 is coded as 69.10, and the 192.1 network as 1.192. The usual cause for failure of reverse lookups is the improper use of these lines. If your reverse name lookups don't work, check the addresses carefully.

Forwarders. This is a list of addresses to which this machine should send forward requests for sites it cannot resolve. First, it will attempt to get an answer from the forwarders and, if that fails, from the root name servers. A good choice for a forwarder is the name server that is authoritative for the zone above yours.

Secondary. A secondary line indicates that you intend this server to be a secondary name server for the listed zone. You should have at least one secondary server for each zone. Proper placement of secondaries can dramatically increase the reliability and performance of your DNS service. In a distributed organization, each area can be primary for its own subdomain and secondary for any other subdomains. Where this gets very tricky is in determining who is primary for the reverse tables. Since most companies utilize either single class B or C networks and physically colocate people and machines in different logical subdomains, it may be a centralized network administrator who maintains the reverse maps.

The secondary line will cause this machine to contact the name server at 10.69.2.1 and request a zone transfer for the adamrachel.com domain and the 192.1 subnet. You can specify multiple IP addresses to query on the secondary line. Named will query those addresses for all the information it can get about the domain, remember it, and act as though it were authoritative for that domain.

named.conf

BIND 8 does not use a named.boot file but, instead, utilizes a named.conf file. You cannot have both of these files on your system at the same time. Sun ships a command called *named-bootconf* that can be used to automatically transform a named.boot file into a named.conf file. No translation is provided for moving backwards.

Although the named.conf contains similar information to named.boot, it is considerably more powerful, adding options that allow for the use of access control lists and categorized logging. The structure of the named.conf differs greatly from that of the named.boot. Not only can you detail what zones a system is authoritative for, but there is a mechanism for restricting access to only those systems that you want using your name server. The named.conf file is split into sections. The major sections are as follows:

Options Sets default values and global settings

Include Essentially the same as an include file for C; inserts the listed file at this point

Logging Details what to log and where

Server Sets options for a remote server

Zone Defines a specific zone

ACL Specifies an access control list using dotted decimal or slash notation

Here is the previous named.boot file expressed in the named.conf format:

```
options {
        directory          "/var/named";
        forwarders         {
                10.69.0.1;
                10.69.1.1;
        };
            };
zone "." in {
        type hint;
        file "named.ca";
};

 zone "foo.com" in {
        type master;
        file "foo.com.db";
};

 zone "0.0.127.in-addr.arpa" in {
        type master;
        file "0.0.127.db";
};

 zone "2.224.in-addr.arpa" in {
        type master;
        file "69.10.db";
};

 zone "adamrachel.com" in {
        type slave;
        file "adamrachel.com.db";
        masters { 10.69.2.1; };
};

 zone "1.192.in-addr.arpa" in {
        type slave;
        file "1.192.db";
        masters { 10.69.2.1; };
};
```

The /etc/named.conf file, like the named.boot, establishes the server as a master, slave, or cache-only name server. It also specifies the zones over which the server has authority and what files it should read to get its initial data.

The Options Section

The options section starts the named.conf file and defines options that are to be applied globally. Within the options section are the following directives:

Directory. Specifies the directory where the DNS data files are located.

Forwarders. Provides the list of machines to send forward requests to when you do not have the data.

Forward. If set, forces any queries to be sent to the forwarders first. If the forwarders do not have the answer, only then is the lookup performed locally.

Notify. Causes messages to be sent to the slave servers when there is a change in a zone for which this server is authoritative. Changes are not pushed to the slaves. Rather, when the slave servers receive the notification, they will check to see if they need to perform a zone transfer. This statement can also be placed in the zone sections to override the default. The default is yes.

Recursion. Allows the server to act as a proxy and attempt to answer when a DNS query requests recursion, even if it does not have the information. If recursion is set to off and the answer is unknown to the server, it will return a referral to the client.

Check-names. Specifies whether names are to be checked for inclusion of illegal characters (such as underscores), and under what conditions. The check-names directive has two parameters. The first parameter states the source of names to be checked. The options are master, slave, and response. *Master* causes names in the master zone files to be checked; *slave* checks names in the slave zone files; and *response* checks responses received back from queries. The second parameter is the level of severity (i.e., how to respond)—warn, fail, or ignore. *Warn* will log invalid names but return them anyway; *fail* will also log invalid names, but will not return them; and *ignore* causes the server to play dumb and simply hand out the results. Unless you change the default behavior, in BIND 4.9.4 and later, a primary name server will refuse to load a zone with bad characters and a secondary will load but complain, while bad characters in responses will simply be ignored.

The next several statements allow you to decide what systems in your network can query your name server, and which machines can perform zone transfers from your machine. If you are serving names out to the Internet community, we highly recommended that you do not allow zone transfers outside of your organization.

Allow-query. Specifies machines from which you will allow queries to your name server.

Allow-transfer. Specifies machines from which you will respond to zone transfers requests.

The Include Section

The include section includes an external file:

```
include "/etc/named.zones-a-e"
```

Named will stuff the /etc/named.zones-a-e file into the current file before processing it.

The Logging Section

The logging section details what to log and where. It is split into two parts—channels and categories.

The *channel phrase* or *channel statement* is used to link output methods, format options, and severity levels with a name that can then be used with the *category phrase* to select how to log different message classes.

All log output is directed to one or more channels. There is no limit to the number of channels you can define. Four are predefined: *default_syslog*, *default_debug*, *default_stderr*, and *null*. These cannot be redefined. The default definitions are shown here:

```
channel default_syslog {
    syslog daemon;         # send to syslog daemon
    severity info;         # send priority info and higher
};

channel default_debug {
    file "named.run";      # write to the file named.run in current
                           # working directory.
                           # Note: stderr is used instead of "named.run"
                           # if server is started with the "- f" option.
    severity dynamic;      # log at the server's current debug level
};

channel default_stderr {   # writes to stderr
    file "<stderr>";       # illustrative only; there's currently
                           # no way of specifying an internal file
                           # descriptor in the configuration language.
    severity info;         # only send priority info and higher
};

channel null {
    null;                  # toss anything sent to this channel
};
```

Every channel phrase must state where the messages for that channel are logged—either to a file, a specific syslog facility, or not at all (i.e., ignored). The channel can also state the minimum severity level that will be logged.

The word *null* as a destination for a channel forces the channel to ignore all messages and to ignore any other options set for that channel.

The *file* clause can include limits on how many versions of the file to save and on how large the file can grow. The size option sets the maximum size of the file. Once the logfile exceeds the specified size, logging to that file ceases. We recommended that you do not limit the size of logfiles that may be needed to debug problems in the future. The default is no limit.

If you choose to use the *logfile* option, versions of files will be saved with a numeric suffix, starting with 0 and ending with n-1, where n is the number of versions you choose to keep. The maximum number that can be kept is 99.

The *syslog* clause takes a single parameter, the syslog facility. (See Chapter 10 for more information on the syslog service.) The important thing to remember is that by using the syslog clause, you are delegating the logging responsibility to your syslog service, and logging will be handled in the same fashion as other process logging is handled by syslog.

The *severity* clause, like the priorities clause, determines the message level at which messages will be logged. Only messages at that severity level or higher will be either written to a log file or sent to the syslog server.

Specific debug levels can also be set with the following syntax:

```
channel specific_debug_level {
    file "debug.txt";
    severity debug 2;
};
```

In this example, messages of severity 2 will be logged to the debug.txt file any time the server is running in debug mode, even if the global debug level is set higher.

If the *print-time* option is enabled, the date and time will be logged. The print-time option should not be used with syslog, since syslog already prints the date and time. If *print-category* is selected, the category of the message will be also logged.

Once a channel is defined, it cannot be redefined. However, there is no limit to the number of new channels you can create.

The category phrase splits logging into four default categories—*default, panic, packet,* and *eventlib*—and, if not specified directly, defaults to the following:

```
logging {
    category default { default_syslog; default_debug; };
    category panic { default_syslog; default_stderr; };
    category packet { default_debug; };
    category eventlib { default_debug; };
};
```

As you can see, the category statement simply connects category names with the type of logging device that will be used. This can be either a file or a call to syslog. If more than one logging device is required, separate them with semicolons.

There can be only one logging statement used to define all of the channels and categories that will be used in the name space. Additional logging statements will simply generate warning messages and their definitions will be otherwise ignored.

There are many categories to choose from. This allows you to send the important logs where they need to be and to prune out the logs that are not important. If you don't specify a default category, it defaults to { default_syslog; default_debug; }

As an example, let's say you want to log security events to a file, but you also want keep the default logging behavior. You'd specify the following:

```
channel my_secure_channel {
file "secure_file";
    severity info;
};
category security { my_secure_channel; default_syslog; default_debug; };
```

To discard all messages in a category, specify the null channel, like this:

```
category lame-servers { null; };
category cname { null; };
```

The categories shown in Table 7.2 are available. Each selects a different type of message.

The Zone Sections

Each zone section corresponds to a specified line in the named.boot file. The basic zone entry contains the name of the zone; whether this server is the master or the slave for that zone; if slave, who the master is for that zone; and the file to read. The directives in the zone section are as follows:

Master. The master copy of the data in a zone. This was called a *primary* in BIND 4.x.

Slave. A slave zone is a replica of a master zone. The following parameter specifies one or more IP addresses that this machine is to contact to update its zone files. If a specific file name is listed, then the replica will be written to that file. This corresponds to a *secondary* in BIND 4.x.

Stub. A stub zone only replicates the NS records of a master zone.

Hint. The hint zone is solely used to find a root name server to repopulate the root cache file. This is the same thing as a *caching zone* in BIND 4.x.

As in the named.boot file, class IN follows, but may be omitted since it is the default class.

Many of the options allowed in the zone section are the same as the options in the options section. The options are:

Check-names. See the description of check-names under "The Options Section."

Table 7.2 Message Categories

CATEGORY	SELECTS MESSAGES
Default	If nothing else is specified, this is what you get: { default_syslog; default_debug; };
Config	High-level configuration file processing.
Parser	Low-level configuration file processing.
Queries	A short log message is generated for every query the server receives.
lame servers	Messages such as "Lame server on. . . ."
Statistics	Statistics.
Panic	Server shutdowns.—If the server has to shut itself down due to an internal problem, it will log the problem both in the panic category and in the problem's native category. If you do not define the panic category, the following definition is used: category panic { default_syslog;default_stderr; };
Update	Dynamic updates.
Ncache	Negative caching.
xfer-in	Zone transfers the server is receiving.
xfer-out	Zone transfers the server is sending.
Db	All database operations.
Eventlib	Debugging information from the event system. Only one channel may be specified for this category, and it must be a file channel. If you do not define the eventlib category, the following definition is used: category eventlib { default_debug; };
Packet	Dumps of packets received and sent. Cannot be sent to syslog, only to files. If not defined, defaults to packet { default_debug; };
Notify	The notify protocol.
Cname	Messages such as ". . . points to a CNAME."
Security	Approved/unapproved requests.
Os	Operating system problems.
Insist	Internal consistency check failures.
Maintenance	Periodic maintenance events.
Load	Zone loading messages.
response-checks	Messages arising from invalid responses.

Allow-query. See the description of allow-query under "The Options Section."

Allow-update. Specifies which hosts are allowed to submit dynamic DNS updates to the server. The default is to deny updates from all hosts.

Allow-transfer. See the description of allow-transfer under "The Options Section."

Max-transfer-time-n. Specifies a time (in minutes) after which inbound zone transfers will be terminated.

Notify. If this server is authoritative for a zone, it sends messages to the slave servers when there is a change. Changes are not pushed to the slaves; rather, when the slave server receives the notify, the slaves will check to see if they need to perform a zone transfer. This statement can also be placed in the zone sections to override the defaults. The default is yes.

Also-notify. Specifies additional machines to be notified of updates. If the notify option is not set, the also-notify will be ignored.

The ACL Section

The ACL section defines who has access to a resource. The choices are *any, none, localhost, localnet,* and *dotted decimal IP addresses*. Note that an address match list's name must be defined with ACL before it can be used elsewhere. The following ACLs are built in:

Any.   Allows all hosts.

None.   Denies all hosts.

Localhost.   Allows the IP addresses of all interfaces on the system.

Localnet.   Allows any host on a network for which the system has an interface.

The Server Statement

The server statement defines the characteristics to be associated with a remote name server. This can be quite useful if there is a remote name server giving bad answers to queries. By creating a server entry marking the server's answers as bogus, you can quickly eliminate problems by preventing further queries from being sent to it.

Two types of zone transfers are supported, one-answer and many-answers. *One-answer* is the default and is understood by all 4.9.x and 8.1.x servers. *Many-answers* is supported only by BIND 8.1.

The Cache File

You should always work with the latest cache file. The easiest way to do this is to periodically retrieve it using FTP from rs.internic.net; get the named.ca file from the domain subdirectory. If you have dig, an excellent available freeware tool, an interesting way to retrieve the file is as follows:

```
dig @ns.internic.net . ns > /var/named/named.ca
```

The cache file contains name server (NS) and address (A) records for the root name servers. The next section details what the different record types are and how they are used.

Figure 7.2 gives an example of a cache file.

```
;            This file holds the information on root name servers needed to
;            initialize cache of Internet domain name servers
;            (e.g. reference this file in the "cache . <file>"
;            configuration file of BIND domain name servers).
;
;            This file is made available by InterNIC registration services
;            under anonymous FTP as
;                file                    /domain/named.root
;                on server               FTP.RS.INTERNIC.NET
;            -OR- under Gopher at        RS.INTERNIC.NET
;                under menu              InterNIC Registration Services (NSI)
;                    submenu             InterNIC Registration Archives
;                file                    named.root
;
;            last update:    Aug 22, 1997
;            related version of root zone:    1997082200
;
;
; formerly NS.INTERNIC.NET
;
.                           3600000   IN  NS   A.ROOT-SERVERS.NET.
A.ROOT-SERVERS.NET.         3600000       A    198.41.0.4
;
; formerly NS1.ISI.EDU
;
.                           3600000       NS   B.ROOT-SERVERS.NET.
B.ROOT-SERVERS.NET.         3600000       A    128.9.0.107
;
; formerly C.PSI.NET
;
.                           3600000       NS   C.ROOT-SERVERS.NET.
C.ROOT-SERVERS.NET.         3600000       A    192.33.4.12
;
; formerly TERP.UMD.EDU
;
.                           3600000       NS   D.ROOT-SERVERS.NET.
D.ROOT-SERVERS.NET.         3600000       A    128.8.10.90
;
; formerly NS.NASA.GOV
;
.                           3600000       NS   E.ROOT-SERVERS.NET.
```

Figure 7.2   Example cache file.

```
E.ROOT-SERVERS.NET.          3600000      A    192.203.230.10
;
; formerly NS.ISC.ORG
;
.                            3600000      NS   F.ROOT-SERVERS.NET.
F.ROOT-SERVERS.NET.          3600000      A    192.5.5.2241
;
; formerly NS.NIC.DDN.MIL
;
.                            3600000      NS   G.ROOT-SERVERS.NET.
G.ROOT-SERVERS.NET.          3600000      A    192.112.36.4
;
; formerly AOS.ARL.ARMY.MIL
;
.                            3600000      NS   H.ROOT-SERVERS.NET.
H.ROOT-SERVERS.NET.          3600000      A    128.63.2.53
;
; formerly NIC.NORDU.NET
;
.                            3600000      NS   I.ROOT-SERVERS.NET.
I.ROOT-SERVERS.NET.          3600000      A    192.36.148.17
;
; temporarily housed at NSI (InterNIC)
;
.                            3600000      NS   J.ROOT-SERVERS.NET.
J.ROOT-SERVERS.NET.          3600000      A    198.41.0.10
;
; housed in LINX, operated by RIPE NCC
;
.                            3600000      NS   K.ROOT-SERVERS.NET.
K.ROOT-SERVERS.NET.          3600000      A    193.0.14.129
;
; temporarily housed at ISI (IANA)
;
.                            3600000      NS   L.ROOT-SERVERS.NET.
L.ROOT-SERVERS.NET.          3600000      A    198.32.64.12
;
; housed in Japan, operated by WIDE
;
.                            3600000      NS   M.ROOT-SERVERS.NET.
M.ROOT-SERVERS.NET.          3600000      A    202.12.27.33
; End of File
```

Figure 7.2   *(Continued)*

The Forward Map File

Let's start with a simple example of a forward mapping file (also referred to as a *zone file*). This file will be used to resolve addresses for machine names in the given zone. The @ sign signifies the start of the definition for the zone. All records will contain IN, denoting an Internet record. Other types of records exist. However, they are rarely, if ever, used. In some implementations of BIND, the IN can be deleted since it is the assumed by default.

```
; Authoritative data for foo.com
;
@               IN          SOA nameserver.foo.com. postmaster.foo.com. (
                            23          ; Serial
                            10800       ; Refresh 3 hours
                            3600        ; Retry 1 hour
                            3600000     ; Expire 1000 hours
                            86400 )     ; Minimum 24 hours
nameserver      IN          A           224.2.130.1
www             IN          A           224.2.130.2
mail1           IN          MX    100   224.2.130.3
mail2           IN          MX    200   224.2.130.4
IN              HINFO       PII350      Solaris 7
ftp             IN          CNAME       www
nameserver2     IN          A           224.2.130.5
East            IN          NS          nameserver2
East            IN          NS          nameserver
```

SOA is the *start of authority* record. It contains the information that other name servers querying this one will require, and will determine how the data is handled by those name servers. Each primary file pointed to in named.boot should have one and only one SOA record.

The two fully qualified names listed after the SOA label are the primary name server for the domain, and where to send problems with the zone or domain via e-mail. Note that since @ signs cannot be used in this field, the postmaster entry should be read as postmaster@foo.com. If your e-mail address contains a dot, such as E.Marks@foo.com, it would have to be escaped with a backslash, and the entry would read E\.Marks.foo.com.

Note that the zone for which this forward mapping file is authoritative is not listed. It is strictly located in the named.boot file in the line that refers to this filename. The SOA record has five magic numbers: *serial number*, *refresh*, *retry*, *expire*, and *minimum*.

The first magic number is the *serial number*. It is used strictly to determine whether secondaries are up to date. Many people like to use the date with a two-digit extension. We find it much easier to start with the number 1 and increment every time a change is made to the file. If changed address information does not seem to be making it to the secondaries, chances are that you either forgot to update the serial number or forgot to restart the name daemon.

Refresh is the time (in seconds) interval within which the secondaries should contact the primaries to compare the serial number in the SOA; in the preceding sample, this is every 3 hours. *Retry* is the interval within which the secondary should retry contacting an authoritative server if it did not respond at the refresh interval. *Expire* is how long a secondary will hold information about a zone without successfully updating it or confirming that the data is up to date (i.e., if it loses contact with the primary). This number should be fairly large, since the loss of your primary name server should not be allowed to impact your network. From experience, we can tell you that it is not unusual to point client machines at the secondaries and have no clients query the primary name server directly. *Minimum* is the default time to live (TTL) for all records in a zone not containing explicit TTL values. In other words, this denotes how long the information will be considered good without needing to check with an authoritative server for changes.

TIP

Decide to use sequential numbers or a date+ scheme for your serial numbers and use it consistently.

There are many types of records that can be used in the forward mapping file. In this example, we show the use of A, CNAME, MX, NS, and HINFO records.

The *A* record is an address record. This is the most straightforward of DNS records. It simply ties a name to an IP address.

The *CNAME* (canonical name) record is for aliasing hostnames and always points to a name that is defined in an A record. A CNAME record cannot point to another CNAME record. It should be noted that a CNAME record can point to A records in other zones that the server is authoritative for. CNAME records should be used to make it easier for users to determine the role that a server plays. For example, if we have our primary Web server, www.foo.com, acting as an FTP server, we can alias ftp.foo.com to that box. People who wish to upload or download files will most likely try the name ftp.foo.com without even thinking. Providing the CNAME results in fewer user calls and a more productive FTP site; this is presumably good for everyone.

The *MX* (mail exchange) record points to a Simple Mail Transfer Protocol (STMP) mail server. It must point to an existing A record. In the preceding example above, there are two mail servers listed, mail1 and mail2. The number after the MX is an arbitrary numeric cost factor. The entry with the lowest cost indicates that this site should be tried first. The greater the cost as compared to other MX records for the zone, the less chance there is of the site being chosen.

Since mail1 has a cost of 100 and mail2 has a cost of 200, mail1 is the preferred mail server. If it cannot be reached, clients will try mail2.

TIP

Set up at least two MX records, maybe three, for your organization. This will make it possible for e-mail to continue to arrive even if your primary mail server is down.

The *NS* record simply delegates a branch of the current domain tree to another name server. In the preceding example, nameserver2 will be authoritative for the east.foo.com subdomain. Why would you want to do this? If you have a large domain that can be broken into autonomous areas that can handle their own DNS information, it is much more practical to distribute the database and the workload. While you still should maintain a central area for the information that everyone needs to see, you should delegate the authority for the other areas of the company so that they can manage their own information. Remember, every domain that exists must have NS records associated with it. These NS records denote the name servers that are queried for information about that zone. For your zone to be recognized by systems outside your zone, the server delegating responsibility for the zone must have an NS record for your machine in your domain. For example, delegating the East.foo.com domain, we have the primary name server for foo.com, called *nameserver*. Within the foo.com mapping, we have an NS record for the machine authoritative for the East.foo.com domain. This machine is nameserver2. The second NS line shows that nameserver is also a secondary for the East.foo.com subdomain.

The *HINFO* record, which is hardly ever used, is put in place to detail system types. The entry consists of two values separated by white space, the first being the hardware type, and the latter being the software version. Some sites use this field for other information, such as contact information or pager numbers for the system. In this case, we are simply stating that www.foo.com is a PII 350 running Solaris 7.0.

The Reverse Map File

Looking at the following sample reverse map, you are probably asking why the file looks like this. Although it may not seem obvious, once you have implemented your reverse map files, you will find them extremely easy to manage and maintain.

The reverse map file starts with the same SOA record that is found in the forward mapping file. The main difference is that the only type of record found in the reverse map file is the PTR record.

The sample reverse map is called *0.0.127.in-addr.arpa*. This file is simply the reverse mapping for the localhost entry. When any machine in the foo.com domain requests the name for the address 127.0.0.1, the name server will return localhost.foo.com. The format of the address is the reverse of a normal IP address. For example, IP address 1.2.3.4 would be found in the 4.3.2.in-addr.arpa file (assuming a class C address) with a PTR record for the address 1. Also note that the PTR records must be fully qualified and end in a period.

```
0.0.127.in-addr.arpa
@               IN          SOA name server.foo.com.postmaster.foo.com. (
; Serial
10800                   ; Refresh 3 hours
3600                    ; Retry   1 hour
3600000                 ; Expire  1000 hours
86400 )                 ; Minimum 24 hours
;
1               IN          PTR         localhost.foo.com.
```

Following is the sample reverse name lookup file for the 224.2.130 network. Note that there are no reverse entries for CNAMEs, and that there can be only one entry for each A record. Also, the network 224.2.130 is implicit for all hosts listed. If this were a class B zone, the host portion would have been 224.2 and the host entries would all have been 130.1 through 130.5.

```
130.2.224.in-addr.arpa
@               IN          SOA nameserver.foo.com.postmaster.foo.com. (
; Serial
10800                   ; Refresh 3 hours
3600                    ; Retry   1 hour
3600000                 ; Expire  1000 hours
86400 )                 ; Minimum 24 hours
;
1               IN          PTR         nameserver.foo.com.
2               IN          PTR         www.foo.com.
3               IN          PTR         mail1.foo.com.
4               IN          PTR         mail2.foo.com.
5               IN          PTR         Name server2.foo.com.
```

It is important to note that the PTR record must point to a machine that can be found in DNS. Also, although reverse mappings are not required, some protocols and applications may not allow your machine to communicate if a reverse entry for it cannot be located.

Starting Up the DNS Server

Before we get to the client side of the DNS configuration, let us mention the command that is used to start up the DNS service and the script that starts this service during normal booting. To start the DNS service, you can enter the following command:

```
/usr/sbin/in.named &
```

The in.named process will read its configuration file (/etc/named.boot or /etc/named.conf) and start up in the background. Under normal conditions, you won't have to start this process manually. If the boot file and the in.named process file both exist on your system, the DNS service will start automatically when you boot a system. It is started in the /etc/rc2.d/S72inetsvc script.

Setting Up Solaris as a DNS Client

In order to set up your Solaris system as a DNS client, you need to know two important pieces of information—the IP addresses of your name servers and what domain you are in (not to be confused with your NIS or NIS+ domain). There are only two files that need to be edited. The first is the */etc/resolv.conf* file. The second is the */etc/nsswitch.conf* file. Here is an example of a simple resolv.conf:

```
domain foo.com
nameserver 224.2.130.2
nameserver 224.2.133.171
```

This file simply states the domain we are in and what name servers (in order) are to be queried for DNS information.

To update the /etc/nsswitch.conf file for DNS, simply add *dns* to the hosts line within the file. Determine the order in which you want the system to check name servers. In most cases, the order will be files then DNS. If you are running NIS or NIS+, you may want DNS last, as shown in the following line:

```
hosts:  files nis dns
```

Troubleshooting Your DNS Environment

The first thing to do in troubleshooting your name server environment is to make sure that your client is configured correctly. If you are using a Solaris client, make sure that the /etc/resolv.conf has the correct domain and name server entries.

Next, type **nslookup.** If nslookup connects to your name server (as shown in the following example), you have at least verified that named is up and running. If nslookup cannot connect, make sure that in.named is running, and, as should be routine, check for messages pertaining to named in your /var/adm/messages file.

```
% nslookup
Default server:  ns.foo.com
Address:  224.2.130.1

>
```

Within the nslookup program, try a few simple queries, such as the name of the name server and localhost. Both of these should resolve without a problem.

If you are connected to a slave, and answers are not correct, try connecting to the master and checking again. If the master and slave differ, chances are that you forgot to update the serial number in the SOA in one of your maps, and a zone transfer did not occur when needed. Update the serial number on the master, kill and restart named, and check again. Remember, this information takes time to propagate.

TIP

Use both nslookup and dig to routinely check the functioning of your name server. Familiarizing yourself with the output when things are working well will help you to spot problems when they are not.

If you can resolve forward but not reverse references, check your PTR records and make sure you have addresses in the reverse order. Also make sure that all of the entries end in *in-addr.arpa*.

Many resolvers will attempt to locate a host by traversing up the domain tree with the hostname. For example, if you are in the domain *a.b.c.com* trying to access a machine called *www*, the resolver will try all of the following names looking for this system:

    www.a.b.c.com.
    www.b.c.com.
    www.c.com
    www.com
    www

If there are multiple machines with the name *www* at different levels in the organization, the resolver might provide the address of a different system than the one you want. Be sure you look at the result you are receiving, and not just that you are receiving a result.

If you are tired of nslookup and would like to use a more revealing tool, try dig. This freeware tool is available from many places on the net and provides much more detail than nslookup. To start it, try:

```
% dig host-name
```

Using dig in this manner causes dig to return the IP addresses (if any) for the given host or domain name along with a variety of additional information, as shown here:

```
dig www.foo.com
; <<>> DiG 2.0 <<>> www.foo.com
;; ->>HEADER<<- opcode: QUERY , status: NOERROR, id: 6
```

```
;; flags: qr rd ra ; Ques: 1, Ans: 2, Auth: 3, Addit: 3
;; QUESTIONS:
;;        www.foo.com, type = A, class = IN

;; ANSWERS:
www.foo.com.    85603   CNAME   evan.foo.com.   ← Hey, it has another name!
    evan.foo.com.   85603   A        224.2.130.2  ← And here's the
address.

;; AUTHORITY RECORDS:                           ← Name servers authoritative.
foo.com.        86257   NS      ns1.yourdomain.com.
foo.com.        86257   NS      ns2.yourdomain.com.
foo.com.        86257   NS      equinox.stockernet.com.

;; ADDITIONAL RECORDS: ← Addresses of those name servers.
ns1.yourdomain.com. 83527               A       198.69.10.27
ns2.yourdomain.com. 83527               A       198.69.10.5
equinox.stockernet.com.   164809 A      199.170.68.11

;; Sent 1 pkts, answer found in time: 0 msec
;; FROM: sweeney to SERVER: default -- 10.69.224.253
;; WHEN: Wed Jan 27 15:14:29 1999
;; MSG SIZE  sent: 37  rcvd: 209
```

There are a number of options available with dig. Each of them is listed in Table 7.3 and more fully explained in the sections that follow.

```
% dig -x ip address
```

The *-x* option of dig is used when you are looking for DNS information using an IP address instead of the usual domain name. For example, the command *dig -x 224.2.130.2* will return the name(s) assigned to the IP address 224.2.130.2, as shown here:

```
% dig -x 224.2.130.2

; <<>> DiG 2.0 <<>> -x
;; ->>HEADER<<- opcode: QUERY , status: NOERROR, id: 6
;; flags: qr aa rd ra ; Ques: 1, Ans: 1, Auth: 1, Addit: 1
;; QUESTIONS:
;;        2.130.2.224.in-addr.arpa, type = ANY, class = IN
```

Table 7.3   dig utility options

OPTION	MEANS
-x	Uses IP address instead of FQDN
@nameserver	Uses a specific name server
Axfr	Performs a zone transfer
Any	Checks for any DNS information

```
;; ANSWERS:
2.130.2.224.in-addr.arpa.    86400    PTR     c235786-
a.blfld1.ct.home.com.                      ← Machine name

;; AUTHORITY RECORDS:
2.224.in-addr.arpa.    86400    NS     dns1.blfld1.ct.home.com.
                                       ← Who's authoritative

;; ADDITIONAL RECORDS:
dns1.blfld1.ct.home.com.    86400    A     224.2.128.33

;; Sent 1 pkts, answer found in time: 0 msec
;; FROM: c235786-a to SERVER: default ñ 224.2.128.33
;; WHEN: Wed Jan 27 15:05:50 1999
;; MSG SIZE sent: 45 rcvd: 125
```

To query a specific name server, simply add the *@ns* option, replacing *ns* with the name server's name or IP address This is also useful for determining if a change in a DNS entry has been propagated. Here's an example:

```
% dig @ns1.home.com www.foo.com

; <<>> DiG 2.0 <<>> @ns1.home.com www.foo.com
;; ->>HEADER<<- opcode: QUERY , status: NOERROR, id: 10
;; flags: qr rd ra ; Ques: 1, Ans: 2, Auth: 3, Addit: 3
;; QUESTIONS:
;;       www.foo.com, type = A, class = IN

;; ANSWERS:
www.foo.com.    86391    CNAME    evan.foo.com.
evan.foo.com.   86391    A        224.2.130.2

;; AUTHORITY RECORDS:
foo.com.        78217    NS     NS0.YOURDOMAIN.NET.
foo.com.        78217    NS     NS2.YOURDOMAIN.NET.
foo.com.        78217    NS     EQUINOX.STOCKERNET.com.

;; ADDITIONAL RECORDS:
NS0.YOURDOMAIN.NET. 168993  A      198.69.10.2
NS2.YOURDOMAIN.NET. 168993  A      198.69.10.5
EQUINOX.STOCKERNET.com.   168993  A      199.170.68.11

;; Sent 1 pkts, answer found in time: 3 msec
;; FROM: sweeney to SERVER: ns1.home.com 224.0.0.27
;; WHEN: Wed Jan 27 15:12:25 1999
;; MSG SIZE  sent: 37  rcvd: 212
```

Note that the results are the same as without the @ option. This is normally the case unless a DNS change has happened recently.

Adding the string *axfr* to the command line will cause dig to perform a zone transfer for the given domain. Zone transfers are useful to check if a name server is properly set up to host a domain name and to track down various DNS problems. For example:

```
% dig foo.com axfr @ns1.yourdomain.com

; <<>> DiG 2.0 <<>> foo.com axfr @ns1.yourdomain.com
;; ->>HEADER<<- opcode: QUERY , status: REFUSED, id: 10    ← Note that this
request was refused.
;; QUESTIONS:
;;      foo.com, type = AXFR, class = IN ← No answers in this section,
either.

;; FROM: sweeney to SERVER: ns1.yourdomain.com  198.69.10.27
;; WHEN: Wed Jan 27 15:18:00 1999
```

Let's try another one.

```
% dig axfr blfld1.ct.home.com @ns1.home.com

; <<>> DiG 2.0 <<>> axfr blfld1.ct.home.com @ns1.home.com
;; QUESTIONS:
;;      blfld1.ct.home.com, type = AXFR, class = IN

home.com.           95226   NS      NS1.HOME.NET.
home.com.           95226   NS      NS2.HOME.NET.
NS1.HOME.NET.      169147   A       224.0.0.27
    NS2.HOME.NET.  169147 A    224.2.0.27
```

Adding the string *any* to the command line will cause dig to check for any DNS information rather than just the IP address.

```
% dig  any www.foo.com

; <<>> DiG 2.0 <<>> any foo.com
;; ->>HEADER<<- opcode: QUERY , status: NOERROR, id: 6
;; flags: qr rd ra ; Ques: 1, Ans: 3, Auth: 3, Addit: 3
;; QUESTIONS:
;;      foo.com, type = ANY, class = IN

;; ANSWERS:
foo.com.            77302   NS      ns1.yourdomain.com.
foo.com.            77302   NS      ns2.yourdomain.com.
foo.com.            77302   NS      equinox.stockernet.com.

;; AUTHORITY RECORDS:
foo.com.            77302   NS      ns1.yourdomain.com.
foo.com.            77302   NS      ns2.yourdomain.com.
foo.com.            77302   NS      equinox.stockernet.com.

;; ADDITIONAL RECORDS:
ns1.yourdomain.com. 78758   A       198.69.10.27
ns2.yourdomain.com. 82924   A       198.69.10.5
equinox.stockernet.com.   164206   A       199.170.68.11

;; Sent 1 pkts, answer found in time: 0 msec
;; FROM: sweeney to SERVER: default -- 10.69.224.253
;; WHEN: Wed Jan 27 15:24:32 1999
;; MSG SIZE  sent: 33  rcvd: 200
```

Summary

DNS is one of the most critical networking components for any organization working on the Internet. Regardless of whether you are directly responsible for its maintenance, knowing how it works and how it is configured will help you in your job:

- Name servers either own information about your systems (in which case they are said to be authoritative) or they know how to get it from other name servers. This is true of the Internet at large, but can also be true within your organization—if you choose to distribute responsibility for your name space across the organization.

- Setting up a DNS server requires that a number of files be carefully, if not painstakingly, prepared. These describe your systems, identify your name servers, and provide a means for ensuring that updates are properly propagated.

  - DNS provides name-to-address as well as address-to-name translations. It identifies mail exchangers and those servers that are authoritative for the given domain.

  - Setting up a client to use a name server is a much simpler operation. There are only two files involved, and the entries are very simple.

- Should you have any trouble setting up your name server or ensuring that it is working correctly, there are two tools that you should be prepared to use—nslookup and dig. Example commands and files included in this chapter should help you use these tools and become proficient at setting up, using, and troubleshooting DNS.

Network Information Services: NIS+ and NIS

Solaris 2.6 and later includes support for any of three network information services—*NIS+*, *NIS*, and (*/etc*) files. If you run your network using files, you ought to use rdist to keep these files synchronized across the systems you manage. This chapter discusses the NIS+ and NIS. We discuss both server side and client side issues. Following are some of the basic differences between NIS+ and NIS:

- The NIS name space is a *flat* namespace, which means that it does not support subdomains. Under NIS, only one domain is accessible from a given host. In NIS+, the namespace is *hierarchical*. This hierarchical structure is similar to the Unix file system structure. Since the NIS+ namespace is hierarchical, it can be configured to conform to the logical hierarchy of the organization. This means that you can create subdomains for different levels of organizations.

- In NIS, even for a small change in the map, the master server needs to push the whole map to the slave servers. In NIS+, on the other hand, the database updates are incremental. This means that only changes in the map are sent to replica servers. Therefore, NIS+ database updates are more efficient in terms of network bandwidth and are less time consuming.

- In NIS, clients are hard bound to a specific server. During the bootup time, the ypbind process on the client side binds to a specific server. However, the NIS+ client library is not a separate process. In NIS, the ypwhich command can tell you to which specific server the client is bound. For NIS+, you can use /usr/lib/nis/nisstat. The binding in NIS+ is soft.

- NIS maps can be searched by only one predefined searchable column, while NIS+ tables allow more than one searchable column.

- NIS supports Unix groups and netgroups. NIS+ also supports the concept of the NIS+ group. One or more NIS+ objects can be grouped together into an NIS+ group. Multiple NIS+ groups can be defined, each with different access and modification rights to the NIS+ namespace.

- NIS+ also has much improved security over NIS. NIS does not support authentication, authorization, or secure remote procedure calling (RPC), whereas NIS+ supports authentication, authorization, and secure RPC.

We're going to start with the newer and more sophisticated of the two—NIS+.

NIS+

Network Information Service Plus (NIS+) was designed to replace NIS, and is one of the naming services available with Solaris. The motivation for developing NIS+ was to provide a number of services that NIS lacks, such as secure authentication, hierarchical naming, and efficient updating. Even though NIS+ is dramatically different in structure from NIS and there is no direct relationship between NIS+ and NIS, it can still serve NIS clients. This makes a transition to NIS+ or support of a network with both NIS and NIS+ clients extremely practicable. However, by supporting NIS clients, you relax some of the security of NIS+.

Along with the robustness of NIS+ comes a good degree of complexity. Whereas NIS uses flat text files and commands are limited to a handful—ypcat, ypmatch, ypinit, ypserv, ypbind, and ypxfr—NIS+ sports a hierarchical organization and more than 20 commands. These are listed in Table 8.1 on pages 148–149; we discuss the most useful of these in this chapter.

There are a number of reasons why you might consider a switch to NIS+ if you are currently running NIS. For one, there is an advantage for large organizations with distinct divisions—the structure of NIS+ can reflect the structure of the organization itself. This is useful both because the organization of NIS+ will seem natural and because responsibility for each division's information can reside within that division. Another reason to consider switching is because the network overhead of NIS+ is extremely small compared with that of NIS. Since NIS+ updates are made individually, rather than through pushing entire tables or maps when only a single record is changed (as with NIS), little network bandwidth is used. The third reason is security.

NIS+ was designed with a secure authentication mechanism from the ground up. Users still have their standard login IDs and passwords as they do in NIS. However, they also have an additional password, known as the *secure RPC password*, for access to the NIS+ system. For most users, the secure RPC password will be identical to the login ID and password, but this is not always the case. The secure RPC password is used to decrypt the user's secret key and can be entered via the *keylogin* command.

Basic NIS+ Objects Explained

One of the first things you need to understand about NIS+ is that it is *object-oriented*. Thus, we introduce the components of the service by first introducing the types of objects that it manages. NIS+ objects are structural elements used to build and define the NIS+ namespace. These objects are always separated by dots when they are expressed. This point will make more sense as we provide examples of NIS+ objects. There are five basic NIS+ object types.

The first type of object is the *directory object*. Directory objects are similar to Unix file system directories. Unlike Unix directories, however, they do not contain files. They can contain one or more other objects, such as table objects, group objects, entry objects, or link objects. Like the Unix file system, directory objects form an inverted treelike structure, with the root domain (root directory) at the top and the subdomains branching downward. They are used to divide the namespace into different parts. Each domain-level directory object contains the *org_dir* and *groups_dir* directory objects for the corresponding domain (the *ctx_dir* directory is present only if you are running FNS). The org_dir directory objects contain table objects for that domain. The groups_dir directory objects contain NIS+ administrative group objects. Here are some examples of directory objects:

```
foo.com.
org_dir. foo.com.
groups_dir.foo.com.
```

Another type of NIS+ object is the *table object*. Tables are similar to NIS maps. They store a variety of network information. Tables may contain zero or more *entry objects*. There are a total of 17 predefined table objects. Tables can be administered with the *nistbladm* and *nisaddent* commands. Table entry objects form a row in the table, and each row stores one record. Here are some examples of table objects:

```
passwd.org_dir.foo.com.
hosts.org_dir.foo.com.
```

Entry objects look like this:

```
[name=user1],passwd.org_dir.foo.com.
```

A fourth type of NIS+ object is the *group object:*. These are NIS+ namespace administrative user groups. They permit controlled access rights to namespace modification on a group basis. They are administered with the *nisgrpadm* command. Here is an example of a group object:

Table 8.1 NIS+ Commands

COMMAND	ACTION
nisaddcred	Creates the credentials for NIS+ principals (stored in the cred table)
nisaddent	Loads information from /etc files or NIS maps into NIS+ tables (i.e., bulk load)
nisauthconf	Optionally configures the Diffie-Hellman key length
nisbackup	Creates backup up NIS directories
nis_cachemgr	Starts the cache manager on an NIS+ client
niscat	Displays the contents of NIS+ tables (similar to ypcat for NIS)
nis_checkpoint	Forces NIS+ to checkpoint data that has been entered in the log but not written to disk
nischgrp	Changes the group owner of an NIS+ object
nischmod	Changes an object's access rights
nischown	Changes the owner of an NIS+ object
nischttl	Changes the time-to-live value for an NIS+ object
nisclient	Initializes NIS+ principals
nisdefaults	Lists an NIS+ object's default values; these include: domain name, group name, workstation name, NIS+ principal name, access rights, directory search path, and time-to-live
nisgrep	Searches for entries in an NIS+ table
nisgrpadm	Creates or destroys an NIS+ group, or displays a list of its members; can also be used to add or remove members to a group, or to test membership in a group
nisinit	Initializes an NIS+ client or server (similar to ypinit)
nisln	Creates a symbolic link between two NIS+ tables
nislog	Displays the contents of the NIS+ transaction log
nisls	Lists the contents of an NIS+ directory

```
admin.groups_dir.foo.com.
```

The last type of NIS+ object is the *link object*. Link objects are pointers to other objects. In other words, they are similar to symbolic links in Unix. They typically point to table or directory entries. Link objects are administered with the *nisln* command.

How NIS+ Works

The NIS+ namespace is hierarchical, similarly to that of DNS and the structure of the Unix file system. As with DNS, this structure allows the name service to

Table 8.1 (Continued)

COMMAND	ACTION
nismatch	Searches for entries in an NIS+ table (similar to ypmatch)
nismkdir	Creates an NIS+ directory and specifies its master and replica servers
nispasswd	Changes password information stored in the NIS+ passwd table (use passwd or passwd -r nisplus instead)
nis_ping	Forces a replica to update its data from the master server
nispopulate	Populates the NIS+ tables in a new NIS+ domain
nisprefadm	Specifies the search order for clients seeking NIS+ information from servers
nisrestore	Restores NIS+ directories from a backup; also useful for setting up replicas
nisrm	Removes an NIS+ object from the namespace (does not remove directories)
nisrmdir	Removes both NIS+ directories and replicas from the namespace
nisserver	A shell script; sets up a new NIS+ server
nissetup	Creates org_dir and groups_dir directories and a set of unpopulated tables
nisshowcache	Lists the contents of the NIS+ shared cache
nisstat	Provides information and statistics about an NIS+ server
nistbladm	Creates or deletes NIS+ tables; adds, modifies, or deletes entries in a table
nistest	Reports the current state of the NIS+ namespace
nisupdkeys	Updates public keys stored in an NIS+ object
passwd	Changes passwords stored in the NIS+ passwd table; can also be used to establish password aging and related password features

mimic the configuration of the organization, divided into subdomains that can be administered independently. Still, hosts anywhere on the network can access information in other domains if they have the appropriate permissions.

The primary server at each domain is called the *master server* for that domain, and the backup servers are called *replicas*. The top-level server for the overall domain is called the *root master server*. It can also have replicas. Figure 8.1 illustrates the relationships between these systems.

Unlike DNS, NIS+ stores information about many aspects of a network, not just the hosts. More like NIS in this respect, this information in stored a set of 16

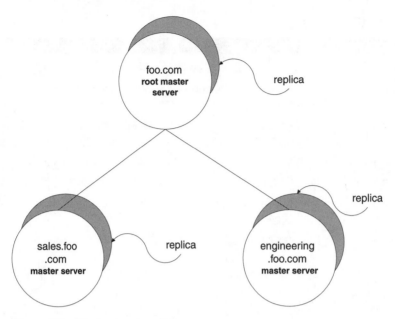

Figure 8.1 Masters and replicas.

standard tables that comprise a special database (see Table 8.2). The master and replica servers run the server software, and both maintain copies of the tables.

As with NIS, changes are made only on master servers and then are propagated to the replicas. This is true of the master server of the root domain (not to be confused with the root domain in DNS), as well as the master server of any subdomain.

NIS+ includes a sophisticated security system that guards not only the information it contains but also its structure. It uses this system to determine whether requests should be answered and what information any particular user is allowed to access or modify. This is in marked contrast to NIS's permissive servicing of any ypcat request.

Updates to the master server are made immediately. However, to be efficient, the master batches changes before sending them to replicas. If no other changes occur within the next 2 minutes or so, the master stores the changes on disk and in a transaction log. The transaction log contains both the updates and time stamps. The updates are actually copies of the changed objects. Once the log has been updated, the master sends a message to each of its replicas. The replicas respond with their own time stamps—indicating the time the last update was received from the master. The master then sends all updates that have occurred since that time. This process ensures that any replica that may have been down for a while will be updated properly when it is again available.

Table 8.2 NIS+ Related Files

TABLE	CONTENTS
hosts	IP address and host name of each system
bootparams	Location of the root, swap, and dump partition for diskless clients
passwd	Password information (username, UID, GID, home directory, etc.) for users
cred	Credentials for principals
group	Group name, group password, group ID, and group members
netgroup	Groups of hosts or users
mail_aliases	E-mail aliases
timezone	Time zone for hosts
networks	Networks in the domain and aliases (canonical names)
netmasks	Netmasks associated with networks and subnet-works
ethers	Ethernet addresses of hosts
services	IP services and related ports
protocols	Protocols
RPC	RPC services
auto_home	Home directory map (used by automounter)
auto_master	Master map information, for example, list of other maps (used by automounter)

Once the replicas have been successfully updated, the master clears its transaction logs.

If a new replica is brought online, the master will notice that its time stamp is earlier than its oldest log entry and will perform a resynchronization operation. It will transfer a full set of objects and other information to the replica. Generally, both master and server will be unavailable until the process is completed. Messages indicating that the server is busy should be expected. For this reason, it's a good idea to bring replicas online during nonprime hours.

Planning Your NIS+ Domain Structure

The configuration you choose should depend both on the structure you are able to support and the structure of your organization. If both clients and system support are naturally spread throughout the organization, you will probably want to select an arrangement that looks similar. Clients that need constant access to other domains will need their credentials added to these domains and will increase traffic. It's possible, of course, to set up a single NIS+ domain for your entire organization, but whether this is practical depends on a number of factors.

NIS+ is currently optimized to support up to 1000 NIS+ clients and up to 10 replicas. If your organization is considerably larger, you might want to create subdomains simply for better performance. If your organization is widely spread out, on the other hand, your reasons may have more to do with record keeping.

A complex domain hierarchy may be more than you want to manage. Think carefully about the size of domains, as well as the difficulty of keeping them up to date. Smaller domains will perform better, but many small domains may require more administrators or more administration than is reasonable for you to assume.

TIP

Consider a switch to NIS+ if your organization is large and distributed management of network information would fit well with your management style. Plan your transition carefully, however, and be prepared to maintain a considerably more complex system.

Common How Tos

The best way to introduce you to the setup and maintenance of NIS+ is to walk you through a number of scenarios. In each of the following how tos, we isolate one aspect of NIS+ and describe what needs to be done. These scenarios are brief and to the point. We encourage you to read additional material and become comfortable with the operations of NIS+ before you convert your site from NIS or /etc files.

How to Prepare Your Site for NIS+

Before configuring your NIS+ namespace, you need to do some planning, including verifying your hardware and software requirements, choosing a name for the domain, determining the security level you should be running at, and planning your domain hierarchy.

In general, you need a Solaris 2.3 or higher operating system, 32- to 64Mb of memory, and about 128Mb of swap space for a medium to large domain. The size of /var/nis is recommended to be about 20Mb. All of these requirements can be found in the *Administering Name Services Manual* included in Sun's

Solaris documentation set. The domain name for the root server should be at least two labels long. The domain name *xyz.*, for example, is not supported, but the domain name *xyz.com.* is a correct domain name.

Another thing to think about is the security level. The default security level is 2. If you want a secure environment, you should run NIS+ at security level 2. If you have SunOS (i.e., Solaris 1.x) client machines on your network that are going to be served by your NIS+ server, you need to run NIS+ in YP compatibility mode. This allows it to respond to both NIS+ and NIS clients. You should also decide what access rights you want to give to users and to your administrative group.

Finally, you should learn all the important NIS+ concepts—such as the difference between the login password and the network password. It's very important to be able to clearly distinguish these two types of passwords when troubleshooting problems related to authentication.

Once you are ready to begin configuring your domain, we strongly recommend that you use the quick startup scripts to configure the NIS+ namespace. You will save yourself a lot of time and trouble. For example, to configure the root server, use the *nisserver* script. To configure clients, use the *nisclient* script. These scripts are well written and easy to use, and reduce your chance of error. In the following sections, we outline the use of these scripts.

How to Set Up a Root NIS+ Master

To set up a root server, become the superuser on the intended root master, and use the *nisserver* script to build the root domain as shown here. You must be ready with the name of your domain. Use the following command:

```
root-server# nisserver -v -r -d domain_name
```

(Here, *domain_name* is the name you've selected for your NIS+ domain.)

Afterward, you will want to populate (i.e., bulk load) the NIS+ tables from a set of ASCII files. It is a good idea to create a separate directory in which to prepare and house the files you will need before you get to this point. For example, create a directory /var/tmp/nisfiles and copy the files from the /etc directory to it. Then, edit the files. You may wish to edit the passwd file, for example, because you only need the entries for the normal users in the NIS+ passwd table.

Table 8.2 lists the standard NIS+ tables that you may wish to include when you populate your maps (although it is not required that they all be included):

To populate the NIS+ tables, change to the directory where the edited files have been stored, and then run the *nispopulate* script:

```
root-master# cd /var/tmp/nisfiles
root-master# nispopulate -v -F
```

One important thing to note is that the network password created in the credential table for all the users is *nisplus*. This should be changed to something more secure. For normal users, every user needs to run keylogin, then do the chkey command and enter a new network password. It is highly recommended that the login password and the network password be the same. In the NIS+ environment, login explicitly runs keylogin; so, if the network password is same as the login password, users don't have to do a separate keylogin to authenticate.

When the nispopulate is done, you should reboot your server. When it comes back up, you can verify that NIS+ is working correctly by running the following standard NIS+ commands:

```
root-master% nisls
root-master% niscat passwd.org_dir
```

How to Set Up an NIS+ Client

To set up an NIS+ client, first become root on the master server, and verify that NIS+ host table has an entry for the client. If it does not, use admintool to add it. Afterward, run the *nisclient* script to create credentials for the client machine:

```
root-master# nisclient -v -d domain_name -c client_machine
```

(Here, *domain_name* is your NIS+ domain, and *client_machine* is the name of your new client.)

Do not worry if nisclient tells you that the credentials for your client machine already exist.

Next, login to your client machine as root, and run nisclient to initialize it:

```
client# nisclient -v -i -h master_machine -a master_ip -d domain_name
```

(Here, *master_machine* is the name of your NIS+ master, *master_ip* is the IP address of your NIS+ master, and *domain_name* is the name of your NIS+ domain.)

How to Set Up a Root NIS+ Replica

First, set the system that will become the root replica up as an NIS+ client (see the previous section).

Next, start the NIS+ server daemon:

```
root-replica# rpc.nisd
```

Then, you can execute the nisserver command on the root-master:

```
root-master# nisserver -v -R -d domain_name -h replica_machine
```

(where domain_name is your NIS+ domain and replica_machine is the name of your root-replica).

Finally, run *nisping*—it forces the master server to propagate the tables to the replica server. This command contacts the replica servers and forces them to check that all of their NIS+ tables are updated. If any are found to be out of date, the updates are then pulled from the master server.

```
root-master# nisping domain_name.
root-master# nisping org_dir.domain_name.
root-master# nisping groups_dir.domain_name.
```

(Here, *domain_name* is your NIS+ domain.)

How to Set Up a Subdomain NIS+ Master

The subdomain server must already be set up as a client of the domain above it (see "How to Set Up a NIS+ Client"). This may be the root domain, or some sub-domain. Once it is a client of its parent domain, you should start *rpc.nisd*:

```
subdomain-master# rpc.nisd
```

Then, you should login to the master of the domain above your current domain, and execute nisserver (*root-master* is used in this example, but this could also be some higher subdomain-master) to identify the subdomain master:

```
root-master# nisserver -v -M -d subdomain_name -h subdomain_master
```

(Here, *subdomain_name* is the name of your new NIS+ subdomain, and *subdomain_master* is the name of your subdomain master.)

You will then want to populate the NIS+ tables for your new subdomain. This is done on your subdomain master, in a similar manner to that previously described in "How to Set Up a Root NIS+ Master." Assuming that you have a set of files with which you intend to populate your subdomain prepared and stored in /var/tmp/nisfiles, you would enter the following commands:

```
subdomain-master# cd /var/tmp/nisfiles
subdomain-master# nispopulate -v -F
```

Afterward, reboot your new subdomain master.

Starting in Solaris release 7, the NIS+ server for a domain can be in the domain it serves. This allows a server to set its domain name to that used by its clients without affecting its ability to communicate with the rest of the domain.

How to Set Up a Subdomain NIS+ Replica

The same procedure as is described in "How to Set Up a Root NIS+ Replica" should be used to set up a subdomain replica. However, the commands will be run on the subdomain-master, not the root-master.

How to Configure the Root Server for an IP Address Change

The assumptions here are as follows:

- Your NIS+ root domain is called *root.dom.*
- The root server is called *master* and has an IP address of 1.2.3.4.
- You want to change the IP address of the root server to 4.3.2.1.
- You have one replica, called *replica*, with an IP address of 1.2.3.5.
- You want to change the IP address of the replica to 4.3.2.2.

Follow these steps:

1. For each of your NIS+ servers, add an entry for its new IP address. The following commands add the master's and replica's new IP addresses.

```
nistbladm -a addr=4.3.2.1 name='"master"' cname='"master"' hosts.org_dir
nistbladm -a addr=4.3.2.2 name='"replica"' cname='"replica"' hosts.org_dir
```

2. Use nisupdkeys to update the IP addresses in the directory objects with these commands:

```
/usr/lib/nis/nisupdkeys -a groups_dir.root.dom.
/usr/lib/nis/nisupdkeys -a org_dir.root.dom.
/usr/lib/nis/nisupdkeys -a root.dom.
```

3. Start up a second logical interface on each NIS+ server with the new IP address. On the master, run this command:

```
master# ifconfig le0:1 4.3.2.1 netmask + broadcast + -trailers up
```

On the replica, run this command:

```
replica# ifconfig le0:1 4.3.2.2 netmask + broadcast + -trailers up
```

4. Push the new directory objects to all the replica servers with this command:

```
/usr/lib/nis/nisping root.dom.
/usr/lib/nis/nisping groups_dir.root.dom.
/usr/lib/nis/nisping org_dir.root.dom.
```

5. Wait for the time-to-live of all the directory objects to expire. This is *extremely* important. Do not skip this step. Typically, the time-to-live is 12 hours, so wait for 12 hours. You can check time-to-live with the command:

```
niscat -o root.dom. groups_dir.root.dom. org_dir.root.dom.
```

6. For each client, follow these steps:

    a) Edit the hosts.org_dir table entry to reflect the new IP address.

    b) Edit the /etc/hosts file.

    c) Reboot the client.

7. Remove the old IP address entries for the NIS+ root servers from the hosts map, so that only the new IP entries remain by following these steps:

    a) Update the IP addresses in the directory objects with these commands:

```
/usr/lib/nis/nisupdkeys -a groups_dir.root.dom.
/usr/lib/nis/nisupdkeys -a org_dir.root.dom.
/usr/lib/nis/nispupkeys -a root.dom.
```

    b) Propagate the changes to all replicas with these commands:

```
/usr/lib/nis/nisping groups_dir.root.dom.
/usr/lib/nis/nisping org_dir.root.dom.
/usr/lib/nis/nisping root.dom.
```

    c) Wait for the time-to-live to expire (usually 12 hours) so that the old server IP address information is cleared from client caches.

8. Once all the clients are done, follow these steps:

    a) ifconfig the old (logical) interfaces on the NIS+ servers down by running, for example:

```
ifconfig le0 down.
```

    b) Remove the old entries from the host table.

    c) Edit the /etc/hosts files.

    d) On the system on which you started the in.routed, turn it off again and reset ip_forwarding to its old value.

How to Add a User to the Admin Group

In your default setup, only root on your master machine will be able to make modifications to most of your NIS+ maps. You will probably want to extend these permissions to all of the system administrators. This is typically done by putting all of the system administrators into the admin group:

```
# nisgrpadm -a admin.domain_name. sandra
# nisgrpadm -a admin.domain_name. evan
```

These commands will give sandra and evan the ability to modify most NIS+ tables from their own accounts. The admin group is the group that has full access to modify any and all NIS+ tables. This can give considerable privilege, so you should make sure that sandra and evan are trusted, and also that their accounts are secure.

How to Change an NIS+ user passwd

Normal users can change their passwords by running the *nispasswd* command:

```
% nispasswd
```

This updates the password in the passwd table, and also updates the credential table. Root can change passwords for users by running the following command:

```
# nispasswd user_name
```

However, this procedure should *never* be used for changing the root passwd.

How to Change an NIS+ root passwd

To change a root passwd, you *must* use the following procedure. First, issue the passwd command, and supply the new passwd:

```
# passwd
```

This will change the passwd in the local /etc/passwd file. Then, run *chkey -p* and enter the new network passwd:

```
# chkey -p
```

Finally, use the command *keylogin -r* to update the /etc/.rootkey file with the new private key for the server:

```
# keylogin -r
```

This changes the private key for the server, while the public key remains the same. This is necessary because clients use the server's public key for authentication.

If you use any other method for updating your root password, you run the risk of seriously damaging your NIS+ domain.

How to Administer NIS+ Credentials

The *nisaddcred* command can be used to create, update, and remove local Data Encryption Standard (DES) credentials. The nisaddcred command is used to create security credentials for NIS+ principals. NIS+ credentials serve a dual role. The first is to provide authentication information to various services; the second is to map the authentication service name into a NIS+ principal name. The DES auth_type is used for Secure RPC authentication (see secure_rpc in section 3N of the man pages), while the LOCAL auth type is used by the NIS+ service to determine the correlation between users identified by UIDs in the domain containing the cred.org_dir table and the fully qualified NIS+ principal names.

To create or update credentials for another NIS+ principal, use the following commands:

```
% nisaddcred -p uid -P principal-name local
% nisaddcred -p rpc-netname -P principal-name des
```

The rpc-netname is unix.uid@domain_name for a user, and unix.hostname@ domain_name for the root user on a host. Note that these domainnames do *not* contain a trailing dot, unlike most NIS+ commands. The principal-name is name.domain_name., where name can be user name or a hostname. For example, sandra (uid 555) in the example.com domain has the following names:

```
principal-name: sandra.example.com.
rpc-netname: unix.555@example.com
```

While root on the machine test has the following names:

```
principal-name: test.example.com.
rpc-netname: unix.test@example.com
```

A few caveats: You can only create DES credentials for a client workstation. Further, DES credentials may only be created in the client's home domain. However, you can create *local* credentials for a client user in other domains. To remove credentials, use this command:

```
% nisaddcred -r principal-name
```

Be careful when using nisaddcred -r. Without the proper arguments, you could accidentally remove the master's credentials.

How to Administer NIS+ Groups

The following commands may all be used to administer NIS+ groups. Be aware that NIS+ groups are not the same thing as normal Unix groups. You can list the object properties of a group with the *niscat* command, as shown here:

```
% niscat -o group-name.groups_dir.domain_name.
```

The *nisgrpadm* command creates, deletes, and performs miscellaneous administration operations on the NIS+ groups. To create a group, use the *-c* option, as shown here:

```
% nisgrpadm -c group-name.domain_name.
```

The group you create will inherit all the object properties specified in the NIS_DEFAULTS variable. You can view the defaults using the nisdefaults command:

```
root-master# nisdefaults
principal name : master.domain_name
domain name : domain_name
Host Name : master.domain_name
Group Name:
Access Rights : ----rmcdr---
Time to live :12:0:0
Search Patch : domain-name
```

To delete a group:

```
% nisgrpadm -d group-name.domain_name.
```

To list the group members:

```
% nisgrpadm -l group-name.domain_name.
```

To add members to an NIS+ group:

```
% nisgrpadm -a group-name member
```

To remove members from an NIS+ group:

```
% nisgrpadm -r group-name member
```

To determine if a member belongs to an NIS+ group:

```
% nisgrpadm -t group-name member
```

How to Administer NIS+ Tables

The *nistbladm* command is the primary NIS+ table administration utility. With this command, you can create, modify, or delete tables and table entries. To create a table, you must have create rights to the directory under which you will create it. To delete a table, you must have destroy rights to the directory. To modify a table, or to add, change, or delete its entries, you must have modify rights to the table or the entries.

Table columns can have following characteristics:

S   Searchable

I   Case insensitive

C   Encrypted

To create a table, use this command:

```
% nistbladm -c table-type column-spec .... table-name
```

For example, to create a table of type *computers* and of name *computers.example.com.*, with two columns, *name* and *model*, which are both searchable, you would use the following command:

```
% nistbladm -c computers name=S model=S computers.example.com.
```

(Here, we assume your domain_name is *example.com.*)

To delete a table, use this command:

```
% nistbladm -d table-name
```

For example, to delete your computers table, you would use the following command:

```
% nistbladm -d computers.example.com.
```

For more information about adding entries or modifying entries, refer to the *nistbladm* man page.

How to Examine NIS+ Tables

The *niscat* command displays the contents of NIS+ tables. To display the object properties of a table:

```
% niscat -o table-name
```

Or:

```
% niscat -o entry
```

To display the contents of a table:

```
% niscat -h table-name
```

How to Modify NIS+ Tables

NIS+ tables may be modified in a number of ways. One note for all of these methods is that an NIS+ principal must be a member of the admin NIS+ group for them to make modifications to most tables (see "How to Add a User to the Admin Group" on page 157).

The best method is to use the admintool GUI to modify them. The only downsides to this approach are that admintool requires X to be running, not all the standard tables are available through admintool, and new tables will never be available through admintool.

If you cannot use admintool to modify a table, *nisaddent* is the best alternative. The nisaddent command loads information from text files or from NIS maps into NIS+ tables. It can also dump the contents of the NIS+ tables back to text files. The following options are used along with the nisaddent command:

-a   *Appends* the contents of the source to the table

-r   *Replaces* the contents of the table with the contents of the source

-m   *Merges* the contents of the source with the contents of the table

-d   *Dumps* the contents of the table to stdout

(With no -a, -r, or -m options, the default is *replace.*)

You can put new entries into a file, and then merge those changes with this command:

```
% nisaddent -m -f filename table-type
```

For example:

```
% nisaddent -m -f /etc/passwd passwd
```

Or, you could dump a table, make changes, and then replace the copy of the table in NIS+. For example:

```
% nisaddent -d passwd > /tmp/passwd
% vi /tmp/passwd
% nisaddent -r -f /etc/passwd passwd
```

If you do not want to use nisaddent, your final option is to use nistbladm to directly modify the table. This can be fairly complex. Examine the nistbladm man page for more information on how to do so.

How to Regularly Administer NIS+

Depending on the updates one performs in the namespace, it is a good idea to frequently perform nisping -C so that log files get written to the disk. You may wish to put this into a cron file on your root-master server, to make sure that it is executed daily.

Another important NIS+ administration task is to regularly backup /var/nis, to make sure that you can recover in the case of a massive failure.

How to Remove NIS+

If you wish to remove NIS+, you should run the following commands on *all* of your NIS+ machines:

```
# cp /etc/nsswitch.files /etc/nsswitch.conf
# /etc/init.d/rpc stop
# rm -f /etc/.rootkey
# rm -rf /var/nis/*
# /etc/init.d/rpc start
```

We suggest that you start with your clients, and do your servers last.

How to Define the Printer Table in NIS+

Run the following command, as root, to set up the NIS+ printers table definition:

```
# nistbladm -c -D access=n+r,o+rmcd,g+rmcd,w+r printers \
```

```
printer_name=S,o+rmcd,g+r,w+r printer_host=S,o+rmcd,g+r,w+r \
description=,o+rmcd,g+r,w+r printers.org_dir.`domainname`.
```

Once you have set up this definition, you can confirm that the permissions are set properly with the following command. You should expect output similar to what is shown here:

```
# niscat -o printers.org_dir
Object Name : printers
Owner : ppp.hans.com.
Group : admin.hans.com.
Domain : org_dir.hans.com.
Access Rights : r---rmcdrmcdr---
Time to Live : 12:0:0
Object Type : TABLE
Table Type : printers
Number of Columns : 3
Character Separator :
Search Path :
Columns :
[0] Name : printer_name
Attributes : (SEARCHABLE, TEXTUAL DATA, CASE SENSITIVE)
Access Rights : ----rmcdr---r---
[1] Name : printer_host
Attributes : (SEARCHABLE, TEXTUAL DATA, CASE SENSITIVE)
Access Rights : ----rmcdr---r---
[2] Name : description
Attributes : (TEXTUAL DATA)
Access Rights : ----rmcdr---r---
```

After this, *admintool* or the *nisaddent* command can be used to populate the printers table.

How to Fix NIS+ Server Breaks with Unable to Authenticate NIS+ Server

NIS+ utilizes three security levels: 0, 1, and 2. These levels determine the types of credentials that a principal must submit in order to be authenticated.

Security level 0 is designed setting up the initial NIS+ namespace and for testing. An NIS+ server running at security level 0 will grant any NIS+ principal full access rights to all NIS+ objects in the domain. Requests that use invalid DES credentials are denied. No credentials are created or maintained within NIS+ at level 0, rendering the nis_passwd command useless since it will not work without credentials. Only if there are credentials existing from some previous higher level will nis_passwd function in a level 0 environment. At this level most of the other NIS+ commands that require access right of some kind will work with the Unix file permissioning system.

Security level is simply for testing level 2 security without DES authentication. This level should not be used unless you are experiencing problems with NIS+ authentication utilizing DES and only on an isolated network. Security level 1 will authenticate requests that use any credentials be they DES or LOCAL. Requests without credentials are assigned only the rights available to the Nobody class.

Security level 2, the default, is the highest level of security currently provided by NIS+. It only authenticates requests that use DES credentials. Any request with LOCAL or no credentials are defaulted to nobody's access rights, and requests with invalid credentials are completely denied access.

First, kill and restart rpc.nisd at security level 0, as shown here:

```
ps -ef | grep rpc.nisd
kill <pid>
/usr/sbin/rpc.nisd -r -S 0
```

Use *keylogout* to remove root's key:

```
keylogout -f
```

Add root's key and push it into the directories, as shown here:

```
nisaddcred des
ps -ef | grep keyserv
kill <pid>
nisupdkeys `nisdefaults -d`
nisupdkeys org_dir.`nisdefaults -d`
nisupdkeys groups_dir.`nisdefaults -d`
/usr/sbin/keyserv
```

Make sure the changes are propagated by using the nisping command, as shown here:

```
/usr/lib/nis/nisping `nisdefaults -d`
/usr/lib/nis/nisping org_dir.`nisdefaults -d`
/usr/lib/nis/nisping groups_dir.`nisdefaults -d`
```

Apply /usr/lib/nis/nisping to any other directories that you may have created. Then, kill and restart NIS at security level 2:

```
ps -ef | grep rpc.nisd
kill <pid>
/usr/sbin/rpc.nisd -S 2
```

NOTE In the following examples, *<master>* indicates the name of the old master server, *<replica>* indicates the name of the old replica server, and '*domainname*' indicates the domainname. Items such as <rpc.nisd pid> indicate the pid for the given process, obtained with the command `ps -ef | grep<processname>`.

How to Promote an NIS+ Root Replica Server to a Root Master Server

```
ps -ef | grep <processname>
```

All other punctuation should be typed as written.

1. Create the master's objects for replica. On the master machine, enter these commands:

```
# nsmkdir -m <replica> groups_dir.`domainname`.
# nsmkdir -m <replica> org_dir.`domainname`.
# nsmkdir -m <replica> `domainname`.
```

2. Copy the root.object of the master. On the replica machine, do this:

```
# rcp <master>:/var/nis/<master>root.object /var/nis/<replica>
```

Or, on Solaris 2.5 or later:

```
# rcp <master>:/var/nis/<data>root.object /var/nis/<data>
```

This moves the root.object from the master's /var/nis/[<master>|data] directory to somewhere else. (Don't delete it, as you may need to reverse the process if it goes wrong.)

3. Kill rpc.nisd and nis_cachemgr on both master and replica:

```
# kill <rpc.nisd pid> <nis_cachemgr pid>
```

4. Restart rpc.nisd and nis_cachemgr on the new replica server. On the new replica machine:

```
# /usr/sbin/rpc.nisd -S 0
# /usr/sbin/nis_cachemgr -i
```

5. Access the domainname directory and verify that the old replica is now the master. On new master machine:

```
# nisshowcache -v
# niscat -o groups_dir.`domainname`.
# niscat -o org_dir.`domainname`.
# niscat -o `domainname`.
```

6. If the contents of the cache still show the old master server to be the old master, do the following on the new master:

```
# nsmkdir -m <newmaster> groups_dir.`domainname`.
# nsmkdir -m <newmaster> org_dir.`domainname`.
```

7. Change the ownership of the directories:

```
# nischown <newmaster> groups_dir.`domainname`.
# nischown <newmaster> org_dir.`domainname`.
```

8. Change the ownership of all the tables within the directories:

```
# for tables in `nisls org_dir | grep -v org_dir`
> do
> nischown <newmaster> $tables.org_dir
> done
# for tables in `nisls groups_dir | grep -v groups_dir`
> do
> nischown <newmaster> $tables.groups_dir
> done
```

9. Check that the tables and directory structures are owned by the correct new master, as shown here:

```
# niscat -o org_dir
# niscat -o hosts.org_dir etc...
```

10. Remove the old replica from replicating the directory structures with the following commands:

```
# nisrmdir -s <oldmaster> groups_dir.`domainname`.
# nisrmdir -s <oldmaster> org_dir.`domainname`.
# nisrmdir -s <oldmaster> `domainname`.
```

11. Checkpoint the domain with the following commands:

```
# nisping -C groups_dir.`domainname`.
# nisping -C org_dir.`domainname`.
# nisping -C `domainname`.
```

12. If they the tables are all now owned and replicated by the correct machine, stop and restart rpc.nisd in security level 2 like this:

```
# kill <rpc.nisd pid> <nis_cachemgr pid>
# /usr/sbin/rpc.nisd
# /usr/sbin/nis_cachemgr -i
```

13. On the old master, clear out the old information and make it a client of the domain. Remove everything from /var/nis except NIS_COLD_START and NIS_SHARED_DIRCACHE. Put the name and IP number of the new master in the /etc/hosts file. Then, run this command:

```
# nisinit -c -H <newmaster>
```

14. Make the old master a replica of the domain. On the new replica, start rpc.nisd. On the master, run these commands:

```
# nismkdir -s <replica> groups_dir.`domainname`.
# nismkdir -s <replica> org_dir.`domainname`.
# nismkdir -s <replica> `domainname`.
# nisping -C groups_dir.`domainname`.   ← Server busy messages generated
# nisping -C org_dir.`domainname`.         because previous command has
# nisping -C `domainname`.                 not finished.
```

15. On each client, kill nis_cachemgr:

```
# kill <nis_cachemgr pid>
```

16. On each client, get a new coldstart file from the new master server:

```
# nisinit -c -H <newmaster>
```

17. On each client, restart nis_cachemgr:

```
# kill <nis_cachemgr pid>
# /usr/sbin/nis_cachemgr -i
```

How to Dump the cred Table

One thing you may want to do in case your credentials become corrupted is dump the cred table and store it in a secure location.

You need to dump the cred table in two parts.

1. To dump the DES credentials, use this command:

```
nisaddent -d -t cred.org_dir publickey > des_cred_table
```

2. To dump the local credentials, do this:

```
nisaddent -d -t cred.org_dir netid > local_cred_table
```

Debugging NIS+

Before trying to debug an NIS+ problem, you should always make sure that you have the recommended patches installed on the system. Otherwise, you may well be struggling in vain against a known (and recently fixed) problem. In particular, the kernel patch should be at the current patch level, and all the systems should have the same patch revision.

Authentication Problems

Most of the problems you are likely to encounter in NIS+ are related to authentication. Assuming that you are running *rpc.nisd* at security level 2 on your master server, you can use *niscat* to determine if a particular user is authenticated. Have the user enter the following command:

```
% niscat passwd.org_dir
```

If the user can see the encrypted passwords, you know that he is being authenticated. If, on the other hand, the user sees *NP* in place of encrypted passwords, you can conclude that the user does not have permission to read the password column. In this case, you should run *keylogin* to reauthenticate the user. If this resolves the problem, as determined by the user being able to see the encrypted password by rerunning the niscat command listed above, the user might still need to run *chkey* to sync the login and network passwords.

If keylogin still does not authenticate the user, it is likely that the user's credentials have not been set up correctly. You can check whether a user has credentials by examining the cred table with the following command:

```
% niscat cred.org_dir | grep username
```

If in fact the user does not have credentials, you can create credentials with the *nisclient* command:

```
% nisclient -c username
```

NOTE Whenever you are having credential problems, you should consider that you might be having a problem with the credentials of the workstation as well as or instead of the credentials of the user. If known-good users fail on a specific workstation, you will probably want to set the workstation back up, as is described in "How to Set Up an NIS+ Client."

Examining NIS+ Tables

Some NIS+ problems occur because information is missing from tables. You can examine the contents of tables with a variety of commands.

- *niscat* will output the entire contents of a table. To view the entire passwd table, for example, use this command:

```
% niscat passwd.org_dir
```

- You can also examine the object properties of a table. This can be very helpful because it will show you, among other things, if a table has incorrect permissions which may be restricting access.

```
% niscat -o passwd.org_dir
```

- *nismatch* can also be used to find things in a table, as shown in this command, where we are looking for sandra's information in the passwd table:

```
% nismatch -h sandra passwd.org_dir
```

- *niscat* and *nismatch* both directly access the NIS+ tables. The command *getent*, on the other hand, will look for information from various sources in the order defined in the */etc/nsswitch.conf* file. A typical getent command would be the following:

```
% getent passwd sandra
```

This command looks up the passwd record for the user sandra. In a typical (i.e., the default) environment, it would first access the */etc/passwd* file, and then would access NIS+. If you find that getent and nismatch give you *different* answers, you should look at your */etc/nsswitch.conf* file. Perhaps the naming service that is listed earlier (before *nisplus*) in this file has different information than NIS+. Alternatively, maybe NIS+ is not listed at all. Look at the line in your /etc/nsswitch.conf file that delineates the search order for the particular information. For example, the following line specifies the search order for passwd data:

```
passwd files nisplus
```

Performance Problems

Some NIS+ problems may be related to performance. You might have problems with NIS+ because your *servers* are overloaded. Alternately, you might get "NIS+ Server Unreachable" errors because your *network* is overloaded. Though we recommend the commands *snoop* and *netstat* as helpful in looking into performance problems, performance tuning is well beyond the scope of this book. We include references in the bibliography which might help you.

Some Frequently Asked Questions

This part of the chapter is meant to be a simple Q&A covering general user questions, setup problems, user login problems, lookup problems, and lookup problems within NIS+.

What Is My Network Password?

In most cases, your network password should be the same as your login password. When NIS+ is just getting set up, network passwords are often set to *nisplus*.

Why Can't I Have Machines and Users with the Same Name?

All machines and users must have credentials created for them. If you have a machine and a user with the same name, only one of them will be able to have credentials. In case of a naming conflict of this sort, you should change the machine's name. You may have to recreate credentials for the user and machine afterward:

```
% nisclient -c user
% nisclient -c machine
```

Where Is NIS+ Data Kept?

Table 8.3 shows where NIS+ data, as well as commands, daemons, and other files are stored.

Why Does nisserver Fail When I Run It as Described in "How to Set Up a Root NIS+ Replica"?

If, for some reason, the nisserver script fails, check the error message. It will give you some ideas about what might have caused the failure. Another option is to do the configuration manually, using nisinit and nissetup, as is described in the *Name Services Administration Guide* (see "Solaris Documentation" in Appendix B). This will help you determine the step at which the script is failing. This information can be vital in diagnosing the problem. If the nisinit -r step hangs, then check if you are running DNI. The DNI installation modifies /etc/netconfig file with this line:

```
nsp tpi_cots_ord - decnet nsp /dev/nsp /usr/lib/straddr.so
```

If you comment this line out and then run the script again, it will work correctly. Why Does My User Get These Errors on Login? "Password does not decrypt secret key for . . ."

This means that the user's login password and network password do not match. After login, users must run keylogin to get their NIS+ credentials, as shown here:

```
% keylogin
```

The user will have to type the NIS+ network password at the keylogin prompt. This may very well be *nisplus* if the user is logging in for the first time. Afterward, the user should run chkey, to synch the login and network passwords:

```
% chkey
```

"/usr/bin/passwd: <user> does not exist Connection closed by foreign host."

Answer 1. This can be the result of selecting *cleared until first login* in admintool when you initially create a user. You should, instead, select a normal password for a user when you create the account.

Table 8.3 Location of NIS+ Components

DIRECTORY	ON	CONTAINS
/usr/bin	Any host	NIS+ commands
/usr/lib/nis	Any host	NIS+ administrative commands
/usr/sbin	Any host	NIS+ daemons
/usr/lib/	Any host	NIS+ shared libraries
/var/nis/data	NIS+ server	NIS+ server data files
/var/nis	NIS+ server	NIS+ working files
/var/nis	NIS+ clients	Machine-specific data files

Answer 2. If you are trying to use password aging, you must install the password aging point patch, as noted under "Patches" for Solaris 2.3 and 2.4 in Appendix B.

Why Can't I Log In via xdm?

Answer: This is a known bug. Appendix B lists the patches for this problem for Solaris 2.3 and 2.4.

Why Do I Get Inconsistent Results When I Do Certain NIS+ Lookups?

In NIS+, the server binding is a soft binding. That is, every query may be accessing a different server. Therefore, if a replica is not in sync with the master, clients will get inconsistent information for every query. When you get inconsistent information for queries, run the *snoop* command (see "The inetd Process" in Chapter 17) to find out which server is providing the incorrect information.

NIS

The Network Information Service (NIS) was designed as a method for sharing critical system files across the network and to maintain consistency across these systems. Files commonly stored in NIS include passwd, hosts, automounter files (auto.master, auto.home, etc.), services, and so on. The client packages for running NIS under Solaris 2.6 are SUNWnisr, and SUNWnisu. The server packages are SUNWypr, and SUNWypu.

There are four major differences between NIS and NIS+—the *name space* itself, *security*, the *update size*, and *key—value pairs*. While NIS+ uses a hierarchical name space, NIS uses a flat name space and stores data in *maps* (as opposed to tables). While this allows NIS+ to scale and evolve without becoming unwieldy, it restricts NIS to a fairly inflexible operational model.

Since NIS was developed in the years prior to the advent of the public Internet, security is pretty much nonexistent. All maps in NIS are transmitted unencrypted over the network. Also, the maps are easily accessible and decoded by anyone with rights to read the files. These things are not true of NIS+.

Incremental updates are another bonus of using NIS+. While NIS requires entire maps to be updated and transmitted, NIS+ allows incremental updating. If you have a password file with 24,000 entries, NIS distributes the entire map to its slave servers even if only a single entry is changed. With NIS+, *only* the changed password entry is transmitted.

For those of you who came from a SunOS 4 (i.e., Solaris 1) background, NIS under Solaris works almost exactly the same way as it did then. However, until recently, obtaining the proper packages to set up NIS was not an easy task. Until release 2.6, Solaris did not come with an NIS server, and the unbundled product NIS Toolkit (SUNWnskit) needed to be installed to obtain this functionality. This toolkit can still be obtained from Sun's SunSolve Web site, although upgrading to a newer version of Solaris is highly recommended. Starting with Solaris 2.6, NIS once again is a part of the base operating system.

NIS is meant to operate in something of a hierarchical fashion, although it uses a flat name space. There is a machine that is called the *master* that holds all of the original files. There are other machines that hold replicated maps received from the master, called *slaves*. Then there is a group of machines that utilize those maps, called *clients*. From the client's perspective, there is no difference between the master and a slave server. A client will bind to any of the servers it can (generally whichever answers first when it first requests service and binds). Also, interestingly enough, the master does not have to be a client in order to serve the maps. The slaves, however, need to be clients. The maps are all served to the clients via the ypserv daemon. The NIS maps are all pertinent to a single domain—not to be confused with DNS or NT domains. Let's look at each type of machine and the role that it plays in more detail.

The NIS Master

The master provides all the files that are converted into NIS maps and, as maps, referenced by clients. The source files are not stored in any special location (thought most of them are in /etc). Rather, the existing system files are used unless otherwise specified. In other words, you don't have to set up a pile of files in preparation of running NIS. The master will make use of a subdirectory called */var/yp*. This directory contains the Makefile and other files used to create and transfer the maps to the clients. Under this directory, a subdirectory with the domain name is created. These files are the converted into the database files—called *maps*—and stored in DBM format under the /var/yp/{domainname} directory.

Here is an example of setting up an NIS master:

```
# /usr/sbin/ypinit -m
```

In order for NIS to operate successfully, we have to construct a list of the NIS servers. Please continue to add the names for YP servers in order of preference, one per line. When you are done with the list, type a <control D> or a return on a line by itself.

```
next host to add:  myhost      ← The master server
next host to add:  myhost2     ← The slave server
next host to add:  ^D

The current list of yp servers looks like this:
```

```
myhost
myhost2
Is this correct?  [y/n: y]  y
```

Installing the YP database will require that you answer a few questions. Questions will all be asked at the beginning of the procedure.

```
Do you want this procedure to quit on non-fatal errors? [y/n: n] n
OK, please remember to go back and redo manually whatever fails.
If you don't, some part of the system (perhaps the yp itself) won't work.
The yp domain directory is /var/yp/mydomain. Can we destroy the existing
/var/yp/mydomain and its contents? [y/n: n]  y
There will be no further questions. The remainder of the procedure should
take 5 to 10 minutes.
Building /var/yp/mydomain/ypservers...Running /var/yp /Makefile...updated
passwdupdated groupupdated hostsupdated ethersupdated networksupdated
rpcupdated servicesupdated protocolsupdated netgroupCurrent working
directory /var/ypmake: Warning: Don't know how to make target
`/etc/bootparams` (This is okay.) Current working directory
/var/yp/var/yp/mydomain/mail.aliases: 3 aliases, longest 10 bytes, 52 bytes
total/usr/lib/netsvc/yp/mkalias /var/yp/`domainname`/mail.aliases
/var/yp/`domainname`/mail.byaddr;updated aliasesupdated publickeyupdated
netid/usr/sbin/makedbm /etc/netmasks /var/yp/`domainname`/netmasks.byaddr;
updated netmasksupdated timezoneupdated auto.masterupdated auto.homemake:
Warning: Target `all` not remade because of errors (The error being no
/etc/bootparams file.) Current working directory /var/yp
myhost has been set up as a yp master server without any errors.
```

If there are running slave yp servers, run yppush for any databases that have been changed. If there are no running slaves, run ypinit on those hosts that are to be slave servers.

The NIS master server now has been set up.

Changing any of the maps is as simple as editing the original file and then changing directories to the /var/yp/domainname and issuing a */usr/ccs/bin/make* command. This will look for any changes in any of the source files listed in the Makefile and update the appropriate maps. After the maps are updated, they are transferred to any slave servers utilizing ypxfr as a transport.

What If You Want to Change Your Master Server to Another Machine?

If the old master is no longer to be an NIS server, it makes things interesting. Any systems that are clients of the old master will need to have the new NIS master added to their local /etc/hosts files and have new bindings created. The best way to do this is to rdist a new copy of /var/yp/binding/{domainname}/ypservers to all client machines. On those machines binding to the old server, ypbind will also need to be restarted once the file is modified for the modification to take effect. To make these changes easily, rdist can be used, providing you have at least one host that has the ability to rdist files to all of the clients. Here's what you need to do:

First, edit the ypservers file to contain the names of the servers that will be providing NIS services—including the new master. Then, rdist the file to the clients only. Following is a sample Distfile. The command Rdist -f Distfile would be the command used to initiate the changes.

```
HOSTS = ( myhost2 myhost3 myhost4 myhost5)
 FILES = (/var/yp/binding/mydomain/ypservers)
        ${FILES} -> ${HOSTS}
        install -R;
        special /var/yp/binding/mydomain/ypservers
"/usr/lib/netsvc/yp/ypstop"  ;
        special /var/yp/binding/mydomain/ypservers
"/usr/lib/netsvc/yp/ypstart";
        special /var/yp/binding/mydomain/ypservers "/bin/echo `172.29.10.1
myhost6 >> /etc/hosts";
```

Once there is no fear of frozen clients, and no clients still pointing at the old master, it is time to set up the new one. Make sure that all of the source files are replicated from the existing master to the new master. Then, on the new master machine, reissue the ypinit -m command and follow the master process just described. Once everything is set, /usr/lib/netsvc/yp/ypstart can be called to start the new master.

The NIS Slave

The machines designated to act as slave servers must have the IP address and name of the master NIS server in their local /etc/hosts files. Without this, ypinit will not run. If at any time the IP address or name of the master changes, all of the local /etc/hosts files will need to be changed, as well.

Next, the NIS domain name needs to be placed in /etc/defaultdomain. This file is read by several rc scripts when determining which daemons to run at system startup. To continue setting up the machine without rebooting, issue the domainname {domainname} command. With out it, the following error message will appear: "The local host's domain name hasn't been set. Please set it." Make sure the domain name is the same as that of the master.

At this point the slave server must be bound to the master in order to enumerate the maps. This process is illustrated by the command and output below.

```
/usr/sbin/ypinit -c
```

In order for NIS to operate successfully, we have to construct a list of the NIS servers. Please continue to add the names for YP servers in order of preference, one per line. When you are done with the list, type a <control D> or a return on a line by itself.

```
next host to add: myhost
next host to add: myhost2
next host to add: ^D
```

The current list of yp servers looks like this:

```
myhost
myhost2

Is this correct?  [y/n: y]
```

Now we can bind to the master with the following command:

```
#/usr/lib/netsvc/yp/ypbind &
```

At this point, the server knows the domain it is in, and is acting as a client to the master. It can now be set up as a slave. Ypinit will not prompt for a list of other servers as it does when you create the master server, nor will it run ypbuild again. This is why we needed to run ypinit -c initially.

```
/usr/sbin/ypinit -s myhost
```

Installing the YP database will require that you answer a few questions. Questions will all be asked at the beginning of the procedure.

```
Do you want this procedure to quit on non-fatal errors? [y/n: n]   n
OK, please remember to go back and redo manually whatever fails. If you
don't, some part of the system (perhaps the yp itself) won't work.
The yp domain directory is /var/yp/mydomain
Can we destroy the existing /var/yp/mydomain and its contents? [y/n: n]   y
There will be no further questions. The remainder of the procedure should
take a few minutes, to copy the data bases from myhost.
```

TIP

Once all of your NIS servers are set up, it is a good idea to make sure they bind to themselves and themselves only. This way, if anything happens to one NIS server, services on all the others will still function. Many times we have seen cases in which systems bound to an NIS server do not automatically rebind to another server after a failure. For the master, it is best to *not* run ypbind. Its /etc/nsswitch.conf should be set to use files and dns only.

Ypinit then calls the program ypxfr, which transfers a copy of the master's NIS map set to the slave server's /var/yp/{domainname} directory, as shown here:

```
Transferring netid.byname...
Transferring auto.home...
```

```
Transferring auto.master...
Transferring timezone.byname...
Transferring netmasks.byaddr...
Transferring publickey.byname...
Transferring mail.byaddr...
Transferring mail.aliases...
Transferring bootparams...
Transferring netgroup.byhost...
Transferring netgroup.byuser...
Transferring protocols.byname...
Transferring services.byservicename...
Transferring services.byname...
Transferring rpc.bynumber...
Transferring networks.byaddr...
Transferring networks.byname...
Transferring ethers.byname...
Transferring netgroup...
Transferring ethers.byaddr...
Transferring hosts.byaddr...
Transferring hosts.byname...
Transferring group.bygid...
Transferring group.byname...
Transferring passwd.byuid...
Transferring protocols.bynumber...
Transferring ypservers...
Transferring passwd.byname...

Myhost2's nis data base has been set up without any errors.
```

The slave server has now been successfully set up. This server will function exactly like the master, with the exception that it cannot be used to generate the NIS maps. To the clients (coming up next) there is no difference.

What If You Want to Add a New Slave Server after the Domain Is Already in Place?

There are several additional steps that must be followed in order to add an additional slave server to a domain once the master has been set up.

First, you need to update the map that contains a list of all of the servers in the NIS domain. This map is called *ypservers.byname* and is used by any broadcast-based clients. This map is also referenced whenever updated maps are to be sent out to the slaves. One of the most common problems that we have seen is the failure to add the new slave to the ypservers map on the master. This results in a functional, but orphaned, slave server. While it will respond to all queries, its maps will not receive the updates from the master, and it will most likely be out of date fairly quickly. Symptoms of this problem are that users are unable to log in with new passwords after they have changed them, new hostnames or IP addresses are not being recognized, and automount maps are not being found.

To see what servers have been defined for your domain, use the command shown here:

```
ypcat -k  ypservers

myhost
myhost2
```

In order to add your new server, myhost3, to the master as a valid server, first add the name and IP address into the /etc/hosts file. Next, change directories to /var/yp/{domainname} and do this:

```
ypcat -k ypservers > ypserverlist
echo "myhost3" >> ypserverlist
```

Or, use vi to edit the file. Next, create the new ypservers map with the following command:

```
/usr/sbin/makedbm ypserverlist ypservers
```

This command will update the ypservers list locally. To update the list on all of the other slave servers, issue a yppush command. This command forces the specified map to the list of servers in the ypservers map:

```
yppush ypservers
```

The NIS Client

Setting up NIS clients is a straightforward process. First, the domainname needs to be set and inserted into the /etc/defaultdomain file. Then, the IP addresses and names of the NIS servers need to be added to the local /etc/hosts file. Next, the */usr/sbin/ypinit -c* command needs to be run. You will be prompted for the names of all of the NIS servers to which this client can bind. Once this is set, the /etc/nsswitch.conf needs to be modified in order to utilize NIS. The system ships with a default nsswitch.nis file that looks like this:

```
passwd:      files nis
group:       files nis

# consult /etc "files" only if nis is down.
hosts:       xfn nis [NOTFOUND=return] files
networks:    nis [NOTFOUND=return] files
protocols:   nis [NOTFOUND=return] files
rpc:         nis [NOTFOUND=return] files
ethers:      nis [NOTFOUND=return] files
netmasks:    nis [NOTFOUND=return] files
```

```
bootparams: nis [NOTFOUND=return] files
publickey:  nis [NOTFOUND=return] files

netgroup:   nis

automount:  files nis
aliases:    files nis

# for efficient getservbyname() avoid nis
services:   files nis
sendmailvars:   files
```

You will note that for password, group, automount, aliases, services, and send-mailvars, *files* is the default. This file can simply be copied to /etc/nsswitch .conf, and NIS will be consulted first for the remaining files.

To start the nis client daemon, ypbind, */usr/lib/netsvc/yp/ypbind* or */usr/lib/ netsvc/yp/ypstart* can be used.

To determine the server to which the system is currently bound, the *ypwhich* command can be used. This command simply echos the name of the NIS server from which the client is enumerating maps. To change the server that the client is bound to, the *ypset* command can be used. In order for this command to function on Solaris machines, the initial ypbind daemon must be started with either the -ypset or -ypsetme options. Neither of these are recommended; allowing a system to be bound to any machine is extremely insecure. The difference between the -ypsetme and -ypset options is that -ypsetme will only function on the local machine, whereas -ypset will allow anyone from any machine to change the bindings. Use these options with care, or preferably not at all.

NIS Commands

Getting information from NIS is frighteningly easy. Simple commands such as ypmatch, ypcat, and ypwhich are part of the NIS toolset.

To list all the values contained in a map, enter:

```
ypcat mapname
```

To list both the keys and the values contained in a map, enter:

```
ypcat -k mapname
```

Note that the ypservers map is one of the few maps with keys but no values.

To list all the map aliases, which are simply shortcuts to the map names, enter any of the following:

```
ypcat -x
ypwhich -x
ypmatch -x
```

They all give the same results.

```
ypcat -x
Use "passwd"     for map "passwd.byname"
Use "group"      for map "group.byname"
Use "networks"   for map "networks.byaddr"
Use "hosts"      for map "hosts.byname"
Use "protocols"  for map "protocols.bynumber"
Use "services"   for map "services.byname"
Use "aliases"    for map "mail.aliases"
Use "ethers"     for map "ethers.byname"
```

To list all the available maps and their master, enter:

```
ypwhich -m
netid.byname myhost
auto.home myhost
auto.master myhost
timezone.byname myhost
netmasks.byaddr myhost
publickey.byname myhost
mail.byaddr myhost
mail.aliases myhost
bootparams myhost
netgroup.byhost myhost
netgroup.byuser myhost
protocols.byname myhost
services.byservicename myhost
services.byname myhost
rpc.bynumber myhost
networks.byaddr myhost
networks.byname myhost
ethers.byname myhost
netgroup myhost
ethers.byaddr myhost
hosts.byaddr myhost
hosts.byname myhost
group.bygid myhost
group.byname myhost
passwd.byuid myhost
protocols.bynumber myhost
ypservers myhost
passwd.byname myhost
```

It is interesting to note that there can be multiple masters in a single domain. *myhost* could be the master for the passwd, group, and services files, while *myhost2* could be the master for the auto_master and auto_home maps. In order for this to work, all of the masters need to send their maps.

To list the master server for a particular map, enter:

```
ypwhich -m mapname
```

To match a key with an entry in a map, enter:

```
ypmatch key mapname
```

Most often this command is used for finding information in the password or hosts file. *ypmatch evan passwd* would return the password file entry for login ID evan. Some of us old-timers prefer combining ypcat with grep. It seems more like raw Unix. *ypcat passwd | grep ^evan* will perform the same function. If you keep phone numbers in the gecos field password file, ypcat | grep is a quick way to do a phone lookup!

Summary

Now that you know how NIS+ and NIS work and how to initiate each service, you can begin making choices about which naming service to use. Other factors in your decision include:

- The size and complexity of your organization
- Your concern for security
- Your concerns over manageability
- Whether you have a homogeneous or heterogeneous environment

We also explained the basic commands and provided some advice that we hope will help you in managing your site.

- Make sure all your NIS servers bind to themselves and themselves only.
- Make sure that you don't run ypbind on the master. Use dns and files only.
- If you can, try setting up NIS+ in a test environment and get used to it before installing it in a production environment. Get used to adding and deleting users, adding users to groups, adding machines to netgroups, and so on.

## PART TWO

Managing Your Systems

When asked if we enjoy being challenged by our jobs, we usually answer yes, but add that we prefer to pick and choose our challenges. When everything you do is difficult, the job is not fun. When most of what you do involves setting services up to run on autopilot and only checking now and then to ensure that they're still flying, you have time for the occasional "learning experience" that might otherwise be the proverbial straw.

The well-managed network is well monitored. None of us has time to read every message written to every log file. On the other hand, if we don't take the time to review these messages at some level, we not only lose an opportunity to stay abreast of how our systems are functioning, but we are likely to run into problems that we might have avoided had we seen the tell-tale signs building up in our log files.

To successfully manage a network of systems, processes, and users, you need to find ways to take the day-to-day out of your daily routine so that you can concentrate on the unusual. Taking the day-to-day out of your daily routine involves automating as much as is reasonably possible. Creating scripts as a way to avoid repetitive work is the single most important task of systems administration. On the other hand, creating scripts isn't the whole job. You also have to remember what each script does, organize your scripts in some manner that allows you to easily use and update them and, when appropriate, run your scripts through services like cron so that you don't even have to invoke them to reap the benefit.

Even a service as straightforward as cron can be difficult to manage and error-prone if your cron files are scattered across many systems and usernames.

When it's time to modify a script that has been running every night for over a year, you shouldn't have to stop dead in your tracks and wonder where the script is being run and where it's located. Organize your work as deliberately and as simply as possible. Complexity will arise on its own.

The well-managed network is also secure. We take the point of view that security is *not* simply keeping a system safe from harm. Security is protecting your system's *function*, not your system's *hardware*. Since we are both parents, we like to use an analogy involving children. If keeping our children safe were to involve locking them in their rooms and not letting them watch TV, life would be easy. Children raised in isolation chambers, however, would not be safe. They would be unprepared for life. Similarly, systems that are too severely protected are not safe. They're unprepared for the kind of work that you and your users need from them. A proper balance of security and functionality is the only strategy that's viable.

Keeping your systems well organized, well monitored, and available is the key to doing a good job and having a good job.

In this part of the book, we discuss many aspects of keeping your systems well organized and usable. In Chapter 9, we address system and network monitoring. We provide some information on commercial network monitoring software as well as monitoring that you can do with scripts and some well chosen tools. In Chapter 10, we provide a roadmap to many file systems, configuration files, log files and processes that make up your system. In Chapter 11, we offer some advice on how and what to automate to make your systems more manageable. Chapter 12 provides an introduction to system security—including a lot of recommendations to help you nail down your systems quickly. Chapter 13 introduces high availability and tells you what you can do, even on a small budget, to keep your network services up and systems available most of the time.

Monitoring Your Environment

Proactive monitoring is looking for trouble before it finds you. With reference to computer environments, monitoring is always proactive. Watching for evidence of emerging or potential problems, checking available disk space and the health of essential processes, and probing systems to ensure that they are reachable are all examples of detecting problems before they disrupt the workflow on your network.

Monitoring is not something you should cavalierly put off until there's nothing else on your busy plate of things to be done. As soon as your computer environment is up and running, it is time to start thinking about protecting it against all the things that can go wrong. A good place to begin is to ask yourself a series of questions. What kinds of problems are possible? Which of these problems will cause serious disruption to your company's productivity? What information do you need to know about the status of your systems to keep them running smoothly? When do you need to know it? How do you want to be notified? These are questions that must be answered fully before you can put any comprehensive monitoring plan into place. This chapter suggests some answers to these questions, discusses the services that network management software offers, and provides you with some useful examples of monitoring and notification scripts.

The key elements of monitoring are as follows:

- Reducing the amount and complexity of data that you need to review. Examples include log files, error messages, quota reports, and the output from scheduled cron jobs.

- Attaching virtual probes to essential services so that you are notified immediately when they become unavailable. Examples of services you might want to monitor in this way include Web servers, database servers, and mail servers.

- Maintaining big-picture connectivity and performance statistics, often through the use of graphical displays of the network being monitored. No service is useful if you cannot access the system on which it is running.

- Assisting in the detection and isolation of faults.

Monitoring is essential because every network, with very few exceptions, is far too complicated for anyone to manage without some kind of automated assistance. In fact, automation is implied in the term *proactive monitoring*. Anyone monitoring a system or a network manually (i.e., without the help of scripts and other software tools) is being reactive, not proactive. Any break in normal processing, any kind of emergency or failure, is likely to steal his or her attention completely from all the other systems and services that need to be watched.

The alternative to monitoring is waiting for things to break and then responding as needed to the resultant emergencies. Most of us, in spite of our best intentions, will find ourselves in this mode from time to time. For the better prepared of us, however, these times are rare. When they occur, we usually have the luxury of being able to focus our attention on the problem at hand, confident that other aspects of our operations are not running on the very edge of usability and likely, themselves, to fail.

Monitoring can take the form of very simple scripts that are invoked through cron, or it can involve large commercial packages and dedicated high-powered workstations. No matter how much computer power or software you throw at the problem of network and system monitoring, however, some manual intervention is required. The analogy of a tree in the forest that falls without anyone hearing is a good one. If no one reads the script-generated reports, looks at the monitoring station's graphical display, or listens for the alarms, is the network being monitored? We think not. For us, therefore, the term *proactive monitoring* implies several factors—automation, detection of problems before they become critical, and reception of reports and alarms by someone who understands their significance.

How much to monitor, how frequently, and at what expense depends on the size and complexity of your network, the degree to which the services it supplies can be considered critical, the window within which your services must be available, and the size and skill of your support staff.

It's easy enough, perhaps, to check disk space using a df -k command, but what if you're responsible for more than 60 servers, all of which have several gigabytes of highly volatile disk space, or thousands of clients? Can you effectively keep track of that much disk space spread across that many systems? How often do you need to check if file systems are dangerously full? How do you do it? Do you telnet to each system and run the df command? Do you set up a cron job to send e-mail to you any time any of the disks on any of the system is more than 90 percent full? Do you set off a script to truncate or compress log files?

Even if you have an answer for managing disk space, what about all the other things that can go wrong? Do you scan messages files for warning messages from your system telling you that there have been memory errors or disk errors? Do you scan sulog for signs that someone knows someone else's password, knows the superuser password, or is trying to guess passwords? Do you routinely look at network traffic? Do you have any idea how high collision rates and error rates are on your clients' network interfaces? Are your users over their disk quotas? Do you know when mail is backing up in your spool directory? Do you check root's mail file now and then, or is mail addressed to root delivered to you? Have accounts for people who have left your company been properly disabled? Are your backups completing properly? Do your systems have the proper patches installed? Are your users' environments set up properly?

So many factors contribute to the overall health and well-being of a network that it is hard to name them all, never mind watch them all. Determining which of the large number of things that can fail should be monitored is a task in itself. If you elect to watch everything you can think of without the benefit of a graphical network display, you can easily be barraged by e-mail or paged so often that you have trouble telling the minor emergencies from the major emergencies.

Commercial network management packages such as HP Openview, Sun Net Manager, Netview 6000, and Robomon are all wonderful products, but not everyone can spend thousands of dollars on a framework for system monitoring. Small companies or offices are not likely to be able to afford the tools or the personnel to support a fully functional monitoring station. We will talk about commercial network management and monitoring systems in enough detail to describe their underlying protocols, basic services, configuration, and ongoing maintenance. But don't lose heart if your budget is small or your boss does not understand how difficult it is to keep track of the health of a network of busy systems. There are many things you can do to monitor your systems directly with customized scripts, Internet access, e-mail, and a pager. We will provide some recommendations for publicly available tools and offer some of our favorite tips and scripts for constructing the poor person's network monitor.

Monitoring Tools: Build or Buy?

In every environment, there is a multitude of items that should be monitored on a continuing basis. For the base operating system, such things as disk space, swap space, CPU usage, and warning/error messages that are written into the /var/adm/messages file are a few that come to mind as needing to be checked periodically. For applications such as DNS, directory services, and Web services, you may have to ensure that these services are operating around the clock.

One thing to remember is that, in every case, there is a chance to spend a boat-load of money on a product that will perform the needed monitoring for you. However, there are two things to keep in mind. First, implementing your own monitoring system may not only prove a rewarding experience, but will allow you to customize your monitoring and alerting process as no purchased program will. And second, even the most fully featured network monitoring software will require some setup and customization as the scope of your monitoring responsibilities changes with changes in your network.

The second thing that you should keep in mind as you make decisions about whether to buy or build your monitoring tools is that it is hard for many companies to get over the "freeware is bad" syndrome. Utilities such as wget, lynx, and perl are the cornerstones for most script-based monitoring. If your management mistakenly believes that basic tools are unreliable and that, conversely, anything that arrives in shrink-wrap is reliable, you might have a hard time getting the backing to "roll your own" or recognition for your efforts afterward.

Some of the major differences between commercial and home-brew monitoring systems involve the approach taken with respect to both protocols and delivery mechanisms. Commercial packages are generally built on top of specially crafted protocols designed to request and obtain information about the systems and processes you are monitoring without overwhelming the network in the process. They generally deliver their reports to graphical displays representing the collection of systems being monitored. Most home-brew systems, on the other hand, rely on a collection of scripts and use a combination of pagers and e-mail to deliver their findings to the interested parties.

As was suggested earlier, one of the most important factors to consider when making the build-or-buy decision is the size and complexity of the network you are monitoring. Large organizations might do well to have a monitoring station that is staffed 24 by 7. One of the authors once worked as an authentication engineer for a company running a global virtual private network (VPN). For this company, round-the-clock monitoring of systems spread across the globe, as well as the network connecting them, was both cost-effective and necessary. At other times in both our careers, this approach would not have been justified.

Evaluating Network Management Systems

The more networks evolve into complex distributed mission-critical networks, the more there is a corresponding need for centralized administration. With the recent exponential growth in the Internet and distributed computing, along with a steady move toward heterogeneity, it is almost impossible to run a network without some level of centralized administration and monitoring.

Commercial network monitoring systems are built to run on top of protocols designed to efficiently gather data from computers and other networking devices (e.g., routers and switches) and deliver it to the management station where, presumably, some human is watching the console for signs of trouble.

These protocols make it possible for a variety of disparate hardware to speak, essentially, the same language. By agreeing on a simple set of primitives for requesting and sending network information and a simple record structure in which to pack and deliver it, the systems involved provide the basis for the exchange and for display of network information at the monitoring station.

Before we go any further into outlining the various protocols and touching upon some of the more prominent network management systems in use today, let's describe the basic operations of network management systems and establish a vocabulary with which we can describe them.

One of the first terms that we need to present is *"agent"*. A network management agent is a process which runs on a client system or network device. Its role in life is to listen for requests from the network management station, retrieve the requested information and then reply. Agents have access to information about the operational status and configuration of the device and are able to respond to requests. They can also control the devices by managing the configuration information. Agents across different devices respond to the same set of commands with responses of the same general form regardless of the type of device or the complexity of the device's internals.

Another term important to understanding how network management systems work is *MIB*. This term stands for management information base, though you will always hear it pronounced as a single syllable word rhyming with "bib." A MIB contains current along with historical information about the local configuration and network traffic. Each agent maintains a base of information about the local system while the management station maintains a global MIB with a summary of information from all of the agents.

MIBs are extremely important, more so than they might initially appear to be. They, in fact, determine the type of information that is maintained by the agent and relayed when a management station requests it with some type of get command. The most common MIB in use today is MIB-II, but there are many additional MIBs, some of which are proprietary. The differences are needed to accommodate additional functionality of the devices being managed and are not a matter of concern.

A *proxy* is an agent which provides support to older devices which do not understand current protocols or any network management protocol at all. In other words, a proxy exists outside of the managed device and provides a means for managing legacy systems.

An *alarm* is a general purpose term used to describe the report of a network event. Alarms are also called traps.

Polling is the periodic action of a network manager to request information from agents.

Discovery is the process by which a management station automatically determines the systems and devices on the network needing to be monitored. In general, the manager sends out requests for descriptive information from each of the devices and then uses this information to assign icons and characteristics for the graphical display.

The *network manager* or *network monitoring station* is the system on which network status information is collected and displayed. This generally involves a fairly powerful graphical representation of the network using icons for each of the network entities, or collections thereof, being monitored. It can, on the other hand, be a simple command line system on which the primitives are typed. Figure 9.1 displays a network monitoring station.

The most widely used and simplest of network management *protocols* is the Simple Network Management Protocol (SNMP). SNMP was intended, initially, as a stopgap—a tool to provide some standardization to network management until an expected transition to an OSI based network framework had been accomplished. While more sophisticated protocols were being specified and the move to OSI was first stalled and later abandoned, SNMP was further developed to accommodate pressing needs. A number of versions now exist and yet, in spite of the existence of other protocols, SNMP continues to dominate the network management scene.

The basic operation of SNMP, and any network management system in fact, involves the agent processes which collect information about the system on which they are running and provide it to management systems either in response to explicit requests (polls) or in response to the severity of things to be reported. Agents can also respond to requests from the management system to alter parameters on the client. Management systems are generally equipped with a graphical display of the network being monitored.

SNMP, therefore, defines a protocol for the exchange of information that relates to the operational status and configuration of network devices, the format for representing this information and a framework involving agents and managing hosts. Current SNMP versions include SNMPv1, SNMPv2, SNMPv2c, and SNMPv2 usec, while SNMPv3 provides security enhancements.

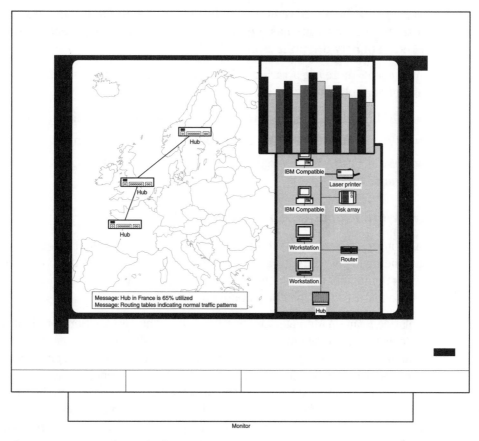

Message: Hub in France is 65% utilized
Message: Routing tables indicating normal traffic patterns

Monitor

Figure 9.1 Network monitoring station.

The four basic operations or primitives that SNMP uses are:

1. *Get.* Used by a network manager, requests information from an agent's MIB.
2. *Set.* Used by a manager, sets a parameter value in an agent's MIB.
3. *Trap.* Used by an agent, sends an alert to a manager.
4. *Inform.* Used by a manager, sends an alert to another manager.

If you delve further into the protocol, you will see these basic operations reflected in actual commands that are run—for example, the get operation is expressed in the Get, GetNext and GetBulk primitives.

Competing and complimentary protocols include CMIP and RMON. RMON is the remote monitoring standard. The goal of RMON is to allow networking monitoring devices which can measure certain aspects of a network without interfering with it. An RMON probe is a network device that runs an RMON agent using the SNMP remote monitoring MIB. Continuously monitoring traffic, it tracks statistics such as the number of packets, octets, broadcasts, and percentage of network utilization.

At present, there are a variety of technologies in common use in network management applications:

- SNMP and CMIP Management Protocols for Network Management
- RPC (Remote Procedure Calls) for Systems Management
- OMG CORBA for emerging Systems and Network Management frameworks

Network Management Products

Although we don't want to endorse any particular product (we're too busy to try them all!), we feel it's appropriate to mention some of the commercial network management products which might answer your needs and explain some of the features that may be valuable to you.

Solstice Domain Manager and Solstice Site Manager (see SunNet Manager) provide centralized management for large multi-site or small networks. SunNet Manager was an early entrant into network management and has grown in features and sophistication. Current versions feature cooperative consoles (for peer-to-peer cooperative management consoles) and support for heterogeneous networks (including accessing Novell NetWare Management Agent). You can choose to fully centralize the management load or spread it around to different groups. Using these tools, you can manage a wide range of system resources, including: communications protocols, network devices (switches, hubs, bridges, routers, etc.), applications, network services, and operating system resources.

Other tools to investigate include Sun's Symon (a Java-based systems management tool), HP OpenView/NetMetrix, Tivoli and Robomon. As these products will all provide many of the same features with different strengths, weaknesses, and price tags, only an evaluation with respect to your network, needs and budget will yield the proper choice.

Any network management system should provide you with a basic set of functions. In our opinion, this set includes the following:

Discovery. Systems administrators are far too busy to manually build up the information base required for network management.

Problem detection. The system should detect and report device and network failures.

Problem resolution. The system should have a means of initiating scripts or taking some action to repair problems (when possible).

Notification. The system should be able to notify you in a number of ways, depending on the severity of a problem. These should include visual cues on the manager display as well as e-mail and paging.

Reporting. The system should be able to prepare a report on the general health of the network, problems detected, and actions taken within some time frame.

Display. The network manager console should be able to assume different views of the managed network and focus in on segments or individual systems when problems occur.

Scalability. Whatever system you select, it should work on both the small and large scale or work seamlessly with other tools to provide you with integrated management of your network.

Additional functions that we think add significantly to the value of network management include trend analysis and correlation of events to support sophisticated problem analysis. Automated trouble ticketing for problems requiring intervention by the systems administrator or support staff is especially useful in large networks.

Poor Man's Network Monitoring

For those of us without the resources to purchase network monitoring software, there are many tools and techniques available to help us perform adequate monitoring, albeit in a less comprehensive and integrated fashion.

Deciding what needs to be monitored, how this can be accomplished, and how we want to be notified when something needs attention are the first steps.

Deciding What You Want to Monitor

There are a number of things that you will undoubtedly want to monitor. They fall into several broad categories—you want critical processes to stay up and responsive, you want system resources to be available and usable, and you want to be on the watch for certain occurrences—signs of break-in and new or impending hardware failures.

Critical processes include most system daemons (network daemons, naming services, file systems, printers, Web servers, logging services, and critical applications).

Disks need to both be available and have available space. Many monitoring systems issue warnings once a certain threshold (say 90 percent) has been reached or exceeded. Better monitors will also warn if space is filling up quickly (especially if more quickly than usual).

Connectivity can be as critical as whether a system is available. If a system and its processes are running, but users cannot access them, they are of little value.

Most system management systems monitor connectivity across the network. If a certain system or a network segment becomes unreachable, you can expect a visual alarm and maybe more. If you have systems that must be reachable, monitoring them from another system (or two) is a good idea.

TIP

Don't forget to consider the possibility that a system used to monitor other systems may itself go down. Don't forget to consider that a process set to warn you about problems might itself be in trouble.

Performance monitoring will help you detect problems of many types—from runaway processes to network attacks meant to disable your services. It will also help you to make decisions to move services or upgrade systems in order to provide an acceptable level of service.

Log files can provide extensive information on how your systems are being used, but only if you look at them. Our preference is to extract certain message types from our log files, digest them into statistics and mail ourselves reports. Log files grow too quickly and are far too numerous for any of us to do a proper job of scanning and understanding all that they have to tell us. Taking the alternate route, ignoring them completely, is worse than trying to read them top to bottom. Fortunately, there are some fine tools to assist you in monitoring log files. We describe some of these later in this chapter.

Deciding How You Want to Monitor

If you decide to use a commercial network application, you'll have a head start on deciding what you want to monitor. Every tool that we have used or looked at provides a number of built-in templates for such things as disk space, cpu utilization, critical processes, and connectivity. If you're going with a home brew approach, you'll want to come up with your own set and then determine how you can best monitor each.

For "live" monitoring (i.e., you're sitting at the screen), perfmeter can be useful. It does, however, require that remotely monitored systems are running the rstatd daemon (rpc.rstatd). If you watch a critical server with perfmeter (see the home brew monitoring screen shown in Figure 9.2), you will notice right way if CPU usage hits the ceiling or the load starts to climb. Keep in mind that the number displayed along with each graph represents the *scale* of the individual panel—not the high value. A flat-line display on a panel showing a 64 is still zero.

Perfmeter displays any or all of a number of values, including:

cpu	the percentage of CPU being utilized
pkts	packets per second coming/going on the network interface
page	paging activity (see Chapter 1)

swap	jobs swapped per second (see Chapter 1)
intr	Device interrupts per second
disk	Disk transfer per second
cntxt	context switches per second
load	average number of runable processes in the preceding minute
colls	collisions per second
errs	errors per second (received packets only)

For times when you might be there and might not, scripts are the ticket. You can write scripts which check almost any measure of system health you're interested in and send yourself mail or page yourself with the results.

You can also install and configure tools which monitor systems resources or digest and analyze log files for you. We mention some of our favorites in the Performance Monitoring section below.

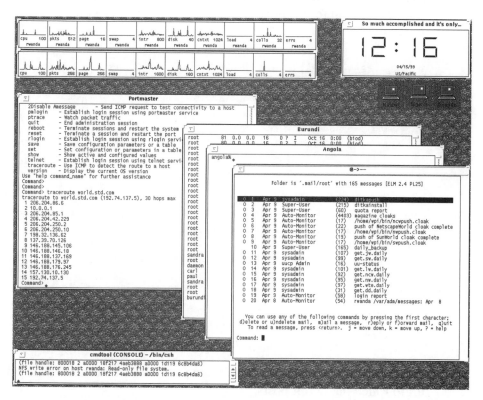

Figure 9.2 Poor man's network monitoring station.

Deciding How You Want to Be Notified

The first thing that you need to set up is the notification mechanism. Let's assume that, depending on the severity of the alert, you will either want to be notified immediately via pager or via e-mail (for less critical problems). We will start by looking at a script that has the capability to do both. The pager script, shown below shows how easily pages and e-mail can be sent. This script requires Internet connectivity as well as having Lynx (a text based browser) loaded on the system. The other requirement is a Web site or other service site from which paging can occur. In this example, pagenet.com is used. The pager script accepts the message using standard in with the alphanumeric paging pin number as a parameter and uses Lynx, a text based browser, to post the message to the paging system's Web site. Here is an example of how you might call this script into action:

```
cat /etc/motd | /usr/local/bin/pager 1234567
```

This command would send a page containing the contents of the message of the day file to a pagenet pager with the specified phone number. These pages are predicated upon html posts performed by these sites and may need to be modified accordingly to get them to function with your paging provider Web site. The Pager Script for pagenet:

```
#!/usr/bin/ksh
#
phonenum="860-524-8123"
read msg
echo "Message=$msg" >>/tmp/pager.log.$LOGNAME
date >>/tmp/pager.log.$LOGNAME
echo $msg | encodedmsg=`/usr/xpg4/bin/awk '
{ for (x=1; x <= NF; ++x) if (x==1 && NR==1) s=$1; else s=s"+"$x }
END { print s }'`
for pin
do
echo "Pin=$pin" >>/tmp/pager.log.$LOGNAME
opts="-post_data -dump -nolist -error_file=/tmp/pager.log.$LOGNAME"
url="http://www.pagenet.net/pagenet/page_gen"
/usr/local/bin/lynx $opts $url >>/tmp/pager.log.$LOGNAME 2>&1 <<__EOD__
SysID=$phonenum860-948-2000&To=$pin&Message=$encodedmsg
---
__EOD__
done
echo "----------------------------------------------------\n"
>>/tmp/pager.log
.$LOGNAME
```

Here is the same script modified for skypage. Note the difference is simply the url to which this script posts.

```
#!/bin/ksh
#
read msg
echo "Message=$msg" >>/tmp/skypager.log
date >>/tmp/skypager.log
echo $msg | encodedmsg=`/usr/xpg4/bin/awk '
{ for (x=1; x <= NF; ++x) if (x==1 && NR==1) s=$1; else s=s"+"$x}
END { print s }'`
for pin
do
opts="-post_data -dump -nolist -error_file=/tmp/skypager.log"
url="http://www.skytel.com/Paging/page.cgi"
/usr/local/bin/lynx $opts $url >>/tmp/skypager.log 2>&1 <<__EOD__
pager=1&pager=2&to=$pin&message=$encodedmsg
---
__EOD__
done
echo "----------------------------------------------------------\n"
>>/tmp/pager.log
```

If you don't have access to the Internet, but know that the paging service you use has a phone number for computer paging access, this is the type of script that can be used. It uses the freeware package "kermit" and requires a modem and phone line to be connected to your system. To get this working, requires patience and knowledge of the prompts that you will receive. As you can see, the entire conversation is scripted. The file with names and pager numbers for this resides in /usr/local/bin/pager/pagers.txt. The format of the entries is simply group name pager#. Pages can be sent either to the entire group or to an individual. Kermit based Pager script:

```
#!/bin/ksh
####################################################################
# Title: kermitpager
#
# Parameters: "number[,number...]" "text message""name,[name...]"
#
 # Mutual exclusion - wait for other beeps to complete
while [[ -f /tmp/beep.mutex ]] ; do
 sleep 20
done
echo $PPID > /tmp/beep.mutex

bft=$PPID$(date +%M%S)
msg=$2
nums="$1"

####################################################################
# Create the preamble to the kermit script we create.
#
print '
```

```
pause 5
set take echo on
set count 10
set line /dev/cua/a
set modem hayes          ← These parameters should be given to you by the
set parity even                              paging company
set terminal bytesize 7
goto DIAL
:AGAIN
pause 30
echo Redialing...
:DIAL
set speed 9600
set input echo on
output at\13
input 5 OK
clear both
echo "Dialing..."
dial t918008325137  ← This phone number should be given to you by your
pause 1                                  paging service
output  \13
input 8 ID=
if success -
 goto M
reinput 0 Too
if success echo "Too slow. Retrying..."
reinput 0 Bad
xif success echo "Bad line. Retrying..."
if count goto again
:M
output M\13' > /tmp/page.$bft
####################################################################
#
# Add a section for each phone number.
# Find the pager numbers in pagers.txt.
#
nums=$(echo $nums|sed 's/,/ /g')
(( tagct=0 ))
for num in $nums
do
(( tagct=tagct+1 ))
 if echo $num|grep "[A-z]"
  then
   num=$(grep -i "$num" /usr/local/bin/pager/pagers.txt/awk
'{print $3}'|sed 's/-//g')
  else
   num=$( echo $num | sed 's/-//g' )
 fi
 print 'input 10 Enter pager ID(s):
output '$num'\13
```

```
input 10 Enter Alphanumeric Message:
if success -
 goto N'$tagct'
reinput 0 Bad
xif success echo "Bad line. Retrying..."
if count goto again
:N'$tagct'
output [AP1] '$msg'\13
input 10 More Pages?
if success -
 goto O'$tagct'
reinput 0 Bad
xif success echo "Bad line. Retrying..."
if count goto again
:O'$tagct'
output Y\13' >> /tmp/page.$bft
done
print 'hangup
pause 5
exit'>>/tmp/page.t
print "$(date +%y%m%d%H%M) $1: $2" >> /tmp/beep.log
/usr/local/bin/kermit /tmp/page.$bft
chmod 777 /tmp/page.$bft
sleep 10
rm /tmp/beep.mutex

Sample Pagers.txt file
Evan    1234567
Sandra 1234566
Jim     1234555
Joe     1234544
Group1 1234567
Group1 1234566
```

E-mail notification is much simpler, since the mail and mailx commands already reside on your Solaris systems. If you use a command like this:

```
cat /etc/motd | mailx -s "Message of the day" emarks@home.com
```

you will send e-mail to Evan containing the same information that we just sent with the paging scripts.

Once your page script and e-mail setup are complete, you can start preparing scripts to monitor your systems and page or e-mail you when problems are detected.

Performance Monitoring

One of the first places to look when a system is slow is, of course, the output of the ps command. The more useful things to notice are:

- The number of processes. Is it larger than usual? Has some system daemon spawned many copies of itself? Can you determine why this might be the case?

- Unusual processes. Are there unfamiliar processes running? Are they using a lot of CPU time?

- Who is running what. Are any users (including root) running processes which seem excessive?

- Are some processes running at high priority?

At one of our sites, a Solaris client was crawling because a user had nearly a dozen textedit sessions running (apparently, he didn't know to exit and was, instead, putting them in the background). Problems like these can go unnoticed until a system gets so slow that the user becomes irritated enough to complain.

There is a lot more information available about processes than the ps command, in its popular forms (e.g., ps -ef), lets on. Should you have any doubt, a quick scan of the structures used to maintain process information (i.e., prpsinfo and prstatus) will convince you otherwise. Some of this information can be extracted by variations of ps commands and some is better highlighted by other tools.

Once you've derived what you can from the output of ps, you might use the *top* command, available from various ftp sites, to gather additional information. Top, as its name implies, reports the process most heavily using the CPU along with addition information including statistics on memory use and the system load (three intervals). The load reports on the number of processes ready to run, but waiting for their turn. If a system load is small (less than 2), your system is not likely being slowed down by processes hogging the processor. If it's approaching or exceeding 4, this is a concern. Top also displays the nice values.

Perfmeter is a built-in graphical tool that will give you a lot of information on a system's performance. Using it, you can determine whether a system is swapping or excessively context switching, the network is congested or disk activity is high. If you don't use perfmeter often enough to have developed a gut feel for what is normal for a system, place two perfmeters side by side—one for the troubled system and one for a similar system performing well—and look into the obvious differences.

TIP

Comparing output on a troubled system with the output from a similarly configured behaving system will almost always provide you with some insights. Be careful in selecting the systems to compare so that your comparisons are not distorted by dramatic differences in the systems' capabilities.

Once you've determined that particular process is slowing a system, you might want to find out why. There are tools for gathering relevant data for this kind of analysis. The *proc commands*, discussed in Chapter 1, provide a wealth of information about running processes, but will require an investment of time before you can use it wisely.

The *truss* command will produce a trace of a process, allowing you to easily see what files it opens (or tries to), what system calls it makes, etc. In the sample output below, the particular process (lynx) tries to open a couple of files which do not exist (i.e., NOENT).

```
open ("/user/local/lib/mosaic/mime.types", O_RDONLY) Err#2 ENOENT
open (".mime.types", O_RDONLY)                        Err#2 ENOENT
open ("/home/nici/.mime.types", O_RDONLY)             Err#2 ENOENT
```

SAR

Sar (System Activity Report) is an excellent package that comes with Solaris. It can be used for data gathering and is extremely helpful when one of your users complains to you that "things started getting slow yesterday around 3 PM." Using the sar reports, you can determine the cause of many performance slow-downs. You might notice, for example, that the CPU was very busy at the time, or that there was a large amount of paging activity on the system. Since sar collects a variety of system activity data and saves it for later scrutiny, it provides a good source of unbiased evidence for your analysis.

By default, sar is turned off, and the corresponding crontab entries are commented out. To run sar routinely on a system, you need to do two things. First, remove the comment (#) character on the crontab lines in /var/spool/cron/crontabs/sys as shown below. The best way to do this is with the command "crontab -e sys" (as root) or "crontab -e" (as sys). Next, uncomment the lines in the startup script /etc/init.d/perf and run it. These two changes will start up system activity data gathering and ensure that it is started up each time your system is rebooted.

TIP

Try out sar on an underused system. Once you're familiar with the insights it provides and how to use its output, begin using it on more critical and heavily used systems.

The data collection takes place as the user "sys". The default crontab entries summarize the data every 20 minutes during the hours 8 AM to 5 PM Monday through Friday and hourly the rest of the time. Notice how this is accomplished in the first two lines. Then, at 6:05 PM every Monday through Friday, the sa2 process runs which xyz. The default crontab entries (with comment characters removed) are as follows:

```
0 * * * 0-6 /usr/lib/sa/sa1
20,40 8-17 * * 1-5 /usr/lib/sa/sa1
5 18 * * 1-5 /usr/lib/sa/sa2 -s 8:00 -e 18:01 -i 1200 -A
```

The data activity reports can be generated via the sar command. The command sar -A will give the most detail. Here is a sample report with some of the important lines annotated for your reading pleasure:

```
SunOS c235786-a 5.7 Generic i86pc    03/14/99 ← The OS version, name of
                                                   the machine and archi-
                                                   tecture
00:00:00    %usr    %sys    %wio    %idle   ← For each hour, the aver-
01:00:00     0       0       0       99         age percentage of time
02:00:00     0       0       0       99         that the cpu spent in
03:00:00     0       0       0       99         usr mode, state, and idle
          ─────────────────────────────────
22:00:00     1       1       1       97
23:00:01     0       0       1       99
24:00:01     0       0       1       98

Average      1       1       1       98     ← Average for the day
```

The next section will show how the disk devices on your system are running. Note that the old style sd devices are listed.

00:00:00	device	%busy	avque	r+w/s	blks/s	avwait	avserv
01:00:00	cmdk0	0	0.0	0	1	0.4	6.5
	fd0	0	0.0	0	0	0.0	0.0
	sd0	1	0.0	0	6	0.0	104.7
	sd0,a	1	0.0	0	6	0.0	105.4
	sd0,b	0	0.0	0	0	0.0	41.0
	sd0,c	0	0.0	0	0	0.0	0.0
	sd0,h	0	0.0	0	0	0.0	0.0
	sd0,i	0	0.0	0	0	0.0	0.0
	sd0,j	0	0.0	0	0	0.0	0.0
	sd0,q	0	0.0	0	0	0.0	0.0
	sd0,r	0	0.0	0	0	0.0	0.0
	sd1	0	0.0	0	0	0.0	0.0
02:00:00	cmdk0	0	0.0	0	1	0.1	6.6
	fd0	0	0.0	0	0	0.0	0.0
	sd0	1	0.0	1	7	0.0	93.5
	sd0,a	1	0.0	0	6	0.0	106.8
	sd0,b	0	0.0	0	1	0.0	19.3
	sd0,c	0	0.0	0	0	0.0	0.0
	sd0,h	0	0.0	0	0	0.0	0.0
	sd0,i	0	0.0	0	0	0.0	0.0
	sd0,j	0	0.0	0	0	0.0	0.0
	sd0,q	0	0.0	0	0	0.0	0.0
	sd0,r	0	0.0	0	0	0.0	0.0
	sd1	0	0.0	0	0	0.0	0.0
22:00:01	cmdk0	0	0.0	0	1	0.3	7.2
	fd0	0	0.0	0	0	0.0	0.0
	sd0	1	0.1	1	10	0.0	56.3
	sd0,a	1	0.0	0	6	0.0	96.9
	sd0,b	0	0.0	0	4	0.0	11.6
	sd0,c	0	0.0	0	0	0.0	0.0
	sd0,h	0	0.0	0	0	0.0	0.0
	sd0,i	0	0.0	0	0	0.0	0.0

	sd0,j	0	0.0	0	0	0.0	0.0
	sd0,q	0	0.0	0	0	0.0	0.0
	sd0,r	0	0.0	0	0	0.0	0.0
	sd1	0	0.0	0	0	0.0	0.0
23:00:01	cmdk0	0	0.0	0	1	0.4	8.1
	fd0	0	0.0	0	0	0.0	0.0
	sd0	2	0.1	2	46	0.0	64.1
	sd0,a	2	0.1	1	36	0.0	77.2
	sd0,b	1	0.0	0	10	0.0	25.6
	sd0,c	0	0.0	0	0	0.0	0.0
	sd0,h	0	0.0	0	0	0.0	0.0
	sd0,i	0	0.0	0	0	0.0	0.0
	sd0,j	0	0.0	0	0	0.0	0.0
	sd0,q	0	0.0	0	0	0.0	0.0
	sd0,r	0	0.0	0	0	0.0	0.0
	sd1	0	0.0	0	0	0.0	0.0
Average	cmdk0	0	0.0	0	2	3.1	6.6
	fd0	0	0.0	0	0	0.0	0.0
	sd0	1	0.1	1	13	0.0	66.8
	sd0,a	1	0.1	1	9	0.0	89.1
	sd0,b	0	0.0	0	4	0.0	17.0
	sd0,c	0	0.0	0	0	0.0	0.0
	sd0,h	0	0.0	0	0	0.0	0.0
	sd0,i	0	0.0	0	0	0.0	0.0
	sd0,j	0	0.0	0	0	0.0	0.0
	sd0,q	0	0.0	0	0	0.0	0.0
	sd0,r	0	0.0	0	0	0.0	0.0
	sd1	0	0.0	0	0	0.0	0.0

This section shows the average runqueue and swapqueue sizes. The lower the number the better.

```
00:00:00 runq-sz %runocc swpq-sz %swpocc
01:00:00    1.0      0
02:00:00    1.3      0
03:00:00    1.0      0
04:00:00    1.0      0

22:00:01    1.4      0
23:00:01    1.2      0

Average     1.1      0

00:00:00 bread/s lread/s %rcache bwrit/s lwrit/s %wcache pread/s pwrit/s
01:00:00       0       1      99       0       1      61       0       0
02:00:00       0       1      99       0       1      61       0       0
03:00:00       0       1      99       0       1      61       0       0
04:00:00       0       1      97       0       1      62       0       0
---
```

21:00:00	0	3	94	1	3	69	0	0
22:00:01	0	1	94	0	1	60	0	0
23:00:01	0	2	93	1	1	61	0	0
Average	0	1	96	0	1	62	0	0

00:00:00	swpin/s	bswin/s	swpot/s	bswot/s	pswch/s
01:00:00	0.00	0.0	0.00	0.0	62
02:00:00	0.00	0.0	0.00	0.0	63
03:00:00	0.00	0.0	0.00	0.0	62
--					
21:00:00	0.00	0.0	0.00	0.0	76
22:00:01	0.00	0.0	0.00	0.0	67
23:00:01	0.00	0.0	0.00	0.0	70
Average	0.00	0.0	0.00	0.0	79

00:00:00	scall/s	sread/s	swrit/s	fork/s	exec/s	rchar/s	wchar/s
01:00:00	65	3	3	0.07	0.07	830	256
02:00:00	65	3	3	0.07	0.07	830	256
03:00:01	2333	104	49	0.08	0.07	28239	19288
04:00:01	187	8	5	0.06	0.06	1309	569
--							
21:00:00	102	8	6	0.21	0.21	7194	1758
22:00:01	76	4	4	0.07	0.07	973	343
23:00:01	85	16	4	0.12	0.12	13751	656
Average	259	13	7	0.08	0.08	4381	2007

00:00:00	iget/s	namei/s	dirbk/s
01:00:00	0	2	1
02:00:00	0	2	1
03:00:00	0	2	1
--			
21:00:00	1	9	4
22:00:01	0	2	1
23:00:01	0	3	1
Average	0	2	1

00:00:00	rawch/s	canch/s	outch/s	rcvin/s	xmtin/s	mdmin/s
01:00:00	0	0	0	0	0	0
02:00:00	0	0	55	0	0	0
03:00:00	0	0	0	0	0	0
04:00:00	0	0	0	0	0	0

14:00:00	1	0	55	0	0	0
22:00:01	0	0	0	0	0	0
23:00:01	0	0	30	0	0	0
Average	0	0	5	0	0	0

00:00:00	proc-sz	ov	inod-sz	ov	file-sz	ov	lock-sz
01:00:00	84/906	0	4660/4660	0	411/411	0	0/0
02:00:00	84/906	0	4744/4744	0	412/412	0	0/0
03:00:00	84/906	0	4829/4829	0	412/412	0	0/0

```
04:00:00   84/906    0  4668/4668    0  412/412    0    0/0
05:00:00   84/906    0  4753/4753    0  411/411    0    0/0
06:00:00   84/906    0  4820/4820    0  412/412    0    0/0
07:00:00   84/906    0  4883/4883    0  412/412    0    0/0
08:00:00   84/906    0  4741/4741    0  412/412    0    0/0
09:00:00   84/906    0  4818/4818    0  412/412    0    0/0
10:00:01   83/906    0  4734/4734    0  407/407    0    0/0
11:00:01   83/906    0  4820/4820    0  409/409    0    0/0
12:00:00   82/906    0  4620/4620    0  405/405    0    0/0
13:00:01   84/906    0  4744/4744    0  415/415    0    0/0
14:00:00   88/906    0  4708/4708    0  424/424    0    0/0
---------
22:00:01   85/906    0  4598/4598    0  415/415    0    0/0
23:00:01   92/906    0  4610/4610    0  435/435    0    0/0
```

If you are running applications that utilized semaphores, that information would show up in the following section of the sar report:

```
00:00:00   msg/s   sema/s
01:00:00   0.00    0.00
02:00:00   0.00    0.00
03:00:00   0.00    0.00
04:00:00   0.00    0.00
05:00:00   0.00    0.00
06:00:00   0.00    0.00
07:00:00   0.00    0.00
08:00:00   0.00    0.00
09:00:00   0.00    0.00
10:00:01   0.00    0.00
11:00:01   0.00    0.00
12:00:00   0.00    0.00
13:00:01   0.00    0.00
14:00:00   0.00    0.00
---------
22:00:01   0.00    0.00
23:00:01   0.00    0.00

Average    0.00    0.00

00:00:00   atch/s  pgin/s ppgin/s  pflt/s  vflt/s slock/s
01:00:00   0.06    0.08    0.08    4.19    6.54    0.00
02:00:00   0.06    0.15    0.15    4.22    6.63    0.00
03:00:00   0.06    0.08    0.08    4.27    6.61    0.00
04:00:00   0.07    0.09    0.09    4.67    7.21    0.00
05:00:00   0.06    0.08    0.08    4.20    6.56    0.00
06:00:00   0.06    0.08    0.08    4.21    6.56    0.00
07:00:00   0.06    0.08    0.08    4.21    6.56    0.00
08:00:00   0.06    0.08    0.08    4.23    6.60    0.00
09:00:00   0.03    0.07    0.08    4.21    6.55    0.00
10:00:01   0.20    2.02    2.39    4.78   23.82    0.00
11:00:01   0.05    0.82    0.89    3.68    6.63    0.00
12:00:00   0.05    0.24    0.25    4.25    6.82    0.00
13:00:01   0.21    0.97    1.09    3.87    7.66    0.00
```

```
14:00:00    0.25    0.97    1.29   11.60   24.43    0.00
----
22:00:01    0.04    0.52    0.53    3.97    6.68    0.00
23:00:01    0.07    1.03    3.80    6.85   12.74    0.00

Average     0.09    0.46    0.69    4.84    9.29    0.00

00:00:00  pgout/s ppgout/s pgfree/s pgscan/s %ufs_ipf
01:00:00    0.08    0.13    0.17    0.29    0.00
02:00:00    0.09    0.16    0.22    0.25    0.00
03:00:00    0.08    0.12    0.14    0.11    0.00
04:00:00    0.09    0.13    0.17    0.13    0.00
05:00:00    0.08    0.13    0.16    0.14    0.00
06:00:00    0.08    0.11    0.13    0.12    0.00
07:00:00    0.08    0.12    0.15    0.16    0.00
08:00:00    0.08    0.11    0.14    0.11    0.00
09:00:00    0.04    0.09    0.13    0.16    0.00
10:00:01    0.32    0.89    2.47    6.58    1.02
11:00:01    0.10    0.48    1.00    2.53    0.00
12:00:00    0.08    0.24    0.36    0.77    0.00
13:00:01    0.16    0.52    1.44    3.55    0.00
14:00:00    0.31    0.87    1.68    3.23    0.00
---------
22:00:01    0.07    0.15    0.48    1.18    0.00
23:00:01    0.17    0.99    3.97    6.69    0.00

Average     0.12    0.33    0.80    1.63    0.18

00:00:00 freemem freeswap
01:00:00    338   347385
02:00:00    336   347407
03:00:00    315   347426
04:00:00    351   347380
05:00:00    338   347393
06:00:00    319   347166
07:00:00    335   347208
08:00:00    312   347388
09:00:00    466   347347
10:00:01    509   374927
11:00:01    323   408684
12:00:00    338   407904
13:00:01    290   409390
14:00:00    555   407033
-----------
22:00:01    448   408629
23:00:01    460   407123

Average     377   371861

00:00:00 sml_mem    alloc fail lg_mem     alloc fail ovsz_alloc fail
01:00:00 2396160 2066764    0 6049792 5587952    0    3993600    0
02:00:00 2392064 2063412    0 6025216 5615632    0    3993600    0
03:00:00 2396160 2064728    0 6041600 5641864    0    3993600    0
```

```
---
14:00:00 2367488 1919364      0 6053888 5603004      0   3993600      0
22:00:01 2347008 1890108      0 5980160 5550592      0   3993600      0
23:00:01 2367488 1927948      0 6012928 5590660      0   3993600      0

Average   169801  142210      0 430501  400356       0    285257      0
```

Log Monitoring

While sar is great at data gathering and reporting system information, it doesn't tell you everything you need to know to determine the health of a system. You might also want to review system logs on a daily basis. The following script, if set to run at 11:59 PM, will e-mail the day's records from the messages file from the system on which it is run. Of course, you would *not* want to do this with syslog!

```
#!/bin/sh

cd /var/adm
MACHINE=`hostname`
if [ `date '+%d'` -lt 10 ]; then
    DAY=`date '+%b %d'|tr '0' ' '`
else
    DAY=`date '+%b %d'`
fi
echo "Subject: $MACHINE Log" > logmon.out
files=`find . -name 'messages*' -mtime -1 -print | sort -r`
for file in $files
do
cat $file | grep "$DAY" >> logmon.out     ← if only concerned about
done                                         certain messages, pipe the
                                             output into another grep
/usr/lib/sendmail -f"Logger" email-id <logmon.out
done
```

Another script that we recommend running at 59 minutes after every hour is called watchlog. It looks for warning messages from the past hour in the messages file, writes any it finds to a log file, and then pages the listed pagers. Warning messages are more severe than the messages commonly written to this file and, sometimes, need to be acted on immediately. By seeing these messages in near real time, you may be able to salvage data from a failing disk before it becomes unusable.

```
#!/bin/ksh -xvf
#
PAGEERM="1234567"
PAGESHS="1234566"
PAGELIST=" $PAGEERM $PAGESHS"
MYNAME=`hostname`
log=""
#
if [ `date '+%d'` -lt 10 ]; then
    DAY=`date '+%b %d'|tr '0' ' '`
```

```
       LASTHOUR="$DAY `date '+%H'`"
else
       LASTHOUR=`date '+%b %d %H'`
fi
#
log=`grep "$LASTHOUR" /var/adm/messages|grep -i warning`
echo $log
if [ ."$log" != "." ]; then
       echo "$MYNAME LOG Alert `date +%H":"%M` $log" |\/usr/local/binpager
           $PAGELIST
       echo "Message Log Alert Logged" | logger -p local0.alert -t watchlog -i
fi
```

In general, Solaris log files cannot be manually monitored. There are simply too many log files and too much information. Digesting the information in the log files of a single busy system could be a full-time job. Our strategies at data reduction involve focussing on the more important messages (i.e., warning messages), summarizing the data in log files by running the logs through analysis scripts (Perl is a great tool for this kind of job) and intercepting messages as they arrive using tools like swatch described in the next section.

Swatch

One of the most useful tools that we have encountered for making effective use of system logging and system log files is swatch. It is extremely valuable if you manage a large number of systems—especially a large number of servers—as its log file monitoring (realtime) and auditing (later analysis).

Swatch was originally designed to monitor messages as they are being written to the log files. It works with any log files written to by the syslog facility. It can also be run in an auditing mode in which an entire log is analyzed for occurrences of certain types of messages.

Swatch is Perl based and this shows. It works on patterns describing the types of messages that it is looking for while doing its analysis. Its basic processing involves patterns and actions to take when messages matching those patterns are detected. You might, for example, want to be notified immediately whenever a "file system full" message appears in your messages file.

The actions that swatch can take when a pattern is detected include:

Echo—display the message

Bell—display the message and signal with an audible alert

Mail—send e-mail to the user running the program

Exec—run a script or command

Pipe—pipe a message to a program

Write—use the system write facility to send a message

Ignore—ignore the message

The configuration file that swatch uses, .swatchrc, contains these patterns and actions. For example, a line like this:

```
/.*file system full/ mail=sysadmin,exec "pager xxxx"
```

will send e-mail to the alias sysadmin and run our pager script if a "file system full" message is written to our log. It follows the general form "/pattern/ action." You can include multiple patterns, like (panic|halt) and multiple actions—as shown in the above example.

You can also include two additional fields in .swatchrc entries. These help to avoid being inundated with messages regarding a single problem. The third field specifies a time interval during which you do not want to take action on identical messages. The fourth further specifies the location of the time stamp in the record. Both are optional.

Swatch can be invoked without arguments or with any of the following options:

-t filename	monitor the log file specified
-f filename	audit the specified file
-p program	monitor output from the specified program
-c filename	use an alternate configuration file
-r time	restart at the time specified
-P separator	use an alternate character (i.e., instead of |) for separating patterns in the configuration file
-A	use an alternate character (i.e., instead of a comma) for separating actions in the configuration file
-I	use an alternate character (i.e., instead of an newline) as a record separator in the input

Swatch was written by Todd Atkins at Stanford and can be downloaded from the ftp site: *ftp://ftp.stanford.edu/general/security-tools/swatch/*.

When first configuring swatch, you should make a decision regarding your basic approach to screening messages with this tool. The two approaches are to specify the messages you want to see or suppress those you don't (using ignore). Consult the sample configuration files included with the tool.

Proctool

An indispensable addition to the poor man's network management toolkit, proctool provides many ways to manage processes and analyze system performance.

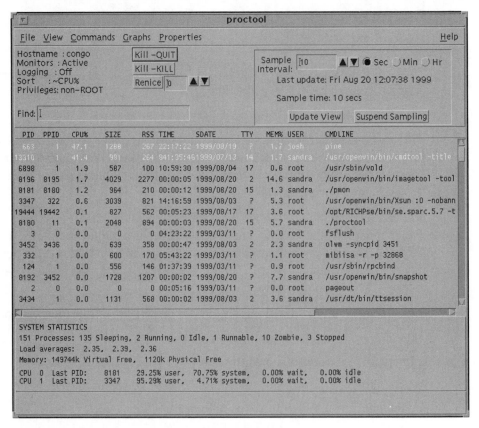

Figure 9.3 Features of proctool.

The first time you start the tool and view its informative panels, you'll wonder how you've ever managed without it. In the screenshot displayed in Figure 9.3, you'll get an appreciation of some of the tool's features. For one, it offers the information as provided by top (written by Bill LeFebvre) in two of its panels. A quick glimpse of which processes are using the most processing resources, load averages and memory usage tell you a lot about the operational state of a system. You can select which process parameters appear if you don't like the defaults.

Proctool provides detailed information on processes that you select and inquire about. These include memory usage, I/O, paging and a memory map.

In addition, the tool provides an easy-to-use renice option. If you are running the tool as root, you can renice any process. If you are running it as a normal user, you can only renice your own. Similarly, you can kill processes (again, depending on your privilege) or send any of a set of signals.

Less obviously, you can also bring up graphs displaying one of a number of items—cpu utilization, system paging, process statistics and page usage. Proc-

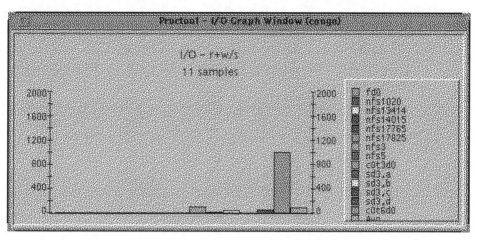

Figure 9.4 One of many proctool graphs.

tool detects the number of CPUs and automatically provides statistics for them. Figure 9.4 shows one of the many graphs available to you.

Proctool also allows you to define monitors—agents that act on criteria you specify. Similar in nature to the configuration rules for swatch, each monitor consists of a logical expression and a set of actions. For example, monitors can be set up to renice any process that uses an excessive amount of the CPU. Alternately, you can simply issue a beep, create a popup, change the color of a process entry, or send e-mail if a monitored event occurs.

Proctool can be downloaded for free from *http://metalab.unc.edu/pub/packages/solaris/freeware/*SOURCES/PROCTOOL. The download also includes a surprisingly nice user's guide. Proctool is not an official Sun product. This means there are no warranties implied. On the other hand, it's a great tool with great documentation and a responsive developer. Once you start using the tool, you can send requests for enhancement, questions, and comments to *morgan.herrington@west.sun.com*.

The SE Toolkit

Another extraordinarily useful, though unendorsed tool from Sun, the SE Toolkit can be thought of as a performance engineer looking over your shoulder. In fact, this tool was created by two such engineers (Richard Pettit from Foglight Software and Adrian Cockcroft from Sun) and provides insights on various aspects of your system without you having to do much of anything at all. Of course, if you want to, you can delve deeply into the tool. It is, after all, a toolkit. That means you can use it as a basis for creating other tools for analyzing your systems' performance—and, indeed, a number of people have.

The tool, as the output below suggests, monitors many aspects of your system and makes recommendations. Overloaded disks, memory shortages, and network load will not escape your notice and the advice offered may help you decide how to best upgrade your systems or your network to achieve better performance.

```
/opt/RICHPse/examples/mon_cm.se Version 0.2: Started monitoring at Tue Aug
31 16:40:14 1999
If the calendar for this user does not exist this program fails

Appointments for Tuesday August 31, 1999:
      1)  4:40pm Startup of RICHPse.mon_cm
                Version: 0.2

You should now see an entry in the calendar, if not you should
use cm as that user to create an initial calendar
Adrian detected slow disk(s) red: Tue Aug 31 16:40:39 1999
Move load from busy disks to idle disks
State         ------throughput------ -----wait queue----- -----active queue--
--
   disk      r/s  w/s   Kr/s   Kw/s qlen res_t svc_t %ut qlen  res_t svc_t
%ut
R c0t3d0   26.9  8.1  108.0   90.0 0.00  0.01  0.01   0 2.01  57.31 12.56
44

Adrian detected slow net(s): Tue Aug 31 16:40:39 1999
Add more or faster nets
State Name        Ipkt/s  Ierr/s  Opkt/s  Oerr/s Coll% NoCP/s Defr/s
red   le0         598.8     0.0   541.3     0.0  0.43   0.07 100.55

Adrian detected RAM shortage (amber): Tue Aug 17 16:40:39 1999
RAM shortage
  procs        memory        page           faults          cpu
  r  b  w     swap   free   pi  po  sr  rt  in    sy    cs  smtx us sy id
  1  1  4  155926   2535   115 340 241 37 2568   787  1317   29 49 24 28
```

It can monitor processes, network interfaces, disks and more. It can monitor Web sites. The best way to become familiar with the tool (other than downloading and using it) is to read Adrian's performance column in SunWorld (http://www.sunworld.com). One of the specific issues to read is May 1999 (*http://www.sunworld.com/swol-05-1999*), but SunWorld has a search engine so that you can easily find other references as well.

The three packages provided with the toolkit include:

1. RICHPsw, the interpreter (called SymbEL).

2. RICHPsex, the extensions package.

3. ANCrules, Adrian's rules and tools.

As the authors like to claim, all the "real work" is done in scripts. This means that you have the flexibility to modify rules if you disagree with them and to create your own. If you're very clever and come up with some useful scripts, consider sending copies to the authors for distribution in their next release. The tool, as of this writing, is in release 3.1.

Summary

Monitoring your network can take all the time you have if you let it. Don't. There are far too many tools—big, expensive and powerful as well as small, free and flexible—that can come to your aid for you to spend your time chasing after the details of what has and might go wrong.

Commercial network management systems have become very sophisticated and can provide you with near instant feedback even if you're managing a large, segmented network. Most also provide the means to manage systems and device configuration from a central station or from cooperating management stations distributed through your organization. Some also provide trend analysis and tools for predicting problems long before they become bottlenecks or failures.

Tools for configuring your own network management console are plentiful as well. We've covered some of our favorites in this chapter and thrown in some scripts of our own to help make sure that you spend your time looking at the more important data available to you.

We encourage you to continue your research into tools by reading online magazines like *SunWorld* and by perusing the Internet for tools contributed by other systems administrators.

Sites such at *http://www.sunfreeware.com* and *http://nce.sun.ca* are great starting points for tools.

## CHAPTER 10

Understanding File Systems—So *That's* What Those Are!

Most of us learned to be system administrators in small steps. We covered the basics—file systems, permissions, creating user accounts—and then started learning more advanced skills as the needs and challenges presented themselves. Yet, even after as many years as we have been managing Solaris systems, we find that we're still learning. It goes with the job and the constant influx of new tools and technologies. Because none of us (unless you, dear reader, are an exception) knows all there is to know about Unix or, in particular, Solaris, this chapter attempts to answer the essential question that so many of us ask ourselves from time to time: What the hell is that? By describing the basic topology of Solaris and then detailing key system processes, configuration files, log files, and so on, we hope to fill in some of the gaps in your understanding of Solaris and provide you with a comfortable familiarity with many of the files and directories you'll run into.

File Systems

We probably don't need to provide much detail about basic file systems, but there is no more natural place to start. The most fundamental breakdown of our systems occurs at this level. The basic Solaris file systems include the following:

/ This is the root of the overall file system tree and superuser's home directory. On some oddly configured systems, the entire file system tree may be housed within root. This configuration provides the maximum flexibility with respect to space (i.e., no file system runs out of space unless the system runs out of space), but there are a number of drawbacks. For one, it's more difficult to back up the system in a manner consistent with the volatility of files; ufsdump expects to dump an entire file system. For another, root is not protected by what is occurring with other file systems. Most systems set up this way, however, are clients that share nothing and mount data and application directories from servers.

/usr The operating system commands and files are stored in /usr. Depending on your particular installation, /usr will house not only the commands that you run every day, but man pages, include files, and other support files.

/usr/local Often a file system, /usr/local is the traditional place for non-OS tools and applications. The word *local* refers to the fact the directory is site-specific, not that it is necessarily resident on the local system. More often than not, /usr/local directories are maintained on file servers and mounted on the client. Contrast this directory with /opt.

/home This is the customary location for user home directories. During the early days of automount, many home file systems were mounted locally as /export/home. With the improved (more natural) naming provided with the autofs automounter, this custom has pretty much fallen out of favor.

/opt This is a file system in which optional software packages, many derived from the OS installation, are kept, along with third-party (i.e., non-OS) tools and applications that arrive in the Solaris package format.

/var The /var file systems contains log files, spool files, cron files, mail files, and more. The name *var* probably derives from the word *variable*, as the contents of /var are among the most volatile on a system. The directory /var/tmp serves the purpose served by /tmp before the latter turned into swapfs. That is, it is used to store temporary user files that may survive a reboot, but which should be periodically wiped out. A find command with a modification time parameter (e.g., find /var/tmp -mtime +3 -exec rm {} \;) is an extremely convenient way to do this cleaning, but watch out for users who know the touch command!

/proc This file system, described in detail in Chapter 1, provides access to running processes. The data available to those that know how to use it rivals information formerly available using sophisticated debuggers and software analysis tools.

/tmp The /tmp system serves as swap space and still is often used as temporary storage. However, its contents are wiped at boot time.

Directories

There are many special directories within each of these file systems that stand out as being worthy of individual explanation and attention. These are the directories in which major system functions are configured and/or managed.

/etc The host-specific configuration files are stored in /etc. If you are not running NIS or NIS+, the hosts, passwd, and shadow files determine which hosts your system knows about (aside from DNS) and who can log in. Other files include important configuration files—for example, those for the init (inittab), the inet daemon (inetd.conf), and the syslog facility (syslog.conf). The /etc directory also includes the configuration file for sendmail (/etc/mail /sendmail.cf), along with other sendmail files, and, at many sites, also contains configuration files for Web and news servers. We discuss some of the directories here.

/etc/cron.d Configuration information for cron (but not the cron files themselves) are stored in this directory. The cron files for each user are stored in /var/spool/cron/crontabs. The files for the at command are in /var/spool/cron/atjobs.

/etc/default The default settings for many services (e.g., policies about whether root can login remotely) are stored in this directory. We discuss the contents of /etc/default later in this chapter.

/etc/dfs This directory contains the dfstab file, which determines what file systems are shared and how.

/etc/mail This directory contains the configuration files for sendmail.

/etc/init.d This directory is the primary location for start/stop scripts. All start/stop scripts should be located here and, then again, in whichever of the /etc/rc?.d directories correspond to the run states in which they should start or stop.

/etc/rc?.d These are the run-state-specific directories for start/stop scripts (/etc/rc0.d is for run state 0, /etc/rc1.d is for single-user, and so on). Any files starting with the letter *K* are executed by the corresponding rc script (e.g., /usr/sbin/rc2) when it enters the particular run state. Afterward, any files starting with the letter *S* are executed. These scripts are executed in alphanumeric order (e.g., a file named *S88httpd* would run before one named *S99mydaemon*).

/dev This directory is the primary location for device files. The most commonly used tape device, for example, is probably /dev/rmt/0, and the most common root directory is probably /dev/dsk/c0t3d0s0. For tape devices, the letters in the name indicate how the device will operate—for example, whether the device will use compression or fail to rewind after use. For disk partitions, the characters in the name specify the controller number, target, disk number, and slice.

/usr/bin The bulk of the system commands are located in the /usr/bin directory. The ls and echo commands, for example, are located here. Some commands (those with origins in the Berkeley side of Solaris's ancestry) are located, instead, in /usr/ucb. There is also a /usr/sbin directory and a /usr/local/bin directory on many systems.

/usr/man The system manual pages are stored in this directory. However, the directory is usually a pointer to /usr/share/man. Most sites that supplement their systems with tools and applications including their own man pages store these man pages in /usr/local/man; for the most part, this is a better choice than individual man directories within the application directories, because it's easier to set up users' MANPATH variables.

/usr/local As previously mentioned, this is a site-specific application directory, often maintained on a file server. Contrast this with /opt.

/usr/local/bin This is a site-specific directory of tools and utilities (*bin* for *binary*). It is also a good place for you to put scripts that you want your users or fellow sysadmins to be able to run.

/usr/include This directory stores the header files for programming and descriptions of system structures (e.g., the record structure for an inode). Subdirectories contain header files for specific functions (e.g., networking or file systems).

/usr/lib/acct This directory holds accounting commands.

/usr/platform This directory contains platform-specific files—for example, the files to create a bootblock for a specific system type.

/var/log Most system log files are stored somewhere in the /var directory. The syslog logs (i.e., syslog and syslog.?) are stored in /var/log. The messages file and login files are stored in /var/adm.

/var/adm This directory contains other log files (e.g., messages and wtmp). The fact that these files are here rather than in /var/log does *not* imply that they are maintained by something other than the syslog facility. The messages file is a syslog-maintained log file. To see what files are maintained by syslog and which are not, look at syslog's configuration file—/etc/syslog.conf.

/var/mail This is the directory where user e-mail is stored. It will be populated with files that have the same names as usernames on your system (e.g., /var/mail/mallory). You may also see some other files in this directory from time to time. Lock files (e.g., /var/mail/mallory.lock) and popper files (e.g., pop.mallory) will appear while users are accessing their mail. You may have to remove these files manually when a mail client crashes, or is otherwise stopped improperly, before the user can again access mail.

/var/yp This directory houses the configuration files for the NIS service on a server. You should see a Makefile; this file contains instructions of what make is to do when you update an NIS map (e.g., make passwd). The times that maps are updated are captured in files with names such as passwd.time. The actual data files are kept in a subdirectory named after your domain. For example, the directory /var/yp/foo.com would house the data files for the Foo NIS domain. These files are named *passwd.dir*, *passwd.pag*, and so on.

/var/tmp   This is user temporary space (preferably used in place of /tmp). Applications requiring temporary space are usually configured to use this location, as well. If you look into the /var/tmp directory, you may see files of many types. Some of these (e.g., those with names such as Ex0005757577) are temporary files used by an editor—maybe vi.

/var/sadm   The /var/sadm directory contains information about packages installed on the system. The /var/sadm/contents file, for example, contains information about every file loaded during installation, along with information detailing its size and permissions when it was installed. This file is used with the ASET (security auditing) tool to detect files that have changed since installation. Obviously, some files need to change (e.g., your /etc/hosts and /etc/passwd files). You should not be alarmed if ASET informs you that they have. This file is also used by the pkgrm utility so that it can located all the files that it must remove when deinstalling software for you.

Mount Points

Any directory can be used as a mount point. In fact, a directory doesn't even have to be empty to serve this purpose, though this is generally the case. Mount points that are used by automounter cannot be used for normal mounts, as the automountd daemon reserves access to them when it starts up. Automount points also look very different from manual mount points, as they appear to be only one or two characters in size. The following mount points are useful to remember.

/mnt   This general-purpose mount point should always be available for temporary mounts. Never mount any permanently as /mnt. Other sysadmins will look at you oddly.

/a   This is the mount point for the existing root file system when you boot from CD-ROM. If you need to change the root password on a system and have no alternative, you can boot from an installation CD, mount the root filing system on /a (e.g., mount /dev/dsk/c0t3d0s0 /a), cd to /a/etc, and edit the passwd file.

/home   This is the mount for home directories, one of those generally reserved by the automounter when you are automounting the home directory (see /etc/auto_home on your NIS master or the corresponding NIS+ map).

Daemon Processes

Daemon processes generally start up in one of two ways: They start up via one of the start scripts in the /etc/init.d (or /etc/rc?.d) directory, or they start up in response to a service request. The daemons listed here are some of the most important on your system.

init Init is the mother of all processes. It is started at boot time, and controls the transition from one run state to the next. The init process reads its configuration file, /etc/inittab, on initial booting and whenever you issue the init command to change run states (e.g., init 2).

cron Cron is the process that runs periodic scheduled jobs (contrast with the at command). Any user can have a cron file. The files are stored in /var/spool/cron and have the format *1 2 3 4 5 command*, where *1* is minutes after the hour, *2* is the hour, *3* is the day of the month, *4* the month of the year, and *5* is the day of the week (0 to 6). The command *1 2 * * 3 /usr/bin/df -k | mailx -s "disk space" sysadmin* would mail a disk usage report to the alias sysadmin at 2:01 every Wednesday morning.

sendmail The sendmail daemon runs in the background, spawns child processes for individual messages, and forks to other sendmail processes to help with the load (the limit is specified in the sendmail configuration file /etc/mail/sendmail.cf).

telnetd The telnetd process supports telnet sessions.

httpd The HTTP daemon, httpd, supports a Web site (the actual name might be different depending on the Web server you are using).

popd Generally POP, the post office protocol provides a simplified protocol for retrieving e-mail. Individual POP sessions will show up in the process list with the process name *popper*.

imapd A more sophisticated protocol for retrieving mail than POP3, imapd supports the concept of folders.

ftpd The FTP daemon, ftpd, supports file transfer sessions.

(flush) This process writes files back to disk from time to time to assist in maintaining a stable file system.

TIP

The /etc/inetd.conf file, described below, is inetd's configuration file. It contains information about processes which are started by inetd—*not* via the /etc/rc?.d files. One easy way to tell whether a process was started by inetd or through the boot process is to look at the parent process (i.e., the second field in the ps-ef display). If the parent process is 1 (init), the process was started during booting. If the process is another number, chances are it's inetd's process number.

Configuration Files

Most Unix configuration files are delimited by white space or the colon (:) character. The /etc/passwd file and the /etc/inittab file use the colon to separate fields. The syslog.conf file, on the other hand, uses white space. Some configuration files are sensitive to whether blanks or tabs are used between fields. If you have odd problems with any configuration file that uses white space, you might want to check whether it expects tabs while you have blanks or vice versa.

/etc/inittab This is init's configuration file. It is read at boot time and when you issue the init command to change run states.

/etc/syslog.conf This is syslogd's configuration file. Syslog routes messages by type to specified files or individuals (via e-mail). Each line in the configuration file specifies a message type (service and priority) and the file that messages are to be logged to (e.g., mail.user HUH /var/log/syslog). The parameter *$loghost* refers to whichever host is listed as the loghost; it may be a synonym for the local host or a host on your network that you wish to use for collecting log messages.

/etc/services This file details system services and the ports they use. For example, sendmail uses port 25 and httpd generally runs on port 80.

/etc/inetd.conf This file details services that start up in response to requests and the process that is started (e.g., the POP service, popper, is usually started this way). When the inet daemon (inetd) intercepts a request for a service it manages (e.g., popper), it uses the line corresponding to the service and starts the process indicated. As you will see in Chapter 12, the best way to disable services that you do not want to run for security reasons is to comment out their entries in this file. Some services, such as sendmail and the print daemon, do not run through the inet service but, instead, do their own listening for service requests and spawn child processes as needed to respond to these requests.

/etc/hosts, passwd, group, netgroup These files contain system configuration information for the local system (some are ignored if NIS or NIS+ is running).

/etc/nsswitch.conf The name service switch file determines where network information is derived from (e.g., host names might be looked up in the /etc files previously shown, in NIS or NIS+, or in DNS). The entry, *hosts files nis dns*, for example, would instruct a system to first look in the local files, then refer to NIS, and last consult DNS to resolve a hostname.

/etc/auto_master This file is the main master map for automountd. It indicates what other maps and files are used.

/etc/auto_home This file is the default map used for automounting home directories.

/etc/auto_direct This file used for automounting direct maps (see Chapter 1).

/etc/auto_whatever You can create additional automount maps and call them just about anything you want. It would be foolish to call your maps anything other than *auto_<something>*, as this would only confuse anyone trying to help run your network.

TIP

Some configuration files are sensitive to whether columns are separated by tabs or blanks. The difference may not be obvious when you look at a file, but you can usually tell if you open the files with an editor, say vi.

Log Files

There are two basic types of log files in Solaris—those that grow indefinitely and those that include a single record for each of *N* items and, therefore, are static or grow rarely. The wtmp file is one of the former. It grows as long as you let it. Some sites have allowed this file to grow for years before space considerations forced them to trim it. The lastlog file is one of the latter. It contains a record for every user that has ever logged in. Because entries are indexed on userid, its size depends on the numeric IDs of your users. There is, therefore, no reason to ever trim or remove this file.

Some log files rotate each night or less frequently. You might have noticed that syslog files turn into syslog.1 files and syslog.1 files turn into syslog.2 files. Once the number reaches 7, the files are no longer retained, but this scheme means that you will always have a good amount of frequent data at your disposal, while your file systems are unlikely to be overwhelmed by syslog entries. Here are log files you should be familiar with:

messages This file contains various system messages, sent to this file via syslogd.

syslog This file contains various system messages. It is heavily dominated by records of sendmail exchanges.

sulog This file contains a log of su attempts, marked as successful or not. It is a good place to check if you suspect anyone is using someone else's password or a particular user knows the root password and is using it.

wtmp This file contains a record of logins and logouts.

lastlog This file contains a record of the last login for each user who has ever logged in.

utmp This file contains a record of current logins.

/etc/mnttab This file describes currently mounted file systems. This is the file that the mount command (without arguments) reads and displays.

/etc/vfstab This file contains the file system mount table (used during boot and with the mountall command).

/etc/dfs/dfstab This file contains the file systems to be shared by local system and the options—for example, -o ro specifies read-only, and -o rw=host1,host2,host3 says that only the three hosts listed can mount the directory.

TIP

It is important to know which log files grow indefinitely and, therefore, need occasional pruning and those which grow to a fixed size (more or less) and stop. It is equally important to know which log files roll over daily or weekly. Contrast the /var/adm/wtmp, /var/adm/lastlog and /var/adm/messages* files.

Devices

Device drivers in Solaris are stored in various subdirectories of /dev. Some of the more commonly needed directories are /dev/dsk and /dev/rdsk. These are used, of course, when you mount files systems and run fsck. Drivers for tape devices are stored in /dev/rmt; /dev/rmt/0 might be your backup tape whether you're using an Exabyte drive or a DSL.

/dev/rmt This directory contains raw tape devices.

/dev/dsk This directory contains the block disk devices.

/dev/rdsk This directory contains the raw disk devices.

/dev/pseudo This directory contains pseudo devices—for example, those devices that correspond to pseduo terminals when you log in with telnet or rlogin.

/dev/pts This directory contains pseudo terminal slave devices.

/dev/sad This directory is an entry point for the streams driver.

Summary

The layout of Unix file systems has maintained a certain consistency from its early days to now. Under the surface, however, a number of new file system types and directories have evolved. These include, but are not limited to:

- /etc/rc?.d and /etc/init.d directories—used in booting and in changing run states
- /proc—an interface into running processes
- /tmp—primarily used as swap space and no longer a standard Unix file system

Familiarity with the basic topology and the major processes and configuration files will help you track down problems and make changes to your systems. Here are some examples:

- Familiarity with the setup of the /etc/rc?.d and /etc/init.d directories will help you determine how a process should be started and to shut down and restart it properly.

- Problems with cron jobs can be more easily tracked down if you search the files in /var/spool/cron.

- New file systems need to be added to /etc/vfstab for local mounting and /etc/dfs/dfstab for NFS sharing.

There are many other directories that we could have described in this chapter. However, we believe that we've touched on the more important file systems and directories and hope that this information will help you locate a particular configuration file or will explain why some particular directory is sitting on your system.

## CHAPTER 11

Automating Everything . . . Well, Almost!

The essence of Unix in general, and Solaris in particular, is how flexible and extensible it is. Extending the OS with software that you create from scratch or borrow from archives on the Internet is the best way to tame your systems and your job. Scripts you build or borrow and tools you acquire will help you manage user accounts, control file systems, and monitor applications. They will also help you configure services and extract from the extensive amount of log data the vital statistics that will tell you how your network is doing and what aspects of it require your immediate attention.

From our perspective as long-time systems administrators, the answer to the question "How much should we automate?" is a resounding "Almost everything!" Any task involving more than a few steps that you're going to do more than half a dozen times is a candidate for automation. The second question to ask in regard to automation is "How well?" Quick and dirty scripts have their place; they can dramatically reduce the drudgery associated with something you have to do a number of times in a row. For the tasks you perform only now and then or automatically under the control of cron, however, anything less than carefully written and tested scripts will, in the long run, prove inefficient and difficult to maintain. We give you pointers in this chapter not only on what to automate, but how to ensure that your scripting efforts will pay off.

Your Fill of Scripting and Then Some

The predominant activity of systems administration is not installing systems, backing them up, or creating and deleting user accounts. It's not tracking hackers, formatting disks, compiling software, or even answering questions. It's *writing scripts*—scripts to manage tasks like these along with a myriad of others.

Anything you can do interactively, with care, you can script. Our advice is to script anything you expect you'll have to do more than half a dozen times—or that you do so rarely that you're not likely to remember the commands if you don't commit them to disk.

If you prepare scripts for your users, they may be able to do a lot for themselves that you might otherwise have to do for them. Not only will this make your workdays easier; it will make their workdays easier, as well. Even the most demanding users are likely to prefer taking care of themselves to waiting for you, with your long list of tasks, to get around to taking care of their latest requests.

Another benefit of scripting is that you can turn your operation over to someone else. Each of the authors has, at times in their careers, inherited a complex setup to administer. Were it not for the body of knowledge contained in our predecessors' scripts, the first few months on those jobs would have been miserable. With them, it was still stressful—but manageable.

If your operation is easy to turn over, you'll have an easier time accepting a promotion when an irresistible opportunity comes along. If you're in the perfect job already, you'll find that you'll benefit from your efforts as much as your replacement would have. Think of your scripts as investments that pay off every time you do a job in a tenth of the time it would otherwise take. Plan for many of your scripts to serve as modules that you can use and reuse as new challenges arise and new solutions are needed.

In general, writing scripts will save you a lot of time and trouble. Any scripts you write will be:

- Faster than running the same commands by hand
- Far less tedious than running the commands by hand
- Reliable and consistent (you might forget a vital step in a complex set of commands)
- Easily scheduled to run at routine, less busy times (often when you're asleep)

Scripting does, however, involve a certain discipline. Like any other software, the scripts you write should be free of bugs and should be written in a style that makes them easy to maintain (i.e., to modify to adjust to changing circumstances).

It almost doesn't matter what language you use, though we recommend that you become adept at programming in several languages. Among these are the

Bourne shell and, optionally, its derivatives (Korn and Bash shells), the C shell, and Perl. You might also consider writing time-intensive routines in C; compiled programs almost always run considerably faster than interpreted shell scripts.

To make the most of your scripting efforts, you should immediately—if you have not already—adopt certain conventions in your scripting styles, naming conventions, and personal habits. Over time, these conventions will save you a lot of time.

- Create a howto directory in which you will store examples of commands that you rarely use—especially those that took you a while to get right—and for which there are no examples in the man pages.

- Develop a migration scheme in which your in-progress scripts are clearly distinguished from those that you've tried and tested.

- Put your trusted scripts in a bin directory—in your personal account if only you are to use them, or in the /usr/local/bin if they are to be made available to other members of your staff or to users.

- Use a script naming scheme that distinguishes between scripts that are to be executed directly and those that are used only by other scripts.

- Use a naming scheme that makes it easy to remember what each script does. Take advantage of abbreviations such as *mk* (make) and *ls* (list); *rm* and *mv* will have obvious meanings because of the corresponding Unix commands. If you're anything like us, you probably won't enjoy recreating a script you well remember writing and testing simply because you can't remember where you put it or what you called it.

- Initialize important parameters at the tops of your scripts, so you'll never have to go hunting through the lines of code to change them.

- Include parameter checks and usage statements to help ensure that scripts are not used incorrectly.

- Use a consistent programming style. Use cut and paste or script templates to save yourself time and effort and avoid annoying syntactical glitches.

- Create simple script utilities for many of the repetitious code segments.

- Decide on a useful organizational style. Will you store scripts by project or by type? Any organizational tricks you can develop will probably end up saving you lots of time.

Essential Elements of Scripting

Systems administrators are presented with an almost endless stream of opportunities to become experts. The tools and languages available to help with our jobs and never-seen-before problems that crop up from time to time keep us from ever settling into a routine. Even so, there is an essential core of scripting skill and technique that, when mastered, will allow us to stay ahead of utter chaos. Our take on these skills and techniques is briefly covered in the sections below. Mastering any of the topics presented here will take a lot more information and practice than we have room for in this chapter. We suggest you take advantage of the many fine texts available on scripting and that you master several languages—including Perl and at least one shell.

Regular Expressions

One of the key concepts for writing scripts or for using the shell in any capacity—perhaps the single most important concept—is that of regular expressions. Though the languages and tools available to you do not use precisely the same expression syntax, there is enough commonality that any familiarity with regular expressions will go a long way.

The essence of regular expressions is pattern matching. In your scripts, you want to match file names and other script data to patterns specified in the script. Take this simple C Shell example:

```
spoon% foreach DATAFILE (`ls *.dat`)
```

The familiar * (match anything) character together with .dat matches file names like 1999-09-09.dat or daily.dat. The ` characters immediately inside the parentheses cause the command between them to be executed. As a result, the command, once the shell is finished processing it, might look like this:

```
spoon% foreach DATAFILE (1999-09-09.dat 1999-09-16.dat 1999-06-23.dat)
```

Regular expressions can become considerably more elaborate. In fact, they can sometimes be very difficult to parse if you don't routinely work with them. Let's look at some more complicated examples.

```
expr $1 : [0-9][0-9][0-9][0-9]
```

This command compares the value of *$1* (i.e., the first argument to the script) with a regular expression that matches any four contiguous digits. The year *1999* will match, but so will *2002* and *1020*, even *0003*, for that matter. Constraining your regular expressions to match as precisely as possible the range of acceptable data will save you subsequent programming steps.

Regular expressions are not just for use in "modern" languages such as Perl. Regular expressions are nothing new. In fact, they lie at the core of every scripting language and tool. The expression

```
grep "^mal" /usr/dict/words
```

is a regular expression that will display all the words in the /usr/dict/words file that start with the three letters *mal*. Similarly, the sed command

```
sed "s/^I am/We are/"
```

will match the string *I am* at the beginning of lines and replace it with *We are*. The pattern

```
s/1999/2000/g
```

matches the string *1999* and changes it to *2000*—not only when used with sed (i.e., sed "s/1999/2000/g") but also when used with Perl (i.e., perl -en 's/1999/2000/g').

Here's a more complex expression like those you're likely to see in a Perl script:

```
(m/^From\s+(\S+@\S+)\s+(.*)/)
```

Before we get into what this expression is actually doing, let's dissect it and label the major features. First, the major form of this Perl expression is for matching—signified by the *m*. The delimiters for the match are emphasized here:

```
(m/^From\s+(\S+@\S+)\s+(.*)/)
```

In other words, everything between the outer slashes is being matched. You shouldn't see any other / marks in a match command—unless they're escaped, as in this expression:

```
m/http:\/\/www.foo.com/
```

This pattern matches *http://www.foo.com.*

Characters that need escaping are any that would otherwise interfere with the interpretation of the command by the shell or language being used to process it. These include $, /, *, (, and even the \ character (to include a \ in an expression, you must use \\).

Getting back to our previous example:

```
(m/^From\s+(\S+@\S+)\s+(.*)/)
```

We can now start looking at the pattern being matched. The \s and \S components are called *metacharacters*. Each represents a certain type of data. In fact, these two metacharacters represent opposites—whereas \s matches any white-space character (blank, tab, new line, or carriage return), \S matches any non-white-space character. Metacharacters are listed in Table 11.1. The + that follows each of these metacharacters signifies that it can be repeated, but must appear at least once. Similarly, the . matches any character, while the * signifies that it can be repeated 0 or more times; in other words, it doesn't need to be present at all. The +, *, and other repeat characters are listed in Table 11.2. Now let's continue our analysis.

This expression is attempting to match lines beginning with the word *From,* followed by white space and then an e-mail address (i.e., *someone@some-where*). This pattern identifies the beginning of an e-mail message. The function of the outer parentheses is to assign the value of the text matched by a portion of the expression [the (\S+@\S+) portion] to the variable $1 and the text at the end of the line [the (.*) portion] to $2. This, of course, facilitates using this information (the e-mail address of the sender) in a subsequent section of the code. The secret to understanding expressions like these is to know what each of the designators means. The slashes delineate the pattern being matched. The (m/ characters at the beginning of the expression and the /) characters at the end are specifying that a pattern is to be matched. There are several forms of matching in Perl—the m//, s///, and tr/// functions (for match, substitute, and translate). The character class represented by \s specifies generic white space (blanks, tabs, and new lines) while a \S represents any regular character. The + sign means that there can be more than one of each of these characters. Since the @ sign is specified, it must appear and have characters on both sides of it. Finally, any amount of additional text may appear at the end of the line. Strings this particular expression are likely to match in your mail file look like this:

From *boss@foo.com* Mon Jan 8 09:15:25 2000

Using regular expressions in your scripts will save you a lot of time and trouble. Instead of having to compare input against a list of possibilities, you can compare it against a pattern that represents all the possibilities. Do not take this to mean that you should use regular expressions for everything. If a simple literal value will do the trick, representing it as a regular expression instead of a literal string is foolish.

Many examples of regular expressions appear in the sample scripts at the end of this chapter.

The Effect of Quotes

You won't get very far in scripting without knowing the way the different sets of quote marks affect the text between them. As previously mentioned, the " marks cause the commands between them to be executed. The command

```
echo "Today is `date +%b`"
```

will print "Today is Monday"

Anything inside double quotes is interpreted, while anything between back quotes is taken literally. For example, the command

```
echo "Welcome, $USER"
```

Table 11.1 Metacharacters

METACHARACTER	MATCHES	EXAMPLE EXPRESSION	EXAMPLE MATCH
.	Any character (except a new line)	.*	A string of any length or nothing at all
\s	White-space characters	\s+	Any amount of white space
\S	Non-white-space characters	\S+	Any one-word string, e.g., sing-along
\d	digit	\d	A single digit, 0–9
\D	Any nondigit	\D+	A string devoid of digits, e.g., Hello world!
\w	Any alphanumeric character	\w+	Windows95
\W	Any nonalphanumeric character	\W+	(*)
\b	Backspace	a\ba\b	Double-struck *a*
\n	New line	2000\n	2000 at the end of a line
\r	Carriage return	\r\n [0-1][0-2]	DOS line ending 00-12
\t	tab	(\S+)\t[0-9]+	Any string, followed by a tab and a number, e.g., apples 15
\f	Form feed	The end\f	*The end,* at the end of a page.
\0	Null character		
\12	The specified octal value	\12	A line feed
\x0A	The specified hex value	\x0A	A line feed
\cS	The specified control character	\cS	Control-S
\\	The specified metacharacter	\\	A \
[a-z]	A single character in the specified range	[a-zA-Z]	Any lowercase or uppercase letter
[A-Z][A-Z]	The number of characters specified in the ranges specified	[A-Z][A-Z]	Any two-letter uppercase string, e.g., CA or JP

Table 11.2 Repeat and Control Characters

METACHARACTER	MATCHES	EXAMPLE EXPRESSION	EXAMPLE MATCH
+	One or more of the specified character	A+ \s+	A string of As (e.g., AAA) Any amount of white space
*	Zero or more of the specified character	A* \/backup*	A string of zero or more As Zero or more repetitions of /backup
|	Expression on either side	1999|2000	1999 or 2000
^	Beginning of a line	^Subject	Subject, at the beginning of a line
$	End of line	2000$	2000 at the end of a string
\b	A word boundary (when not within [])	\b2000	2000 at the beginning of a word
\B	A nonword boundary	\B2000	2000 not at the beginning of a word
\A	Beginning of a string		
\Z	End of a string		
\G	Where previous m//g left off		

in a .login file prints "Welcome, nici" when user Nici logs in. If the string were enclosed in back quotes instead, it would print "Welcome, $USER" as shown here:

```
echo `Welcome, $USER`
Welcome, $USER
```

Make sure you use the proper quotes for your intended purpose.

Delimiters and Escape Characters

Some utilities, such as awk and sed, make heavy use of delimiters. The default delimiter is always *white space*—which represents any combination of blanks and tabs. Alternate delimiters need to be fed as arguments to the command. Thus, the command

```
spoon% cat /etc/passwd | awk -F: '{print $1}'
```

uses a colon character as the field delimiter and prints the first field of each line of the passwd file. Delimiter substitution is important. If you couldn't adjust commands to the data they are to process, scripting would be a limited and unrewarding activity. You not only have to adjust delimiters to match delimiters in data; you need to adjust delimiters to avoid conflicts in data. The command

```
sed "s/this/that/"
```

is no different than

```
sed "s,this,that,"
```

On the other hand, the command

```
sed "s/this,/this /"
```

is *not* the same as

```
sed "s,this,,this ,"
```

In fact, the latter command would result in an error; sed will be confused by the appearance of the delimiter within the text.

Some characters will cause problems when commands are parsed by the shell, unless they are *escaped* (i.e., preceded by a special character that tells the shell to ignore them). For example, the command

```
spoon% echo "System crashing... Panic\!"
```

will print "System crashing . . . Panic!" Without the \ escape character, the shell would choke on the exclamation point.

Assignment Statements

Each command interpreter (shells and Unix utilities) has its own way of assigning values to variables. If you code in several languages or must maintain scripts written in a number of languages, it's a good idea to keep this straight. Table 11.3 provides examples of assignments in each of the major shells and languages discussed here.

Table 11.3 Assignment Statements

LANGUAGE	ASSIGNMENT	PRINTING
Csh	set file = $1	echo $file
Sh	limit = $1	echo $limit
Perl	$defaultmbox = "/var/mail/sys";	print "$defaultmbox\n";
Awk	CNT = 1	print CNT

Table 11.4 The for Command

#!/bin/csh	#!/bin/sh	#!/usr/bin/perl
	for var in [item1 item2 . . .]; do	for ($n = n1; $n < N; $n++) {
	command	command;
	done	}

for, while, if, and case Statements

Branching and looping in shell programming is essentially the same as in almost any programming language. The basic programming constructs are for loops, while loops, and case statements (also known as *switch* commands).

Though for loops and while loops are very similar, they have an essential difference. Though each command iterates over a set of values, the for command is usually executed at least once; the conditions for termination are tested *after* the command loop is executed. While loops, on the other hand, test the termination condition on their onset. An easy way to think about these commands is to say to yourself, "While TRUE do . . ." and "for VALUE1, do until VALUE2." Table 11.4 illustrates the syntax of the for command.

Like the C shell, Perl also has a foreach statement. Table 11.5 illustrates the syntax. Notice that the sh for statement behaves like a foreach (not like the Perl for command).

The while command is illustrated in Table 11.6.

If/then/else commands provide a mechanism for simple testing and branching. The syntax differs in minor ways across languages. Whether the then is expressed or implied and how the end of the command is expressed (e.g., endif or fi) is a minor detail. The three if/then/else commands shown in Table 11.7 illustrate the basic syntax in the C shell, the Bourne shell, and Perl

TIP

Indenting code is not anal! It's a low-cost way to make your scripts more readable and can help you avoid a lot of mismatches between statement beginnings and endings.

Table 11.5 The foreach Command

#!/bin/csh	#!/bin/sh	#!/usr/bin/perl
foreach var (item1 item2 . . .)	N/A	foreach $var (item1 item2 . . .) {
command		command;
end		}

Table 11.6 The while Command

#!/bin/csh	#!/bin/sh	#!/usr/bin/perl
	while [condition]	while (condition) {
	do	action;
	action	action;
	action	};
	done	

Table 11.7 The if/then/else Command

#!/bin/csh	#!/bin/sh	#!/usr/bin/perl
if ($1 == "test") then	if [$1 -eq "test"]; then	if ($1 == "test") {
echo "testing"	echo "testing"	echo "testing"
else	else	} else {
echo "Prepare yourself"	echo "Prepare yourself"	echo "Prepare yourself"
endif	fi	}

A case statement effects a similar decision structure as an embedded if/then/else, but does so much more efficiently. Given an embedded if/then/else with five tested conditions (if) and one fall-through (else), the average execution will run through three tests before it finds the matching conditions. Case commands work differently and branch directly to the matching choice.

Although Perl doesn't include a formal case statement, its advanced pattern-matching capabilities can be used to effect a makeshift case statement. Table 11.8 illustrates case statements and the Perl equivalents.

One clever way to use case statements efficiently is to use them to hold parameters for a script that performs a similar function for a number of different items. For example, the following script fragment is a *push* script used to fire off the mirror script to support a number of Web sites. Each site is represented by a block in the case statement. The remainder of the script uses the assigned parameters to determine the source and destination of the Web site to be pushed.

```
#!/bin/sh

PATH=/usr/ucb:/usr/local/bin:$PATH ; export PATH
me=`basename $0 2>/dev/null`
umask 022

case ${me} in
site1)
    tag=site1
```

Table 11.8 The case (switch) Statement

#!/bin/csh	#!/bin/sh	#!/usr/bin/perl
switch ($arg)	case ${arg} in	CASE: {
case "1":	1)	$arg == 1
commands	actions	&& do { action;
breaksw	;;	action;};
case "2":	2)	$arg == 2
commands	actions	&& do { action;
breaksw	;;	action;};
default:	*)	$arg > 2
commands	fall-thru	&& do { fall-thru;
breaksw	;;	};
endsw	esac	}

```
    vers=v6
    config=/usr/local/conf/site1.conf
    ;;
site2)
    tag=site2
    vers=v4
    config=/usr/local/conf/site2.conf
    ;;
site3)
    tag=site3
    vers=v3
    config=/usr/local/conf/site3.conf
    ;;
site4)
    tag=site3
    vers=v6
    config=/usr/local/conf/site4.conf
    ;;
site5)
    tag=site5
    vers=v6
    config=/usr/local/conf/site5.conf
       ;;
*)
    echo "unknown command: $0"
    ;;
esac
content=`(grep `^local_dir' $config | cut -d= -f2) 2>/dev/null
```

This style of script provides certain advantages. For one, the information that is different for each Web site is clearly organized near the top of the script. For another, the script determines which set of parameters it is to use by how it is called. The ${me} parameter holds the name of the script. The various script names are created as hard links. Therefore, a single file with multiple names is then used to perform the same function for any number of sites. To add a site, a new entry must be added to the case statement, and a new hard link, reflecting the new name, must be created.

If a script is exited because of an error, a return code might be useful in deciding what to do next. If one script calls another and has to proceed to the next step only if the first was successful, return codes can provide the most natural mechanism for communicating this information.

Dealing with Limits

Sooner or later, if you haven't already done so, you're going to run into limits. Your standard way of solving a problem is suddenly not going to work. A tool that modifies links in html files—for example, to change them from (fixed) to relative—will be asked to use one more pattern than it can handle and will issue an error message and stop. The sed utility can only handle so many patterns before it balks. The awk tool can only handle so many fields before it just says "too many fields" and quits. Elegant workarounds to problems like these are few and far between.

In our testing, the foreach command in the C shell balked and issued the error "Too many words" at just over 1700 items in its expanded list. Our sed command gave up the ghost and told us "Too many commands" with just under 200 patterns in our file. Our awk script refused to budge when we passed it data with 100 fields.

You can use regular expressions as one possible workaround to these kind of limits. If you can reduce the number of patterns that you are trying to match by using regular expressions instead of literals, you may stay below the tool's threshold. At other times, you can break the problem into pieces and build your output file gradually rather than in a single step.

Often the best workaround is to use another tool. A newer member of the awk family, such as gawk or nawk, might be able to work with a larger file. A compiled language such as C or C++ will offer little resistance when called into battle against large problems, but will probably take considerably more effort in preparation. Finding ways to works against limits is one of the signs of a seasoned sysadmin.

Using the Right Tool for the Job

One thing that can and has, many times, been said about Unix systems is that there is always more than one way to solve a problem. Most of the time, there's even more than one *good* way to solve a problem. However, each of the tools and languages that comprise our systems has its particular strengths and weaknesses. Though you might be able to use either sed or tr to solve a problem, one might have decided advantages over the other.

The *Bourne shell* is one of the most popular shells. One reason is that it is ubiquitous; you will not find a Unix system without it. Another is that Bourne shell scripts will run with newer shells in the same shell family—such as the Korn shell and Bash (the Bourne Again shell).

The *C shell* is a nice shell with easy-to-use features such as the foreach command and interactive file completion. It has fallen out of favor with many sysadmins because of an earlier bout of security problems and because it lacks many of the features found in more modern languages such as Perl (e.g., reading multiple files). However, it has many nice features and is extremely useful for quick and dirty scripts.

An easy favorite, *Perl* is capable of being extremely terse. It makes extensive and fluid use of regular expressions. Once familiar with Perl, you're likely to use it almost exclusively. It provides numerous features of other Unix tools—for example, sed and awk. Freely available, and popular partly due to its use in cgi scripts for Web sites, Perl promises short development time for those who know it. It also includes a number of features missing from older languages—good array handling, string functions, and, of course, *impressive* regular expressions. It is very straightforward in its file handling (note in the mh script how it evaluates each line in a file and sends data to the proper output files).

Expect is the tool to use when you can't be there. Expect will interact with some utility that expects real-time answers and provide these answers on your behalf. You basically prepare a script of what to expect and how to answer.

C and *C++* are two of the more popular languages in use today and are usually available on Solaris systems, whether as commercial software or the GNU versions. When you need speed, it's hard to beat the running time of a compiled program.

Awk is a pattern-matching language, great for grabbing the *n*th column in a delimited file, and good for writing simple filters. To grab the third field in the passwd map using awk and NIS, you would use *enter: ypcat passwd | awk -F: '{print $3}'*.

Sed, the Unix stream editor, is good for processing changes in a file. It is generally used inline (e.g., cat file | sed "s/this/that/"), but can be also be used with a prepared file of expressions.

Grep is another tool for use with regular expressions. It provides one of the easiest ways to select and deselect patterns. Contrast grep with fgrep, which allows you to do greplike things with a file of patterns.

Tr is a tool for translating characters or strings to other characters or strings. A common example of this command is *cat file | tr "A-Z" "a-z"*. It changes all uppercase letters to lower case. Similarly, *cat file | tr -d "\015"* gets rid of carriage returns in a DOS text file (turning it into a Unix text file), while *cat file | tr "\015" "\012"* turns Macintosh text file endings into Unix text file endings by replacing carriage returns with new lines.

Wc is a command that counts lines, words, or characters. Combined with grep, for example, wc can tell you how many times a particular pattern appears in a file.

Good Scripting Practice

There are some simple techniques that can make script writing more reliable and less frustrating. One that we recommend, especially to those just getting started in the business of automating their work, is to start simple and build up to complexity. One practice that we consider almost essential when starting a script that is destined to be complicated is to first build the control structure. Later, you can fill in the commands. Inserting simple comments at each level in the looping or case structure will help you to verify that it's working properly before additional details weigh down the process. You could start with something as simple as this:

```
foreach FILE (`find ./* -name *.dat -print`)
  echo $FILE
end
```

Once you see that you're picking up the correct files, you can start adding the commands to process the file. But wait! Another idea that we've used on occasion is to next echo the commands that you will be using. You then verify that the generated commands appear to be proper before you remove the echo command and allow the commands to be executed in your first trial.

TIP

Build up your scripts gradually. By getting the annoying details (control loops and such) our of the way first, you can work on the more difficult details knowing that your basic control structure is intact.

By following techniques such as these, you're far less likely to run into problems with mismatched begins and ends or similar problems. In the following Bourne shell code, you can see how we've used this technique to display the mv and ln commands before allowing this script to impact the actual files. After we're confident that we've constructed our file names correctly, we'll remove the echo commands.

```
#!/bin/sh

PATH=/usr/ucb:/usr/local/bin:$PATH ; export PATH
me=`basename $0 2>/dev/null`
year=`date +%Y`
mo=`date +%m`
umask 022

echo mv /www/index.html /www/index.html$$
echo mv /usr/tmp/$me/new.html /www/$me/$year-$mo.html
echo ln -s /www/$me/$year-$mo.html /www/index.html
```

Another important rule of thumb for developing scripts is to test them with increasingly more realistic amounts of data. Early tests should be run with a *very* small sample, both because this allows you to closely examine the results before proceeding and because you'll get these results quickly. A process that runs an hour or more and then proves to have generated bogus results can waste an hour or more of your time.

Scripts that you create should also be well behaved. There are certain characteristics of a well-behaved script that we would like to share. For one, well-behaved scripts make sure that a file exists before they try to use it. If the file doesn't exist, a well-behaved script will generate an error and return (exit). If the file should have been included as an argument, a well-behaved script will issue a usage statement, trying to assist the user, and return (exit).

It is also good practice for any script that exits prematurely to exit with an error code (i.e., exit 1). Although you may never use these return codes, you might use them if you ever call one of these scripts from another script. In this case, knowing whether the called script completed properly or abended might be important in determining how the calling script should react.

TIP

Include error messages and usage statements in your scripts—especially if they will be used infrequently. You'll save yourself and anyone else who uses the scripts a lot of time. They won't have to read you code to figure out how to use it.

One way to combine testing and script buildup is to run your commands interactively, as shown in the following example, and then, when you're satisfied with the results, cut and paste the commands into a file. This technique generally works better with simple scripts. Once you've put the effort into typing the commands for a useful functioning, save them in the form of a script, give them a name you can remember, and store them in a bin directory. The small effort involved might save you some time someday when you need as much of it as you can find. If you type the following commands interactively:

```
spoon% foreach file (`ls /logs/*`)
? gzip $file
? echo $file compressed
? end
```

Your cut-and-pasted script will have to be modified slightly to look like this:

```
#!/bin/csh

foreach file (`ls /logs/*`)
  gzip $file
  echo $file compressed
end
```

Don't overlook the utility provided by Sun's cmdtool windows for saving the results of your processing. A right mouse button click brings up, among other things, the option to store or clear the contents of the log file. This can be provide a useful way to recover commands that worked especially well—a little while ago. Since many of our efforts might initially be hit and miss, you might not always recognize a good approach to a problem until after you've tried it again. It's nice to know that these gems of scripting wisdom can still be retrieved—either from your command history or from a cmdtool log.

Once you've captured your gem, another option (besides depositing the commands into a script) is to create an alias—at least for the single liners—and store it in your shell dot file (e.g., .cshrc).

Whenever you're scripting for general use, be careful with permissions. An output file owned by root might not allow appending to a file if the next person to run it is a normal user. If you do your testing as root, be sure to watch for potential side effects. Running your tests as a normal user will help ensure that they'll work for normal users.

Another good practice is to write your scripts to be as general as possible. You might be able to use them in a variety of situations. The count_same script is, admittedly, extremely simple, but it can be thrown into many situations to save time where counting the repetitions of the same string or pattern is important.

Another good idea is to leave your debugging lines in your code, but to comment them out; or, even better, provide a verbose mode with lines like this chunk of Perl so that you can run the script with helpful comments if you need to:

```
if ($verbose) {
  print $_;
}
```

Temporary files can be made to be almost certainly unique by adding $$ (the process id) to the end of them (procid of current shell) in the Bourne and C shells. The likelihood of a conflict is exceedingly small, and this practice will save you from being concerned about whether previous output may interfere with your results.

Make a practice of storing results from potentially time-consuming operations rather than running them again. For example, note how the set command in the example shown here is both easier to understand and more efficient than putting the two grep . . . wc commands and the expr command inside of the two echo commands:

```
set SUBS = `grep "Subject: subscription" subfile | wc -1
set DROPS = `grep "Subject: remove" subfile| wc -1
echo "$SUBS newsletter subscriptions"
set PCT = `expr $DROPS \/ $SUBS \* 100`
echo "$PCT % drops"
```

As is the rule in any programming situation, carefully watch those *end points*— one of the most troublesome parts of scripting is dealing with the first and last instances of anything. Be careful of these as you write and test your scripts. In counting lines that are the same, the first line is an exception, since there *are* no preceding lines, and the last line is an exception, since you have to remember to print the count accumulated thus far (usually done when you encounter a different line).

Take care to ensure that your scripts will not run into problems if they are executed more than once. Getting rid of temporary files at the ends of scripts is generally a good idea, especially if the script appends data to these files. If it is important that a script not be run more than once (e.g., not more than once a month), be careful to implement that restriction in your logic. Make sure that you can easily and reliably identify when a script has been run.

Add comments to your scripts, but *not* excessively. A foreach DAY (Monday Tuesday Wednesday . . .) command does *not* need a corresponding comments that says # *for each day of the week*. It's obvious. On the other hand, a complex regular expression like (m/^From\s+(\S+@\S+)\s+(.*)/) deserves a comment # *At beginning of e-mail message. . . .*

Don't fail to test your scripts. If necessary, create clones of data files and make sure you get the results you expect before you turn them lose on important files. There is no worse feeling than realizing that your brand-new clever script has just demolished a critical data file because a command was just a little wrong. At the same time, be careful, *and* forgive yourself for your mistakes. We all make them.

Running Scripts at Regular Intervals

There is nothing like cron when it comes to running your scripts at regular intervals. Using cron, you can schedule jobs to run at any minute of any day. You can run a script as infrequently as every time January 8 falls on a Tuesday (approximately once every seven years). Most scripts run once a day, once a week, or once a month.

Running your scripts through cron is easy. The cron fields are listed in Table 11.9.

The cron entry corresponding to the examples in Table 11.9 would be listed as follows:

```
10 9 8 7 6 /usr/local/bin/runme 2>&1 | mail sysadmin
```

This would cause the script runme to run at 9:10 on July 8 if it's a Saturday. Any field can include more than one value (e.g., 9, 21) or an * representing any possible value. Unfortunately, there isn't any easy way to specify that you want a script to run on the last day of the month, so monthly scripts are usually run on the first, shortly after midnight. If you needed to run a script on the last day of the month, you could schedule it to run every night and quickly exit if it isn't the last day of the month.

If you want a script to run shortly after midnight, but to wrap up log files and such from the day before, start the job shortly before midnight and insert a sleep command, as shown in the following example. This will cause it to wait the appropriate amount of time before it starts to process the previous day's files.

```
#!/bin/sh
YR=`date +%Y`
MO=`date +%m`
DAY=`date +%d`

sleep 120
```

Table 11.9 The Fields on a crontab File

FIELD	RANGE	EXAMPLE
Minutes	0–59	10
Hours	0–23	9
Day of month	1–31 (but watch out!)	8
Month	1–12	7
Day of week	0–6 (Sunday to Saturday)	6

If this script is run at 23:59, it will pick up the date of the day that is ending and hold it for use after the brief period of sleep. This is a good technique if you want to be sure to include a complete day's data.

Updates to the cron files should always be made using the crontab -e command. This gives cron a chance to balk on your syntax if you make a mistake (e.g., omitting one of the five scheduling fields). Cron, like a number of Unix daemons, reads the crontab files only when it starts up or when crontab -e is used.

It is common practice for sysadmins to send e-mail to themselves at the completion of a cron job. The *2>&1* part of the line corresponding to the Table 11.9 example redirects both standard output and standard error to the mail program. This helps to assure you that cron processes have been run. On the other hand, if you run a lot of jobs through cron, you might not notice if the output from a single job never arrives. For this reason, you probably don't want to inundate yourself with e-mail from cron. Another option is to set up cron to log its activities and periodically check the log file. To enable cron logging, set the option *CRONLOG=YES* in the file /etc/default/cron.

When you are setting up a script to run through cron, test it on its own (i.e., invoking it on the command line) and then test it through cron—even if you have to change the running time so that you get the e-mailed notification soon afterward. Keep in mind that cron jobs run with reference to the environment of the particular user. If you, as yourself, are preparing a script that will be run by root, make sure that it runs properly when initiated by root (whose environment may be very different from your own). If you're careful to do this and can keep the fact that 2 means Tuesday, and so on, straight, you should have no problems setting up your cron jobs to run when and how you want them to.

Sample Scripts

We've included a couple of scripts in the following subsections to illustrate some of the points we've been making in this chapter. Extract code from these scripts or modify them to suit your needs as you like.

Scripted FTPs

Most of the time, the ftp process is run manually. The user issues the ftp command, enters username and password, and then uses get and put (along with other commands) to move files from one system to another. For processes that you want to happen automatically, you can script your ftp moves as shown in the sample script below. Note that the password is included in this script in plain text. If this is a security problem, you may not want to use processes like these.

```
#!/bin/sh

site=ftp.xyz.org
local=/logs
remote=/www/logs

cd $local
ftp -n $site <<EOF 2>&1 /dev/null
mylogin mypassword
cd $remote
binary
prompt
mget *
end

EOF
```

Mass Mailings

If you need to send mail to a large population of users and don't want to include your distribution list with each message, you can do so easily with a script like that shown below. It sends each piece of mail out individually and keeps a log of what it has done.

```
#!/bin/sh
# mass mail a message (from a file) to addresses (from a file)

# defaults:
recipfile=recip.list
msgfile=msg.txt
subject="mass mailing"
log=massmail.log
returnadd=$USER@`domainname`
admin=$USER
USAGE="massmail -s subject -r recipient-list -m message-file"


# prompt with usage statement if no arguments are given

while [ $# -gt 0 ]
do
   case $1 in
   -s) subject=$2
       shift ;;
   -r) recipfile=$2
       shift ;;
   -m) msgfile=$2
       shift ;;
   *)  echo $USAGE
       exit 1 ;;
   esac
   shift
done
```

```
sendmail=/usr/lib/sendmail
mail=/usr/ucb/mail
delay=1

if [ ! -f $recipfile ]; then
    echo "cannot find $recipfile"
    exit 1
fi
if [ ! -f $msgfile ]; then
    echo "cannot find $msgfile"
    exit 1
fi

#
# calculate time estimated
ndat=`wc -l $recipfile 2> /dev/null | awk '{print $1}'`
time=`echo "$ndat $delay" | awk '{printf("%.2f",($1*($2+1.88))/3600)}'`

(
echo "Mass mailing started at `date`"
echo
echo "subject line:    $subject"
echo "recipient list: $recipfile"
echo "message file:    $msgfile"
echo "logfile:         $log"
echo "return address: $returnadd"
echo "delay:           $delay seconds"
echo "time required:   $time hours ($ndat addresses)"
echo
) | tee -a $log
sleep 3

j=0;
while read rec
do
    j=`expr $j + 1`
    echo "sending #$j to: $rec" | tee -a $log
# dispatch outgoing parcel to addressee
(
cat << EOF
From: $returnadd
Subject: $subject
Reply-To: $returnadd
To: $rec
EOF

cat $msgfile
) | $sendmail -f "$returnadd" $rec

    if [ $? != 0 ]; then
        echo "dispatch of #$j returned with non-zero exit status" |
        tee -a $log
    fi
```

```
        sleep $delay
done < $recipfile

(
echo " "
echo "Mass mailing completed at `date`"
echo
) | tee -a $log

echo "$0 done at `date`" | $mail -s $0 $admin

exit 0
```

Web Link Updates

Here's a script which automatically updates some Web pages. Note how it is composing html. This is a simple script, only intended as an extremely simple example of how this might be done.

```
#!/bin/sh
PATH=/usr/ucb:/usr/local/bin:$PATH ; export PATH
me=`basename $0 2>/dev/null`
year=`date +%Y`
mo=`date +%m`
umask 022

case ${mo} in
01) month="January";;
02) month="February";;
03) month="March";;
04) month="April";;
05) month="May";;
06) month="June";;
07) month="July";;
08) month="August";;
09) month="September";;
10) month="October";;
11) month="November";;
12) month="December";;
esac
case ${me} in
update.site1)
    tag=site1
    vers=v6
    ;;
update.site2)
    tag=site2
    vers=v4
    ;;
update.site3)
    tag=site3
```

```
        vers=v3
        ;;
update.site4)
        tag=site3
        vers=v6
        ;;
update.site5)
        tag=site5
        vers=v6
          ;;
*)
          echo "unknown command: $0"
          ;;
esac

awk '{if (index($0,"Insert new month here") > 0) {
  print "<!-- Insert new month here -->"
  print " "
  print "<H2>",MO,YR,"</H2>"
  print "<LI><A HREF=\"/data/" YR "-" M ".rep." VER ".html\">"MO
"Report</A>"
  print "<LI><A HREF=\"/data/" YR "-" M ".cgi\">" MO "Graph</A>"
else
  print $0
}' < /www/$tag/index.html MO=$month YR=$year VER=$vers >
/www/$tag/index.html.$$

mv /www/$tag/index.html /www/$tag/index.html.prev
mv /www/$tag/index.html.$$ /www/$tag/index.html
```

Summary

There is probably nothing you can do that will save you more time and effort than preparing well-crafted, reusable scripts. By adopting a set of good habits with respect to naming and coding techniques, you will benefit properly from your scripting efforts.

There are many choices of languages and tools, but using the proper tool for the job can make a difference in how hard it is to tackle a particular problem. Perl is clearly our favorite for versatility and programming ease, but requires considerable effort to get over the initial hump of its heavy reliance on regular expressions. Whatever scripting (or programming) language you use, follow good development techniques, create well-behaved scripts, and don't forget to do proper testing.

## CHAPTER 12

Keeping Your Solaris Systems Secure

There are two prevalent views of what computer security is. The first and most obvious of these is that computer security involves protecting your systems from break-ins and malicious attacks. Following this definition, the most secure systems are turned off, boxed, and stored in a vault. The second view is that computer security involves maintaining the usability, reliability, and availability of your systems. According to this definition, your systems aren't secure unless they behave as expected, files are stable, processes are executing properly, and work is getting done.

It's probably safe to assume that none of us is tasked with maintaining the security of computers boxed and stored in vaults. Therefore, our working assumption in this chapter is that we are securing systems that must be, first and foremost, usable by their intended users and for their intended uses. This attitude imposes a vein of practicality on security. Our jobs are to secure our systems as well as possible without making it difficult or impossible for our users to get their work done.

Nothing in this attitude is meant to imply that you should be cavalier when it comes to system security. In this day and age, there are numerous and very serious threats to your systems. They include thefts of proprietary data, disruption of service, destruction of data and process files, and unauthorized use of your systems—sometimes in conjunction with criminal activity. If your systems are compromised, your organization may well end up enduring considerable disruption to work, embarrassment, and expense.

This is not a book about security, of course. In the space allotted to this chapter, we can only give you some of our best advice, without going into a lot of detail. We suggest that you read other texts on security; to that end we have listed some of our favorites in the bibliography and recommended reading list.

Network Security

Network security involves protecting systems from vulnerabilities that exist because of their local area network (LAN) or Internet exposure. The basic strategy that any sysadmin should adopt is twofold:

1. Restrict network services to those that are needed for the system's proper and intended function.

2. Protect the system from network-based damage, whether intentional or inadvertent.

Since any network service potentially provides opportunities for abuse, only required services should be run, and even then, the more vulnerable of these should be replaced with security-hardened equivalents. In addition, careful configuration of systems and enforcement of security guidelines, along with routine scanning of systems for evidence of tampering, should be the norm. In most cases, you will want to provide many services to a limited set of known systems and only a few services to systems in general.

To examine network security, we must first look at the processes, or daemons, that provide network and system services. The most intrinsic of the network services is the Internet daemon itself, inetd.

Security through Service Elimination—inetd

Most network services in Unix run from a central dispatcher called *inetd*. The file /etc/inetd.conf tells inetd what to do. It is a straightforward, column-oriented text file that lists most of the network services available to the operating system and, in turn, to the user. Services run through inetd are run *on demand*; that is, they are started by inetd on a request made on behalf of a user. For example, a user on another system enters ftp *ftp.foo.com* and inetd starts up an instance of in.ftpd to support the user's ftp session. Contrast this with daemons—processes that are started via the init process during system bootup and run-state changes (see Chapter 4).

One of the simplest yet most effective moves you can make to improve network security is to comment out the services that are not required and those that may prove to be an unwarranted security risk.

NOTE
You must be root user to edit this file.

After you make changes to this file, you must force inetd to reread the file by sending it a hangup signal. The command is *kill -1 (or kill -HUP) <pid of inetd>*. In general, we recommend the -HUP form of the command since you are less likely to make a mistake and enter *kill 1 123*, which would kill the init process.

The line *<service_name> <socket_type> <proto> <flags> <user> <server_pathname> <args>* describes the fields in each tab-separated line. The line for the ftp service, for example, has the following fields: *ftp, stream, tcp, nowait, root, /usr/sbin/in.ftpd*, and *in.ftpd*. Reading this, we see that the ftp service uses the tcp protocol and runs without additional arguments. Here is a sample /etc/inetd.conf file:

```
#ident"@(#)inetd.conf   1.33   98/06/02 SMI"   /* SVr4.0 1.5 */
#
#
# Configuration file for inetd(1M). See inetd.conf(4).
#
# To re-configure the running inetd process, edit this file, then
# send the inetd process a SIGHUP.
#
# Syntax for socket-based Internet services:
# <service_name> <socket_type> <proto> <flags> <user>
<server_pathname> <args>
#
# Syntax for TLI-based Internet services:
#
#   <service_name> tli <proto> <flags> <user> <server_pathname>
<args>
#
# Ftp and telnet are standard Internet services.
#
ftp    stream tcp   nowait   root   /usr/sbin/in.ftpd   in.ftpd
telnet stream tcp   nowait   root   /usr/sbin/in.telnetd in.telnetd
#
# Tnamed serves the obsolete IEN-116 name server protocol.
#
name   dgram  udp   wait     root   /usr/sbin/in.tnamed in.tnamed
#
# Shell, login, exec, comsat and talk are BSD protocols.
#
shell  stream tcp   nowait   root   /usr/sbin/in.rshd   in.rshd
login  stream tcp   nowait   root   /usr/sbin/in.rlogind in.rlogind
exec   stream tcp   nowait   root   /usr/sbin/in.rexecd in.rexecd
comsat dgram  udp   wait     root   /usr/sbin/in.comsat in.comsat
talk   dgram  udp   wait     root   /usr/sbin/in.talkd in.talkd
```

```
#
# Must run as root (to read /etc/shadow); "-n" turns off logging in
utmp/wtmp.
#
#uucp   stream  tcp   nowait   root   /usr/sbin/in.uucpd in.uucpd
#
# Tftp service is provided primarily for booting.  Most sites run this
# only on machines acting as "boot servers."
#
#tftp   dgram   udp   wait   root   /usr/sbin/in.tftpd in.tftpd -s
/tftpboot
#
# Finger, systat and netstat give out user information which may be
# valuable to potential "system crackers."  Many sites choose to disable
# some or all of these services to improve security.
#
#finger   stream  tcp   nowait   nobody /usr/sbin/in.fingerd in.fingerd
#systat   stream  tcp   nowait   root   /usr/bin/ps     ps -ef
#netstat  stream  tcp   nowait   root   /usr/bin/netstat netstat -f inet
#
# Time service is used for clock synchronization.
#
time    stream   tcp   nowait   root   internal
time    dgram    udp   wait     root   internal
#
# Echo, discard, daytime, and chargen are used primarily for testing.
#
echo       stream   tcp   nowait   root   internal
echo       dgram    udp   wait     root   internal
discard    stream   tcp   nowait   root   internal
discard    dgram    udp   wait     root   internal
daytime    stream   tcp   nowait   root   internal
daytime    dgram    udp   wait     root   internal
chargen    stream   tcp   nowait   root   internal
chargen    dgram    udp   wait     root   internal
#
# RPC services syntax:
#  <rpc_prog>/<vers> <endpoint-type> rpc/<proto> <flags> <user> \
# <pathname> <args>
#
# <endpoint-type> can be either "tli" or "stream" or "dgram".
# For "stream" and "dgram" assume that the endpoint is a socket descriptor.
# <proto> can be either a nettype or a netid or a "*". The value is
# first treated as a nettype. If it is not a valid nettype then it is
# treated as a netid. The "*" is a short-hand way of saying all the
# transports supported by this system, ie. it equates to the "visible"
# nettype. The syntax for <proto> is:
#   *|<nettype|netid>|<nettype|netid>{[,<nettype|netid>]}
# For example:
# dummy/1   tli   rpc/circuit_v,udp   wait   root /tmp/test_svc   test_svc
```

```
#
# Solstice system and network administration class agent server
100232/10   tli   rpc/udp   wait root /usr/sbin/sadmind sadmind
#
# Rquotad supports UFS disk quotas for NFS clients
#
rquotad/1   tli   rpc/datagram_v   wait root /usr/lib/nfs/rquotad   rquotad
#
# The rusers service gives out user information.  Sites concerned
# with security may choose to disable it.
#
rusersd/2-3   tli   rpc/datagram_v,circuit_v   wait root
/usr/lib/netsvc/rusers/rpc.rusersd   rpc.rusersd
#
# The spray server is used primarily for testing.
#
sprayd/1   tli   rpc/datagram_v   wait root
/usr/lib/netsvc/spray/rpc.sprayd   rpc.sprayd
#
# The rwall server allows others to post messages to users on this machine.
#
walld/1      tli   rpc/datagram_v   wait root
/usr/lib/netsvc/rwall/rpc.rwalld   rpc.rwalld
#
# Rstatd is used by programs such as perfmeter.
#
rstatd/2-4   tli   rpc/datagram_v wait root
/usr/lib/netsvc/rstat/rpc.rstatd rpc.rstatd
#
# The rexd server provides only minimal authentication and is often not run
#
#rexd/1  tli  rpc/tcp wait root /usr/sbin/rpc.rexdrpc.rexd
#
# rpc.cmsd is a data base daemon which manages calendar data backed
# by files in /var/spool/calendar
#
#
# Sun ToolTalk Database Server
#
100083/1 tli  rpc/tcp wait root /usr/dt/bin/rpc.ttdbserverd rpc.ttdbserverd
#
# UFS-aware service daemon
#
#ufsd/1   tli   rpc/*   wait   root   /usr/lib/fs/ufs/ufsd ufsd -p
#
# Sun KCMS Profile Server
#
100221/1   tli   rpc/tcp   wait root /usr/openwin/bin/kcms_server
kcms_server
#
```

```
# Sun Font Server
#
fs    stream   tcp   wait nobody /usr/openwin/lib/fs.auto    fs
#
# Print Protocol Adaptor - BSD listener
#
printer   stream tcpnowait  root   /usr/lib/print/in.lpd in.lpd
#
# CacheFS Daemon
#
100235/1 tli rpc/tcp wait root /usr/lib/fs/cachefs/cachefsd cachefsd
#
# Kerbd Daemon
#
kerbd/4    tlirpc/ticlts wait    root    /usr/sbin/kerbd  kerbd
#
# GSS Daemon
#
100234/1   tli   rpc/ticotsord   wait   root   /usr/lib/gss/gssd gssd
dtspc stream tcp nowait root /usr/dt/bin/dtspcd /usr/dt/bin/dtspcd
100068/2-5 dgram rpc/udp wait root /usr/dt/bin/rpc.cmsd rpc.cmsd
```

Our suggestion is to go through the /etc/inetd.conf file, line by line, and comment out all of the entries that you don't actually need. In some cases, you might go as far as to comment out every entry except those labeled "echo" (If you comment out the echo lines, you could cause the network operations group problems.) Assume that each entry is guilty until proven innocent.

Here are some of the entries you may want to leave in:

1. *Telnet.* If you need to login over the network, especially from other platforms not likely to be equipped with rlogin, you'll probably want to preserve telnet. Telnet is a fairly safe tool in terms of security vulnerabilities. At least, it hasn't been a source of security holes over the years. The main risk with telnet is that passwords are sent over the network in plain text and can be easily sniffed.

   Ways around this inherent insecurity of telnet include one-time password software (e.g., OPIE) or a package that allows fully encrypted telnet sessions, two of which we will discuss shortly. One-time passwords require their users to manage lists of passwords, which they might easily misplace or fail to take with them when they travel. Secure telnet or telnetlike sessions, on the other hand, require software on both the client and server end of the secure communications channel. It is also possible to use token encryption that uses a randomly generated number (which changes every 10 seconds or so), which, along with your password, makes a *passcode*. In systems that use this method to secure logins, such as SecurID, the passcode is transmitted in plain text, but there are clear advantages. First, the passcode is half of the user's choosing (i.e., the user's password) and half generated by a device the size of a credit card. If the device is lost, it does the finder no good. Someone would need your password in addition to the device to log in—and your username. Similarly, if someone learns your password and does not have your device (not any card will do), they cannot log in. In fact, even if your passcode were sniffed, it would soon be invalid. The window of opportunity is small enough that the likelihood of systems such as these being vulnerable to any kind of attack is very small.

With systems such as SecurID, there is some cost in terms of administration. The software that runs on your server maintains a small database and stays in sync with the cards themselves. One of the authors was once responsible for supporting a SecurID server and found the task extremely manageable, though bulk loading of information for large collections of SecurID users was more easily accomplished using a Tcl/Tk script than by maneuvering through the database interface.

Our recommendation is to use SSH, discussed later in this chapter, as a replacement for telnet, and preserve telnet only if you have platforms for which client software is not available.

2. *Ftp.* If you work at home or need to share files with others, you may want to use ftp to exchange files. Even though this may fall into the category of being a necessary evil, and most people have this turned on, we need to warn you that the ftp daemon has been a continuing source of security holes. We know of no holes in the current program, but where there's been one bug, we often suspect there may be others. One way to get around this risk is to have a separate *expendible* ftp server. By exchanging files through a "vanilla" system that lacks sensitive or proprietary data and can be easily rebuilt from backups or installation media, you avert risks to your valuable servers.

Better yet, since user passwords are easily sniffable (they are transmitted over the wire in cleartext) with ftp just as with telnet, we recommend disabling the service and using instead a secure file transfer mechanism that encrypts the entire session (such as kerberized ftpd or SSH). If ftp access is a must, the service should be wrapped, as discussed later in this chapter.

3. *Finger.* The use of finger is controversial. A lot of users like to have the finger daemon running, so that other people can find out whether they're around. Since the *finger* command reads the user's profile as well as reporting on their recent login activity, others users can use the command to *finger* to obtain this information. However, most security experts recommend against it. When someone wants to break into your system, one of the first things they need to do in determine its vulnerabilities is to find out about

the machine and its users. Finger is a great way to do that. We'd be inclined to recommend against running it. A bug in finger was one of the major holes exploited in the famous Internet worm a number of years ago. That bug is fixed now, of course. But where there was one bug . . . We recommend disabling this service or using a more secure version, such as *cfinger*.

Here are some common services that may be of concern, along with our recommendations. Many of these you will probably want to remove. It is not difficult, nor a particularly bad idea, to turn these services on briefly, on an as-needed basis, and then turn them back off. For example, if you want to send an image to a remote system using tftp, you can start up the service, transfer the file, and then shut the service down.

TIP

By commenting out an entry rather than removing it, you can easily return the service to operational status should you need to.

bootp and bootps. Used for boot parameter services. We recommend disabling these unless you are running a bootp server.

comsat. Used for incoming mail notification via biff. We recommend disabling it unless you rely heavily on biff.

echo, daytime, discard, and chargen. Used largely for testing and largely unnecessary. We recommend disabling them.

exec. Allows remote users to execute commands on a host without logging in. It also exposes these remote users' passwords on the network, and it thus insecure. We recommend disabling the service.

login. Allows remote users to use the Berkeley rlogin utility to log in to a host without supplying a password (via the trusted hosts mechanism established by .rhosts). It is considered highly insecure. We recommend disabling the service and using SSH instead. If rlogin access is a must, the service should be wrapped.

netstat. Designed to provide network status information about a host to remote hosts. This is considered a potential security hazard. We recommend disabling the service.

shell. Allows remote users to run arbitrary commands on a host using the Berkeley rsh utility (via the trusted hosts mechanism established by the .rhosts file). It is considered highly insecure. We recommend disabling the service and using SSH instead. If rsh access is a must, the service should be wrapped.

systat. Designed to provide status information about a host. It is considered a potential security hazard. We recommend disabling the service.

talk and ntalk. Allows remote users to use talk to have a real-time conversation with a user on a host. It is considered a security hazard. We recommend disabling the service.

tftp. Allows remote users to transfer files from a host without requiring login. It is used primarily by X terminals and routers and is considered insecure. We recommend disabling the service. If tftp access is desired, we recommend that the *-s* option be used and that the service be wrapped.

time. Used for clock synchronization. We recommend disabling the service and using xntp to synchronize your system clock to WWV.

uucp. Allows remote users to transfer files to and from a host using the UUCP protocol. Unless you use UUCP, we recommend disabling the service.

Services Based on RPC

RPC-based services such as NFS and NIS are considered major security hazards unless you are using secure RPC (under DCE, for example), as they are vulnerable to spoofing attacks (discussed later in this chapter). In a highly security-conscious environment, you might consider outlawing use of NFS and NIS—especially if the physical network segments are not protected from physical access (i.e., they can be accessed by sniffing equipment). In these environments, RPC-based services should be disabled in inetd.conf.

Alternatives to NIS include Sun Microsystem's NIS+. However, availability is currently limited to only a handful of vendors, so this will not be a suitable tool for a highly heterogeneous environment. Another is rdist, which can be used, along with SSH, to securely distribute /etc/passwd, /etc/group, and similar files to clients from a central server.

Common RPC-based services defined in inetd.conf include:

rexd. Allows remote users to run RPC programs on a host. It can be used to run an arbitrary shell on the host; thus, it is highly insecure. We recommend disabling the service.

rquotad. Returns quotas for a user of a local file system that is mounted by a remote machine over the NFS. We recommend disabling it.

rstatd. Extracts performance statistics from the kernel for use by programs such as perfmeter. We recommend disabling it.

ruserd. Used to return a list of users on a network. We recommend disabling it.

sprayd. Records the packets sent by spray, and sends a response to the originator of the packets. We recommend disabling it.

walld. Used for handling rwall and shutdown requests. We recommend disabling it.

ypupdated. Used for updating NIS information. Since we recommend against the use of NIS in general, this service should be disabled.

Replacing Services with Secure Counterparts

Replacing services that are vulnerable to security abuses with those that are more secure is another simplistic yet powerful strategy for increasing security on your servers. In this section, we introduce a number of tools to consider.

SSL

SSL is a security protocol that was developed by Netscape Communications Corporation, along with RSA Data Security, Inc. This protocol ensures that data transferred between a Web client and a server remains private. It allows the client to authenticate the identity of the server.

Once your server has a digital certificate, SSL-enabled browsers such as the IBM Secure WebExplorer, Netscape Navigator, and Microsoft Explorer can communicate securely with your server using SSL. With SSL, you can easily establish a security-enabled Web site on the Internet or on your corporate TCP/IP network.

SSL uses a security handshake to initiate the TCP/IP connection between the client and the server. During the handshake, the client and server agree on the security keys that they will use for the session, and the client authenticates the server. After that, SSL is used to encrypt and decrypt all of the information in both the https request and the server response, including:

- The URL the client is requesting
- The contents of any form being submitted
- Access authorization information such as user names and passwords
- All data sent between the client and the server

We consider SSL a must for any site involved in e-commerce or that wishes to keep its Web interactions private for any reason.

SSH

ssh (Secure Shell) is a program used to log into another computer over a network, to execute commands in a remote machine, and to move files from one machine to another. It provides strong authentication and secure communications over unsecure channels. It is intended as a replacement for rlogin, rsh, and rcp, which do not provide these security features.

Basically, when you can use ssh instead of telnet, your session between your computer and the remote machine is encrypted and mischievous people can't get your password by running a sniffer on the wire. As sysadmins, we have converted from telnet to ssh because we don't want our passwords being sniffed or our activities monitored by anyone not authorized to know what we're doing.

Why should you use it? The traditional r- commands (rsh, rlogin, and rcp) are vulnerable to different kinds of attacks. Anybody who has root access to any system on your network, or physical access to the wire, can gain unauthorized access to systems in a variety of ways. It is also possible for such a person to log all the traffic to and from your system, including passwords (which ssh never sends in the clear).

The X Window System also has a number of severe vulnerabilities. With ssh, you can create secure remote X sessions transparently to the user. As a side effect, using remote X clients with SSH is more convenient for users.

Users can continue to use old .rhosts and /etc/hosts.equiv files; changing over to ssh is mostly transparent for them. If a remote site does not support ssh, a fallback mechanism to rsh is included.

SSH protects against the following kinds of attacks:

- IP spoofing, where a remote host sends out packets that pretend to come from another, trusted host. ssh even protects against a spoofer on the local network, pretending to be your router to the outside.

- IP source routing, where a host can pretend that an IP packet comes from another, trusted host.

- DNS spoofing, where an attacker forges name server records.

- Interception of cleartext passwords and other data by intermediate hosts.

- Manipulation of data by people in control of intermediate hosts.

- Attacks based on listening to X authentication data and spoofed connections to the X11 server.

In other words, SSH never trusts the net; somebody hostile who has taken over the network can only force ssh to disconnect, but cannot decrypt or play back the traffic, or hijack the connection.

This holds only if you actually use encryption. ssh does have an option to use encryption of type *none*; this is meant only for debugging purposes, and should not be used routinely.

Sendmail

Clearly valuable, sendmail is generally not a service that you will want to shut off. However, we recommend that you give some thought to turning it off on servers that do not require it. Sendmail has been a source of numerous attacks on systems over the years and, even when it is running properly, can provide opportunities for malicious attacks by people interested in slowing down or disabling your server. Sendmail will process each piece of mail that it receives regardless of whether it is properly formed, properly addressed, or intended for your domain. It will return many of these with errors, of course, but it needs to process them. For systems on which you need to run sendmail, make sure you are running a recent release; each release of sendmail fixes problems detected in earlier versions and many include significant enhancements. Make sure you configure the service to limit the number of messages that sendmail will reply to in a given time period to keep sendmail processing from overwhelming the system. The antispam feature in current releases of sendmail is also a significant bonus.

Don't depend on your Solaris OS to include the latest version of sendmail. Compare your version with the latest available at http://www.sendmail.org.

Security through Wrappers

Wrapper software evaluates every access to services running through inetd before the particular service is invoked. By doing this, an opportunity is provided to evaluate the connection before it is established and, in doing so, to accept or reject it.

In order to invoke a wrapper—and we shall discuss the TCP Wrappers (tcpd) software available from the Computer Emergency Response Team (CERT) Web site—the /etc/inetd.conf entry for the service must be modified to invoke the TCP daemon (tcpd). The wrapper software, in turn, invokes the service, but only after checking whether the request is allowable. The two files that determine whether a given connection will be accepted are the hosts.allow and hosts.deny files.

TCP Wrappers

TCP Wrappers is a program that is run before any configured TCP daemon is started by the inet daemon. It also provides for greater logging capabilities through syslog, along with restricting access to specific daemons from specific machines. TCP Wrappers is similar to a firewall in that it restricts access and allows only certain user IDs and nodes to execute authorized server processes. It secures and monitors incoming service requests such as ftp, rpc, rsh, rlogin, telnet, exec, rcp, and many others that have one-to-one mapping. You do not need to modify system files or configurations to install TCP Wrappers—except for inetd's configuration file, /etc/inetd.conf—and it works on all Unix systems. The TCP Wrappers daemon, tcpd, is positioned between inetd and the network services it manages. You modify the inetd.conf file to invoke tcpd, instead of the service directly. For each service you want to run through TCP Wrappers, you replace the pathname in the /etc/inetd.conf file with the pathname to the tcpd program. For example, this section of the /etc/inetd.conf file:

```
# Ftp and telnet are standard Internet services.
#
ftp     stream  tcp   nowait   root   /usr/sbin/in.ftpd       in.ftpd
telnet  stream  tcp   nowait   root   /usr/sbin/in.telnetd    in.telnetd
```

would be changed to look like this:

```
# Ftp and telnet are standard Internet services.
#
ftp     stream  tcp   nowait   root   /usr/local/bin/tcpd     in.ftpd
telnet  stream  tcp   nowait   root   /usr/local/bin/tcpd     in.telnetd
```

It simply replaces the network services by moving them to another location and putting the TCP daemon tcpd in their place. As with a firewall, you can specify which hosts can execute certain processes by utilizing the host-allow and host-deny tables.

How the service process flows before TCP Wrappers is installed:

user -> FTP client -> listening inetd host -> ftpd -> transfer files

How the service process flows after TCP Wrappers is installed:

user -> FTP client -> inetd -> tcpd -> ftpd -> transfer files

The TCP wrappers can also prevent access to UDP-based services, though their functionality is more limited due to the nature of the protocol. Implementing TCP Wrappers will involve editing several files (these examples are based on the advanced configuration).

TIP

When installing TCP Wrappers, we would make two suggestions:

■ First, go with the paranoid setting, as this does a reverse lookup for all connections.

■ Second, use the advanced configuration option, which is actually quite simple. This configuration keeps all the binaries in their original locations, which may be critical for future patches.

Once compiled, the tcpd binary will be installed in the /usr/local/bin directory. The file /etc/inetd.conf must be configured for the services that are to be wrapped, as shown. Note how inetd first launches the wrapper, /usr/local/bin/tcpd, then the actual server daemon.

```
# Ftp and telnet are standard Internet services.
#
#ftp    stream  tcpnowait  root     /usr/sbin/in.ftpd  in.ftpd
#telnet stream  tcpnowait  root     /usr/sbin/in.telnetd    in.telnetd
#
ftpstream  tcpnowait  root     /usr/local/bin/tcpdin.ftpd
telnet  stream  tcpnowait  root     /usr/local/bin/tcpdin.telnetd
/etc/syslog.conf must be edited for logging tcpd. TCP Wrappers were
compiled for logging at local3.info
# Log all TCP Wrapper connections
#
local3.info    /var/adm/tcpdlog
```

WARNING

Don't forget to send signals to syslogd and inetd once you make the changes (kill -HUP).

hosts.allow and hosts.deny

Once you've modified your /etc/inetd.conf file, you need to set up your hosts.allow and hosts.deny files. The /etc/hosts.allow and /etc/hosts.deny files are access control files that allow you to control what particular people or hosts have access to specific parts of your Unix machine. The tcpd process looks at hosts.allow first, so you can permit a few machines to have telnet or ftp access and then deny access to everybody else in hosts.deny. This is often called a *default deny* policy. The /etc/hosts.allow file determines for each service which hosts connections will be allowed to connect, while the /etc/hosts.deny controls which hosts tcpd will be rejected. The format of a hosts.{allow,deny} entry is as follows:

service1,service2: host1,host2 [/path/to/program]

The first field specifies a service name, such as sendmail or telnetd. The keyword *ALL* matches all daemons. The second field lists which hosts will be allowed or denied access for the given daemon (depending, of course, on which file it appears in). For example:

- *foo.bar.com:* matches foo.bar.com exactly

- *.bar.com:* matches *.bar.com

- *10.22.6.:* matches 10.22.6.*

- *ALL:* matches all hostnames

Here is an example of a hosts.allow excerpt with more features:

```
ALL: 172.16.3.0/255.255.255.0
Fingerd   : borg klingon Q
Rshd, rlogind: LOCAL EXCEPT borg
Telnetd, ftpd: LOCAL, .starfleet.com, 188.12.5
```

This set of specifications allows any user on any host on the 172.16.3.0 network to have access to all of the services (telnet and ftp) on your machine. Each such user will still have to supply the appropriate password. Always use IP addresses in the hosts.allow file, because hostname information can be spoofed (if you are using the Internet Domain Name Service, or some other name service, such as NIS).

The second entry grants access to the remote finger service to users on any of the listed hosts. Hostnames may be separated by commas and/or spaces. The third entry allows rsh and rlogin access by users from any local host (defined as one whose hostname does not contain a period), with the exception of borg. The fourth entry allows telnet and ftp access to all local hosts, all hosts in the domain starfleet.com, and all hosts on the subnet 188.12.5.

Deny all hosts by putting *all:all* in /etc/hosts.deny and explicitly listing trusted hosts that are allowed access to your machine in /etc/hosts.allow:

```
    ALL: ALL: /usr/bin/mailx -s "%d: connection attempt from %c"
root@mydomain.com
```

Not only does this deny access to all services from all hosts (except for those just established, of course), it causes tcpd to send an alarm via e-mail that somebody is trying to get unauthorized access to the machine. Substitute the e-mail address of somebody who reads e-mail regularly for root@mydomain.com in the example line.

System Security

Unlike network security, system security involves the protection of a system and its assets from users who are logged in locally. This is the domain of traditional Unix security—from the times before bored kids and cybercriminals had little better to do than attack computers. Passwords and file access permissions, group memberships, and wtmp files were once all you had to understand to secure a Unix system.

Even though the commands and the mechanics of file security may be simple, the seasoned sysadmin still has challenges to face in determining how to best turn organizational policy into practice. In general, you'll want to facilitate file sharing among groups of people who work together, and keep this access away from anyone else. Similarly to the federal government's need-to-know policy, you want to operate on a need-to-access basis. This is a bigger issue than it might at first appear. After all, you don't have exclusive control over your user's files. Your users can themselves introduce risks by creating files with world read/write access, by choosing obvious passwords, and by being careless in other ways. You, as sysadmin, should be on the lookout for sloppy users and hope to be backed up by strong organizational policies should you proactively enforce good security.

System security is a much bigger issue than simply whether you trust your users. As a human being, you may trust your users. As a sysadmin, you must be wary. Imagine that one of your users is about to go cyberpostal or that someone has just managed to break into your server with your boss's password. The more consistently you have enforced proper access controls, the less damage will likely be done.

For most readers, the bulk of this section may be a review. We suggest you skim through it, looking for anything that may be new.

Permissions

File permissions are your first line of defense against others' potentially being able to read files and execute programs or scripts that you don't want them to. Though they offer no protection against superusers and anyone who has somehow usurped this authority, they remain the primary control that users and sysadmins alike have at their disposal to protect the integrity of files.

Unix protects files and directories by keeping track of what level of permission is granted to the owner of each file, to others in the file's group (this is usually the same as the owner's group), and to anyone else—commonly called *the world.* For each file, each category (owner, group, world) can have the right to read the file's contents, write new information to the file, and execute the file.

The permissions for files in the current directory are displayed when you issue the *ls -la* command:

```
net% ls -l foo
-rw-r--r-- 1 spock staff 4 Mar 12 18:18 foo
```

Starting in the second column (the first displays a *d* for directories), the permissions for owner, group, and world are displayed as three sets of three characters—nine consecutive columns. The first column for a set can have a value of *r* or -, to indicate whether permission to read has been granted. The second column shows *w* or -, to indicate write permission. The third shows *x* or -, to indicate execute permission. For a file that is not a directory and for which the owner has all permissions, the group has read and write permissions, and the world has no permissions, the pattern is -*rwxrw----*.

How to Read Common Permissions

The following examples show some common sets of Unix file permissions, which are often expressed as a three-digit number, such as 644.

NUMERIC	UNIX EQUIVALENT	OWNER R	W	X	GROUP R	W	X	OTHER R	W	X
777	rwxrwxrwx	✔	✔	✔	✔	✔	✔	✔	✔	✔
755	rwxr-xr-x	✔	✔	✔	✔		✔	✔		✔
744	rwxr--r--	✔	✔	✔	✔			✔		
640	rw-r-----	✔	✔		✔					

TIP

Here's an easy way to remember how the numbers work:

4 = read

2 = write

1 = execute

So, if the world (i.e., other) is set to read (4) and execute (1), the last digit would be 5.

File permissions are changed using the command *chmod*. The chmod command can be used in two different ways—with numeric or with alphabetic arguments. If you're setting all the permissions on a file, the *numeric* mode is easier. If you are adding or removing one or more particular permissions, the *alphabetic* mode is easier.

TIP

Check the man pages for more details (man chmod).

The letters *u, g, o* represent the owner (*user*), the owner's group (*group*), and everybody else (*other*). You grant or revoke privileges to these, using + or – and the letters shown in an ls -l display—*r*, *w*, and *x*. For example, to give group and others read access to a file named *info*, you would use the following command:

```
net% chmod go+r info
```

To revoke others' read access, but leave group's read access in place, you would use the command:

```
net% chmod o-r info
```

One of the authors has trouble remembering whether the *o* means *owner* or *other*. She now repeats the word *Yugo* to herself to keep it straight.

In general, you are only going to want to give others read access to a few files you want to share. But before you can do this, you will need to either put the file in a directory that anyone can access, such as */tmp*, or make your home directory accessible to everyone.

The /tmp directory is useful for making a file available to someone else without mailing it to them or putting it into a personal directory with open permissions. You might want to do this if, for example, the file is large, or it is not a text file, and you don't want to bother with encoding it for mailing. Simply copy the file into /tmp and set it readable by others:

```
host% cp filename /tmp
host% chmod o+r /tmp/filename
```

The person you are sharing the file with can now read it or copy it to his or her directory. Note that anyone on the system can also read or copy this file, so you should not use this method to exchange information you don't want others to see. The *tmp* in /tmp stands for *temporary*; files in /tmp are automatically removed when the system is rebooted. If you want files to be available on a more permanent basis, you will need to keep them in your own or a shared directory.

By default, your home directory is inaccessible to others, as are all files you create. If you allow only execute access on your home directory, others will not be able to list the names of your files and subdirectory. Execute permission on a directory allows users to read its contents. Without execute permission, they will be able to read accessible files or *cd* to accessible directories if they know the names of the files and directories that you've given them access to. The easiest way to do this is to create a subdirectory with both read and execute permission for others, and place your files in it.

```
host% chmod o+x ~
host% mkdir public
host% chmod o+rx public
```

The chmod command can also be used in numeric form. For example:

```
host% chmod 755 ~/readme
```

As previously mentioned, this is an easier command to use if you want to set all permissions at once, but you need to be comfortable with the octal notation. Octal 7 is binary 111—all bits on means all permissions on. Octal 5 is 101—lacking write permission. The alphabetic equivalent of chmod 755 is as follows:

```
chmod u+rwx; chmod go+rx
```

ACLs

The current and recent releases of Solaris include a facility for expanding on the access permissions of files. Access control lists (ACLs) allow a file to be associated with more than one group and to exclude access to a particular individual. ACLs are covered in considerable detail in Chapter 1.

Users and Groups

In a Unix system, a group ID (GID) is a number that associates a system user with other users sharing something in common (perhaps a work project or a department name). It is often used for accounting purposes and to provide a means for file sharing. A user can be a member of more than one group and thus have more than one GID. Only one group, however, is associated with the user in the passwd file or map. This group, the user's primary group, is the one with which the user's files will be associated by default. Any user using a Unix system at any given time has both a user ID (UID) and a group ID (GID). Both are associated with rights and permissions, as previously described for files and directories.

Process UID and GID

Processes are associated with UIDs and GIDs, as well. In order for the operating system to know what a process is allowed to do, it must store information about who owns the process and what group it is associated with (UID and GID). In general, these permissions are associated with the user running the process, not the owner and group of the process file (i.e., they differentiate the executing process from the process as it exists as a file on your disk).

The Unix operating system stores two types of UIDs and two types of GIDs—real and effective. A process's *real* UID and GID will be the same as the UID and GID of the user who is running the process. Any process you execute, for example, will execute with your UID and GID. The real UID and GID are used for accounting purposes.

The *effective* UID and GID are used to determine what operations a process can perform—its access to system files and resources. In most cases the effective UID and GID will be the same as the real UID and GID. In other words, a running process will have the same access privileges as the user running it. This is not always the case, however. When a process is set to run as a *setuid* or SUID process, it runs with the privileges of the owner of the process. Similarly, a process set to run as a *setgid* or SGID process runs with the privileges of the group of the process. We discuss SUID and SGID processes later in this chapter.

Groups

The /etc/group file associates names with groups as well as members. This file defines which group (or groups) you are a member of in addition to your primary group. An example of a /etc/group is shown here. Note how many groups root is in:

```
# more group
root::0:root
other::1:
bin::2:root,bin,daemon
sys::3:root,bin,sys,adm
adm::4:root,adm,daemon
uucp::5:root,uucp
mail::6:root
tty::7:root,tty,adm
lp::8:root,lp,adm
nuucp::9:root,nuucp
staff::10:
daemon::12:root,daemon
sysadmin::14:
nobody::60001:
noaccess::60002:
nogroup::65534:
webmast::100:
dba::25:
oper::30:
```

umask

The umask command displays or sets the creation mask setting—that is, it determines what permission will be used when you create a file or directory. If no argument is included, umask displays the current setting. To change the creation mask setting, type **umask <value>,** where *value* is a three-digit octal number similar to the one defined in the chmod section (numerical values only). It is important to note that umask is a mask. It negates rather than sets

Table 12.1 Summary of umask Permissions

NUMBER	PERMISSION GIVEN (DIRECTORIES)	PERMISSION GIVEN (FILES)
0	rwx Read, write and execute	rw- Read and write
1	rw- Read and write	rw- Read and write
2	r-x Read and execute	r-- Read
3	r-- Read only	r-- Read only
4	-wx Write and execute	-wx Write
5	-w- Write only	-w- Write only
6	--x Execute only	--- No permissions
7	--- No permissions	--- No permissions

bits. Also note, as is shown in Table 12.1, that the effect of umask on a file and on a directory is different. Files are not given execute permission, regardless of the umask setting.

Using this table, you can see that a umask setting of 022 would give the owner full privileges while the group and all others would not have write privileges if a directory were created with this umask in effect.

Following are examples of using the umask command:

1. To give yourself full permissions for both files and directories and prevent the group and other users from having any access whatsoever:

```
umask 077
```

This subtracts 077 from the system defaults for directories (777) and 066 from the value for files (666) and results in files with 600(rw------) and directories with 700 (rwx------).

2. To give all access permissions to the group and allow other users read and execute permission:

```
umask 002
```

This subtracts 002 from the system defaults to give a default access permission for your files of 664 (rw-rw-r--) and for your directories of 775(rwxrwxr-x).

3. To give the group and other users all access except write access (the default umask):

```
umask 022
```

This subtracts 022 from the system defaults to give a default access permission for your files of 644 (rw-r--r--) and for your directories of 755(rwxr-xr-x).

TIP

To make changes to the default access permissions that last until you next change them, place the umask command in your .login file. Which file this is depends upon the shell that you use:

SHELL	LOGIN INITIALIZATION FILES
Bourne shell	.profile
Korn	.profile, .kshrc (if specified)
BASH	.bash, .login, .bashrc
C shell	.login, .cshrc
TC shell	.login, .cshrc or .tcshrc

Logging and Log Files

One of the best ways to keep an eye on what's happening (or has happened) on your systems is to pay attention to their extensive sets of log files. The log files will tell you everything from who has logged on recently, to who has sent mail from your system, to every command that every user has executed. A security-conscious system administrator will have extensive logging and auditing installed on the server. This allows the sysadmin to determine where errors might have occurred, recover the system after a crash, or work out the details of a break-in by a hacker.

One pair of log files, *wtmp* and *wtmpx*, keeps track of who has logged into the system and for how long. Solaris never clears the wtmp and wtmpx files. Therefore, as the system runs, the log files increase in size. Eventually you need to clear them out to ensure that the system can continue to operate properly. If you delete these files, the system won't be able to perform any logging to them. The login program expects these files to exist and will not recreate them. In addition, the wtmp and wtmpx files need to have a particular owner and set of permissions or the login program can't update them. You can't just rm the files and make new ones. The best way to recreate these files is to touch new ones and change the permissions and ownership, or, better yet, empty their contents without changing ownership and permissions by using *cat/dev/null > wtmp* and *cat/dev/null > wtmpx* commands.

The proper ownership and permissions for these file is illustrated with these long listings:

-rw-rw-r-- 1 adm adm 63972 Jul 14 21:54 wtmp

-rw-rw-r-- 1 adm adm 661044 Jul 14 21:54 wtmpx

WARNING
When you empty these two files, you erase most of the log information available to you about the users who have logged into your computer over a long period of time. Therefore, you must first make sure that you don't need to keep this information or that you have a backup of these files.

To read a small portion of these files, just type in **last:**

```
host% last |more
neth pts/3    205.245.153.141  Thu Jun 24 10:24 - 11:06  (00:41)
lkirkconsole:0Tue Jun 22 15:57 - 16:05  (00:07)
ingres    pts/5   205.245.153.72   Tue Jun 22 14:55 - 15:56  (01:01)
neth pts/3    205.245.153.72   Tue Jun 22 14:42 - 14:42  (00:00)
ingres    pts/6   205.245.153.72   Tue Jun 22 13:00 - 13:19  (00:19)
neth pts/5    205.245.153.72   Tue Jun 22 12:59 - 13:19  (00:20)
neth pts/3    205.245.153.72   Tue Jun 22 12:56 - 12:56  (00:00)
mx   console:0Mon Jun 21 07:51 - 11:59  (04:07)
neth ftp10.0.20.170 Sun Jun 20 20:22 - 20:35  (00:13)
neth pts/3    10.0.1.176  Sun Jun 20 16:07 - 16:09  (00:02)
neth console:0Sun Jun 20 15:56 - 16:00  (00:04)
mx   console:0Tue Jun 15 09:46 - 15:55 (5+06:09)
```

The *last* command may also be followed by username or terminal identifiers to display only the last time that particular user was logged in or that terminal was used. The fields show the name (login) of the user, where the user logged in from, the IP address where the user logged in, the date and time the user logged in, and the duration of the session. The file that gets read is /var/adm/wtmp. This file isn't cleartext to help prevent modification of the file if the system is compromised. The /var/adm directory is where some of the system logs are kept, including system startup logs and logs listing who has *su*ed to other accounts. There are other directories for logging, as well.

Another file used to store information about user logins is the *lastlog* file. This file, however, maintains only a single entry for each user. In fact, it is indexed on the userid and, thus, is a fairly stable size.

The most common directories for log and auditing files in Unix are the following:

```
/usr/adm
/var/adm
/var/log
```

Remember, these are common locations for log files, and 9 times out of 10, this is where they reside (often in subdirectories of these locations). However, log files can be anywhere on the system, and a sysadmin with even a drop of healthy paranoia will use far less obvious locations for these files.

Log files normally located in /var/adm include:

messages. Console messages.

messages.x. Archived console messages.

sulog. List of users that *su*ed to other accounts, including root.

aculog. Log of dial-out modem use. Entries are stored in plain text.

Other log files include:

/var/spool/cron/log. Cron log file.

/var/log/maillog. Logs inbound and outbound mail activity.

/var/spool/lp/log. Log file for printing.

The syslogd reads and forwards system messages to the appropriate log files and/or users, depending upon the priority of a message and the system facility from which it originates. The configuration file /etc/syslog.conf controls where messages are forwarded. The syslog is an easy, built-in mechanism to direct error messages from a number of systems to one that can be easily monitored.

Tripwire

Tripwire is an indispensable tool for detecting changes to system files. It compares the state of important system files to attributes stored as a result of an earlier examination. It can compare all of the file attributes stored in the file's inode or base its comparison on file signatures. By using more than one checksum calculation, Tripwire is extremely hard, if not impossible, to fool.

Tripwire uses an ASCII database that is created the first time you use the tool. It bases the comparisons that it makes on instructions provided in its configuration file, tw.config.

To get the most benefit out of Tripwire, run it immediately after installing or upgrading a system.

Swatch

With all the log files that we are likely to create using TCP Wrappers, we now need a way to do something with them. That's where Swatch (Simple Watchdog) comes in. Swatch is a utility that allows a system manager to log critical system- and security-related information to a dependable, secure, central-logging host system. Swatch examines messages as they are written to system log files, monitoring these messages in real time and responding. Alternatively, it can make a one-time pass over a file, evaluating its contents. Swatch monitors log files and acts to filter out unwanted data and take one or more user-specified actions (ring bell, send mail, execute a script, etc.) based upon patterns it is looking for. It is extremely useful when logging to a central host in conjunction with TCP Wrappers to provide extra logging info.

The sysadmin's friend, Swatch has a simply formatted configuration file. The first column contains patterns describing what it is looking for. The pattern */*file system full/*, for example, directs it to watch for this message. The second column, which tells Swatch how to respond, might say *echo,bell,mail=sysadmin*. Swatch echos the message to standard out, sends an audible signal to the terminals, and sends e-mail to the user sysadmin. More detail on Swatch is included in Chapter 9.

Patches and Security

The first thing you want to do to be sure your system is secure is to be certain that you are at the latest patch levels for your operating system. A *showrev -p* command will list the patches that are currently installed. As emphasized in Chapter 5, regular but guarded (install only what you know you need) installation of patches will go a long way toward protecting your systems from discovered security weaknesses.

Summary

The best advice we have to offer on the subject of system and Internet security is that you take it seriously. You face real threats—from targeted attacks to mischievous vandals. There are a number of steps you can take to reduce the risk:

- Turn off services you don't need.
- Replace vulnerable services with more secure tools.
- Configure the tools you keep for maximum security.
- Wrap your services to limit the users and hosts that can access them.

- Put a firewall between your systems and the outside world.
- Track security updates issued by Sun and other security organizations (e.g., CERT).
- Patch your systems appropriately and periodically.
- Monitor your systems for security holes and evidence of tampering.

## CHAPTER 13

Implementing High Availability: Eliminating Single Points of Failure

You've bought your shiny new Enterprise servers with their extremely high levels of reliability, availability, and scalability (RAS). You've been given impressive mean time between failure (MTBF) numbers and an assurance from your Sun-Service sales rep that your systems will never fail. Now, you have Internet applications that you're expected to keep up 24 hours a day, 7 days a week. What will happen if there is an outage? How will you keep your applications running and your data available while maintenance is performed? Have you considered that planned outages, just like any catastrophe that takes down your servers, are downtime? Maybe it's time to start looking for a high-availability (HA) solution.

Many people confuse high availability with fault tolerance. High availability delivers up to 99.5 percent uptime, while fault tolerance will gain you that extra half percent. Though 100 percent availability is an attractive concept, that extra half of a percent can push your costs off the scale. Unless you can't survive without round-the-clock uptime, a high-availability solution might be quite sufficient. With the proper architecture and planning, HA can bring peace of mind to you and your organization—without the considerably higher cost of a fault-tolerant operation.

There is also confusion over the difference between High Availability and Disaster Recovery (DR). Disaster Recovery is the ability to recreate the environment in the event of a catastrophic event, such as flood or hurricane. Most DR planning revolves around making sure that reserve hardware and system backups of primary systems are available at an alternate site in case the primary site becomes unavailable.

There are also many ways to implement HA solutions. The more elaborate, the higher the price tag. Don't be discouraged by the range of choices; if implemented properly, any solution to increase availability will save you time and headaches.

The Mission Plan for High Availability

Planning for high availability is not rocket science. Simply take a look at your systems and applications and eliminate single points of failure. Consider each component in turn. Start with the power source, move to the server hardware and system software, proceed to connectivity, and then finish with each application.

It still amazes us that people will implement elaborate HA schemes and yet not use appropriate power protection. This puts the onus for providing a source of clean, adequate power on someone else—and risks your hard work to elements beyond your control. Power is one of the most overlooked components of mission-critical systems. Don't make this mistake yourself. A good uninterruptible power supply (UPS) can make the difference between a normal business day and an extended outage. Most systems administrators don't have the luxury of a hardened data center. Even today, many servers are located in office environments. If you are one of the systems administrators who manages servers in the office environment and have to protect your systems, there are several rules you should follow. They may seem intuitively obvious, but we have seen them ignored enough times to feel they're worth saying.

- Do not put all of your HA servers on the same UPS. A UPS failure should not take down your entire HA solution. If your setup includes two servers, two A1000 arrays, two monitors, and so on, put each set of components on its own UPS.

- Do not consider a system safe unless every power cord is plugged into a UPS. During a power outage, you want every system component to work— the monitors and tape drives are not exceptions.

- Test the batteries on your UPS devices to make sure you will have enough time to shut systems down gracefully. An underpowered UPS is almost as bad as no UPS at all.

To avoid single points of failure within your server hardware, use as much redundancy as possible. If you're using the Ultra Enterprise line of servers, you need enough internal power supplies to absorb the loss of one. Mirror your OS and swap disks. If multiple CPU boards are installed and you have only two CPUs, be sure to place one on each board. Mirror your disks across multiple controllers; if you lose a controller, you won't lose the data on both disks. When using SPARC storage arrays for your storage, mirror across arrays or, if you have only one array, throw in a spare optical module in each system.

If using an E10000, don't assume failover within the box will always be an option. Cluster with another server able to handle minimally the most mission critical domains, and preferably all domains, although at degraded performance. Within the E10K there are still single points of failure, such as the centerplane which can render the entire box inoperable. Planning ahead is always a good idea. And please . . . don't try to use your SSP as one of your failover devices. . . .

For any specific piece of external hardware that is not redundant, such as a tape jukebox or modem, you should have interfaces ready and waiting that can accommodate those devices on your other servers. This might involve having a kernel ready, but a reboot with a -r (i.e., boot -r) with the device attached will serve the purpose. In the case of moving tape drives or jukeboxes, running both the drvconfig and tapes command will make those devices immediately accessible.

Install additional network interfaces to be employed in case of adapter failure. A failover to the second adaptor can be accomplished easily and allow you to postpone repairs indefinitely; a couple of ifconfig commands—one to shut down the malfunctioning interface and one to start up the second—and moving the network cable and you're back in business. Please don't consider multiple ports on a QFE (Quad Fast Ethernet) board sufficient. Chances are, when you lose one port, you lose them all. Also, for completeness, primary and alternate interfaces should be plugged into separate network switches or hubs. If the hub or switch is the problem, you could have your system looping between adapters with no way to get messages out.

For example, if there are two hme (hundred meg ethernet) interfaces on a system, one live, hme0—ip address 1.2.3.4 subnetted to a class C, and one dormant, hme1, the commands needed to migrate the ip address from hme0 to hme1 would be:

/usr/sbin/ifconfig hme0 0.0.0.0 down

/usr/sbin/ifconfig hme0 unplumb

/usr/sbin/ifconfig hme1 plumb

/usr/sbin/ifconfig hme1 1.2.3.4 netmask 255.255.255.0 up

If hme1 were already live with another address on the same subnet, hme1 would be replaced with hme1:1, as Solaris allows up to 255 virtual addresses per adapter.

One can argue that if Failover software is used, these redundancies are not needed. While HA software will provide proper failover within a specified time frame, the best HA solution is one where system failover never happens. In other words, make each system in itself highly available, then couple these independently highly available systems with other highly available systems. Regardless of how good HA software is, in most cases that software will be restarting on an alternate system and all network connections will be severed and system states will not be retained. By having redundant components within the system itself, the system can heal itself without having to take down any of the running applications.

You must determine if you will need any of your own scripts, programs, or third-party utilities during a failover. If so, these should either be located on shared disks, copied to all HA servers, or mirrored to the other servers. For products requiring license keys, ask your vendors for a key to be used only in case of a failure. For a tape jukebox and backup software, be sure you can use any of the servers in the HA configuration as the backup server.

In regard to your applications, decide which ones are mission critical and should be part of the HA environment. Determine their system requirements. If the worst possible calamity happened and everything was failed to a single server, could that server handle the load? Nothing should be hard coded in any application that would preclude its operation on another server.

Once single points of failure have been eliminated, it will be time to get the hardware and software fully prepped for a smooth failover (i.e., a takeover of data and applications elsewhere on your network) when a server fails completely or partially.

HA Configuration

Originally, HA solutions were all one-into-one configurations, each server requiring a twin server as an idle hot standby. Only complete system failovers—all services migrating to the standby—were performed when any failure occurred on the primary server. A one-into-one configuration is depicted in Figure 13.1. Today, there are many types of HA solutions to choose from that can provide M-into-N, symmetrical, and asymmetrical failovers. Figure 13.2 depicts a many-into-one configuration.

An asymmetrical HA configuration consists of two servers, with failover occurring in one direction only. Symmetrical HA involves possible failovers in either direction. M-into-N involves M services running on N servers, with any of the services able to fail over to any of the other servers. HA packages all perform some sort of or clustering. Clustering can be defined as the combination of multiple systems with shared resources. In most cases those shared resources are disk space and IP addresses. Most clustering HA packages have two major facets to their operation: heartbeats and service groups. The *heartbeat* provides the connection between all of the systems in your HA cluster. Most heartbeats

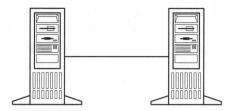

Figure 13.1 One-into-one.

require at least one private network—although two such networks is recommended, both for redundancy and elimination of the heartbeat as a single point of failure. Some HA packages utilize multicasts or broadcasts to determine the members of the cluster. We recommend, therefore, that you not place heartbeats on your public network, lest your corporate network evangelist club you over the head with a sniffer. Also, if you cannot use a separate hub for each private network, crossover cables are recommended for one-into-one configurations, as a single hub would constitute an unacceptable single point of failure.

For partial failovers (i.e., only some services fail), applications are split into service groups. Each service group is a logical unit that can be failed over on its own. For example, a server that is running two instances of Sybase SQL server and one instance of Oracle and providing NFS home directory services would have four logical service groups. Each of these groups would be assigned its own IP address. Port numbers for the database instances should be kept distinct among all instances within the cluster.

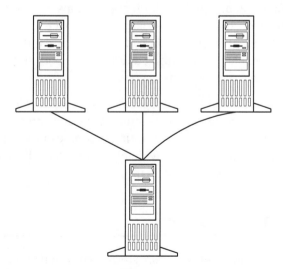

Figure 13.2 Many-into-one.

All drives and volumes for each service group should be placed in their own disk groups if using Veritas Volume Manager. If you're using Solstice Disk Suite, make sure your metadevices for each service group don't share drives, and that you have enough configuration copies of the metadb defined. If this is a small HA configuration with dual-ported SCSI disks between two systems, the SCSI targets (Logical Unit Numbers of LUN's) must not conflict for the controllers that are dual ported. Also, when planning out the disk layouts, keep in mind what will happen if one of those devices fails. If using multiple disk arrays, try to keep each side of a mirror on one array. The authors have seen cases where volumes consisted of discs across two arrays, then the mirror of that volume was across the same two arrays. When one array failed, both sides of the mirror were toast. In a shared disk HA configuration, you still need something to share in order for failover to work. Keep this in mind when applications start requiring additional disk space or business areas don't want to pay for the added costs of mirrored disk. Disk is cheap, lost business is not.

The key to service groups is remembering that IP addresses need to be distinct for each service. No multiple adapters? Don't worry—Solaris supports up to 255 virtual IP addresses for each adapter. For those that don't know, the syntax for starting up a new virtual address is *ifconfig interface:virtual# IP-address*. For example, *ifconfig hme0:1 191.29.71.48* starts up a second virtual address for the hme0 interface.

Why would we want to fail over a single service? There are a number of good reasons. Let's examine two examples:

In the first example, a controller failure on an application's primary system (machine one) causes a failover of that one service to the secondary system (machine two). Performance will be much better if applications not affected by the failure continue running on machine one than if all services fail over to machine two. By allowing a single application to fail over, hardware maintenance can be scheduled for machine one during a noncritical period when the rest of the services can be failed over with little consequence.

In the second example, you are testing a new operating system. If you have an asymmetrical configuration with two machines—one production and one test—with dual-ported storage between them, the operating system can be upgraded on the test box and each service failed over individually to methodically test how each application runs on the new operating system.

Rolling Your Own—Can It Be Done?

Once you've built redundancy into your servers, determined which applications are critical, and thoroughly thought through your failover scenarios, your environment is ready for HA. With the purchase of Open Vision by VERITAS, there are now three major vendors of HA software for the Sun Solaris environment: Legato, Sun, and VERITAS. Each of the HA packages offered by these companies has strengths and weaknesses. Should you consider rolling your own? Is it possible? Is it worth doing?

The first thing you need to determine is what type of availability is really needed. If you have mission-critical applications, buy the software. If, on the other hand, you can get by with modest lapses in service, but want to improve the uptime of non-mission-critical projects, then it is possible to create your own HA on a shoestring.

But while it is possible, we don't recommend it. Buy the software if you have the budget. If you cannot buy the software, consider whether you have the time to write and support a custom solution. This is probably the time to bring management in to help weigh the pros and cons of in-house development of an HA solution. One major plus for purchasing an HA package is the ability to point a finger and know whom to call when there is a problem.

Disclaimer: If you are planning to develop your own HA solution, a lab environment is highly recommended to test and verify your work. A misconfigured or misbehaving HA product can wreak havoc on an otherwise well-functioning network. You should insist that you be given opportunities to test your failover routines in an environment where no one else will be affected.

If you decide to proceed with an in-house solution and feel that you know the risks, here are the major components you will need to implement in your HA solution:

- The ability to start, stop, and test each service from all servers
- The ability to bring physical and virtual network interfaces up and down and to add and delete virtual IP addresses
- The ability to import, export, and start disk groups and volumes
- The ability to monitor the status of service groups and servers
- The ability to send notification

How much downtime and manual intervention you are willing to accept will determine how much functionality you need to implement into your HA solution. If you can accept a manual failover, you can simply write a script to import the drives and disk groups, configure the interface, and start the application. Procedures can then be written for operators to run these scripts as required. Figures 13.3 and 13.4 show a user oblivious to a failover that moves his access from one server to another. Do you need this level of seamlessness or can failovers be allowed to cause brief interruptions in service?

Any of the components listed can be built via scripts. Most applications you are running should already have start scripts (see Chapter 4). Developing methods to determine whether an application is up and how to bring it down (hopefully other than kill -9) should be rudimentary. Using ifconfig to start an interface is also simple, but you don't want to bring up an IP address on one machine while it is still being used on another. Before you use ifconfig, ping the address and make sure that you don't get a response; if you get a response, the address is in use. The same goes for the importing of disk groups: VERITAS Volume Manager makes it quite easy to import a disk group (vxdg import disk group) and start volumes (vxrecover -g disk group). It even has a force option (-f) to ensure that the group is imported. To make your HA solution, the group needs to be

Figure 13.3 Before failure.

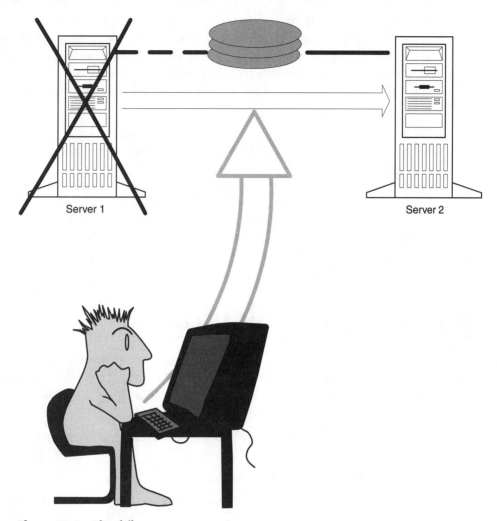

Figure 13.4   After failure.

exported when the application is brought down on the original server, if possible, and imported file systems should be *fsck*ed prior to being mounted.

Probably the toughest task in rolling your own is the communication between the servers. Determining what is up, what is down, and who holds the ball for each service is not as simple as it sounds. For reliability, this should be accomplished across the private network. For each service, you need to maintain where the service is currently being run, and the machine to which it is to fail over in case of a failure.

Once your solution in place, the hard part begins. HA is now a part of your system. Any system upgrade, patch, or added application will most likely require modifications to both the other systems in the cluster and your failover software. Mirroring changes on all systems means that Operating System levels and patch clusters need to be synchronized in order to prevent unforeseen circumstances. Test failovers regularly, both on a system and service group basis. The worst time to find out your HA solution doesn't work is when you need it.

The HA cluster can also be used to test applications in a new operating environment. This is recommended for use in development environments only, as changes can cause unforeseen consequences. In this scenario, a node in the development cluster would be backed up then the OS would be upgraded or patched to the new releases for testing. Then, applications can be failed over to the new node and tested on the new OS or patch level and failed back. This works well in most cases. Beware incompatibilities in raid software such as VERITAS Volume Manager or Online Disk Suite. Keep good backups in case the testing corrupts the data.

Choosing a Third-Party HA Solution

When choosing a third-party HA vendor, you should consider all the options prior to making a decision. As we mentioned earlier, each vendor's product has pluses and minuses. Here is a list of questions that you should ask of each HA vendor:

- Is the installation simple? Can a cluster be installed in hours, days, or weeks?
- Are the test intervals customizable?
- Does the solution provide for symmetric, asymmetric, or N-node cluster capabilities?
- Are service groups supported, or is it system-level failover only?
- Does the solution support the servers and OS versions you are currently using or plan to use in the future?
- Are kernel modifications required to implement the solution?
- What types of disks and RAID software are supported?
- Can the solution be customized for in-house applications?
- What type of modules or agents are available (Sybase, Oracle, NFS, or HTTP)?
- Is root access required for all access to the applications?
- How is planned application downtime handled?

After these questions have been answered, you can make an intelligent informed decision on which vendor to choose.

Implementing Your Solution

You have chosen a vendor and are ready to proceed to implement the solution. Remember the old adage—KISS (keep it simple, stupid)? Try to keep your configuration as clear and understandable as possible. The more complex the solution, the greater the chance for error. If you hire a consultant to implement your solution, be sure that internal employees also understand exactly how and why things are being set up. Establish procedures for anyone needing to interact with the HA system, so that mistakes can be confined to a minimum. Look for products that complement the HA package—like paging software. Finally, test all permutations of failovers on a regular basis. We can't reiterate this point enough. A nontested HA solution is probably a nonworking HA solution. Besides, you and other staff members will likely feel more comfortable with your solution if you have experience with it.

Summary

High availability solutions offer near-continuous availability of data and applications using redundant hardware and prepared software to accomplish or facilitate a smooth failover of services. You now know what HA is and isn't, how to plan for an HA configuration, and how to choose and implement an HA solution. These simple guidelines can help you create a highly available environment:

- Eliminate all single points of failure.
- Test failover regularly.
- Watch disk configurations and keep mirrors separate.
- Use redundant network components.
- Remember changes to one system should be applied to all systems in the cluster.
- Test failover regularly—especially after making changes. (It's important so it's listed twice!)
- Keep the design as simple as possible.

## PART THREE

Looking After Your Hardware

I
f you are a typical Systems Administrator, hardware is something that you try to
deal with as little as possible. If you are in a large corporate environment,
chances are you have Sun or a third party maintaining your equipment. No, this
section is not a SunService Field Guide nor is this section a detailed explanation of what every piece of Sun hardware is and does. Rather, this eclectic collection of chapters details items that will assist you with the software and
methodologies required to install and troubleshoot your hardware and keep it
running.

Chapter 14, "Maintaining Your Hardware," deals with system commands used
to troubleshoot your hardware and assist you in determining when a service
call should be placed. Also, for older Sun hardware, some common problems
and remedies are discussed.

Chapter 15, "Peripheral Vision," brings up a sysadmin's favorite subject:
modems and printers. Since the first Sun systems first rolled off the assembly
line in 1982, serial ports and the configuration of devices hung off them has
always been a challenge. This chapter is meant to assist you in understanding
how to install and troubleshoot these pesky devices.

Definitely not commonplace, Sun's crowning achievement—the Starfire—is the
subject of the last chapter in this section, Chapter 16: "Starfire—Not Just a Big
Unix Box." In it, we describe in detail the methodologies and commands used
to install, implement, and troubleshoot Sun's most prestigious and heaviest
piece of iron. Though it functions like any other Enterprise box from an OS

standpoint, the E10000 has many other features and peculiarities that make its administration unknown territory for even the most seasoned Solaris administrators. The E10000 is an extremely scalable, yet temperamental machine. If you support Starfires in your corporate environment, or just want to learn about its fascinating architecture, this section is a must read.

## CHAPTER 14

Maintaining Your Sun Hardware

While many of us use SunService or other third-party vendors for our systems maintenance, it is becoming increasingly important that we understand the details of what our hardware is and does. This knowledge is crucial if we are to assist our vendors in troubleshooting problems when they occur. A disturbing trend among service companies is to have a clear separation between service technicians who support software and those who support hardware. Most systems administrators, working in the trenches, realize that problems are not always that cut and dried.

This chapter discusses maintenance procedures that should be followed to keep your equipment running at peak efficiency and details what some of the more mysterious hardware is. Also, a long section on NVRAM should tell you everything you've ever wanted to know about your machine's identity and hardware parameters.

Troubleshooting Your System Hardware

Sun systems are renowned for running forever. The authors, in fact, have encountered numerous Sun systems that, aside from occasional OS upgrades, have run for 5 to 10 years without downtime. It is imperative, however, that the people administering Sun systems know how to test and maintain them. Many of the newer systems (sun4u, sun4d, etc.) come with impressive diagnostics that not only will report hardware faults, but will tell you the temperature of the boards in the system. This section provides an example of using the *prtdiag* command for troubleshooting, and then discusses both the OpenBoot PROM and NVRAM—the core of every SUN system.

First, here is a sample output from the prtdiag command on an E450. Note that, even if the hardware is thousands of miles away, you can get quite a bit of information about it by running this command in a telnet (or ssh) session.

```
./prtdiag -v
System Configuration:  Sun Microsystems  sun4u Sun Enterprise
450 (2 X UltraSPARC-II 400MHz)
System clock frequency: 100 MHz
Memory size: 512 Megabytes
```

As you can see, this system has two 400 MHz processors and 512Mb of RAM.

```
========================== CPUs ==========================

                       Run    Ecache   CPU     CPU
Brd   CPU   Module    MHz      MB     Impl.    Mask
---   ---   -------   -----   ------   ------   ----
SYS    1      1        400     4.0     US-II    9.0
SYS    3      3        400     4.0     US-II    9.0
```

This output shows that there are two system boards (labeled 1 and 3), each with a single CPU module installed.

```
========================== Memory ==========================

         Interlv.  Socket   Size
Bank     Group     Name     (MB)   Status
----     -----     ------   ----   ------
  0      none      1901     128     OK
  0      none      1902     128     OK
  0      none      1903     128     OK
  0      none      1904     128     OK
```

On this E450, there are four 128Mb dual in-line memory modules (DIMMs) installed. All of them are reportedly running fine.

```
========================== IO Cards ==========================

      Bus   Freq
Brd   Type  MHz   Slot  Name             Model
---   ----  ----  ----  -------------------------------   -------
--------------
SYS   PCI    33    5    pciclass,001000                   Symbios,53C875
SYS   PCI    33    7    pciclass,068000
SYS   PCI    33    10   SUNW,m64B  ATY,GT-B

No failures found in System
```

Next, we see that prtdiag has found nothing wrong with the system. Note that if NVRAM has been replaced, all failure information is cleared.

```
========================= Environmental Status
=========================

System Temperatures (Celsius):
------------------------------
AMBIENT   23
CPU 1     40
CPU 3     40

==================================
```

The temperature on the system boards is one of the more important things to watch. The higher the temperature becomes, the more the chance there is of developing a problem. If the temperature exceeds 50 degrees Celsius (122 degrees Fahrenheit), you run the risk of the system shutting itself down to prevent further overheating. Note that if your system keeps shutting itself down because of temperature, you have a cooling issue that should be resolved. When the temperature gets too hot, the displayed message will show up as *WARNING* or *CRITICAL*.

```
Front Status Panel:
-------------------
Keyswitch position is in Diagnostic mode.

System LED Status:    POWER       GENERAL ERROR      ACTIVITY
                      [ ON]          [OFF]            [ ON]
                      DISK ERROR  THERMAL ERROR  POWER SUPPLY ERROR

  [OFF]        [OFF]                [ERROR]

Disk LED Status:       OK = GREEN      ERROR = YELLOW
                DISK 10: [EMPTY]    DISK 11: [EMPTY]
                DISK  8: [EMPTY]    DISK  9: [EMPTY]
                DISK  6: [EMPTY]    DISK  7: [EMPTY]
                DISK  4: [EMPTY]    DISK  5: [EMPTY]
                DISK  2:   [OK]     DISK  3:   [OK]
                DISK  0:   [OK]     DISK  1:   [OK]

==================================
```

This display is equivalent to the status lights on the box and will show errors when they occur. In this case, it looks like one of the power supplies is bad and should be replaced.

```
Fans:
-----
Fan Bank  Speed   Status
--------  -----   ------
CPU        49      OK
PWR        31      OK
```

```
Power Supplies:
---------------
Supply    Rating   Temp   Status
------    ------   ----   ------
  0       550 W    37     OK
  1       550 W    35     OK
  2       550 W    34     OK

========================= HW Revisions =========================
```

The next section shows all of the hardware revisions of the boards in your system. You should check prior to performing OS upgrades to make sure there are no upgrades in hardware required, as well. Hardware compatibility lists can be found at http://sunsolve.sun.com.

```
ASIC Revisions:
---------------
STP2223BGA: Rev 4
STP2223BGA: Rev 4
STP2223BGA: Rev 4
STP2003QFP: Rev 1
STP2205BGA: Rev 1
FEPS: SUNW,hme Rev c1

System PROM revisions:
----------------------
  OBP 3.12.2 1998/09/14 11:28   POST 6.0.6 1998/07/16 18:40
```

The OpenBoot PROM (OBP) level is extremely important to correct system operation. Make sure that OBP levels are checked at least quarterly, as many seemingly hardware problems can be related to boot PROM levels.

Upgrading the OpenBoot PROM Level

Upgrading your boot or flash PROMs is as simple and painless as a tooth extraction. And, while you won't get sued for malpractice if you mess up, you can render your system totally inoperable and require a system board replacement.

E3X00/4X00/5000/6X00

If you are especially lucky, you'll have Ultra Enterprise machines. These are the only systems that can be safely upgraded *while* they are up and running. A reboot is required to activate the new firmware. You should write down the values of all of your NVRAM settings in case the variables are reset to their defaults during reprogramming. Also, make sure that the front panel key switch is in the secure position and that Jumper P601 is off. If the jumper is on, the system board's flash PROMs will be write-protected and you will see an error to this effect. The series of steps required to upgrade is as follows:

1. Download the update from SunSolve.

2. Execute the *flash-update* binary with the highest revision level. It will extract and install the flashprom driver on the system. Then, it runs the executable to start the update process. The program displays the current revision of the PROMs in your system and the versions that are available. You will be asked whether you wish to proceed with the update. Once you answer yes (i.e., y), the reprogramming begins automatically. The program will then display its progress at every step. Here is a sample output where a machine has boards 0, 2, and 3, and its flashproms are being updated:

```
# ./flash-update-<latest-rev>
Generating flashprom driver...
Generating SUNW,Ultra-Enterprise flash-update program...

Current System Board PROM Revisions:
------------------------------------
Board  0:        cpu OBP   3.4.2 1998/01/20 11:17 POST  3.0.3
1998/02/19 13:54
Board  2:        cpu OBP   3.4.2 1998/01/20 11:17 POST  3.0.3
1998/02/19 13:54
Board  3: dual-sbus FCODE 1.7.0 1998/03/20 07:07 iPOST 3.0.3
1998/02/16 13:55

Available 'Update' Revisions:
-----------------------------
cpu OBP   3.4.3 1996/04/04 20:23 POST  4.1.4 1998/04/04 20:23
dual-sbus FCODE 2.7.0 1998/03/04 20:23 iPOST 4.1.4 1998/04/04 20:23
upa-sbus FCODE 2.7.0 1998/03/04 20:23 iPOST 4.1.4 1998/04/04 20:23

Verifying Checksums: Okay

Do you wish to flash update your firmware? y/[n] : y   ← Enter y here
Are you sure? y/[n] : y ← Enter y here

Updating Board 0: Type 'cpu'
1 Erasing ... Done.
1 Verifying Erase ... Done.
1 Programming ... Done.
1 Verifying Program ... Done.

Updating Board 2: Type 'cpu'
1 Erasing ... Done.
1 Verifying Erase ... Done.
1 Programming ... Done.
1 Verifying Program ... Done.

Updating Board 3: Type 'dual-sbus'
1 Erasing ... Done.
1 Verifying Erase ... Done.
1 Programming ... Done.
1 Verifying Program ... Done.
```

The number displayed on the leftmost column is the pass number. If any of the four steps listed here fail, all four steps have to be repeated and the pass number will be incremented.

Desktop Flash PROM Update

For desktop machines (Ultra 1, 2, 5, 20, 30, 250 or 450), the process is more painful. Essentially, a new boot image needs to be installed that boots a single purpose kernel used for updating the flash PROMs. Download the appropriate flash files from SunSolve. Copy the boot image to the root directory and give it a name you can remember.

```
# cp flash*latest   /flashboot
# chmod 755 /flashboot
Now bring the machine down to the ok prompt then physically
power off the system.
#init 0
ok
```

Next, jumper J2003 on each machine needs to be set to write enable (pins 2 and 3) in order to enable updating of the flash PROMs.

NOTE

These jumpers should be touched only while the power is *off* and you are wearing an antistatic strap.

Once the jumper is set and the machine is put back together, power the system back on. Hit the Stop-A keys when you see the banner. You should then be back at the ok prompt.

Issue the command *boot disk /flashboot*, replacing *disk* with the appropriate alias if you are not using *disk* as your disk alias. If you are booting over the network (i.e., boot net), the flashboot file should have been placed in the corresponding root directory for this client on the server providing the files. In other words, if the system machine1 is booting off of machine2, the flashboot file should be /export/root/machine2/flashboot.

A version of the following menu will appear:

```
Standalone Flash PROM Update Utility, Rev. 2.0
  Ultra(tm) 1
  Ultra(tm) 2
  Ultra(tm) 5/10
  Ultra(tm) 30
  Ultra(tm) 60
  Ultra(tm) Enterprise(tm) 250
  Ultra(tm) Enterprise(tm) 450
```

This utility allows you to interactively update the firmware
revisions in specific system Flash PROM components.

Type h for help, q to quit, Return or Enter to continue: ← **Hit Enter here.**

Every precaution should be taken to prevent the loss of system
power during the Flash PROM programming process!

Type h for help, q to quit, Return or Enter to continue: ← **Hit Enter here.**

```
         Firmware Release(s)              Firmware Release(s)
Currently Existing in the System     Available for Installation  /  Install?
--------------------------------     ------------------------------------------
OBP  3.1.2 1996/03/28 17:08          OBP  3.1.5 1996/08/27 16:13       no
POST 3.1.4 1996/04/09 03:23          POST 3.1.5 1996/06/28 11:54       no
```

Type sa if you wish to select all available firmware releases for
installation. Type h for help, quit to exit, or cont to continue: ← **Enter**
sa **to update all PROMs.**

```
         Firmware Release(s)              Firmware Release(s)
Currently Existing in the System     Available for Installation  /  Install?
--------------------------------     ------------------------------------------
OBP  3.1.2 1996/03/28 17:08          OBP  3.1.5 1996/08/27 16:13       YES
POST 3.1.4 1996/04/09 03:23          POST 3.1.5 1996/06/28 11:54       YES
```

Type sa if you wish to select all available firmware releases for
installation. Type h for help, quit to exit, or cont to continue: ← **Enter**
cont **at this point.**

The Flash programming process is about to begin.

Type h for help, q to quit, Return or Enter to continue: ← **Once again hit**
Enter.

Erasing the top half of the Flash PROM.
Programming OBP into the top half of the Flash PROM.
Verifying OBP in the top half of the Flash PROM.

Erasing the bottom half of the Flash PROM.
Programming OBP into the bottom half of Flash PROM.
Verifying OBP in the bottom half of the Flash PROM.

Erasing the top half of the Flash PROM.
Programming POST into the top half of Flash PROM.
Verifying POST in the top half of the Flash PROM.

Programming was successful.

Resetting

At this point, physically power off the system. Then power it back on and let it come back up. Your programming is complete!

NVRAM—The Heart of the System

The nonvolatile random-access memory (NVRAM) problems are among the most annoying. The contents of the NVRAM chip can become corrupted for a variety of reasons, most commonly, failure of the embedded battery. The battery embedded in the NVRAM chip keeps the clock running when the machine is off and also maintains important system configuration information. This section tells you how to reprogram your NVRAM chip and where to buy a new one, should you need to replace your current NVRAM chip. If your NVRAM is no longer functional, you'll need to purchase a new chip. For some problems, it is possible to reprogram your NVRAM, as long as your system retains its hostid and MAC address and the clock keeps time when the machine is turned off.

NVRAM problems can usually be easily identified. Your system looks like it is trying to come up, but, because of its identity crisis, cannot do so. The output when the system is powered up will usually show an Ethernet address of all zeroes or all ones. Sun erroneously calls the media access control (MAC) address the "Ethernet" address. For those with asynchronous transfer mode (ATM), fiber distributed data interface (FDDI), Token Ring, or other network cards, this is not a correct term; however to keep things simple and sane, we will continue with this mistake.

Here is an example of what one would see in the case of an NVRAM failure:

```
Sun Workstation, Model Sun-XXXXXX Series.
ROM Rev X.X, XXMB memory installed
ID PROM invalid.
Testing 0 Megabytes of Memory ... Completed.
ERROR: missing or invalid ID prom
Requesting Internet address for 0:0:0:0:0:0
```

or

```
Sun Workstation, Model Sun-XXXX Series.
Type 4 Keyboard
ROM Rev X.X, XXMB memory installed, Serial #16777215
Ethernet address ff:ff:ff:ff:ff:ff, Host ID ffffffff

Invalid format type in NVRAM
The IDPROM contents are invalid
```

How do you fix this? The solution is to replace the NVRAM chip. The NVRAM chip holds the hostid, MAC address, and most of the system boot parameters. When this chip fails, replacement is usually required. Another possibility is that the onboard battery has failed. If replacing the NVRAM chip fails, the battery or system board may need to be replaced, depending on whether the battery is soldered onto the system board. This is an extremely common error on older Sparcstation 1, 2, IPC, and IPX devices. The information in this section applies to the following Sun architectures: sun4c, sun4m, sun4d, sun4u, and sun3x (but not to sun4 and sun3).

Changing the Ethernet Address

People can be asking either of two different questions when they ask how to change the Ethernet address of a workstation. If you merely want to change the Ethernet address of an *interface* on your system, you can use the ifconfig command and forget about the procedures in this document. The Ethernet address in NVRAM is the default address for all interfaces. If, for some reason, you want to change this default Ethernet address in NVRAM, then the instructions in this document will tell you how. Sun workstations are a little strange in this regard; they don't get their MAC addresses from the hardware itself.

Every Sun 3/80, sun4c, sun4u, and sun4m architecture machine contains an NVRAM chip. This NVRAM chip stores various configuration parameters (e.g., the boot device, amount of RAM to test, and so on), maintains the system clock, and also contains the IDPROM data, which is composed of the MAC address, date of manufacture, hostid, a version number, and a checksum. The name *IDPROM* is historical. On older machines—such as the sun2-, sun3-, and sun4-architecture machines—the hostid and Ethernet address were stored in a PROM called the IDPROM.

The sun4d machines (e.g., the SS1000) also have an NVRAM chip. However, the IDPROM information is stored in a flash EEPROM and is downloaded into the NVRAM during POST. You can also upload the IDPROM information from the NVRAM chip to the flash EEPROM, so you can change the value of IDPROM in the flash EEPROM by merely changing the NVRAM and uploading the new values.

This document is for people who want to accomplish one of the following tasks:

- Install a new NVRAM chip in a Sun 3/80, sun4c, or sun4m machine. Usually, this will be due to an NVRAM failure or the loss of the NVRAM password in full security mode.

- Change the hostid or Ethernet address of a Sun 3/80, sun4c, sun4m, sun4u, or sun4d machine.

- Restore a Sun 3/80, sun4c, sun4u, or sun4m machine with a corrupted NVRAM chip to working order.

We're going to focus on methods that involve reprogramming the chip from the Forth OpenBoot monitor (i.e., the ok prompt). As you may recall from Chapter 3, the OpenBoot monitor uses a modified version of Forth. Forth is a language similar to that used on the HP calculators and uses a Reverse Polish Notation (RPN) syntax. You don't really need to know any Forth to reprogram your IDPROM, but the following instructions below might make a little more sense if you do.

The NVRAM chip will usually have a white or yellow barcode label on it (except for sun4d). Given the barcode, Sun can reconstruct your original hostid and Ethernet address. On newer machines (some SS5 and SS20 and all Ultras), the number printed on the barcode is the last 3 bytes of the Ethernet address (the same as the last 3 bytes of the hostid). The first 3 bytes of the Ethernet address are always 8:0:20 and the first byte of the hostid is determined by the system type (see Table 14.1), so, on these machines, you can trivially reconstruct the hostid. We have no idea how to do it on the machines with the old-style barcode label but, if nothing else, the label makes the NVRAM chip easy to identify.

Table 14.1 gives the location of the NVRAM chip for various models of Sun workstation.

The NVRAM chips are SGS-Thomson Timekeeper (formerly Mostek) chips. They contain an embedded battery with a fixed life. When the machine is off, the battery runs down. It is very common for the battery embedded in the Timekeeper chip in an older Sun (sun4c, sun3x) to fail. Table 14.2 lists the NVRAM chip type by machine architecture.

The NVRAM chips used to be designated Mostek MK48T02, and so on. These chips come in various speeds. The newer SGS-Thomson part numbers are M48T02-200PC1 for the 200 ns systems and M48T02-, M48T08-100PC1 for the 100 ns M48T08. The 200-ns chips are adequate for any Sun, but often the faster chips are easier to come by, and there is no harm in buying them. If you have trouble tracking down a local SGS-Thomson distributor, Mouser electronics also sells the SGS-Thomson Timekeeper chips (telephone: 1-800-346-6873, 1-817-483-5712). You can also order from Mouser on the Web at www. mouser.com. The Mouser stock numbers as of 1995 are slightly different than the usual part numbers, as shown in Table 14.3. As of October 1995, the prices for these chips from Mouser ranged from U.S. $16.00 to $23.12. We have no affiliation with Mouser other than as customers.

Dallas Semiconductor makes a clone of the SGS-Thomson M48T02 chip, the DS1642. We've had mixed experience using the Dallas chips in Suns. Our experience is that these chips do not work properly in the following machines: 3/80, SS2, and IPX (they fail POST, but otherwise seem okay). However, the Dallas chips are reported to work in the following machines: SS1, SS1+, and IPC. We

Table 14.1   NVRAM Chip Location on Various Sun Workstations

MODEL	SOCKET NUMBER
3/80	U0205
4/60 (SS1)	U089
4/40 (IPC)	U0901
4/65 (SS1+)	U089
4/20 (SLC)	U1011
4/25 (ELC)	U0813
4/50 (IPX)	U0512
4/75 (SS2)	U0512
4E	U1101
4/10 (SPARCclassic X)	U0707
4/15 (SPARCclassic)	U0707
4/30 (LX/ZX)	U0707
Sparc Xterm 1	U1605
SS4	U1605
SS5	U1506
SS10	U1004
SS20	U1004
SS600MP	U2701
SS240 (Voyager)	U1506
SS1000/1000E	U1007
SS2000/2000E	U1205
U1/170	U2006

Table 14.2   NVRAM Chip Type in Various Sun Machine Architectures

MODEL	NVRAM
sun4c	M48T02
sun4m	M48T08/18
sun4d	M48T08
sun4u	M48T59Y
sun3x	M48T02

Table 14.3 Mouser Stock Numbers as of 1995

SGS-THOMSON PART	MOUSER STOCK NUMBER	SPEED	CAPACITY
M48T02-200PC1	511-M48T0220PC1	200 ns	2K
M48T02-150PC1	511-M48T0215PC1	150 ns	2K
M48T02-120PC1	511-M48T0212PC1	120 ns	2K
M48T08-150PC1	511-M48T0815PC1	150 ns	8K
M48T08-100PC1	511-M48T0810PC1	100 ns	8K
M48T59Y-70PC1	511-M48T59Y70PC1	70 ns	8K

have no idea whether the Dallas chips work properly in the SLC and ELC systems. You can order the DS1642 chips in 120- or 150-ns speeds (150 ns is fine) directly from Dallas in quantities up to 10 by calling 1-800-336-6933 and giving Dallas a credit card number. Data sheets and distributor lists for Dallas are available from www.dalsemi.com. Stanislav Sinyagin <stas@isf.ru> reports that the M48T12 is another acceptable alternative for the SS1.

General sun4c, sun4m, sun4d, and sun4u IDPROM Programming

If you have a valid NVRAM chip installed (IDPROM is okay) then, before doing anything else, write down a copy of the IDPROM information. You can get it by executing the command */usr/sbin/prtconf -vp*. Alternatively, you can get the IDPROM information at the OpenBoot monitor ok prompt by typing the command *.idprom* (yes, the dot is part of the command). You'll need this information if the NVRAM gets screwed up and you need to back out.

Step 1: Go to the OpenBoot Monitor

Go to the OpenBoot monitor (ok prompt). You can do this by turning on your machine, pressing L1/Stop-A to interrupt the boot sequence, and entering *new command mode*. Alternatively, if your machine is running, just shut down your operating system (e.g., init 0).

If you are installing a new NVRAM, type **set-defaults** followed by the Enter key and then **setenv diag-switch? False** followed by the Enter key.

Generally, a machine will reset the NVRAM to the default values (excluding the IDPROM information) when it detects a new NVRAM. Still, it is good to do a set-defaults just in case this fails.

Step 2:

The command to reprogram the IDPROM part of NVRAM is *mkp*. The format for the command is:

```
<value> <location> mkp
```

Here, location is read off Table 14.4 (all values are in hexadecimal). Note that some Sun clones (e.g., Tatung COMPstation 25 with TWS boot PROM REV 1.7), don't have an mkp command. If mkp doesn't work on your system, see the later section entitled "Other More Arcane Methods for Modifying the IDPROM."

As previously mentioned, you can look at the complete IDPROM by executing the command *.idprom*. Bytes c through e in Table 14.4 are collectively referred to as the *serial number*. If you convert the concatenation of bytes c to e to decimal, this is the serial number you see when you turn the machine on.

Alternatively, you can use the *idprom* command to get a particular byte from the IDPROM, like this:

```
<location> idprom@
```

This returns the IDPROM value of byte <location>. So,

```
<location> idprom@ .
```

prints the IDPROM value of byte <location> because the dot is the Forth command to print the value on the bottom of the stack.

Next, make the changes using mkp. Be very careful and be sure to compute the checksum after making changes. If you don't, you'll get nasty warnings about an incorrect IDPROM checksum on boot. A quick-and-dirty way to compute and store the checksum in location f is to execute the following at the ok prompt *after* you have made your changes to locations 0 to -e:

Table 14.4 IDPROM Location Values

BYTES	CONTENTS
0	Always 01—format/version number
1	First byte of hostid (machine type)
2-7	6-byte Ethernet address (first 3 bytes should be 08,00,20)
8-b	Date of manufacture (usually all 0s, doesn't really matter)
C	Second byte of hostid
D	Third byte of hostid
E	Fourth byte of hostid
F	IDPROM checksum—bitwise XOR of bytes 0-e

```
0 f 0 do i idprom@ xor loop f mkp
```

Don't change the first byte of the hostid to something that doesn't correspond to your system type (see Table 14.5). Similarly, the first 3 bytes of the Ethernet address should be 08, 00, 20. The first byte of the hostid is often used to determine the architecture when booting from CD-ROM on some Sun models. If you don't set the first 3 bytes of the Ethernet address to 08, 00, 20 you might get a message that says you have a defective system board. We don't know of any other consequences of changing this to some reasonable value, but especially avoid ff:ff:ff:ff:ff:ff!. On some systems, you can get away with changing the first 3 bytes of the Ethernet address to more or less anything you want.

If you'd rather not use Table 14.5, you can find out what you should make the first byte of the hostid by typing **real-machine-type .** at the ok prompt. Note that this command may not be defined on some machines with older boot PROMs.

Here's an example. Here, we modify the hostid of an IPX to be 57c0ffee and the Ethernet address to be 08:00:20:c0:ff:ee. At the OpenBoot monitor ok prompt, do this:

```
1 0 mkp
real-machine-type 1 mkp
8 2 mkp
0 3 mkp
20 4 mkp
c0 5 mkp
ff 6 mkp
ee 7 mkp
0 8 mkp
0 9 mkp
0 a mkp
0 b mkp
c0 c mkp
ff d mkp
ee e mkp
0 f 0 do i idprom@ xor loop f mkp
```

Step 3:

If you are on an SS1000, type **update-system-idprom** at the OpenBoot PROM ok prompt.

For any of these machines, you next type **reset** at the ok prompt. Your machine should then attempt to reboot with your new hostid/enet addr.

Table 14.5 matches Sun system models with the first byte of the hostid.

Table 14.5 Sun Models and Hostids

BYTE	MODEL
01	2/1x0
02	2/50
11	3/160
12	3/50
13	3/2x0
14	3/110
17	3/60
18	3/e
21	4/2x0
22	4/1x0
23	4/3x0
24	4/4x0
31	386I
41	3/4x0
42	3/80
51	SPARCstation 1 (4/60)
52	SPARCstation IPC (4/40)
53	SPARCstation 1+ (4/65)
54	SPARCstation SLC (4/20)
55	SPARCstation 2 (4/75)
56	SPARCstation ELC
57	SPARCstation IPX (4/50)
61	4/e
71	4/6x0
72	SPARCstation 10 or SPARCstation 20
80	SPARCstation Classic, LX, 4, 5, SS1000, Voyager, and Ultra 1

A Quick-and-Dirty Guide to Restoring the NVRAM of a sun4c/m/u Machine

This section is for folks who need to replace the NVRAM chip in a sun4c, sun4m, or sun4u machine and don't want to bother with the XOR calculations or with the details provided in the preceding sections on how to do this with mkp. We are assuming that you have a brand-new NVRAM chip in hand. All the numbers in the following discussion are in hex.

First, decide what Ethernet address you want to use and what you want for the last 3 bytes of the hostid. The Ethernet address should begin with 08:00:20. There are no restrictions on the last 3 bytes of the hostid. Say the Ethernet address is 08:00:20:E3:E4:E5 and the last 3 bytes of the hostid are H1, H2, H3. The first byte of the hostid will automatically be set according to the system type (real-machine-type variable in the OpenBoot monitor).

Turn off the machine. Remove the old NVRAM chip after noting the orientation. Insert the new NVRAM chip. Be sure to insert it in the correct orientation, as installing it in the wrong orientation and powering on the machine will generally destroy the chip. Power up the machine and bring it to the ok prompt. At the ok prompt execute the following commands:

```
set-defaults
setenv diag-switch? false
8 0 20 E3 E4 E5 H1H2H3 mkpl
```

The *mkpl* command expects some input (but it doesn't prompt you). The input is a Ctrl-D followed by a Ctrl-R. If mkpl does *not* print a copyright notice, then it changed the IDPROM. You should make sure by looking at the idprom after using mkpl by executing the .idprom command.

For example, the command *8 0 20 13 de ad c0ffee mkpl* will set the last 3 bytes of the hostid to c0ffee and the Ethernet address to 08:00:20:13:de:ad.

NOTE

mkpl will work only if the IDPROM checksum is *invalid.* Otherwise, it will simply print a copyright notice after you type the Ctrl-R. So, if you can't get mkpl to work as described, you can try making the IDPROM checksum invalid. You can invalidate the IDPROM checksum in an NVRAM with a valid IDPROM checksum by executing *f idprom 1 xor f mkp* (it seems that invalidating the version number will also do the trick, e.g., *17 0 mkp*). If you still can't get mkpl to work, then you should try using mkp as described in the preceding section. This note was added because, on some machines, set-defaults will set the IDPROM checksum according to the other values in the IDPROM.

Examples of Restoring the NVRAM

As we said earlier in this chapter, you should be careful that the first byte of the hostid matches the system type.

1. Modify the hostid of an IPX to be 57c0ffee and the Ethernet address to be 08:00:20:c0:ff:ee. At the OpenBoot PROM monitor prompt, do this:

```
01 0 mkp
57 1 mkp
08 2 mkp
0 3 mkp
20 4 mkp
c0 5 mkp
ff 6 mkp
ee 7 mkp
57 8 mkp
0 9 mkp
0 a mkp
0 b mkp
c0 c mkp
ff d mkp
ee e mkp
29 f mkp
```

Note the simplification in this example. If you make the Ethernet address 08:00:20:H1:H2:H3 and the 4 bytes of the hostid ST, H1, H2, H3, where ST is the system type byte, and you put ST, 0, 0, 0 in the date-of-manufacture field, then the IDPROM checksum will always be 29 (remember, all of these numbers are hexadecimal). This makes things a bit easier. You can, in general, just enter the following:

```
01 0 mkp
real-machine-type 1 mkp
08 2 mkp
0 3 mkp
20 4 mkp
H1 5 mkp
H2 6 mkp
H3 7 mkp
real-machine-type 8 mkp
0 9 mkp
0 a mkp
0 b mkp
H1 c mkp
H2 d mkp
H3 e mkp
29 f mkp
```

And you don't need to calculate the checksum, since it will always be 0x29.

2. Change the hostid of an SS10 to be 72c0ffee and the Ethernet address to be 08:00:20:c0:ff:ee as shown here:

```
01 0 mkp
72 1 mkp
08 2 mkp
0  3 mkp
20 4 mkp
c0 5 mkp
ff 6 mkp
ee 7 mkp
0 8 mkp
0 9 mkp
0 a mkp
0 b mkp
c0 c mkp
ff d mkp
ee e mkp
0 f 0 do i idprom@ xor loop f mkp
```

3. Change the hostid of an SS1000 to 80c0ffee. Leave the Ethernet address and the date of manufacture intact. Note that the system type byte for the SS1000 is 0x80.

```
c0 c mkp
ff d mkp
ee e mkp
0 f 0 do i idprom@ xor loop f mkp
update-system-idprom
```

4. Install a new NVRAM in an IPX. Set the hostid to 57c0ffee and the Ethernet address to be 08:00:20:c0:ff:ee.

   a) Turn the machine off.

   b) Remove the old NVRAM chip.

   c) Install the new NVRAM chip. Be sure to get the orientation right.

   d) Turn the machine on.

   e) At the OpenBoot monitor prompt, execute the following commands:

   ```
   set-defaults
   setenv diag-switch? false
   8 0 20 c0 ff ee c0ffee mkpl
   ^D^R
   ```

Here, ^D represents Ctrl-D, and so on.

Tips and Tricks for Your Hardware Adventures

This section provides some tips for use when your hardware is especially uncooperative. NVRAM problems do not occur often. Still, it's good to know something about how they look and what you can do about them.

Resetting the NVRAM When Stop-N Doesn't Do It

You might need to recover from the loss of an NVRAM password (in full security mode) or if you mess up your nvramrc. The safest thing to do is pay the $20 for a new timekeeper chip. Compared to the trouble you might run into, this is a small price to pay.

Other More Arcane Methods for Modifying the IDPROM

The mkp and mkpl commands are not the only ways to modify the IDPROM. Before we discovered these commands, we used to use procedures like those shown following. The material in this section assumes that you have access to the OpenBoot PROM manual, which is part of the Solaris 2.x Answerbook and can be found online at http://docs.sun.com.

You can use the OpenBoot monitor to find the virtual address of the NVRAM by following these steps:

1. First, cd to the EEPROM device (you can find its exact name via show-devs)

2. Execute *.attributes* or *.properties* depending upon whether you have V2 or V3 of the OpenBoot PROM.

3. Execute *device-end* followed by *reset*.
   For example:

```
ok show-devs
...
/obio/eeprom@0,200000
...
ok cd /obio/eeprom@0,200000
ok .attributes
address: ffee9000
...
ok device-end
ok reset
```

From this point, you can modify and look at the NVRAM by using the *c!*, *dump* and *c?* commands in the OpenBoot PROM. You can also get the virtual address of the NVRAM by looking at the output of */usr/etc/devinfo -vp* under Sun OS 4.1.x or */usr/sbin/prtconf -vp* under Solaris 2.x. On sun4c machines, the IDPROM starts at offset 0x7d8 from the start of the NVRAM. On sun4m, sun4d, and sun4u machines, the offset is 0x1fd8.

From here, one can also find the physical address of the NVRAM using *pgmap?*. In the preceding example, if you type *ffee9000 pgmap?* at the OpenBoot prompt, you get a few lines of output, one of which is:

```
Physical: 0.7120.0000
```

Which means that on this machine the physical address is 71200000 in address space 0.

You can also use *map-page* to map the physical address of the page containing the IDPROM to virtual address 0. To do this, you need to know the physical address of the NVRAM. You can find it as already shown or just use Table 14.6.

For the sun4m and sun4d machines, the page size is 4K (0x1000)—so the simplest thing to do is map the second page of the NVRAM. This is because we're using map-page and it maps only one page at a time.

For example, to modify the hostid of an IPX to be 57c0ffee and the Ethernet address to be 8:0:20:c0:ff:ee, enter the following commands:

```
02000000 obio 0 map-page
1 7d8 c!
57 7d9 c!
08 7da c!
0 7db c!
20 7dc c!
c0 7dd c!
ff 7de c!
ee 7df c!
57 7e0 c!
0 7e1 c!
0 7e2 c!
0 7e3 c!
c0 7e4 c!
ff 7e5 c!
ee 7e6 c!
29 7e7 c!
```

To modify the hostid of an SS10 to be 72c0ffee and the Ethernet address to be 08:00:20:c0:ff:ee, do the following:

```
f1201000 f 0 map-page
01 fd8 c!
72 fd9 c!
08 fda c!
```

Table 14.6   Machine Type and NVRAM Addresses

MACHINE TYPE	ADDRESS	SPACE	ARCH −K
SS1, SS1+, SS2, ELC, IPC, IPX, and SLC	02000000	Obio	sun4c
Classic, LX, SS5, SS4, and Voyager	71200000	0	sun4m
SS10, SS20, and 6x0/MP	f1200000	f	sun4m
SS1000	00280000	f	sun4d

```
0 fdb c!
20 fdc c!
c0 fdd c!
ff fde c!
ee fdf c!
72 fe0 c!
0 fe1 c!
0 fe2 c!
0 fe3 c!
c0 fe4 c!
ff fe5 c!
ee fe6 c!
29 fe7 c!
```

Note that we added 0x1000 to the physical address in the table, as previously explained.

The hostid on Solaris 2.5 x86 and Up

Intel processor machines don't have an IDPROM. Sun uses a different mechanism to generate the hostid. When the operating system is initially installed, a pseudo random hostid is generated. It appears that this pseudo randomly generated hostid will always be between 1 and 3b9aca00. The hostid is based on 8 bytes of serialization information in the kernel module /kernel/misc/sysinit. This is in contrast to the situation on SPARC machines, where the hostid is based on the IDPROM.

The file */kernel/misc/sysinit* contains code that initializes the variable *hw_serial* in the kernel based on the serialization information. On both SPARC and x86 versions of Solaris 2.5, hw_serial stores the hostid as a decimal C string.

Other than the 8 bytes of serialization information, the /kernel/misc/sysinit files do not differ between machines. Four of the serialization bytes depend upon the other four bytes, so the hostid is somewhat tamper resistant. If the serialization information is tampered with carelessly or the sysinit module fails to load for some other reason, the hostid of the machine will be 0. A little more obfuscation is done in the code; hw_serial is not referenced directly in the module, but indirectly via the pointer _hs1107.

This means that, if you need to have two machines with the same hostid for some reason (say, to have a backup server with the same hostid in case your primary server malfunctions), you can simply copy the /kernel/misc/sysinit file from one machine to another.

Moreover, it seems that initializing hw_serial is the only function performed by the sysinit module. Hence, it is a simple matter to replace /kernel/misc/sysinit, yielding a machine with whatever hostid one wants, by compiling a simple C program for a loadable kernel module that sets hw_serial to the desired value.

C code for a generic replacement sysinit module is included in *change sun hostid*, which is available from www.squirrel.com/squirrel/sun-stuff in the file change-sun-hostid.tar.gz. Replacing part of the operating system is probably not the best way to achieve this effect. In general, we recommend using one of the other modules to change sun hostid, as there is less risk of damaging things and rendering the system unbootable, but a few people have asked for this.

The NVRAM in sun4 Architecture Machines

The sun4 machines (e.g. Sun 4/1xx, 4/2xx, 4/3xx, and so on) also have M48T02 chips. These chips do not store the hostid and Ethernet address, which are in an actual PROM, but they do keep track of the time of day and the system configuration information. Replacing the NVRAM chip is a relatively simple matter; the only trick is to set the appropriate values in the Sun PROM monitor using the **q** command, then boot the operating system to kick-start the clock. You can use the table for the Sun 3/80 to set the values in the old Sun PROM monitor. The only significant difference is that normal/diagnostic boot is controlled by a physical switch instead of the byte at location 0x70b. See the *Sun Hardware Reference* (online at http://www.si.unix-ag.org/faqs/SUN-HW-FAQ.html), your machine documentation, or the *Sun FE Handbook* if you need more information on the Sun PROM monitor.

Enterprise Server NVRAM Programming

This procedure works the same as is listed for other systems: *<value> <location> mkp 80* is the system type for all Enterprise X000 systems. As has been the recent trend, the last three digits of the Ethernet address are also the ones used for the hostid.

The checksum procedure works the same, too:

```
0 f 0 do i idprom@ xor loop f mkp
```

When writing to the Enterprise X000 NVRAM, you are writing to the one located on the clock board. Once it is programmed, you can copy its contents to the NVRAMs on the I/O boards by using the following command:

```
copy-clock-tod-to-io-boards
```

You can also program a blank or corrupt NVRAM on a board by copying a valid copy from another board. Only the clock board and I/O boards have NVRAMs. The CPU and memory boards do not have NVRAMs.

Here is an example of copying from an I/O board NVRAM in slot 1 to the clock board NVRAM:

```
01 copy-io-board-tod-to-clock-tod
```

Note that 01 is the slot number of the I/O board.

After selftest, you may get a message saying that the clock TOD does not match any I/O boards. This may have been caused by swapping the clock or I/O board without keeping the original NVRAM. It can also be caused by a glitch in the Boot PROM code that causes the system to think there is a mismatch after you power off the system. Sun has a patch or fix for this problem. You can reprogram the flash memory with an update.

To fix the mismatch, you have a choice of updating the clock NVRAM from an I/O board or the other way around. Keep in mind that the one displayed in the banner is the one on the clock board. If the clock board has the correct hostid, then update all the I/O boards with a single command:

```
copy-clock-tod-to-io-boards
```

If one of the I/O boards has the correct hostid, then copy its contents to the clock board (change 01 to equal the slot number of the valid I/O board) with this command:

```
01 copy-io-board-tod-to-clock-tod
```

You should be able to examine the contents of each I/O board's NVRAM to see which one has the correct hostid and Ethernet address.

Summary

Hardware problems are almost always painful. Even if you never do any hardware maintenance yourself, knowledge of the symptoms of various types of failure and the commands available for bringing a system back to operational status will help you determine what's wrong and make sure that problems are resolved.

Hopefully you've found something relevant to your systems in this chapter, as it will come in handy if ever a system refuses to boot.

The most common reasons systems don't boot are because file systems are corrupt or there is a problem with the boot block on the disk. Less frequent problems, like those mentioned in this chapter, can occur, however, and you'll be ahead if the game if you know what other things can go wrong.

## CHAPTER 15

Peripheral Vision: Understanding and Configuring Other Hardware

P robably one of the most annoying and repetitious things that we sysadmins have to do is add certain external devices to systems. Back in the old days (SunOS 4.x, circa 1990), this task involved simply editing a few files and making a few devices. Then came Solaris with its admintool and other ease-of-use "enhancements." Settings were hidden behind a GUI and we didn't *have* to understand how printing really worked. We thought to ourselves, "Okay!" but our complacency lasted only until the first printing or connectivity problem.

Back in those days, many things were simpler. The Unix network didn't have to worry about printing to the PC network, and most modem connections supported only remote administration or simple Unix-to-Unix copy program (UUCP) file transfers. How times have changed! Now, networks are becoming dramatically more heterogeneous and point-to-point protocol (PPP) is the order of the day.

In this chapter, we detail the installation and configuration of both printers and modems, then show some handy tips and scripts for making these installations easier.

Managing Your Printers

Managing printers is quite a bit like managing your children. Just when you are certain that they understand your instructions to the letter, they run off and do something else entirely. Setting up printers through admintool almost guarantees that at some point, something will not print correctly.

Under SunOS, we had it easy. We had a single printcap file, NFS-mounted to all machines and then linked to /etc/printcap. A midnight cron job ran a script that created the spool directories for printers, added to it the printcap file of the day, and then restarted lpd. The simplicity and reliability of administrative solutions such as these made each of our lives as sysadmins a dream. Just for historical purposes, we added comments to our printcap file (which, in time, contained several hundred printers) describing the name and the location of each printer. They looked like this:

```
#@  ws23045a    East BLDG     Column-3J    East Nowhere CT ttyb on ws23045
```

Back then, Evan's organization owned a class B network and all workstations and printers were named after the IP addresses they were using. The dynamic host configuration protocol (DHCP) had not yet entered the picture. If a printer was attached to a workstation, it was given the workstation's name with the port appended to the address. If it was a network printer, it was given the name pr######. For some strange reason, leading zeroes were dropped.

The makespool script lived under /usr/remote/bin, which was automounted to all systems. The script read as follows:

```
#! /bin/csh -f
#
# Make spool directories and restart printers
#
foreach printer (`grep "#@ " /etc/printcap | awk '{print $2}')
if ( ! -e /var/spool/$printer) then
mkdir /var/spool/$printer
lpc restart $printer
endif
```

Note how simple a script this is. Yet, it happily updated several thousand workstations nightly. But let's get back to reality—and today.

Solaris 2.X Printing

You have probably already added printers to your system using admintool. If you're a Unix command-line person at heart (like us), you most likely want to know what the print manager within admintool is actually doing, and how the process could be scripted. This was certainly one of our first priorities on using the new print system.

The heart of the Solaris print engine is the *lpadmin* command. This command is used to add, remove, and change printers; to set the system's default printer; and to configure the LP print service. Our friend the /etc/printcap file is gone, and now configurations are saved in the /etc/lp/printers/printername/configuration files.

Here's an example of a local printer configuration file:

```
Banner on
Content types: postscript
Device: /dev/bpp0
Interface: /usr/lib/model/standard
Printer type: PS
Modules: default
```

For Solaris 2.6 and above, remote entries will look like the following:

```
Banner: on
Content types: postscript
Device: /dev/null
Interface: /usr/lib/lp/model/netstandard
Printer type: PS
Modules:
Options: protocol=bsd,dest=hp
```

Note the difference in the device lines and the addition of the Options line for the remote printer.

To configure a new printer, the *-p* parameter is used with lpadmin. To create a new printer from the command prompt, enter a command of the following form:

```
# lpadmin -p printername  [-v device | -s system!printername | -U dialup]
[-e printer_interface_to_copy | -.i interface | -m model]
```

The *-v* parameter is for the name of the device to which a local printer is attached. The entire path must be included in the device name for the printer to function. Here's an example—adding a local printer called *mickey* via command line to the parallel port 0:

```
lpadmin -p mickey -v /dev/bpp0
chmod 600 /dev/bpp0
chown lp:lp /dev/bpp0
accept mickey
enable mickey
```

The *-s* parameter refers to the name of the remote system where the printer is physically attached. If the remote printer name differs from the local name, the remote printer name is appended with a *!* separator. For example, if the printer *hplaser* is known on the system to which it is connected (say, sparc10) as printer hp, the command will read as follows:

```
lpadmin -p hplaser -s sparc10!hp
```

The *-T* parameter is used to define what type of print this printer can accept as defined in the /etc/termcap file. To have a complete remote install for the remote printer hplaser, which in this case we are saying is a postscript printer, we would need to issue the following command to define the printer as a post-script printer:

```
lpadmin -p hplaser -T postscript -I any
```

For versions of Solaris prior to 2.6, the system_name (sparc10) also needs to be identified in the systems table located in the /etc/lp/Systems file. This is accomplished with the *lpsystem* command, scheduled for complete removal in Solaris 2.7.

```
lpsystem -type bsd
```

The *-U* parameter tells the LP print service that the printer is connected remotely through a dial-up device, such as a modem. This parameter is almost never used.

To remove a printer, use the *lpadmin -x printername* command.

The *-c* class parameter places the printer into the specified class and creates the class if it doesn't already exist.

The *-e* printername parameter copies the interface program of the printer specified as the interface for hplaser.

The *-i* interface parameter creates a new interface program for the printer. The full path to the interface should be specified.

The *-m* model parameter selects the model interface program for the printer provided by the LP print service.

The *-o* options parameter shows the options that should be set in the printers.conf file.

The lpadmin command gives you considerable flexibility for defining printer features, filters, and alerts. The *-D* parameter allows the administrator to add a comment about the printer, such as its location, or the data types handled. This comment will be displayed by the *lpstat* command. The *-A* parameter allows you to specify the type of alert the LP print service should send when it detects a printing error. By default, the print service is configured to send e-mail to root for every error encountered.

Another added feature is the ability to set up forms for printers. The default is *no forms*. Forms can be added with the *lpadmin -f allow:formlist* command. Form definition is handled by the *lpforms* command

The printer can be made the default for a machine with the *lpadmin -d* command.

Table 15.1 Print Commands

COMMAND	ACTION
accept and reject	Accepts or rejects print requests
enable/disable	Enables or disables specified printers
lpadmin	Defines printers and devices
lpfilter	Adds, changes, deletes, and lists filters used with the LP print service
lpforms	Administers the use of preprinted forms with the LP print service
lpmove	Moves print requests from one destination to another
lpshut	Stops the LP print service
lpsystem	Registers remote systems with the LP print service; not needed in 2.6 and higher
lpusers	Sets printing queue priorities
lpsched	Operates on files that are located within the /etc/lp tree

You can also enable or disable banner pages with lpadmin. However, we recommend that you edit the /etc/lp/interfaces/printername file instead. There is a line in the file that contains *nobanner="no"*. This can be changed to "*yes*".

The traffic cop for the print services under Solaris is the *lpsched* daemon. This daemon handles multiple functions, including scheduling local and network print requests, applying filters when needed, executing programs required to interface with the printers, tracking forms and job status, and delivering all alerts. The lpsched daemon does not accept any commands directly. Instead, other LP print service commands communicate with it. These commands are shown in Table 15.1.

The LP system files shown in Table 15.2 are used by lpsched to clarify information from a print request before printing.

New Printing Options in Solaris 2.6

Starting with Solaris 2.6, many changes were made to the printing subsystem to make life easier for us. Unfortunately, this happened at the same time we were just getting used to the other new way of doing things.

The new SunSoft Print Client is contained in the following packages: SUNWpcr, SUNWpcu, SUNWpsr SUNWpsu, SUNWpsf, and SUNWscplp. If you perform a

Table 15.2 LP System Files

FILE	CONTENTS
LP	System files contents (/etc/lp)
Systems	LP spooler system information
classes	User-defined printer classes (fd) Printer filter forms User-defined forms and interfaces Printer
logs	LP print service logs (linked to /var/lp)
model	Printer interfaces for specific types of printers (linked to /usr/lib/lp)
printers	Printer definitions
pwheels	Printwheel definitions

pkginfo | grep {packagename} and you see the package displayed, you already have the new printing system installed.

One major thing to remember is that this subsystem is *not* System V. Any remote machine attempting to print to a 2.6 or higher machine needs to refer to it as type BSD.

For Solaris 2.6 and above, there is a new file, called the *printers.conf* file, which seems to behave quite a bit like the old Berkeley Software Distribution (BSD) printcap file. Here is a sample printers.conf file:

```
hplaser:\
     :bsdaddr=sparc10,hp,Solaris:
_default:\
     :use=hplaser
_all:\
     :use=hplaser
```

In order to set up a remote networked printer under 2.6 or higher, the commands would look like this:

```
    lpadmin -p hplaser -o protocol=bsd,dest=sparc10!hp -T PS -I postscript
-v /dev/null -i /usr/lib/lp/model/netstandard
    chmod 666 /dev/null
    chown root:sys  /dev/null
    accept hplaser
    enable hplaser
```

A new command, *lpset*, can be used to add printers into the printers.conf file. The syntax is as follows:

```
lpset -n fns -a bsdaddr=server,<printername>,Solaris <printername>
```

If you are not using the federated naming system, the -n fns can be ignored.

The printer can even be aliased with new names by using the *lpadmin -p print-ername -c aliasname* command. Then issue the command *accept aliasname ans*, and that alias can now be used as well.

You can remove a printer with the new lpset command if it was added in a similar fashion. For example, the command

```
lpset -x printername
```

will remove the printer. The *lpget list* command will list all of the printers in your printers.conf file.

One nice thing about the printers.conf file is that it can live in the NIS and the NIS+ world. A new map called *printers.conf.byname* can be configured into NIS for ease of sharing. This would have come in handy in the SunOS days. Also, the master list can be pared down by the user, since users can now have their own printers.conf files located under $home/.printers. This file has the following format:

```
<alias><tab><printer>
_default<tab><printer>
_all<tab><printer1,printer2,printer3>
```

Note that *_default* becomes the default printer for the particular user, while *_all* is the list of printers that will be accessed via the lpstat or cancel command.

Tips and Tricks for Solaris 2.x Printing

To create a printers.conf file from the print system on a system prior to Solaris 2.51, use the following command:

```
conv_lp -d / -f /etc/printers.conf
```

If you have diskless clients, change the *-d* parameter to reflect the root directory for that client, and the *-f* parameter should reflect where the printers.conf file lives.

One problem that has plagued all of us is the watched kettle problem. How many times have we sent prints to a postscript printer and watched the light blink, only to get no output? This is one of the most frustrating problems we've seen. The usual cause of this problem is one of two things. Either the output type setting is incorrect, or the serial port setting is incorrect.

Sun provides a program located in /usr/lib/lp/postscript called postprint, for Post-Script printing of ASCII files. This program resides in /usr/lib/lp/postscript. It translates text files into postscript and adds formatting with the following operations as follows:

-c num   Print num copies of each page. By default, only one copy is printed.

-f name   Print files using font name. The default is courier, but any PostScript font can be used.

-l num   Set the length of a page to num lines. This is defaulted to 66 but will set based upon font and point size if set to zero.

-n num   Print num logical pages on each piece of paper, this is defaulted to one.

-o list   Print pages whose numbers are given in the comma separated list.

-r num   Selects carriage return behavior. 0 is ignore, 1 is carriage return, 2 is Carriage Return/Newline.

-s num   Print files using point size num. Use with -l 0 to automatically scale lines per page.

It is not widely known that postscript printers attached to Solaris systems must have the type set to either postscript or simple (ASCII). The printing subsystem cannot autodetect postscript and will most likely send incorrect data to the printer. For printers that autosense, setting the type as shown here will allow both postscript and ASCII to print without a problem:

```
lpadmin -p printername -T PS -I postscript
```

Or, for HP Laserjet printers:

```
lpadmin -p printername -T hplaser -I simple
```

TIP

Printing an ASCII Text file to an HP LaserJet or compatible printer from a Solaris machine may cause a strange effect where each succeeding line will be indented:

Line 1

        Line2

              Line3

                    ad infinitum

To fix this, edit /etc/lp/printers/printername/configuration and make sure it has the correct content type and printer type defined.

Content types: postscript

Printer type: hplaserjet

For settings on the serial ports, see the serial port section of this chapter. One EEPROM parameter should also be checked with the EEPROM command—*tty[a|b]-ignore-cd=true*. If the setting is false, the serial port will not transmit the data to the printer. If you reset this to true, a reboot will be needed for it to take effect.

How to test the serial port is a common question. First, make sure that you are using a null-modem cable. A null-modem cable crosses the send and receive wires (pins 2 and 3). If the baud rate is matched between the system and the printer, you should be able to cat a file out the port. Then, *echo "^D" >> /dev/cua/[a\/b]*. The Ctrl-D character forces an end-of-job to the printer, and the file should then print. This little trick utilizes none of the print subsystem, but it verifies that your settings are correct. If printing works here, but not when you use the lp command, you should check that the baud rate is correctly stated in the printer definition. The baud rate can be changed by issuing the following command:

```
# lpadmin -p <printername> -o "stty=19200
```

Or, for a HP PCL plotter:

```
# lpadmin -p <plottername> -o "stty='19200 -opost'"
```

TIP

Testing a printer by cat'ing a file to it with a proven null-modem cable is a good way to be sure your printer and port are working properly. Any ensuing problems would clearly be related to your print system and not these components. Don't forget the Ctrl-D (^D) as explained in the text.

Another common problem is when root is the only user that can print. This is usually caused by a permissions problem with /dev/null. The file should be 666 and should be owned by root:sys. This can be accomplished by issuing the following two commands:

```
chown root:sys /dev/null
chmod 666 /dev/null
```

TIP

The root:sys argument changes both the owner and group of a file in a single command. This is useful shortcut.

The last issue we tackle with respect to printers is the situation in which local printing works fine, but remote systems cannot print. This gets a little tricky. First, we must verify that the tcp listeners are still functioning. To do this, try the following:

```
# pmadm -l -p tcp
PMTAG          PMTYPE        SVCTAG        FLGS ID
<PMSPECIFIC>
tcp            listen        0                -    root
\x00020ACE00000000000000000000000000 - c - /usr/lib/saf/nlps_server #
tcp            listen        lp               -    root    - - p -
/var/spool/lp/fifos/listenS5 #
tcp            listen        lpd              -    root
```

```
\x0020203000000000000000000000000000 - p -
/var/spool/lp/fifos/listenBSD #
```

If these services are *not* running, set up a *local* printer on the print server with admintool. Here's the command line to set up the listeners:

```
# sacadm -a -p tcp -t listen        -c "/usr/lib/saf/listen tcp"
-v `nlsadmin    -V` -n 9999
#  pmadm -a -p tcp -s lp -i root -m `nlsadmin -o
/var/spool/lp/fifos/listenS5` -v `nlsadmin -V`

# pmadm -a -p tcp -s lpd -i root -m `nlsadmin -o
/var/spool/lp/fifos/listenBSD -A
'\x0020203000000000000000000000000000'` -v `nlsadmin -V`

# pmadm -a -p tcp -s 0 -i root -m `nlsadmin -c
/usr/lib/saf/nlps_server -A
'\x00020ACE0000000000000000000000000000'` -v `nlsadmin -V`
```

Also, make sure that there is a process running that is listening on tcp port 515:

```
#  netstat -a | grep printer
*.printer            *.*              0     0     0     0  LISTEN
```

Hopefully, this brief guide will bring you to a better understanding of Solaris printing.

Serial Port Configuration (Terminals and Modems)

After printers, serial ports just *has* to be our favorite subject. Luckily for us, since the advent of the public Internet, use of directly attached modem devices has shrunk considerably.

Those of us who come from the old SunOS 4.1 school remember how difficult setting up terminals and modems was back then. Editing the /etc/ttytab and making sure the correct getty process was or wasn't forked took some amount of trial and error, but, sooner or later, our terminals and modems worked—and they worked well.

TIP

Make sure you get the correct modem settings from your modem manufacturer. Incorrect modem settings usually cause more problems than system configuration.

With Solaris, our notions of the old regime went right out the window. Getty processes were replaced with port monitors, and simple files to be edited were replaced by a slew of commands, all difficult to remember.

For those of you just starting out, admintool is probably a good place to start. However, don't be fooled into believing that all of your serial port configuration can be performed through the admintool GUI. Knowing what happens under the covers will assist you in being able to determine whether you can use admintool and also whether it will work.

TIP

Never try to use the Admintool GUI to set the baud rate for a serial printer. Always use the lpadmin command if you are not going to use the default of 9600 baud 8 bits no parity. The syntax is lpadmin -p printername -o "stty=speed,characterset,parity" where speed is the baud rate, character set is either cs8 (8 bit) or cs7 (7 bit) and parity is either -parity (for no parity) or parity.

This section explains in detail how serial ports should be configured for both terminals and modems and explains the processes used to troubleshoot both types of devices.

Sun's serial ports come preconfigured with archaic settings. While most of the companies out there set their serial ports to 8 bits, no parity, and no stop bits, Sun's are preconfigured at 7 bits, even parity, with 1 stop bit. One of the first things that you will want to do is set the serial port modes to something useful.

Setting Serial Port Attributes

The first thing that you need to do is set the EEPROM settings for the port you are working with. The EEPROM commands still refer to the ports as *ttya* and *ttyb*; however, these translate into */dev/term/a* and */dev/term/b* in Solaris. To see the defaults, issue the following command:

```
#eeprom | grep tty
ttyb-rts-dtr-off=false
ttyb-ignore-cd=true
ttya-rts-dtr-off=false
ttya-ignore-cd=true
ttyb-mode=9600,8,n,1,-
ttya-mode=9600,8,n,1,-
```

To configure the ports as 34,800 baud with 8 bits, no parity, and 1 stop bit, issue the following commands. These settings require a reboot to activate.

```
#eeprom ttya-mode=38400,n,1,h
#eeprom ttyb-mode=38400,n,1,h
```

The /etc/ttydefs File

The /etc/ttydefs file contains all of the serial port mode definitions. The format of the entries in ttydefs is defined as follows:

```
ttylabel:initial-flags:final-flags:autobaud:nextlabel
```

For example:

```
contty:9600 hupcl opost onlcr:9600 sane::contty1
```

Following are some definitions for this example:

ttylabel. In the example, contty (ttylabel) is a port mode name, and is used as a parameter to the ttyadm part of the pmadm command when configuring a new port monitor. It is usually descriptive of the configuration parameters, such as 9600 or 38400E; however, the name has no bearing on the settings themselves.

initial-flags. This parameter contains the initial port settings taken from termio (7I). For example, the system administrator can specify what the default erase and kill characters will be. The initial-flags must be specified in the syntax recognized by the stty command. In the preceding example, the initial flags are 9600 baud; close the connection on last close (hupcl); map line feed to carriage return-linefeed (onlcr); and post process output (opost). There are a myriad of different settings, which can all be found in the man page for stty(1).

final-flags. The final-flags must be specified in the same format as initial-flags; ttymon sets these final settings after a connection request has been made and immediately prior to invoking a port's service. In the preceding example, the serial port is set to 9600 baud and reset (sane) to default values.

autobaud. If the autobaud field contains the character *A*, autobaud will be enabled. Otherwise, autobaud will be disabled. The ttymon process determines what line speed to set the port to by analyzing the carriage returns entered. If autobaud has been disabled, the hunt sequence is used for baud-rate determination.

TIP

Don't use the autobaud field with modems supporting speeds higher than 9600 baud, as it does not function with speeds in excess of 9600. Using a combination of hitting the break key and a circular hunt group will perform the same function for speeds above 9600!

nextlabel. If the user indicates that the current terminal setting is not appropriate by sending a <break>, ttymon searches for a ttydefs entry whose ttylabel field matches the nextlabel field. If a match is found, ttymon uses that field as its ttylabel field. A series of speeds is often linked together in this way into a loop called a *hunt sequence*. For example, 9600 may be linked to 4800, which in turn is linked to 2400, which is finally linked to 4800.

Note that the order of the flags within the initial-flags and final-flags fields is extremely important. The fields are processed from left to right. The *sane* command is extremely dangerous if used incorrectly. A long string of parameters ending with sane will reset the serial port to the default settings.

There are many ways to define the same thing. For example, *evenp* and *-parodd parenb* are the same. Both will set the port to even parity. There are many such possibilities.

The most common settings for use with modems and terminals are locked for sanity at 9600 or 38400 baud, 8 bits, no parity, hardware flow control. The entries in /etc/ttydefs would look like the following:

```
9600L:9600 -parenb cs8 ignpar opost onlcr:9600 hupcl -clocal -parenb
-ignpar cs8 -istrip -ixon -ixany::9600L
38400L:38400 -parenb cs8 ignpar opost onlcr:38400 hupcl -clocal -parenb
-ignpar cs8 -istrip -ixon -ixany::38400L
```

Now that we understand the /etc/ttydefs entries and how they function, the next step is to delve into the world of port monitors.

Port Monitors and sacadm

As we mentioned previously, Solaris is quite different from its predecessor in its method of monitoring ports. Starting with Solaris 2, the notion of the Service Access Facility (SAF) was introduced, and the BSD getty method of port monitoring was abandoned. Now, instead of having *n* number of autonomous gettys, we have a single process (/usr/lib/saf/sac) controlling a group of independent port monitors. The tools used to administer these functions are the *sacadm* and *pmadm* commands. There can be multiple sacs running, and each can control its own grouping of devices. For example, one SAC process can control a group of PPP-enabled modems, while another can control hardwired terminals.

If you have never dealt with the SAF before, initial setup of the port monitors might prove to be an issue in futility. Since there isn't a simple set of files to edit, as with most Unix processes (and the inittab and ttytab in SunOS), all settings are initialized via sacadm and pmadm commands. The steps required in order to configure a working service are as follows:

The sacadm command is used to add, remove, or modify service access controllers (SACs). Here is an example of a sacadm command that will add a sac with a port monitor tag (pmtag) called *terminal*. The pmtag is actually the name by which this sac is referenced. The type is *ttymon*; the command to run is */usr/lib/saf/ttymon -v 1*.

```
sacadm -a -p terminal -t ttymon -c /usr/lib/saf/ttymon -v 1
```

The sacadm command can also be used to enable, disable, or remove the SAC with the -e, -d, and -r parameters.

To check to see what sacs are running, *sacadm -l* can be used. To show all running controllers of a specific type (e.g., ttymon), the command would be *sacadm -l -t ttymon*. To remove one controller, use the *sacadm -l -p {pmtag}* command. There is a default sac that runs called *zsmon*. To delete it and recreate it, use the following procedure:

#sacadm -r -p zsmon

Add a new one:

```
# sacadm -a -p zsmon -t ttymon -c /usr/lib/saf/ttymon -v `ttyadm -V`
```

At this point, no services should be running on this port monitor. This can be checked with the *pmadm* command. This command looks and acts very similar to the sacadm command, but operates on a lower level. Within the pmadm command is embedded the ttyadm command. The *ttyadm* command is used to format and display information specific to port monitors. The major parameters to both the pmadm and ttyadm commands are as follows:

1. pmadm parameters:

    -a   Adds a port monitor.

    -l   Lists the port monitors.

    -r   Removes a port monitor.

    -e   Enables a port monitor.

    -d   Disables a port monitor.

    -f u Sets the *flag* field such that a utmp entry is created and a port monitor is enabled.

    -p   Defines which SAC it should run under (pmtag reference).

    -s   Identifies this port monitor under its SAC. This is called the *service tag* (svctag). You use this with the pmtag to specify this port monitor when you want to manipulate it.

    -S y Tells ttyadm to enable the *softcarrier* flag for this port. If an *n* follows the *-S*, it will be disabled, as for a modem-type port monitor.

2. ttyadm parameters:

    -d   The device file (tty node file) to run on.

    -l   The /etc/ttydefs entry to use.

    -s   The actual command to run.

    Use the pmadm command to list the services running:

```
# pmadm -l
```

Check to see if there is already a service running on the port you wish to use. For this example, let's use /dev/term/a. In the following example, there is already a process running on /dev/term/a with the svctag of ttya. The svctag is equivalent to the pmtag, since it is the unique identifier for the ttyadm process on that port.

```
# pmadm -l
PMTAG          PMTYPE         SVCTAG         FLGS ID          <PMSPECIFIC>
zsmon          ttymon         ttya           u    root        /dev/term/a I
- /usr/
bin/login - 9600 ldterm,ttcompat ttya login:  - tvi925 y  #
zsmon          ttymon         ttyb           u    root        /dev/term/b I
- /usr/
bin/login - 9600 ldterm,ttcompat ttyb login:  - tvi925 y  #
```

Next, we remove the existing service by issuing the following command with the pmtag and svctag found in the prior command:

```
# pmadm -r -p zsmon -s ttya
```

If there was no pmtag with the port we are configuring, we are all set. Since we already removed and added zsmon, there should currently be no services running.

Next, we need to configure the port for one of four types:

- Terminal use (vt100/vt320/wyse, etc.)
- Modem dial-in
- Modem dial-out
- Bidirectional modem

Configuring Ports for a Dumb Terminal

To configure the port for a terminal, first set up the port monitor based upon the terminal sac set up previously, as is done with this command:

```
pmadm -a -p terminal -s terma -i root -fu -v 1 -m "`ttyadm -S y -d
/dev/term/a -l 19200 -s /usr/bin/login`"
```

This command will set up a service that runs /usr/bin/login on port /dev/term/a at a baud rate of 19,200. The terminal should be configured to the same parameters as the port itself. In this case, we are running at no parity, 8 bits, and 1 stop bit (N/8/1).

Make sure you are using a null-modem cable. As mentioned earlier, a null-modem cable crosses the send and receive wires. Without a cable of this type, communication will not take place.

Configuring a Dial-in Modem

When configuring modems on serial ports, you *must* communicate with the modem via the *tip* or *cu* commands. These two commands allow you to test connectivity, and also allow you to configure the modem through the serial port.

For the tip and cu commands to be used, several things first need to happen. For one, the permissions on the port must be set such that you can read and write to it. This can be accomplished by changing the permissions on the appropriate device to 666 (rw-rw-rw-). The standard devices used are */dev/term[a-z]* for incoming data and */dev/cua/[a-z]* for outgoing data, although we have found that /dev/term[a-z] works fine for both. For another, the owner of /dev/cua/[a-z] should be uucp:tty and root:tty should own the /dev/term/[a-z].

The port monitor settings for a dial-in modem are similar to those for a terminal, with two exceptions. Primarily, the -S flag should be set to *n*. This ensures that there is a real carrier by changing the soft carrier flag to no. Also, the -b flag is set to allow bidirectional communication. Although we are configuring for dial-in only, the best way to test initial connectivity is with tip, and the -b flag is required for this testing. For a 38,400-baud connection, the pmadm line would look like this:

```
pmadm -a -p terminal -s terma -i root -fu -v 1 -m "`ttyadm -S n -d
/dev/term/a -l 38400 -s /usr/bin/login`"
```

Tip utilizes a file called */etc/remote* to determine its own settings. It contains information on how the Sun and the modem should communicate. Do not confuse this with modem-to-modem communication. Although the modem may be able to transfer at 56K per second, it is only possible to set the Sun modem speed to 38.4K per second. This speed is also called the *data terminal equipment (DTE) speed*.

Let's take a look at the /etc/remote file. There is a standard entry called *hardwire* that every administrator uses to test communications with modems. The default entry on Solaris looks like this:

```
hardwire:\
        :dv=/dev/term/a:br#9600:el=^C^S^Q^U^D:ie=%$:oe=^D:
```

Modify this entry to reflect the correct port-to-modem speed (i.e., 38,400) and outgoing device (/dev/cua/a). The resulting entry will look like this:

```
hardwire:\
        :dv=/dev/cua/a:br#38400:el=^C^S^Q^U^D:ie=%$:oe=^D:
```

After this change, you can use the tip command to talk to the modem. The command is simply *tip hardwire*. When you run this command, make sure you are in a nonscrollable window, as we have had problems with scrollbars in the past.

If everything is connected properly, you will see a *connected* message. At this point, you should be able to enter modem commands. If the modem understands, the industry-standard Hayes command set *ATZ <carriage return>* should return *ok*. If you see the *ok* returned, it is working. If you don't, you are not talking to the modem: Make sure that your cable is straight through and *not* a null-modem cable. Check that the baud-rate settings are correct, the modem is plugged in, and the /etc/remote and pmtag settings are correct. To exit this mode, use [carriage return] [tilde][period].

If you leave the port set as bidirectional and don't want others to dial out, change the ownership of /bin/tip to yourself, or make it not executable. If you want to change the port from bidirectional, you can either use admintool to unclick the bidirectional button, or delete and re-add the svctag without the *-b*.

Configuring Dial-out Modem

The interesting thing about configuring a modem for dial-out only is not what you need to do, rather it is what you don't need to do. For a dial-out-only modem, all the steps mentioned previously for dial-in modems should be followed to confirm communication with the modem. Once communication is verified, entries for your users to dial should be added to the /etc/remote file.

Although we briefly discussed this file in the preceding section, here is a more in-depth look at the /etc/remote file and the settings for dialing out.

The attributes that can be set in the file are as follows:

dv   Device to use for the tty

du   Dial up; used to make a call flag

pn   Phone numbers

at   ACU type

ie   Input end-of-file marks (default is NULL)

oe   Output end-of-file string (default is NULL)

cu   Call unit (default is dv)

br   Baud rate (default is 300)

tc   To continue a capability; point to another entry for the rest of the settings

Setting up entries in /etc/remote for dialing out is fairly simple. For example, if you want to set up the phone number for Acme Widgets, 212-555-1234, using /dev/cua/a, you can create the following entry in /etc/remote:

```
acmewidget:pn=14155551234:tc=UNIX-38400:
```

Where Unix-38400 looks like this:

```
UNIX-38400:\
        :el=^D^U^C^S^Q^O@:du:at=hayes:ie=#$%:oe=^D:br#38400:tc=modem1:
```

And modem1 looks like this:

```
modem1:\
        :dv=/dev/cua/a:
```

When the users enter *tip acmewidget,* the phone number is looked up, the correct settings are applied, and the phone number 212-555-1234 is dialed via the Hayes command set (atdt2125551234).

Once connectivity is verified, the service running on the port that the modem is connected to should be removed via the *pmtag -r* command. This will prevent anyone from dialing into the system.

Summary

Setting up printers and modems is one of our least favorite tasks. The command syntax is fussy, the settings have to be right on target for anything to work at all, and our users think we should be able to do this kind of stuff by twitching our noses. Yet every time we get a printer or modem working after struggling with it for a while, we feel like slapping ourselves on the back.

The pointers and commands provided in this chapter should make the task a little less stressful and a little less error-prone.

## CHAPTER 16

The E10000 (Starfire)—Not Just a Big Unix Box!

This chapter is intended as a relatively in-depth guide to Sun's largest and most unique Enterprise server, the Enterprise 10000. Although many of the readers of this book will never get a chance to breathe in the direction of this beautiful machine, our intention is to make administration of such a beastie accessible to all Solaris sysadmins. The E10000 has many features above and beyond those of any other machine made by Sun. Of course, there are many eccentricities that make this machine particularly daunting at first glance, but we hope to dispel any fears you may have and bring a coherent working picture of this *very* serious machine to light. We also would like to provide a solid foundation and reference to current owners and administrators of these boxen.

What's the Difference?

The original concept for Sun's Enterprise 10000 (or Starfire) was acquired from Cray Research. Despite the UltraSparc II heart and Solaris kernel, the E10000 was a new direction for Sun—to provide all the power and flexibility of a Unix system with the armor and reliability of a mainframe. What was forged was an utterly unique machine, with a whole new set of ideals behind it.

Even from the outside, you can see that something is *different* about the Enterprise 10000. Physically, it is far larger than its Enterprise line cousins. It's striking lines scream *power*. Under the hood, it's even more impressive. With up to 64 CPUs and 64Gb of memory, the E10000 is a performer through and through. Its layout is intelligent and eminently usable: 16 system boards divide up the whole—each with the capacity for 4 CPUs (ranging from 250 to 400 MHz), 4 I/O cards, and 8Gb of memory. The system boards are connected through an intelligent high-speed backplane, which creates virtual links between the components for seamless symmetric multiprocessing (SMP). The backplane actually scales its allocated bandwidth to the size of the domain, allowing true flexibility, even on the fly. The system has one control board and two centerplane support boards (CSBs) that allow for system configuration and booting.

Although this machine is decidedly a Sun, it differs from the rest of the Enterprise line in several noteworthy ways:

Partitioning. The E10000 can be segmented in up to eight separate logical machines. Each segment or *domain* is a fully functional Solaris system. *Ex unum, pluribus.* Each domain is also *completely isolated* from the next; thus a hardware or software error on one domain will never affect the others.

Dynamic reconfiguration. You can add or remove system boards on the fly from a running domain, allowing for greater flexibility of scaling.

Component-level blacklisting. If portions of the system board (including memory, CPU, I/O, etc.) are determined to be bad, they can be deallocated from the machine without physical removal, or detriment to the system. The one stipulation is that this must be done before booting.

Floating network console. Domains have no physical console. Instead, they are fronted by the network console or *netcon.* This allows a system administrator to fix even the most serious problems without being physically present at the machine.

System service processor. The SSP is a front-end of sorts to the Starfire. It not only provides a front-line connection into the E10000, but also manages many of the features that make it so dynamic. SSPs are usually lower-end Sparcs, such as Sparc 5 or UltraSparc 5.

Private network. A special network comprised only of domains and the SSPs is mandatory with every E10000, providing unique new twists on network administration. However, it also provides an unmatched level of system accessibility (for sysadmins, at least).

Of course, having all of these fantastic features means having more administrative overhead, specifically in the arena of commands to remember. The intent of this chapter is to remove some of the mystique from this powerful machine, and allow the reader to gain a clearer understanding of its more apocryphal features.

NOTE

The use of *domain name* or *domain* in this chapter always refers to the name of a reconfigurable system partition on the Starfire, and never to DNS or other domain names.

Hardware Configuration

When you uncrate your E10000, there's a bit more work to be done than there is on your standard Enterprise machine. Planning is a necessity: You should know how you are going to configure your first domain or set of domains before the machine even arrives. Your domain is, of course, reconfigurable at any time, but planning will expedite machine setup immensely. The physical system is quite easy to get used to. There can be up to 16 system boards. Each side of the machine holds eight system boards and one control board, oriented vertically and arranged horizontally across the bottom of the system. You should have already discussed physical domain layouts on these boards with your Sun service rep, so we will merely gloss over this. Each domain must have not only the appropriate number of system boards (procs and memory) to support your application needs, but also the correct I/O on these boards to allow for all of the disk and peripherals you will need. Since each board has four sbus slots, you should have plenty of room unless you are partitioning your machine into a multitude of one-board domains.

The absolute minimum configuration for any domain would be one Quad [Fast] Ethernet (QFE) card. An array or a boot disk is recommended, but one could technically boot a domain over the network. In regard to networks, you will need to use two ports on your QFE for each domain to correctly set up the Starfire. One should plug in to your public network (i.e., where the rest of your machines reside) and the other into a private network. Sun provides two small four-port Ethernet hubs for this purpose, but most users find them utterly inadequate (they are literally $49 off-the-shelf 10-baseT hubs). On our Starfires, we saw fit to replace them with 24-port 10/100 hubs. Though this may be overkill, the added potential capacity certainly will not be detrimental on a machine of this size. Plugged into this hub should be one Ethernet port from each domain, one from each control board, and one from the SSP. IP addresses will need to be allocated for the private network for domains and control boards. You should probably be consistent with regard to which QFE port you use on each domain, just for clarity's sake. The reason the control boards are plugged into the private network is for continuous access. This connection, called the JTAG, allows you to communicate with the host (albeit slowly) without any network drivers loaded or Ethernet interfaces configured and, indeed, without the system being up at all.

We have seen recommendations that suggest making the private network the only network—actually plugging the private hub into your LAN. This is an exceptionally bad idea. The separation afforded by the private/public split will help you avoid problems in the future. Also, you probably would not want the snmp traffic generated by the SSP software's monitors and such on your LAN.

The best solution is to configure your SSP with two Ethernet interfaces, so each domain and your SSP have both public and private interfaces.

With all of that planned out, the next step is to actually install the I/O where it belongs. This is generally be done by a Sun-authorized service professional—as you probably wouldn't want to void your warranty on this machine!

An important point should be made about domain naming conventions: Domain names should differ decidedly from the actual hostname of the domain. So, if you plan the hostname of one domain to be *frood*, the name the SSP knows it as should *never* be frood. The reasoning behind this is simple. There are times when having both names the same could lead to confusion as to which Ethernet interface you are talking to or from on the domain, with possibly cataclysmic results. To alleviate this, the simple convention which we use is to add a *-dn* to the end of the domain name on the SSP, where *n* is simply the next number in a sequence. So, when we create the first domain, it would have *frood-d1* as a domain name on the SSP and *frood* as a hostname when we set up the OS.

A shareware Java app called the *Java Starfire Planner* is available to assist in configuring your Starfire. This is available as shareware on the Web at *www.starplanner.com* for the Solaris, Microsoft NT or Windows, and Linux operating systems for personal computers installed with Java 1.1.6 or higher.

Now you are almost ready to configure your domains. However, before this can happen, you will have to familiarize yourself with the SSP.

The System Service Provider—Intimidation at Its Finest

The soul of this machine resides within its *system service processor* (SSP). This standalone machine acts as the software controller for most of the Starfire's unique features. In fact, most of this chapter is devoted to commands and concepts that reside on the SSP. The machine generally has a standard Solaris build (either 2.5.1 or 2.6), with the one difference of having the SSP packages installed. These are provided by Sun on a separate CD. Installation is as simple as a pkgadd command and a few brief configuration questions after reboot, but using it is an entirely different matter. When setting up the SSP, you will need to specify a *platform name*. This is the name by which the SSP will reference the actual E10000, and is used in many domain-configuration commands and tasks. For example, at the site where Evan works, there are two Starfires. On one, the platform name is *mercury*, and on the other it's *orbifold*. This is simply for clarity. We also named our SSPs accordingly: The hostname on the first is *mercury-ssp01*, and on the other it's *orbifold-ssp01*.

Another important note is that the SSP software setup will prompt you for whether the machine you are setting up is to be a main or a spare SSP. There are generally two SSPs shipped with each E10000. To state the bluntly obvious, one should be main, one spare. The purpose of this configuration is that, in theory, if you were to lose an SSP due to a crash, the act of a deity, or the use of a Tesla coil in the nearby vicinity, you could set the secondary up for use and continue without much problem. The actual functionality to support this feature comes in the SSP startup files, located in /opt/SUNWssp/bin.

The setup of the SSP v3.2 software follows. You will be prompted with this screen after you install the packages on the SSP CD-ROM and reboot. In the following example, the control board IP addresses are not listed in /etc/hosts. Though it is generally recommended that you do this (once you assign the IPs), it is not absolutely necessary. Obviously, the values here are fictitious. Your mileage may vary depending on the version of SSP you're installing, as well:

```
Beginning setup of this workstation to act as a MAIN or SPARE SSP.

The platform name identifies the entire host machine to
the SSP software. The platform name occupies a different
name space than domain names (hostnames of bootable systems).

Please enter the name of the platform this ssp will service: gedanken
Do you have a control board 0? (y/n): y
Please enter the host name of the control board 0 [gedankencb0]:
I could not automatically determine the IP address of gedankencb0.
Please enter the IP address of gedankencb0: nnn.nnn.nnn.nnn
You should make sure that this host/IP address is set up properly
in the /etc/inet/hosts file or in your local name service system.
Do you have a control board 1? (y/n): y
Please enter the host name of the control board 1 [gedankencb1]:
I could not automatically determine the IP address of gedankencb1.
Please enter the IP address of gedankencb1: nnn.nnn.nnn.nnn
You should make sure that this host/IP address is set up properly
in the /etc/inet/hosts file or in your local name service system.

Please identify the primary control board.
Is Control Board 0 [gedankencb0] the primary? (y/n) y
Platform name    = gedanken
Control Board 0 = gedankencb0 => nnn.nnn.nnn.nnn
Control Board 1 = gedankencb1 => nnn.nnn.nnn.nnn
Primary Control Board = gedankencb0
Is this correct? (y/n): y
Are you currently configuring the MAIN SSP? (y/n) y

MAIN SSP configuration completed
```

There are several directories on the SSP with which you will need to familiarize yourself, as you will undoubtedly be frequenting them. The actual SSP binaries and libraries are installed by default in /opt/SUNWssp. This can be referenced by the SSP user as the environment variable *$SSPOPT*. The bin directory under this hierarchy is included in your path as the user *ssp* by default. Most of the important commands for administering an E10000 (and the ever-important man pages to back them up) can be found here. A slightly more hidden but nonetheless important directory is /var/opt/SUNWssp. This can be referenced by a similar environment variable, *$SSPVAR*. Many of the actual configuration files for your specific E10000 can be found here, along with the domain-specific and SSP-specific message files and error logs. These are discussed in detail in the section "Know Your SSP."

Though the default environment for the SSP user is obfuscated, or even obnoxious to some, it is an unfortunate necessity. The intricate ways in which the SSP user's environment interfaces with the E10000 domain commands require some very specific environment variables, and, quite unfortunately, csh. It is not recommended that you alter the SSP user's environment in any more than superficial ways, such as the background color in OpenWindows, or the number of command tools that are brought up for netcons.

The SSP User

The first thing you will have to adjust to when learning Starfire administration is *not* logging in as root. Instead, most of the important work can be done as the user *ssp*. This user is installed by default with the SUNWssp package. This account will allow you to execute all of the important commands that will be discussed in this chapter. Logging in as *ssp*, you will notice an immediate difference.

```
Login: ssp
Passwd:
Last login: Tue Jun 29 15:11:51 from 167.69.134.221
Sun Microsystems Inc.    SunOS 5.5.1    Generic May 1996

Please enter SUNW_HOSTNAME: foonly-d1

gedanken-ssp01:foonly-d1%
```

Upon initial login as ssp, what you enter as a default domain (SUNW_HOST-NAME) is not important. At this point, there are no domains to communicate with. This will become important later—the domain you set is the one you will be talking to with Starfire commands. Upon initial setup, there are no domains created. The easiest way to determine domain configuration is with the command *domain_status*. The output of this command will look as thus upon initial setup:

```
gedanken-ssp01:foonly-d1% domain_status
domain_status: No domains configured.
```

In order to configure a domain, you will need an EEPROM image. Since the E10000 is dynamically configurable, it made little sense to have physical EEPROM chips. Instead, the EEPROM images are stored as data in $SSPVAR/ SUNWssp/etc<platform_name>. This is generated from a template image in $SSPVAR/.ssp_private/eeprom_save by domain_create. Sun will provide you with one EEPROM image for each domain you have requested. If a new EEPROM image needs to be generated, Sun can provide you with a key and hostid for use with the *sys_id* utility. You should make sure that you have a written copy of the initial Sun-provided hostid and serial number, should anything catastrophic ever happen to the machine.

The next important concept to understand before a domain can be created is the software-controlled power feature of the Starfire. Each system board and control board can be powered on or off from the domain, and the status of each can be checked. The command to accomplish such feats is *power*. At its simplest usage, power is invoked like this:

```
power -on -sb 0
```

or

```
power -on -cb 0
```

These commands power on system board 0 and control board 0, respectively. Control boards, realistically, do not need to be powered up or down often, only upon initial 10k setup. The antithesis of the above command would be replacing *-on* with *-off*. The power command is considerably more powerful than that, though. Used with no arguments, it will display the power status for each subsystem on each board. It can also be used to adjust acceptable voltage margins, turn off the entire machine, or bring the center plane up or down. If you substitute the *-all* option for the system board option, the command will affect all system boards and control boards. It is generally advised that any functions besides the most mundane of cycling power on system boards be left to Sun service professionals.

Now, you are ready to create your first domain. Make sure that all of the system boards you will be using are powered on. The command to accomplish this is *domain_create*. The syntax is as follows:

```
domain_create -d domain name -b sysboards -o os_version -p platform
```

So, if your first domain is *foonly-d1*, the platform name you decided on is *gedanken*, it will live on system boards 0 1 and 2, and you will be running Solaris 2.5.1, the command would look like this:

```
domain_create -d foonly-d1 -b 0 1 2 -o 2.5.1 -p gedanken
Domain foonly-d1 created!
```

The same command can be used to create any future domain. Care should be taken (through use of the domain_status command) to make sure that the system boards you want to use in a domain creation are not already in use by another.

```
gedanken-ssp01:foonly-d1% domain_status
DOMAIN          TYPE                      PLATFORM    OS        SYSBDS
foonly-d1       Ultra-Enterprise-10000    gedanken    2.5.1  0  1 2 3 4
```

Also, it is worthwhile to note the somewhat obvious point that the boards you utilize for a domain must have the minimal configuration that any Sun machine would use: enough memory and CPU, an Ethernet interface, and so on.

Of course, since the machine is dynamic, you may want to remove a domain at some point. This is very easy to do, and it can be done on a domain that is up and running, so be careful. The command is polite enough to prompt you in this situation, though. The syntax is simple:

```
domain_remove -d domainname
```

You will then be asked if you want to keep subdirectories related to the domain. We generally recommend answering yes, because you never know when you might want to check old logfiles. Beyond that, the directories are keyed by name, so if you recreate the domain (which is often the case), you will have everything just as you left it. Here is an example:

```
domain_remove: The following subdirectories contain domain specific
information such as messages files, configuration files, and hpost dump
files.
You may choose to keep these directories if you still need this
information.
This domain may be recreated with or without this information being saved.
                /var/opt/SUNWssp/adm/foonly-d1
                /var/opt/SUNWssp/etc/gedanken/foonly-d1

Keep directories (y/n)? y
Domain : foonly-d1 is removed !
```

The command *domain_history* will show you a complete history of domains that have been removed. Its output looks like a domain_status.

Bringup—Your Key to the E10000

Now you are undoubtedly at a loss. The domain is set up, so the machine is essentially *there*, but how does one access it? How can one even power it up, or run a post? The answer lies in the *bringup* and *netcon* commands. The bringup command acts as a virtual system key; it lets you start your domain up and access the OpenBoot PROM, or bring it up to the OS if one exists. Before issuing this command, the status of the domain can be determined with *check_host*. This command will return a straightforward "Host is UP" or "Host is DOWN" for the domain currently set as $SUNW_HOSTNAME. It is generally not advisable to run bringup on a running domain unless it is an emergency or recovery situation.

This command has a very specific set of functions that it executes, in this order:

1. First, bringup runs power to check that all of the system boards in the domain are powered up. If not, it will abort with a message to this effect.

2. Next, it runs check_host to determine the status of the domain (see more on this command following). If the domain is determined to be up, bringup will prompt you on whether or not to continue. This is useful if you are using this command to recover from a hung host.

3. The *blacklist* file, located in $SSPVAR/etc/<platform name>/blacklist, is checked. This file allows components, from I/O units and CPUs to entire system boards, to be individually excluded from the domain at start time. This is incredibly useful, and will be described in detail later.

4. Then, bringup will check the status of other domains on the system. If no other domains are active, it will prompt you with the fact that it intends to configure the centerplane, and ask if you want to continue. If the center-plane is already configured, reconfiguring it will not bring any harm.

5. Next, bringup runs *hpost* on the domain. This is a very valuable tool, which can be run (on a domain that is not up) interactively at any time. It runs the domain through a series of tests that can often shake out hardware errors. By default, it will run at level 16. It can be configured to run up to level 127, which we will discuss a bit later.

6. Finally, bringup starts the obp_helper and the netcon_server, both of which are final handoffs to the system itself.

The most important thing to keep in mind when running a bringup is that the domain that is currently set as the $SUNW_HOSTNAME environment variable is the one the command will affect. This is true of most E10000-specific commands. This is the hostname that you enter upon logging in as SSP, and the one that will be prominently displayed in your PS1 prompt. It is important to *always* check what this value is set to before executing a domain specific command. To switch between domains, use the command *domain_switch <domainname>* (pretty straightforward).

Bringup can be run with many options, which are profiled at the end of this chapter. The most basic and important option is *-A*. A *bringup -A off* will bring the system to the OpenBoot PROM by default, whereas a *bringup -A on* will boot the system normally (that is, if an OS is installed in one way or another). You can also pass boot arguments to the obprom by specifying them at the end of the command line.

Here is the complete output from the successful completion of a bringup command. This is what the output should look like (with the exception of the configuration-specific lines) when bringup runs with no errors:

```
gedanken-ssp01:foonly-d1% bringup -A off
This bringup will configure the Centerplane. Please confirm (y/n)? y
Starting: hpost  -C
Opening SNMP server library...

Significant contents of /export/home/ssp/.postrc:
#
logfile

phase cplane_isolate: CP domain cluster mask clear...
phase init_reset: Initial system resets...
phase jtag_integ: JTAG probe and integrity test...
phase mem_probe: Memory dimm probe...
phase iom_probe: I/O module type probe...
phase jtag_bbsram: JTAG basic test of bootbus sram...
phase proc1: Initial processor module tests...
phase pc/cic_reg: PC and CIC register tests...
phase dtag: CIC DTAG tests...
phase mem: MC register and memory tests...
phase io: I/O controller tests...
phase procmem2: Processor vs. memory II tests...
phase lbexit: Centerplane connection tests...
phase npb_mem: Non-Proc Board MC and memory tests...
phase npb_iopc: Non-Proc Board IOPC register tests...
phase npb_io: Non-Proc Board I/O controller tests...
phase npb_cplane: Non-Proc Board centerplane connection tests...
phase nmb_procmem2: Non-Mem Board Proc vs. memory II tests...
phase final_config: Final configuration...
Configuring in 3F, FOM = 215040.00: 20 procs, 7 Scards, 12288 MBytes.
Creating OBP handoff structures...
Configured in 3F with 20 processors, 7 Scards, 12288 MBytes memory.
Interconnect      frequency is 83.284 MHz, from SNMP MIB.
Processor external frequency is 124.926 MHz, from SNMP MIB.
Processor internal frequency is 249.851 MHz, from proc clk_mode probe.
Boot processor is 0.0 =0
POST (level=16, verbose=20, -C) execution time 6:53
Boot proc 0 is written to /var/opt/SUNWssp/etc/mercury/sifp-d1/bootproc
Updating the bootproc and IntVector MIB
Starting: obp_helper -m 0  -A off
Starting: netcon_server -p 0
```

If the hpost phase of bringup does, in fact, uncover any hardware problems, bringup will exit immediately with the error encountered. If this occurs, it may be worthwhile to capture the information on the screen. Open a call with Sun immediately, as hpost failures are generally quite critical. You may also want to run the domain through a more thorough hpost, depending on Sun's assessment of the situation. This can be accomplished with an hpost -1127 command on the current $SUNW_HOSTNAME, but be forewarned that this can take many hours, depending on the size of the domain in question.

TIP

The default run level for hpost, within a bringup or otherwise, is 16. This runs basic tests on the proc, memory, and I/O devices. If you decide (due to a hardware failure, or simple paranoia) that this is not sufficient, the default level can be modified with the file *~ssp/.postrc* (SSP's homedir, wherever that may lie). This is a simple-format ASCII text file, in which the following can be put:
level n

where *n* is an integer, 7 to 127. Detailed descriptions of the important levels can be displayed by running *hpost -?level*. It should be noted that many other options can be added to the .postrc, but *level* is the only one of real use. Most of the others are for debugging or Sun Service engineer use. Full descriptions can be found in the man page for postrc. Once bringup completes, the system is ready to be accessed. The important question here is: How do you access it? This is a perfect segue to netcon.

Netcon—It's Your Friend

Netcon is an unbelievably versatile and convenient tool. In fact, we would list it as our favorite feature of the Starfire. *Netcon* stands for *network console*, and it is just that: a free-floating console for your domain, accessible from the SSP. This functionality is extremely useful in two ways. First, there is no need to connect physical consoles to each domain. This could be exasperating, depending on how much domain reconfiguration you do. Also, if problems occur with the system, physical console presence is no longer necessary. All of the console functions that would generally require a sysadmin on-site can now be accessed from anywhere, anytime. This is a life saver if a system goes down in the middle of the night. Instead of driving in to fix a problem, it can be done from a dial-up terminal, or anyplace from which SSP access can be gained. It has been noted that many people feel this functionality should be implemented across the Enterprise line, as it adds significantly to ease of administration, not to mention the well-being of sysadmins.

Before netcon will work, however, the domain must be brought up. If a netcon session is started when the host is down, it will sit idly and wait for the netcon server to be started on that domain. The process on the SSP that needs to be running in order for this scenario to work is *netcon_server -p <boot_proc>*. This will be started automatically at bringup. The process that runs on the domain (once at the OS level) is the *cvc daemon (cvcd)*. The cvcd allows the domain to communicate with the SSP over the private Starfire network interface. Prior to the cvcd being brought up, all communications are transacted over the JTAG. The JTAG is the Ethernet interface on the control board, which is also plugged into the private Starfire network. This is generally painfully slow, but it grants the access necessary to bring the system up. It should be noted that if you are connected with netcon in multiuser mode, and the system is still responding over the JTAG (you will notice immediately, it's *that* slow), you can manually restart the cvcd. You should probably kill the previous one if it is still running, then simply run /sbin/cvcd.

There are situations in which the netcon_server may become unavailable, or you find yourself unable to issue a netcon. If this is the case, first consult the *ps -ef | grep netcon_server* on your SSP. There should be one running for each domain that is up. This can be a little cryptic, since the only way to differentiate between domains is by viewing the *-p <n>* option on the netcon_server and deciphering which board that boot proc is located on. Fortunately, we have included a handy formula for just this situation in the section on blacklisting. If you have determined that it is not running, then make sure your $SUNW_HOST-NAME is set to the domain you're attempting to connect to, and issue a *nohup netcon_server -r &* command. This option attempts to read the boot processor info from the SNMP daemon.

Connecting with netcon is as simple as issuing the command. Once connected, your terminal becomes a virtual console for that domain. You can interact with the system at the OpenBoot PROM, in single-user mode, or in multiuser mode. However, keep in mind that until the cvcd is running in multiuser mode on the domain, all communication will be over the JTAG. Now, since netcon is a generally accessible system tool, it follows that multiple users can run it at once. Confusion is alleviated by allowing only one user at a time to have write access, but an indefinite number to have read access. There are several modes in which a netcon window can be opened: *locked write* permission, *unlocked write* permission, and *read-only* permission. Unlocked write permission is not particularly secure, as it can be revoked by several command-line options to another netcon session, or by ~@, ~&, or ~*, discussed in the list following this paragraph. Locked write permission is probably the mode you would want to be in if you're doing work on the console, as it can be revoked only by another session opening with a *-f* (force) option or with ~*. Tilde (~) acts as an escape character to a netcon session, and there are several important commands that can be issued in this manner:

~#   Analogous to Stop-A on a normal system. This will take the system down to OBP. Be careful with this.

~?   Shows the current status of all the open netcon sessions by pts number.

~=   Switch between the SSP private interface for the domain and the control board JTAG interface. This feature works only in private mode.

~*   Private mode. This sets locked write permission, closes any open netcon sessions, and disallows access to netcon from any other terminal. This is the same as the -f option.

~&   Locked write mode. This is the same as opening a session with the -l flag.

~@   Unlocked write mode. This is eminently revocable. This is the same as opening a session with the -g option.

~^   Read-only mode. Releases write permission (if currently set) and echoes any other session with write permission to your terminal.

~.   Release netcon. This will exit the netcon session and return you to the SSP.

For an initial system installation, follow the normal procedures that you would for a JumpStart boot from the OpenBoot PROM. The only notable difference between this and any other Enterprise system is that the install will always be in character mode, so just be sure to set your terminal type correctly when prompted. From the SSP, assuming you are using cmdtool or something similar, X-Terminal usually works well.

So, if you run a netcon immediately after running a bringup -A off, you might see this:

```
gedanken-ssp01:foonly-d1% netcon
trying to connect...
connected.

SUNW,Ultra-Enterprise-10000, using Network Console
OpenBoot 3.2.4, 12288 MB memory installed, Serial #00000000.
Ethernet address 0:0:be:a6:00:00, Host ID: 00000000.

<#0> ok
```

Hey, that looks familiar! So, you're up and running—and you've hit upon many of the important E10000 system topics along the way. From here on in, you can address the system much as you would any Enterprise server. There you have it.

Know Your SSP

To become a true acolyte of the Starfire, you must learn the inner workings of the SSP software. To a great extent, this involves plying through the directories related to the SSP and looking at the log files, scripts, and configuration files therein. The SSP also runs various daemons to keep the state of the environment constant and monitored. Although in most cases it is not necessary to directly interact with any of these programs, having a working knowledge of them does indeed aid in administration.

For the most part, the salient bits of the SSP (besides the binaries themselves) are located in $SSPVAR. As discussed earlier, the default value for this is /var/opt/SUNWssp/. The most directly important subdirectory in this hierarchy is adm. This contains the SSP message file (similar to the system's /var/adm/messages, but very specific to the SSP software), and also domain-specific message and log files.

The $SSPVAR/adm/messages file is, for the most part, relatively incomprehensible, and contains primarily messages from some of the daemons we will elucidate shortly. Occasionally, though, very helpful messages come through, dealing with the powering on or off of a system board, temperature warnings, or fan failures. These are generated by the event detector daemon. We have included a Perl script in the "Hints and Scripts" section that can monitor multiple SSPs for such messages from a remote location. It can then perform an action, such as page or e-mail you.

The most important files are located in subdirectories of $SSPVAR/adm. Within this directory, there will be directories with the same names as your domains. Each of these contains domain-specific message files, records of each hpost run, and any error dumps you may incur. These become important after a crash or panic, as the information collected there can allow Sun (or you, if you know how to read cores) to determine the root cause of the problem. We discuss core files in the section entitled "Recovering from Crashes." For now, let's look deeper at the domain-specific files.

messages. A messages file for the domain from the SSP's point of view. It contains specific information about the interaction of SSP daemons and the domain. Most of these messages are generated by the event detector daemon.

post. Subdirectory of date/time-keyed files containing the output of each hpost run.

last_edd_bringup.out. The output of the last bringup run.

Edd-Arbtstop-Dump, Edd-Record-Stop-Dump, hostresetdump. These are dumps, discussed in "Recovering from Crashes."

As for the rest of $SSPVAR, no other directories contain files that are particularly interpretable by humans; most of it is state or configuration files for the various SSP daemons. The contents of these folders should *never under any circumstances* be edited, with the one exception of the blacklist. Changing these files could lead to system failures. Here are some brief descriptions:

$SSPVAR/etc/<domainname>. Contains the blacklist file, and domain-name subdirectories containing the EEPROM images.

$SSPVAR/pid. Contains the PIDs of various SSP daemons.

$SSPVAR/data/Ultra-Enterprise-10000. Contains the E10000 JTAG scan database, used by the cbs daemon.

$SSPVAR/.ssp_private. Contains lockfiles created by the file access daemon, and some resource files for the control board. In here also exist several files containing domain and SSP configuration information, which are accessed by ssp commands. These include *domain_config*, *domain_history*, *ssp_resource*, and *ssp_to_domain_hosts*.

There is another SSP directory, $SSPETC. The default location for this is /etc/opt/SUNWssp. Within this directory resides the ssp_startup script. This starts the daemons which allow communication between the SSP and the domains. These should never be run manually. They are as follows:

cbs. Control board server. This provides a conduit to the control board for the rest of the SSP servers and clients. It also manages the JTAG functions.

edd. Event detector daemon. This listens for events such as temperature warnings, fan failures, and panics, and creates SNMP traps to handle the response. It also creates dumps, such as arbstops or recordstops.

snmpd. Simple Network Message Protocol daemon. Handles the management information base (MIB) for the E10000.

straps. Monitors the SNMP traps and passes them to any SSP client software, such as EDD.

fad. File access daemon. This provides file locking for client programs.

machine_server. Handles port lookup or allocation requests for snmpd and netcon_server.

obp_helper. Also reexecuted every time a bringup is run, this downloads the OpenBoot PROM to the domain's memory.

netcon_server. One for each domain, also reexecuted at bringup.

The Dynamic Domain

The more static features of the Starfire have been discussed thus far, but, by now, you're probably asking how all of this matters. Where, outside of the multiple domains, does the E10000 bring a strong advantage as opposed to multiple Enterprise systems? The answer lies within its dynamic reconfiguration functionality. There are two ways to access these features, either the pretty graphical (read: slow, buggy, and less than reliable) method, or the command-line interface. You've probably noticed our preference.

Hostview—Since When Do Un*x People Need GUIs?

The GUI, named *hostview*, can perform many functions beyond dynamic reconfiguration that can be invoked from the command line, such as domain creation and removal, the opening of network consoles, and so on. The graphical interface also allows manipulation of the blacklist file for selected components, but we will delve into doing this manually later on. For simple components, such as an entire system board or a single CPU module, it may be easiest to use hostview to modify the blacklist. The reason for our negativity regarding this tool is that use of it has displayed numerous weaknesses. From our experience, it is notoriously flaky. It certainly has memory leaks, and will tend to eat free memory on your SSP if you leave it running. If you try to use it remotely (i.e., log in as ssp from your desktop workstation, export the display, and run hostview) it has a decent chance of crashing, and probably at a very inopportune time. Beyond that, it is slow and not terribly intuitive in some cases. Though most documentation you will find focuses directly on this tool, the scope of this guide focuses on the command-line interfaces.

The dr Is In

The preferred method for reconfiguring your domains is the shell-like tool called *dr*. Like hostview and most other SSP binaries, it can only be invoked by the user ssp, and will affect whatever domain is currently set in $SUNW_HOSTNAME. To bring it up, simply invoke *dr*. You will be prompted with information that looks like this:

```
gedanken-ssp01:foonly-d1% drChecking environment...Establishing Control
Board Server connection...Initializing SSP SNMP MIB...Establishing
communication with DR daemon...foonly-d1: System Status - Summary

BOARD #: 5 6 7 8 9 10 physically present.BOARD #: 0 1 2 3 4 being used by
domain foonly-d1.

dr>
```

You'll note that this is acting like a shell. Commands passed in at this point affect only dr. At any time, you can enter *help* for a synopsis of commands. Here is a brief listing of the functions of dr, and the commands used to achieve them.

Attaching a system board:

`init_attach <sysbd>`	Begins the attach process for the specified system board
`complete_attach <sysbd>`	Finalizes board attach, only to be run after init_attach
`abort_attach <sysbd>`	Aborts the attach after init_attach, or a failed complete_attach

Detaching a system board:

`drain <sysbd>`	Drains the memory on the system board to prepare for detachment
`complete_detach <sysbd>`	Finalizes detach, to be run only after drain
`abort_detach <sysbd>`	Aborts a detach if drain or complete_detach fails

It is important to note that while dr will list all of the system boards not in the current domain as being physically present, this does not necessarily mean that they are eligible for attachment to the system. These may be used in running domains! Although the program should not allow you to actually attach a used board, it is suggested that you consult the output of domain_status before actually attempting an attach.

Here is a sample attach. Note that a complete hpost is run on the board to be attached to ensure its hardware integrity. This is generally the only place that you should encounter a failure on an attach, it is otherwise generally smooth.

```
dr> init_attach 5
Initiate board attachment, board 5 to domain foonly-d1.Adding board 5 to
domain_config file./opt/SUNWssp/bin/hpost -H20,0
Opening SNMP server library...

Significant contents of /export/home/ssp/.postrc:
#
logfile

Reading centerplane asics to obtain bus configuration...
Bus configuration determined to be 3F.
phase cplane_isolate: CP domain cluster mask clear...

<STANDARD HPOST OUTPUT (DELETED)>

phase final_config: Final configuration...Configuring in 3F, FOM = 2048.00:
2 procs, 4 Scards, 2048 MBytes.memboard_cage_swap(): INTERNAL:
memboard_sort_order not known.Creating OBP handoff structures...
```

```
Configured in 3F with 2 processors, 4 Scards, 2048 MBytes memory.
Interconnect       frequency is  83.284 MHz, from SNMP MIB.
Processor external frequency is 124.926 MHz, from SNMP MIB.
Processor internal frequency is 249.851 MHz, from proc clk_mode probe.
Boot processor is 5.0 = 20
POST (level=16, verbose=20, -H0020,0) execution time 3:08
hpost is complete.
/opt/SUNWssp/bin/obp_helper -H -m20
Board debut complete.
Reconfiguring domain mask registers.
Probing board resources.
Board attachment initiated successfully.

Ready to COMPLETE board attachment.

dr> complete_attach 5
Completing attach for board 5.
Board attachment completed successfully.
dr> exit
gedanken-ssp01:foonly-d1% domain_status
DOMAIN          TYPE                   PLATFORM     OS        SYSBDS
foonly-d1       Ultra-Enterprise-10000 gedanken     2.5.1 0   1 2 3 4 5
```

There is also a handy dr command called *reconfig*. Run from within the dr shell after a board attachment, it runs the standard Sun online configuration sequence on the domain—that is (in order), drvconfig, devlinks, disks, ports, and tapes. The same caution should be used as when running these commands manually, as they can move devices about.

Detachment is a bit more tricky, and the *drain* command deserves a special note. After running this command, dr returns immediately as if it has completed. *Do not* run a complete_detach immediately. Drain can take from seconds to hours, depending on the usage of the system board you are trying to detach. The reason for this is that the command actually moves the pages of physical memory from the system board specified to any free memory it can find on the domain. If you're trying to remove the system board that has the kernel resident, it may seem as if it hangs forever. One instance had us waiting for 3 hours for the final 4K of memory to finish draining. The general rule for detaching a system board is that system usage must be generally low, unless the domain is exceptionally large. Do not expect to be able to reliably detach a system board from a 2-board domain with a load average of 25. Also, keep in mind that the lowest system board (the first one in the domain) can *never* be removed, as it contains the boot processor.

The command used to view the status of an in-progress drain is *drshow*. For the purposes of viewing a drain, the syntax is as follows:

```
drshow <sysbd> drain
```

Here is a sample detach:

```
dr> drain 5Start draining board 5Board drain started. Retrieving System
Info...

                Bound Processes for Board 5

cpu   user  sys  procs
---   ----  ---  -----
20    0     2
22    0     2

No active IO devices.

                Memory Drain for Board 5 - IN PROGRESS

Reduction = 2048 MBytes
Remaining in System      = 12288 MBytes
Percent Complete         = 0% (2097152 KBytes remaining)

Drain operation started at Tue Aug 03 15:05:59 1999
Current time             Tue Aug 03 15:06:00 1999
Memory Drain is in progress...
When Drain has finished you may COMPLETE the board detach.

dr> drshow 5 drain

                Memory Drain for Board 5 - COMPLETE

Percent Complete         = 100% (0 KBytes remaining)

Drain operation started at Tue Aug 03 15:05:59 1999
Current time             Tue Aug 03 15:06:03 1999
dr>dr> complete_detach 5Completing detach of board 5.Operating System has
detached the board.Reconfiguring domain mask registers.Processors on board
5 reset.Board 5 placed into loopback.Removing board 5 from domain_config
file.
Board detachment completed successfully.
dr>
```

Now for the caveats. While dr is an extremely powerful tool, great care should be taken in its use. We have crashed our share of production systems by using it wantonly, or without proper research beforehand. You should *never* attempt to detach a system board with active I/O on it of any kind. It is fairly obvious that attempting to remove a board with an attached array containing, say, your root file system would be an extremely bad thing. However, what are not so obvious are issues arising with I/O attached to a target system board even if it is *not apparently active*. Sometimes (for whatever reason), domains decide to panic when dr attempts to detach something that they are not ready to let go of. For this reason, at our sites we instituted the convention of a *floater board* resource. What this means is that we have one (or two) system boards on the E10000 that are allocable. They have no I/O cards, just processors and memory. This way, we can bring the horsepower to whatever domain needs it, then detach it after the bulk of major processing is done with little to no problem. We would strongly suggest that if you are investigating the purchase of a Starfire, you equip it with said boards. The headache reduction will be worth it.

There is a way from within dr to see if there is active I/O on a board. This is with another option to drshow, *io*. First, a board with I/O:

```
dr> drshow 0 io

                I/O Controllers and Devices for Board 0

----------------------- I/O Bus ) : Slot 1 : qec0 ----------------------

device    opens  name                    usage
------    -----  ----                    -----
qe0              qe0
qe1              qe1
qe2              qe2
qe3              qe3

---------------------- I/O Bus 1 : Slot 1 : QLGC,isp0 --------------------

device    opens  name                    usage
------    -----  ----                    -----
sd0         25   /dev/dsk/c0t0d0s0       /
             0   /dev/dsk/c0t0d0s1       swap, /tmp
             8   /dev/dsk/c0t0d0s5       /var
sd1          0   /dev/dsk/c0t1d0s0
sd2          0   /dev/dsk/c0t2d0s0
sd3          0   /dev/dsk/c0t3d0s0
```

This board should *never* be detached. As for a candidate for detachment:

```
dr> drshow 4 io

                I/O Controllers and Devices for Board 4

No devices present.
```

This is a much healthier choice. You should probably run the drshow command against any board you plan to detach, even if its I/O is completely physically disconnected from any cables. You never know what the kernel may be holding open. If dr does decide that your choices are somehow inferior, and refuses to actually complete them, you can always bail out with the abort_attach or abort_detach commands. These are relatively nondestructive, and we have never personally run into a problem using them.

Don't let these warnings prevent you from using dr. Just make sure that your usage is logical, necessary, and does not interfere with the system's current functioning. If you're doubtful that there's enough memory available on the system to drain a board, or that the I/O is completely unused, don't attempt a detach.

Blacklisting for Fun and Profit

Having perused dynamic reconfiguration, we should now touch upon not-so-dynamic configuration, embodied in the blacklist. The blacklist is located in $SSPVAR/etc/<platform_name>/blacklist. This is read by hpost during a bringup or a dr. The syntax of this file is very straightforward, though the keywords may not be. Each line can have a case-insensitive keyword and a number or set of numbers. If this item is recognized, it will be ignored during hpost and left out of the physical configuration of the system once it is up. Here is a list of some important keywords:

sysbd <board num>. Any physically present system board (0 to 15). This means that if the board is listed as being a member of a domain, it will be left out of the configuration. This will also prevent dr from adding the specified board to a domain.

mem <board num>. The memory on the referenced system board.

scard <system board>.<I/O controller>.<slot>. The named sbus I/O adapter card. There are two I/O controllers on each system board, the upper half being 0, and the lower half being 1. The same is true for the slot, the upper one within the specified I/O controller being 0, and the lower being 1. So, if you wanted to ignore an Ethernet adapter in the third slot from the top of system board 3, the blacklist entry would be:

```
scard 3.1.0
```

proc <system board>.<proc>. A single processor, listed by its number on the board. There can be up to 4 processors on each board, so the integer will be between 0 and 3. Example: proc 5.2 is processor 2 on system board 5. Of course, since a panic string usually will list the CPU as an absolute number (i.e., 32), this is less than intuitive. In the past, this might have required the aid of a Sun Service professional. (They have the *secret* books and incantations.) But, instead, here's a simple homebrewed formula to decode the sysboard.proc number from the absolute processor number, where n is the absolute proc number:

int(n / 4) = system board number <the integer of n divided by four>
n % 4 = processor number <n modulo four>

So, if the CPU listed in a panic string is 42, then the system board would be 10 (int (42 / 4)), and the processor number would be 2 (42 % 4). Your blacklist entry for this situation would be:

```
proc 10.2
```

Or, if you prefer hexadecimal:

```
proc A.2
```

There are also some more in-depth components that you can blacklist, but it is highly recommended that you know precisely what you're doing before attempting any of these:

mgroup <board>.<bank>	The specified bank of memory (0 to 3) on a given system board
mlimit <board>.<group>.<mbytes>	Restricts the memory of a given bank to <mbytes>, either 64 or 256
ioc <board>.<io controller>	An I/O controller on a given system board, 0 (upper) or 1 (lower)
xdb <board>.<data buffer>	The data buffer (0 to 3) on a given system board
abus <abus>	An address bus, 0 to 3
dbus <dbus>	Half of the centerplane data bus, 0 or 1
ldpath <board>.<dbus>	Half of the data bus on a given system board, 0 or 1
pc <board>.<controller>	A port controller, 0 to 2
cic <board>.<interface controller>	A coherent interface controller (0 to 3) on a given system board
cplane <centerplane>	The half-centerplane, either 0 or 1

The disadvantage of using the blacklist functions is that you will be unable to allow any of these components back into the system until another bringup. The one slight exception is that if you can dr the board in question out safely (i.e., there is no attached I/O), remove the entries from the blacklist, then dr the board back in, you can bypass a bringup.

You will probably stumble across the *redlist* in your wanderings through the Starfire. This is a near-useless file. It has the same syntax as the blacklist, and winds up behaving exactly the same, as well. It prevents the listed components from being tested by an hpost. Since only passed components will be handed to the obp_helper, redlisted components wind up being ignored. This is probably a Sun engineering feature, and its use is strongly discouraged, as the way it is handled makes it far less stable than the blacklist. Your safest bet is to ignore it.

All of these features become especially useful when a hardware failure is encountered. An example scenario: A domain panics, and Sun determines that a CPU is the culprit, and must be replaced. Instead of risking further downtime, you can blacklist the system board containing the CPU in question if the domain is down, or if you manage to get it back up, you can dr out the afflicted board if there is no dependent I/O. This would then allow you to safely power down and remove the system board in question with *no further downtime*. In all, this is a very nice, very forgiving set of features, which is particularly pleasant when customers are constantly screaming about the <expletive deleted> downtime.

Recovering from Crashes

Now for the fun part—what does one do when all of this wonderful technology has utterly (and messily) failed? All machines are wont to do this at some point, so it is best to be armed with the proper information beforehand to ensure a quick and smooth recovery.

Before diving into situations, here is a look at the tools you can use. These should obviously be used with caution; they can and will perform their functions on a running domain as invoked. These commands all affect the domain set as $SUNW_HOSTNAME. They are listed in the order in which they should be attempted, from least severe to most:

hostint. Processor interrupt. This will force a panic on the domain, which will dump before rebooting.

hostreset. This sends an externally initiated reset to the domain, resetting it. The domain then goes into limbo, but you should then be able to run a bringup on it. This is also useful at the OBP level—if you are hung waiting for a boot, it can be used to get you back to the ok prompt.

sys_reset. Very, very, harsh. This resets all of the system boards in the current domain. This will not work against a running domain without the -f (force) option. The system will be left in limbo, and you will probably need to run a bringup.

bringup. Our old friend, with a new option, -f (force). This will run the bringup even if the host is up.

The most common problem for which these commands may be useful is a hung domain. Normally, if an event is discovered that should cause a panic, the EDD will initiate a reboot. If for whatever reason this does not happen, your domain will hang. When this occurs, the goal is to recover with minimal system impact and data loss. Use of these commands assumes that you are unable to reboot the machine by normal means, and that issuing a Stop-A (~# from netcon) will not work.

If your domain panics, there is a bit more to do than if a normal Enterprise system were to panic. We would tend to insist that every domain on your E10000 have savecore enabled, as it is direly important to have panic dumps from these machines. Now, the first step in recovery is readily apparent: Get the system back up. Hopefully, this should be accomplished with the commands already given. If the crash has rendered your system unusable, general Solaris procedures are to be followed for recovery of the actual domain. In any case, Sun will also need any messages files from $SSPVAR/adm and $SSPVAR/adm/<domain-name>. The most important component, however, is the collection of dumps located in $SSPVAR/adm/<domainname>. Here are the various types you may encounter, all of which will be time and date stamped:

Edd-Arbstop-Dump. This is a fatal error, usually caused by a CPU panic. When this is created, EDD will try to do a complete bringup on the domain after the dump completes.

Edd-Record-Stop-Dump. These errors are actually fairly common. They are often left by a crash, but they can be caused by ECC memory errors and other correctable conditions, as well.

hostresetdump. This is the dump left behind by the execution of a hostreset on a domain.

watchdog-redmode-dump. The dump when a processor enters a watchdog condition. This will cause EDD to do a complete bringup on the domain.

When a crash is encountered, any of these files, along with the message files (both SSP and domain-specific), post output, bringup output, and anything else you have is relevant. One thing we always try to do is capture the console output, so we generally leave one netcon session open per domain on the SSP. Even if the write access to that netcon is stolen away when we access it remotely, we still have a record that we can scroll back to and copy to a text file when next we visit the SSP.

A very important hint is to keep in mind that the SSP is the hub of all Starfire activity, and can in fact get itself into strange states. The thing is, you can reboot it at just about *any time*. The only ill effect you will notice is that the sudden loss of fan control will cause a sound like a jet engine to emanate from your E10000. It is certainly not recommended that you leave it down for extended periods of time, but we cannot tell you how many times rebooting the SSP has actually cleared a condition that had every sysadmin around dumbfounded. Keep in mind, there will be no error detection or environmental control while the SSP is rebooting. The good news is that it is *not* a single point of failure.

We have also encountered more esoteric problems on the Starfire. Once, a domain crashed, and every time we tried to run a bringup, the bringup itself would crash and attempt to redlist components. Odd behavior, indeed. Eventually, we deciphered that it was attempting to redlist a particular system board's ASICs, powered off that offending board, and powered it back on. This did indeed work. Often, if a problem like this is encountered, it is best to analyze any data and draw the best conclusion you can from it. Then, step back and assess what (if any) action can be taken. Keep all of the various aspects of this often complex machine in mind, and you will find yourself coming up with innovative solutions. Of course, there are the occasions on which hardware does fail catastrophically, and in these cases it is best to rely on your blacklisting or dr skills. Downtime avoidance is the key.

Above all else, we recommend getting any information available (cores, logs, etc.) to Sun as soon as possible after the dump. They have been extremely responsive and helpful on any problem we've ever encountered on our Starfires.

Hints and Scripts

The script *sspmon.pl.* will monitor the $SSPVAR/adm/messages on the listed SSPs. The assumption is that the machine you run this from is in the .rhosts file of the user you are running it as on the SSP. The reason it is set up for remote access is to monitor multiple SSPs at once.

```perl
#!/usr/local/bin/perl

# Remotely monitors $SSPVAR/adm/messages on ssp. Run every 15 mins
# from cron
# There is absolutely no implied warranty. Use at your own risk!
# 8/26/98 Jeff Ruggeri
# Last modified 04/08/99, JRR

#Put the platform name (or any handy referential bit of info)
#and the SSP's IP in this hash table.
%hosts = ( "STARFIREone" => "127.0.0.1",
           "STARFIREtwo" => "127.0.0.2"
         );

#Action - the actual binary to run. This should take the message as an
#argument. Listed below is an example - it calls an external paging
#script. It would be very easy to mail as well.
$action = "page.ksh RUGGERI";

$date = '/usr/bin/date +"%b %e "';
$hour = '/usr/bin/date +"%H"';
$min = '/usr/bin/date +"%M"';
chomp($date, $hour, $min);
if ($min < 10) {
   $hour--; }
$mdate = $date . $hour;

if (-e "/tmp/.sspmon.state") {
   open (STATE, "/tmp/.sspmon.state");
   flock STATE, 2;
   @state = <STATE>;
   flock STATE, 8;
   close (STATE);
   unlink ("/tmp/.sspmon.state"); }
```

```
HOSTLOOP: foreach $host (keys %hosts) {
  @msgs = 'rsh $hosts{$host} cat /var/opt/SUNWssp/adm/messages | grep
\"$mdate\"';
  if (scalar @msgs == 0) {
    next HOSTLOOP; }
  else {
   @fail = grep /(FAILED)|(OFF)|(911\stemp)/, @msgs;
   if (scalar @fail == 0) {
     next HOSTLOOP; }
  foreach $grr (@fail) {
    chomp($grr);
    $grr =~ s/^.*\(.*\).*:\s//;
    $argh{$grr} = 1; }
  foreach $failu (sort keys %argh) {
    $message = "E10K Alert ($host): " . $failu;
    if (scalar @state) {
      foreach $old (@state) {
        chomp($old);
        if ($message eq $old) {
          $oldmess{$message} = 1; } } }
    if (!exists $oldmess{$message}) {
      system "$action \"$message\"";
      $oldmess{$message} = 1;
      print "$message\n";  } }
  } }
open (STATE, ">/tmp/.sspmon.state") || die "Can't open state file";
flock STATE, 2;
foreach $mess (keys %oldmess) {
   print STATE "$mess\n"; }
flock STATE, 8;
close (STATE);

exit 0;
```

SSP Command Reference

You can find additional information about the Starfire along with a command reference at the Sun Web site, *http://docs.sun.com*. This site provides online access to an expanding library of Sun's documentation. The site provides tools with which you can search or browse the collection. If you choose to browse, you can do so by subject, collection or product. You can also search by OS (e.g., Solaris 7) or product classification (e.g., servers). Much of the site is organized as document collections. You'll find release notes as well as user guides and installation manuals. For the Starfire, you'll find user guides as well as reference manuals. The site also provides links to other documentation sites. We strongly encourage you to browse the material available here.

Summary

The Enterprise 10000 is a *stunning* system. This alternative to a mainframe allows you to:

- Add processors.
- Add memory and I/O.
- Take down portions of the machine without bringing down the whole thing.

If you are fortunate enough to have the E10000, don't let its radical design or the differences between how this machine and other Sun systems are managed keep you from appreciating what this system can do for you. In the most data-intensive environments, the E10000's speed and reliability will *make* you love it.

## PART FOUR

Surviving in the Real World

T oday's networks are complex. Because they're connected to the Internet, the complexities and the problems are not all within your control. Some of the problems you'll run into will happen because of something out there impacting something in here. Not only will your users want to access services and systems outside of your organization; people outside of your organization will want to access services and systems inside your organization—both legitimately and not so.

Keeping your systems manageable in the context of these demands involves several critical steps: understanding the configuration of network services—especially those provided to the outside world; configuring services properly so that they provide the intended service and nothing more; and monitoring services so that you are able to detect when a problem is developing.

Of course, the difficulties are not all on the boundaries between your organization and the rest of the Internet. You may have many difficulties and, in fact, many boundaries within your organization if your systems and your users cannot work together effectively. The reality of today's networks is that they are increasingly heterogeneous. A network with Unix servers and clients, Windows NT servers and clients, Windows 95/98 clients, Linux PCs, and Macintosh systems interspersed randomly is not at all uncommon. In fact, some version of this mixed network is probably the norm. How you manage system services will determine, to a large extent, whether you and your users are constantly bumping up against problems sharing data, files, printers, and applications.

This *is* the real world. There is no escaping the Internet or the attraction of desktop systems with increasing power and decreasing price tags. Then, again, we wouldn't *want* to. Along with the challenges of surviving in today's complex computing environments, there is a lot of excitement in the process of configuring and managing our networks. Even after as many years as we have spent doing Unix systems administration, we still get a thrill the first time some device or network service we're setting up suddenly springs to life. Today's networks are complicated and, at times, frustrating. Today's networks are fun. We really wouldn't have it any other way.

In Chapter 17, we talk about the problems and responsibilities associated with running an Internet site. In Chapter 18, we provide suggestions and techniques for co-existing with the Evil Empire—in other words, managing the heterogeneous network. Both situations—being on the Internet and working within a mixed client environment are more the norm than the exception these days. We hope that something within these two chapters will manage your role in these real-world situations.

## CHAPTER 17

Running an Internet Site

W hat does it mean to run an Internet site? Most of us are on the Internet, more or less. We get mail from around the globe. We search for technical answers and new hardware using our Netscape browsers. Running an Internet site is more than being on the Internet, however. It's participating on the Internet, often being a source for tools and expertise, rather than just a consumer.

This is true for businesses small or large, whether technical or not. Diners in Pennsylvania post their menus on the Web. Artists display collections of their works. Poets, sailors, architects, and accountants—all manner of craftsmen are offering their works for purchase or admiration on the Internet. Not just a population explosion, however, the trend toward near-universal Internet participation is also giving rise to new organizational structures. Increasingly, corporations are forming partnerships and taking advantage of the ease with which information can be shared and distributed. Corresponding changes, both technical and political, are needed to manage the delicate balances of competition and cooperation, threat and opportunity.

Along with our participation on the Internet comes a new set of responsibilities and concerns. Security is one of the top concerns. How do we protect our assets from malicious and inadvertent damage? Liability is another. How do we keep our systems and our users from becoming active or unwitting participants in fraudulent activities? How do we ensure that our systems don't become repositories of unauthorized copyrighted materials? How do we avoid becoming conduits for spam? We offer some guidance with respect to these concerns and suggest some avenues for further exploration of security issues in Chapter 12.

The Dangers of Internet Presence

There are several reasons why connection to the Internet is inherently dangerous:

- TCP/IP services are flawed.
- The Internet is growing every minute.
- Hackers are motivated.

Initially designed to be open, services that run on and run the Internet are now being retrofitted with restrictions and security extensions. With every security enhancement, there is an increased sophistication (read: *complexity*) and, as is often the case, a new and different set of problems. In addition, Internet connections are based on protocols that break network connections (whether connection-oriented or connectionless) into packets that travel freely across whatever routes seem best at the time. Unless precautions are taken to obfuscate their contents (i.e., by using encryption), they can be intercepted and, possibly, altered en route to their destination.

At the same time that we are facing these old and new dangers, use of the Internet is increasing faster than the ozone is diminishing. The steady rise of netizens brings additional problems—both advertent and inadvertent. Increased traffic leads to potential bottlenecks, service overruns, and increasing activity at Internet sites. There is also a growing population of hackers; most of them grew up on the Web and now use the Internet as a kind of cyberplayground for their malevolent hobby.

Many network services could, at least theoretically, be secured, but they cannot necessarily be secured in isolation (i.e., without consideration to other network services) or across the board on a highly heterogeneous network or the Internet. The most practical solution for many organizations is, therefore, to invest their efforts in single connections to the Internet that are both highly constrained and not very interesting.

Fortunately, tools for limiting the risk of participating on the Internet are, more or less, keeping pace with the dangers. Firewall technology and security-hardened network services are helping sysadmins to maintain some semblance of security on their networks. Office workers are dialing in to their ISPs and then using VPN products to securely connect to their offices. Sendmail is refusing to provide lists of e-mail addresses or to relay messages for strangers. Encrypting messages in most client e-mail products is now as simple as clicking a button.

The DMZ

The term *DMZ* stands for *demilitarized zone* and derives from international conflicts where a neutral buffer is established between warring parties. In a networking context, it's a barrier between your network and the outside world. A DMZ is not part of your network in the strictest sense of the word nor part of the Internet. By putting what is essentially an informational air lock between critical resources and a myriad of unknown dangers, you reduce the risk of anyone on the outside taking advantage of your systems.

A DMZ is, typically, the networking between your Internet router and your bastion host. This can be accomplished in one of two fashions. Either the DMZ can be the segment between two physical firewalls, or it can be a third network interface off of your existing firewall. In either case, the normal access controls allow traffic to flow from the Internet to the DMZ, and from the DMZ to the internal network, but never would anything be allowed directly from the Internet to your internal network. Figure 17.1 depicts a typical configuration where a bastion host is deployed to restricts access to a network. The router only permits traffic to and from the bastion host.

Firewalls

Firewalls are like traffic cops. They look at all connections that try to make it across the barrier and decide whether to let them through, based on protocols or addresses. The name, of course, derives from firewalls in other contexts—

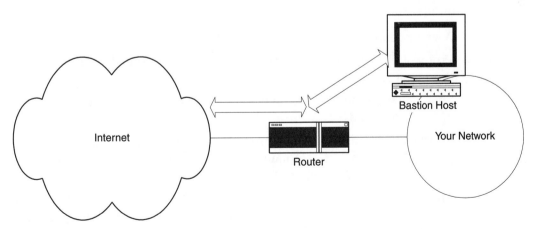

Figure 17.1 A bastion host.

between you and the engine in your car or your townhouse and the one next door. The idea is similar; a firewall is a barrier against danger. On a network, a firewall can be a device unto itself, but is usually software running on a router or on a single-purpose host. It is unwise to use a firewall for any other purpose. It is unwise to allow logins (other than those that are needed for its maintenance) or provide any additional services—for the simple reason that these services might be exploited and might provide ways around the firewall's constraints.

Firewalls are located at boundaries between organizations that do not want any and all traffic passing between them. Firewalls can be configured to pass or block data based upon port, IP address, authenticated user, and other criteria. The more sophisticated you make your firewall implementation, the more chances there are for error. The best policy is to start with a blanket "Deny all traffic" statement, then open up specific external hosts and ports for access to specific DMZ hosts and ports, and do the same for access between the DMZ and the internal network.

Decisions regarding the purchase and configuration of firewalls involve a number of factors. These include your basic goal, your organizational policies, your staff, and your budget. Whether you are trying to provide remote access service to a handful of roaming employees or ward off service attacks determines the solution you should choose. Without strong security policies and control over your organization's networking architecture, a firewall may be next to useless. You'll need to gauge the extent to which you can ensure that connections around the firewall are not permitted. You also have to take a hard look at your budget. A commercial firewall package will likely cost upwards of $100,000.

Firewalls provide these basic functions:

- A single control point for Internet security
- Protocol filtering—blocking protocols that are not needed, especially those that are risky
- Source/destination filtering—blocking sites you don't trust (or allowing *only* those you do)
- Information hiding—making information that is readily available inside your organization (e.g., usernames and host names) unavailable from the outside or on the firewall itself
- Application gateways—stop points through which services users must connect before proceeding further, providing opportunities for extensive logging and application-level control
- Concentrated and extended logging of activity across the firewall

Firewalls cannot protect against every possible type of damage or attack. In fact, the best firewall is one that is turned off. The worst is one that's improperly configured. One of the biggest misconceptions out there is the thought that just because you have a firewall, you are safe. Most attacks are not against firewalls; rather, they go through the firewalls on ports that are already open. Also, they can't protect you from data walking out the door in someone's breast pocket. They can't protect you against break-ins if someone leaves a modem hooked up to a workstation. They can't protect you if they're not configured properly or if someone knows an authorized user's username and password (and remote login is allowed). They can't protect you from viruses except when they're specially configured to do so.

NOTE In spite of the simplicity of the filtering examples provided in the following section, do *not* get the impression that configuring and maintaining a firewall is easy. There is a lot of thinking and testing needed before you'll be ready to establish the seemingly simple rules and meet the continuing need for monitoring and updating.

In the following sections, we describe the basic types of firewalls and mention some alternatives.

Understanding Ports and Protocols

Before we begin discussing how firewalls work, a review of the basics of the Transmission Control Protocol/Internet Protocol (TCP/IP) and the role of ports and protocols is in order. TCP/IP is used on local area networks (LANs) as well as on the Internet itself. You don't have to know much detail about the internals of TCP/IP in order to use it, but any knowledge you have will undoubtedly come in handy when you run into problems.

TCP/IP refers to a family of related protocols. The specifications are published so that anyone can build compatible tools and products. The major protocols comprising the protocol suite are the Internet Protocol (IP), Transmission Control Protocol (TCP), and User Datagram Protocol (UDP).

IP is the foundation for the other protocols and provides addressing—the familiar IP addresses in dotted octet notation (e.g., 192.90.200.2) that identify each host. IP provides addresses (IP or network addresses—*not* hardware or MAC addresses), but doesn't guarantee delivery of packets from one host to another. It leaves that part of the work to other protocols.

TCP provides for guaranteed packet delivery. This doesn't actually mean that packets always get where they're supposed to go, of course. Systems crash, routers fail, and problems with the receiving applications can result in data failing to reach the far end of a connection. Instead, it means that there is a mechanism built into the protocol for acknowledgment and for retransmission. Packets frequently don't reach their destination. Were these mechanisms not in place, few of our connections would seem reliable from our vantage point as sysadmins and as users.

TCP is called a *connection-oriented* protocol. This means that there are three phases to a TCP connection—setup, data transmission, and shutdown. In addition, packets are serialized and can be reordered if they arrive at the far end out of sequence. TCP also incorporates an important addition to the addressing structure of packets-*ports*. Ports identify particular services on the communicating systems that are active in the connection.

UDP is a *connectionless* protocol. There are no setup and shutdown phases involved in UDP transmissions. UDP is used by services that do not require anything more than the transmission of data. The common analogy is to say that TCP is similar in character to a phone conversation, while UDP is similar in character to a letter that arrives in the mail.

TCP/IP involves other protocols, such as ICMP, which we will not discuss here. There are many extremely good books written on the subject, and we encourage you to do further reading if you are interested in understanding the Internet extremely well.

Services

Most Unix servers support a wide range of network services, including FTP, telnet, sendmail, POP, printing services, news and Web servers and more. Each of these runs (i.e., listens for requests) on its own port. Some use UDP and others TCP; some services use both.

There are two basic ways that these processes are initiated—starting up as background tasks in the start/stop scripts (see Chapter 4) or starting up as requested through the services of inetd. To determine which of the processes on your systems start during bootup and changes of run state, examine the /etc/init.d and /etc/rc?.d directories. These include the inetd service itself, NFS, and sendmail and httpd processes, along with numerous others. Though many services could be initiated either way, there is generally a good reason for the choices made. For some services, like inetd, this is clearly the only option. For others, it's only practical for them to run constantly in the background. Services that run through the auspices of inetd are more likely to be run *infrequently*. In addition, the services are often simpler, since some of the overhead involved in making and breaking connections is managed by inetd rather than by the services themselves.

The inetd Process

The inetd process is sometimes referred to as the *superserver*. It listens on many ports and starts the appropriate service as needed. To determine which of your services runs through inetd, you have only to examine your /etc/inetd.conf file. This is inetd's configuration file. Here are a few lines excerpted from a typical inetd.conf file:

```
#  <service_name> <socket_type> <proto> <flags> <user> <server_pathname>
<args>

# Ftp and telnet are standard Internet services.
#
ftp          stream        tcp       nowait     root    /usr/sbin/in.ftpd
in.ftpd
telnet stream tcp nowait        root       /usr/sbin/in.telnetd
in.telnetd
```

Like most files on Unix systems, comment lines start with a pound sign (#). The seven fields that comprise each service line are as follows:

1. *Service_name.* As specified in the /etc/services file, which associates services with particular ports.

2. *Socket_type.* The type *stream* is used with TCP connections, and *dgram* (meaning datagram) is for UDP.

3. *Protocol.* The protocol used by the server. These are almost always TCP or UDP, but you will see some RPC types as well.

4. *Wait/nowait.* This is a flag used to determine whether inetd will resume listening immediately (nowait) or only after the service terminates (wait).

5. *User.* The username the process runs under.

6. *Service_pathname.* The full pathname to the service.

7. *Args.* The service's arguments. This includes the service name (and often no additional arguments).

Ports also fall into three broad categories—*well-known* (also called *reserved*), *registered,* and *ephemeral* (the rest). Ports with numbers below 1024 should only be used for the service for which these ports are reserved. If you ran sendmail on any other port than 25, after all, no other system would know how to communicate with it. Ports above 1023 are often used without concern for their official registrations. For example, you will often see user Web sites running on port 8000 (root's port is 80). Ports above 49151 are officially available for any service you might want to build or configure to run on them.

Now let's briefly run through a typical connection. A user starts a telnet session with a *telnet spoon* command. The user's telnet process is allocated an unprivileged port on the local machine. That process connects with the privileged port on the system the user is trying to reach (telnet uses port 23). The remote telnet daemon, telnetd, then responds to the assigned port on the client. The connection is established and the telnet session proceeds to completion. If you wanted to block telnet sessions on spoon, therefore, all you would need to do is inactivate port 23. That's the only port that telnet is listening on, even though the originating (client) process will be on some random port above 1023. This snoop excerpt shows the ports in an active telnet session (from the server side):

```
spoon# snoop port 23
. . .
TCP: Source port = 23
TCP: Destination port = 1026
```

Some services do not use privileged (i.e., known) ports and are, therefore, harder to block. Your firewall may make it easy to block all ports with port numbers below 1024 (i.e., all privileged ports), but this will block all services. A combination of rules and exceptions may be what it takes to select the proper set of services.

Poor firewall management can be worse than having no firewall at all. Make sure that you get a firewall product that is easy to configure or that you spend enough time to fully understand what you are blocking and what you are allowing through.

Packet Filtering

The primary function of a firewall is to filter packets—basically, allowing them through or stopping them at the firewall. Packets can be filtered on a number of criteria—protocol, IP address of the source or destination, or port (TCP/UDP) of the destination or source. If you want to prevent ping attacks, for example, blocking ICMP traffic at the firewall prevents these requests from reaching your hosts. This is very similar to the functions performed by access lists on routers.

The decision as to what protocols you want to filter depends on the particular policies your organization has in effect and what you are trying to accomplish. Typically, protocols that are blocked at the firewall include FTP, TFTP, X, RPC (including NFS, NIS, and NIS+), r commands (e.g., rlogin), telnet, RIP, and UUCP. If you're running a Web site, you'll need to support HTTPD and maybe also FTP. You probably need to allow e-mail through, using SMTP. We suggest that you spend some quality time with your network services files (e.g., /etc/services) and determine what services you must support and which you can filter without impacting the productivity of your organization.

Packet filtering rules take a general form including packet type, source and destination addresses, source and destination ports, and what is to be done with

Table 17.1   Sample Deny Rule

FIELD	SAMPLE VALUE
Type	tcp
Source IP address	0.0.0.0/0
Destination IP address	0.0.0.0/0
Source port	any
Destination port	< 1024
Action	deny

Table 17.2   Sample Permit Rule

FIELD	SAMPLE VALUE
Type	tcp
Source IP address	220.203.27.0/24
Destination IP address	0.0.0.0/0
Source port	any
Destination port	23
Action	permit

packets that match the specified criteria. For example, a rule that looks like Table 17.1 would reject requests for any privileged port, regardless of where they derived. The network designator 0.0.0.0/0 matches *any* address. An address like 220.203.27.0/24 would match any host on the 220.203.27.0 network; the 24 indicates that the first 24 bits are significant with respect to the matching. The rule shown in Table 17.2 allows telnet from one particular class C network.

The more sophisticated packet filtering firewalls also allow you to configure when filtering happens—when a packet is received or when it is sent. These options are usually referred to by the terms *on input* and *on output*. They can also filter packets leaving your network as easily as those that are arriving; not every danger is out there. Other features include filtering, the ability to avoid the use of routes learned from other systems, and the ability to disable source routing. Firewalls that cannot be reprogrammed remotely provide an additional level of security; the last thing you want is for your firewall to fall into the hands of a hacker.

Packet-filtering firewalls are also called *network-level* firewalls.

Proxy Servers

A proxy server (also called an *application gateway*) is an application that sits between a network service and the Internet. Because it must speak and understand whatever protocol the application uses, it also can manipulate the data and commands that it intercepts. Most proxies, therefore, can effect finely tuned control over whatever service they are proxying for. They also provide fairly extensive logging and can add more rigorous authentication support than is generally enforced (e.g., they could authenticate with another system before making the connection to the target service). They can also replace network addresses as they pass packets to the application and to the caller.

Proxies are tied to specific network services. You might set up a proxy for telnet, ftp or http, and so on. A set of proxy servers, the TIS Internet Firewall Toolkit, is available from http://www.tis.com. There is also a generic proxy system called Socks that can be used to make a client-side application work through a firewall. Information on Socks is available from www.socks.nec.com.

When you use proxy servers, no network traffic goes directly to the services in question. Some proxy systems are less transparent to end users than their packet-filtering counterparts, especially older systems.

Application-level firewalls permit no traffic directly between networks but, instead, run proxy servers.

Because these types of firewalls run processes to handle each application or port range separately, CPU usage and scalability is an issue. Make sure you define your requirements adequately prior to sizing a machine as an application firewall.

Stateful Inspection

Many modern network-level firewalls now maintain internal information about the state of connections passing through them. Similar to proxies in the level of application control available, firewalls equipped to do stateful inspection examine the contents of data streams without requiring a proxy for each service to be monitored and without the performance hit that is easy to imagine might be possible. FireWall-1 and VPN-1 Gateway, both products of Check Point, include a Security Policy Editor that allows you to configure stateful inspection options.

Patented by Check Point, stateful inspection allows content-level inspection of traffic crossing a firewall. For example, you can:

- Check for malicious code (e.g., applets).
- Scan e-mail attachments for code or viruses.
- Use built-in APIs to integrate third-party screening and antivirus applications.
- Ignore other than basic SMTP commands (hiding information and preventing SITE EXEC commands).

- Remove malicious code and viruses before forwarding the contents of the communication.

- Scan URLs for specific pages or content types—using wildcard specifications, file specifications, or third-party databases.

- Strip Java and ActiveX code and tags (protecting against attacks).

- Block spam relays.

- Block suspicious addresses.

- Hide internal addresses.

- Drop mail (i.e., filter) from given addresses.

- Strip attachments of given types from mail.

- Strip the received information from outgoing communications (concealing organizational information).

- Drop mail messages larger than a specified size.

- Run filename and virus checking for ftp.

- Implement optional blocking of ftp get requests.

Firewall Alternatives

Firewalls have also been constructed using dual-homed hosts—systems with two network interfaces, one connected to the outside and one to the inside network. With IP forwarding disabled, users would have to log in to the dual-homed system before proceeding past it. The system would then act as a choke point. Systems like these were more popular before the advent of the Web. Figure 17.2 illustrates the position of a dual-homed host. Figures 17.3 and 17.4 illustrate two additional firewall techniques—a screened subnet and a screening firewall. In a screened subnet, the router is acting at a network level. In the screening firewall, only certain protocols are allowed to pass.

Another alternative to a standard firewall is software, such as TCP Wrapper (described in Chapter 12), which adds access control to standard network services that are invoked through inetd (e.g., telnet and FTP), but does not protect other services.

Firewall Security

For a firewall to provide security, it must itself be secure. Here are some general rules of thumb to help you keep your firewall functioning well and safe from tampering.

- Maintaining extensive logs on a firewall is important to help determine if the firewall is indeed working and to detect suspicious activity

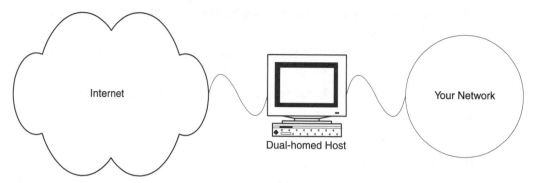

Figure 17.2   A dual-homed host.

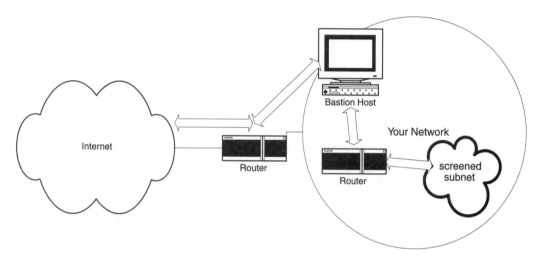

Figure 17.3   A screened subnet.

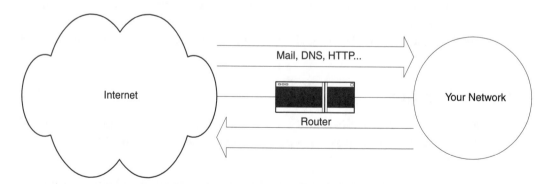

Figure 17.4   A screening firewall.

(which could be a precursor to an attack of some kind). Review these logs periodically.

- Do not assume the integrity of your firewall. Examine it from time to time.

- Install patches as required. (Don't think your firewall can't possibly need them.)

- Make sure your firewall is configured with adequate memory and be attuned to any sign of hardware failure.

- Provide a backup strategy should your firewall fail.

- Limit or ban network logins to your firewall. If you must log in, use Secure Shell (SSH) or a similar encrypted method of access. Do not use telnet, as your entire session can be sniffed and your IDs and passwords determined.

- Use authentication tokens (e.g., SecurID) if you must log in over the net.

- Do not run any services on the firewall that don't relate to and are not needed by the firewall-, no NIS, no NFS, and so on.

- Disable finger.

- Don't allow host trust (~/.rhosts or hosts.equiv type access) on your firewall.

Solaris Firewalls

The overall goal for a firewall is to create a virtual network perimeter around your network and enforce rules consistent with organization policy about who and what gets through. There are a number of firewall products available for Solaris systems. Those that we know of by experience or reputation include the following:

- Checkpoint Firewall 1
- Sun SPF300
- Raptor
- Gauntlet / TIS Toolkit

DNS and E-mail Configuration

In Chapter 7, we discuss the configuration and management of DNS. Setting up your name server is an essential step in establishing your Internet presence. You should be sure to set up the obvious servers. If your domain were foo.com, you would want to set up *www.foo.com* and probably also mail.foo.com and ftp.foo.com. Set up a single mail exchanger, but back it up with a secondary, maybe even a tertiary, to ensure that your mail services will not be disrupted if your primary mail server has problems. For many organizations, the movement of mail in and out is one of the primary conduits for business, and significant work comes to a halt if this exchange of messages stops. As with hostnames, the use of obvious e-mail addresses for organizational functions will facilitate communications with your customers and users. We suggest that you consider establishing some additional predictable e-mail addresses in addition to the standard ones (e.g., postmaster): info, webmaster, jobs, and sysadmin.

You can distribute mail to groups of individuals by using e-mail aliases if this is appropriate. For example, if mail addressed to *sysadmin@foo.com* should be received by four different individuals, you can set up an alias that causes this to happen.

Having a single mail server will simplify e-mail addressing for everyone who writes to your users and also makes it easier to manage e-mail services for individuals who move from one part of the organization to another. The only real drawback is that the larger your user base, the more likely it will be that there will be username conflicts. Though maintaining unique UIDs and unique usernames across an organization is the ideal, you might have a Jane Doe and a John Doe strongly identifying with the username jdoe. Another useful technique for reducing the identity conflicts in your organization is to provide aliases for such users. If Jane Doe can have mail addressed to *jane doe@foo.com* or *jane.doe@foo.com* as well as *jdoe2@foo.com*, she might be happier handing out her business cards.

Sendmail Configuration

They used to call it *sendmail hell*, and anyone with guts enough to get into sendmail's rewriting rules had an instant reputation for being a hacker (in the good sense of the word). It's getting much better. Recent versions of sendmail (e.g., 8.9.3) allow you to configure major features by adding them to an m4 configuration file and then using the m4 tool (e.g., GNU m4) to create your sendmail configuration file, sendmail.cf. The following file is the generic_solaris2.mc file with one additional line at the bottom.

```
divert(-1)
#
# Copyright (c) 1998 Sendmail, Inc.   All rights reserved.
# Copyright (c) 1983 Eric P. Allman.   All rights reserved.
# Copyright (c) 1988, 1993
#      The Regents of the University of California. All rights reserved.
#
# By using this file, you agree to the terms and conditions set
# forth in the LICENSE file which can be found at the top level of
# the sendmail distribution.
#
```

```
#
#
#  This is a generic configuration file for SunOS 5.x (a.k.a. Solaris 2.x)
#  It has support for local and SMTP mail only.  If you want to
#  customize it, copy it to a name appropriate for your environment
#  and do the modifications there.
#

divert(0)dnl
VERSIONID('@(#)generic-solaris2.mc     8.8 (Berkeley)
5/19/1998')
OSTYPE(solaris2)dnl
DOMAIN(generic)dnl
MAILER(local)dnl
MAILER(smtp)dnl
define('confDOMAIN_NAME,'foo.com')
```

We added the last line to illustrate how you can further tweak the sendmail.cf file you will be creating. The sendmail 8.9.3 distribution includes more than a hundred of these variables. This particular one represents the variable that will be used (if you specify it) to compose the domain. This line would be needed only if your host could not determine this on its own. For those of you've who have spent any time inside the sendmail configuration file, this corresponds to the $j macro.

In addition, since sendmail's default behavior is better in terms of security (e.g., no relaying for outsiders by default), you don't have to work as hard to configure it with more conservative options. There are several features you'll probably want to use. You can also set up a database of known spammers and populate it from one of the sites keeping track of the more vigorous spam generators. In addition, you can modify some of your sendmail parameters to lessen the chance that your sendmail service will be used against you. You want to be sure that no one can overwhelm your mail system by sending volumes of large messages, straining the system. By limiting the speed with which sendmail responds as well as its timeout options, you can prevent this from happening. You should browse through the sendmail release notes for the particulars. It's almost as thick as the O'Reilly book *sendmail* by Brian Costales—so find a comfortable chair.

Sendmail security is significantly improved, it seems, with every release. A significant amount of sendmail security, however, still rests with you. Here are some important pointers:

- Don't leave your aliases, /etc/aliases, file, or the NIS map writable.

- Ensure that all files that sendmail reads—its configuration file, lists of domains for which it accepts mail, spammer databases, and so forth—can be altered only by root.

- Make sure .forward files cannot be created or changed by anyone other than their rightful users.

- Outlaw :include: files in your aliases.

Another e-mail issue that you should be concerned with is user privacy. User mail files (stored, by default, in /var/mail) should not be readable by anyone other than the owner. Under certain circumstances, anyone reading someone else's e-mail is guilty of a violation of privacy. Be cognizant of organization policy as well as federal law in managing your users' inboxes.

Client Mail Protocols

Sendmail isn't the only software that sysadmins have to deal with in today's networks. Most client non-Unix systems will use POP or IMAP to fetch their e-mail from your mail servers. The typical mail client—such as Eudora or Microsoft Outlook—uses POP or IMAP to retrieve mail and SMTP to send it. Generally, the protocols used are POP version 3 (POP3) and IMAP version 4 (IMAP4).

POP3 is a dead-simple protocol. In fact, it has only the following commands: *user, pass, stat, list, retr, dele,* and *quit.* Their meanings are listed in Table 17.3.

Note the conversation ensuing between a POP3 user and the popper process on the host:

```
telnet spoon 110
Trying 220.203.27.111...
Connected to spoon.
Escape character is '^]'.
+OK QPOP (version 2.53) at spoon starting. <2512.935598886@spoon>
user sandra
+OK Password required for sandra.
pass NotMyPswd
```

Table 17.3 POP3 Commands and Actions

COMMAND	ACTIONS
user	Identifies the user connecting to the service
pass	Announces the password
stat	Makes a status request (tells you how many messages are in your inbox)
list	Lists the messages and lengths
retr	Downloads a message
dele	Deletes a message
quit	Exits

```
+OK sandra has 2282 messages (32289278 octets).
stat
+OK 2282 32289278
dele 1
+OK Message 1 has been deleted.
quit
+OK Pop server at spoon signing off.
Connection closed by foreign host.
```

To set up POP3, you need the popper executable plus the line in your /etc/inetd.conf file/, as shown in the following example. Users can retrieve their mail from almost anywhere. The most complicated part of running POP is keeping your users in touch with where their e-mail is at any point in time. Unless they are careful to select the *leave mail on the server* option when they are popping in, their mail will be gone when they come back to the office. Make sure that they understand this. Once some of their mail is on their home systems, some is on their laptops, and some is at work, they will begin to feel more fragmented and frustrated than usual.

```
# for the popper daemon:
pop3    stream  tcp    nowait  root    /usr/sbin/popper    popper -s
# for IMAP clients:
imap    stream  tcp    nowait  root    /usr/local/etc/imapd    imapd
```

IMAP4 is another mail service, but one that supports e-mail folders. Many PC mail clients now use IMAP4. Again, be careful to inform your users about the implications of downloading mail from a particular location.

One problem that you need to watch out for with POP and IMAP clients is a mail buildup on the server. Many mail clients keep a map of which messages have been deleted by the user but do not actually delete the messages on the server. From the users' point of view, they are managing their mail holdings responsibly. Meanwhile, their mail on the server may be larger than 100Mb per user, dominating the space available for incoming mail.

Configuring FTP Services

Don't use Solaris ftp for your Internet services. The Solaris ftp is a perfectly functional, but limited, FTP service. For your Internet services, download and install *wuarchive-ftpd* (commonly referred to as *wu-ftpd*)—a replacement FTP daemon for Unix systems, and the most popular FTP daemon on the Internet. With considerably better security, logging, and differentiation between users and virtual users, wu-ftpd is the choice of responsible sysadmins. The following URL, a site maintained by Kent Lanfield, is a source of lots of useful information and sample scripts:

www.landfield.com/wu-ftpd

Abuses of FTP include using it as a repository for pirated software and other copyrighted material and pornography. In addition, misconfigured FTP setups have sometimes allowed processes to be run under the FTP userid.

To set up anonymous FTP service, you should determine the purpose of the service—whether it is intended to serve as a drop-off only, as an archive only, or must support both functions. If your FTP service is an archive, restrict access so that it is read-only to the FTP user. If your FTP service is for drop-offs only, don't provide read access.

FTP sites can also impact the performance of the system on which they are running. In a prior position, one of the authors noted that a Sun client had slowed to a point at which it was almost useless. As it turned out, an undergrad assistant in the department had mirrored a collection of image files (including "Todd in Tights"). The explosion of logins dragged the system to its knees.

To avoid abuses of your FTP site, scan its contents regularly, looking for suspicious files. Don't forget to use the -*a* option so that you will spot any hidden files or directories. We also strongly suggest that you read the following guidelines produced by CERT:

- ftp://ftp.cert.org/pub/tech tips/anonymous ftp config
- ftp://ftp.cert.org/pub/tech_tips/anonymous_ftp_abuses

Make sure that the wu-ftpd package you install is the correct one for your Solaris version. It may not compile or work properly otherwise.

Managing Your Web Presence

There's a very conspicuous billboard on Route 101, south of San Francisco. It says something like "My grandma can make a better Web site than your grandma." If you're putting up a Web site for your company, you've got a lot of grandmas competing with you for browsers' eyeballs. You've also got a lot of other companies, a lot of independent contractors, a lot of college students, a lot of hobbyists, and a lot of kids. You'll want your site to be not only attractive, but also effective and responsive. But that's only the *fun* part of building a Web site. You'll also want to keep it up as close to 24 by 7 as possible. Configuring a Web site involves a series of steps. There are a number of important configuration files to set up once your Web server software is installed—and some new log files to maintain, process, and clean up after.

The most popular Web server at this point in time is Apache—and for good reason. Its configuration files are easy to understand and modify. It performs well and has all the features most of us could want. The remainder of this section provides an overview of an Apache Web site.

Specifying Ports and Protocols

As indicated earlier, the well-known (or *reserved*) port for httpd, the HTTP daemon, is port 80. Whenever you visit a Web site without specifying otherwise, your browser is communicating with this port. To specify an alternate port, you include it at the end of the home page URL, like this:

www.somesite.com:8888

You are seldom likely to use this syntax, but might run into it if the site is run by an ordinary (not a system) user or if the site is *cloaked* (i.e., hidden by virtue of running on an unexpected port).

The HTTP protocol, as you probably well know, includes directives-*get, put, post, link, unlink,* and *delete.* Specifications for the HTTP protocol also identify the form of a URL as http:// followed by the hostname (e.g., *www.foo.com*), an optional colon and port number (e.g., :8888) and an optional path (needed if you are accessing other than the home page). If you wanted to go directly to a subsidiary page on a cloaked site, you might use an address like this:

www.foo.com:8888/contributor/notes

Processes

The HTTP daemon, httpd, is started up through the init process. A typical start/stop script would look like this:

```sh
#!/bin/sh

#
# Start WWW httpd for www.foo.com.
#

httpd="/usr/sbin/httpd-apache"
httpdconf="/etc/httpd-apache.conf"
startbanner="Starting Apache WWW daemon for www.foo.com."
stopbanner="Stopping Apache WWW daemon for www.foo.com."
pidfile="/etc/httpd-apache.pid"

case "$1" in
'start')
     if [ -f $httpdconf -a -f $httpd ] ; then
         echo "$startbanner"
         $httpd -f $httpdconf &
     else
         echo "$0: unable to find $httpdconf or $httpd"
```

```
            exit
       fi
       ;;
'stop')
       if [ -f $pidfile ] ; then
            echo "$stopbanner"
            PID='cat $pidfile'
            /usr/bin/kill ${PID} 1> /dev/null 2>&1
       else
            PID='/bin/ps -ef | grep httpd-apache | grep -v grep | awk '{print
$2}''
       if [ ! -z "$PID" ] ; then
                echo "$stopbanner"
                /usr/bin/kill ${PID} 1> /dev/null 2>&1
            fi
       fi
       ;;
*)
       echo "Usage: $0 { start | stop }"
       ;;
esac
exit 0
```

If stored as /etc/init.d/httpd and hard-linked as /etc/rc3.d/S98httpd and as /etc/rc2.d/K55httpd, the daemon would be stopped in run state 2 and start in run state 3. If you needed to restart the daemons manually, you might do this:

```
cd /etc/init.d
./httpd-apache stop;./httpd-apache start
```

We said *daemons* because there will likely be many more than one running. The Apache server will fork additional processes as needed to help support the load.

Configuration Files

Apache configuration files are fairly straightforward and easy to locate. If you were called to modify the configuration on an unfamiliar system, you could find the configuration files by first looking at the startup script. As previously shown, this file indicates the location of the configuration files and the daemon process.

The noncomment lines in the configuration file will include lines such as these:

```
BindAddress foo
ErrorLog logs/www.foo.com-errors
Group staff
HostnameLookups on
KeepAlive 5
```

```
KeepAliveTimeout 15
MaxClients 150
MaxRequestsPerChild 30
MaxSpareServers 10
MinSpareServers 5
PidFile /etc/httpd-apache-foo.pid
Port 80
ScoreBoardFile logs/www.foo.com-status
ServerAdmin webmaster@foo.com
ServerName www.foo.com
ServerRoot /var/WWW/apache_1.1.1/foo
ServerType standalone
StartServers 5
Timeout 400
TransferLog logs/www.foo.com-access
User nobody
```

As you can see from this list, the base of the Web directory (/var/WWW/apache_
1.1.1/foo in this case) is specified as the *ServerRoot*. The configuration (conf)
and log directories are within this directory. The conf directory contains the
remainder of the configuration files:

access.conf. The access permissions configuration file. It is used to set
access permissions on files, directories, and scripts.

httpd.conf. The primary configuration file. It tells the server how to run—
identifies the port, the ServerRoot directory, and the username to which
e-mail regarding problems should be sent.

mime.types. This file is not a configuration file in the same sense as the
others but lists mime types (e.g., text/html).

srm.conf. The resource configuration file. It identifies what resources should
be offered from your Web site and how they should be offered. Included in
this file is the specification for the root of your document (i.e., Web content) directory. It will look something like this:

```
DocumentRoot /var/www/spautlacity/docs
```

Directory Structure

The directory structure that your site will use depends, of course, on your pref-
erences and the setup on the configuration files listed previously. However, the
form most Web sites take looks roughly like this:

```
                +--- conf
                |
ServerRoot --+--- logs

                   +--- cgi-bin
                   |
```

```
DocumentRoot --+--- icons
               |
               +--- images
               |
               +--- [content subdirectories]
               |
               index.html
```

Your visitors will have access only to files within the DocumentRoot subdirectory and below. They will not have access to your configuration and log files. Directories included within your directory structure should have permissions set to 755 (rwxr-xr-x), html files to 644 (rw-r-r—), and cgi scripts to 755 (rwxr-xr-x) for the Web site to work as intended. If you have multiple people supporting your Web site, you may open up group permissions, but continue to restrict general access.

Busy Web sites will generate lengthy log files. You should be careful to monitor space usage and to compress and archive older files as needed. To collect this information and not use it, on the other hand, is inadvisable. Log files are a source of considerable information on the popularity and use of your site. Because none of us has the time or interest to read megabytes of get requests each and every day, there are tools that can help you digest your log files. Of the free tools, the best we have found is *Analog*. It runs through even very large log files quickly and generates an HTML report including graphs detailing file accesses and displaying your hits over the span of a month or daily averages, depending how what you specify in your configuration file. We found it extremely easy to set up and use, and the reports it created provided some insights we didn't expect. You can learn more about or obtain Analog from this Web site:

www.statslab.cam.ac.uk/~sret1/analog

If you can afford the resources, it's a good idea to maintain both an internal development Web site and a public Web site. This permits you to test changes to your Web site and then *push* (i.e., mirror) your Web site when the changes have been verified; duplicate your site if it is appropriate to do so; or quickly overwrite your site if, in spite of your efforts, someone breaks in and replaces your corporate image with pictures of Todd (see "Configuring FTP Services"). We recommend the Mirror script (mirror.pl). Mirror is a package written in Perl that uses FTP to duplicate an entire directory hierarchy on another system. It is not necessarily restricted to use as a push resource for Web sites, but it serves this purpose very well. Simple configuration files identify the source and destination hosts, user, and password (be careful to protect these files), along with expressions that detail what should be excluded from the push, and so forth. You can learn about Mirror and obtain the package from this Web site:

sunsite.doc.ic.ac.uk/public/packages/mirror/mirror.html

Summary

Running an Internet site is a major responsibility. While you are providing your users with access to Internet resources, you are also providing the outside world with limited access to your organization's resources, and therefore influencing its public image.

A firewall is strongly recommended, whether you spend the money to buy a commercial tool or set one up yourself with a spare system—but do the latter only if you have the time and resources to do it right. How successful you will be at limiting what comes into and goes out of your Internet site will depend on how well your organization's policies are specified and implemented and the degree to which your organization backs your efforts to limit access.

Regardless of whether you are able to sit behind a firewall, you cannot take security for granted. Some other helpful security reminders include the following:

- Your services are secure only if they are properly configured. Take advantage of organizations like CERT that report on security problems and fixes.

- It is important to use the latest versions of services, such as sendmail, that tend to be vulnerable to attack. The latest software will include the fixes for security holes discovered in earlier versions and may provide you with some useful configuration options you didn't have with the older release.

- Never assume that, just because there are dangers *out there*, that there are no dangers deriving from the inside. Be conscious of security in general, not just as it pertains to the Internet.

- Don't allow your Internet security setup to lull you into a false sense of security. Know how to monitor your systems and watch for signs of trouble. Consider scanning your systems from the outside, but only *with* official permission to do so!

## CHAPTER 18

Coexisting with the Evil Empire

O ne of the authors once worked in an office where everyone's desk, from the office chief to the lowliest of workers, held a Sparcstation. There was bandwidth to boot and fiber just under the floor awaiting our move to the next generation of networking. Administering this network involved writing scripts that called other scripts, and several hundred clients or user accounts could be updated with an easily constructed one-liner (e.g., *ask_clients "run_script2"*). The heart of the simple ask_clients script was a *foreach 'ypcat hosts'* command and the argument one of a number of scripts or a Solaris command. Once it was set up, managing this network was so easy that it bordered on boring. The dominant Sun network was managed by two sysadmins—from a desktop or two.

Most offices today bear little resemblance to this ideal of roughly 10 years ago. Today's networks consist of a mix of systems—Sun servers, PCs running Solaris, PCs running Windows, PCs running Linux, and Macintosh systems—running different programs for users with vastly different sets of needs and skills. It's hard to define a set of tools to manage this diverse collection of systems with the same ease that we managed homogeneous networks of Suns. Yet, this is the environment that we work in today. This is the environment that we expect you work in, as well.

Of the non-Unix systems that we have to deal with, an increasing number are running some version of Microsoft Windows—the motivation for the title of this chapter. The ability to share resources and interoperate with other types of systems is *not* one of Windows' (even Windows NT's) strengths; in fact, this is probably its greatest weakness. Microsoft Windows is what some of us like to call an "80 percent operating system." Were we left with only what we can get from Microsoft, our fate as systems administrators in mixed Unix/Windows environments would be unbearably difficult. Thanks to scores of third-party developers, we have many technologies to help bridge the gap between these two diverse technological camps. We also can't overlook the efforts of Sun Microsystems and other devotees of open systems in making it possible for such technologies to exist.

Years ago, collections of Windows or Macintosh systems seemed to be grouped together somewhere far from the Unix systems that were ours to manage. Today, they're sitting side by side with Unix systems, cabled into the same network equipment, and using the same files. In this chapter, we hope to provide some guidance on how you can manage a mixed architecture environment like this while averting chaos.

Windows Essentials

If you're not already steeped in the proper terminology to use when describing Windows systems, a little vocabulary is in order. Windows NT can be purchased in one of two versions—*Windows NT Server* and *Windows NT Workstation*. Windows NT Workstation has one basic configuration, though it can be used by multiple users and maintains separate environments for each of them with separate startup files and desktop choices. Windows NT Server, on the other hand, can provide additional services and can act as a *domain controller*—similar to a NIS/NIS+ server. From a security point of view, the important distinction is between workstations (NT Workstation or NT Server performing as a workstation) and domain controllers.

Another important difference is that between *local accounts* and *domain accounts*. Local accounts are those that are used only on the local system. They don't exist as far as the domain is concerned. Most NT accounts are, however, domain accounts. These are stored on domain controllers responsible for maintaining them and authenticating requests for service (e.g., logins). Although domain controllers can provide file serving, they are not necessarily used for this; their primary role is maintaining account information and authentication.

Users and groups are not implemented identically in Windows NT and Unix systems though the concepts exist in both. Both support groups and access control lists (ACLs). Every user in either system is a member of at least one group and can be a member of more. The mechanisms are different, of course.

The Administrator account on a Windows NT system is not precisely the same as a root account on Solaris. The Administrator account cannot be served via the domain manager; it is *always* a local account. The root account can be set within NIS or NIS+, but we strongly recommend that you maintain a root login in your /etc files. If ever your NIS/NIS+ service isn't working, you can still log in and fix things.

If you don't remotely administer your Administrator accounts, you can still set the passwords remotely by logging in and using the following command:

```
net user Administrator *.
```

This command will prompt you for a new password.

Windows NT does not have the concept of a *nobody* (i.e., superuser on a remote host) user and comes with a guest account that works very differently from the guest accounts that came enabled in much older versions of SunOS. On NT servers, the guest account is assigned when the server can find no match among its valid accounts. This is markedly different from the guest account in old SunOS systems, which simply lacked a password (or maybe the password was set to *guest* or *welcome*). Both of these accounts are considered very poor practice today. The guest account should be disabled immediately following installation.

Another difference between Windows and Solaris is that Windows does not enforce the concept of a primary group. In Unix systems, the group assigned to a user in the /etc/passwd file is the user's default or primary group. On Windows systems, all user group memberships are set up within the User Manager for Domains tool. Another difference is that Windows systems have an *everybody* group—a supergroup composed of members of any group and, therefore, all users. Unix systems do not have a group that contains all users. The closest match is the *world* group, which, in general terms, refers to anybody *except* the owner and the group associated with the file. Solaris ACLs, now extended to provide secondary owners as well as specifications like "everybody *but* Mallory," are not available in Windows NT. At the same time, Solaris does not have an equivalent to NT's *take ownership* attribute; by default, only the owner of a file in Solaris can give it away (i.e., make someone else the owner).

Domain controllers are subdivided into *Primary Domain Controllers* (PDCs), of which you must have one, and *Secondary Domain Controllers* (SDCs) which act like slave NIS (or replica NIS+) servers. Changes are made on PDCs and propagated to SDCs in the same manner, and changes are made on NIS servers and propagated to slaves. Each workstation in an NT domain is a member of only one domain.

Domain controllers can establish *trust relationships* between themselves which work in a single direction only. This allows them to share account information from one domain to the next.

Associated with each NT account are the same kind of access controls you might expect, coming from a Unix background:

- Groups (so that you can manage service access by group rather than by individual user)
- Password expiration
- Password parameters (e.g., minimum length and whether a user can reuse a password)
- Whether a user can change his or her own password
- The hours during which a user can log in
- Account locking if a wrong password is used some number of times

You can use a tool available with the NTResKit to lock administrator access for anything other than local logins—the antithesis of what we're trying to do in this chapter (facilitate remote administration), but similar to the feature in Solaris (see /etc/default/login). You can do this locally through the User Manager for Domains tool by choosing Policies → User Rights, then selecting "Access this computer from network" and removing Administrator from the list (i.e., select Administrator and hit Remove).

Windows NT uses ACLs, but only with the NT file system (i.e., *not* the DOS FAT file system). Every file or object in an NT file system can have an associated ACL detailing who can access the file or object and how. ACLs are as essential to security in NT systems as they are in Solaris (refer to Chapter 1 for a description of file permissions and ACLs). Directories in NT have default ACLs that will be applied to any subsequently created file.

One oddity in the NT file system bears mentioning. There is an ACL right called *Bypass Traverse Checking* that is given by default. This particular right allows users to bypass directories for which they do not have permission; they can enter and access files further embedded in the directory structure as long as they know the full path. Unix systems, on the other hand, prevent anyone from entering or listing the contents of directories if they do not have proper permissions on the directory itself (regardless of whether they know pathnames or the embedded directories are open). We advise that you disallow this right, and thereby enforce the expected blockage when a directory is locked.

As with Unix systems, the policy of least privilege holds in Windows NT. Anyone with administrator access should be instructed to use the least privilege necessary for the task at hand. Doing so, the risk associated with any faux pas is reduced. So is the risk associated with running a malicious program or one contaminated with a virus. For those of us with enough history to admit that we make mistakes, the least-privilege policy is a matter of professionalism, not a questioning of our status or competence.

Other groups in the Windows NT system can be given the privilege required for many administrative tasks. For example, the Backup Operators, Server, and Account groups can be given privileges so that full administrator privilege is not required by the members of these groups to perform the given tasks. Administrative groups can be created on the domain, thereby providing privileges at a network level.

One of the most critical elements of Windows systems that you will need to become familiar with is the *Registry*. A large and complex tree-structured data store for native as well as third-party applications, the registry in NT systems is implemented as a hierarchy of files in Windows NT and is modified with the regedit (regedt32) command. Although the registry is binary (i.e., you look at its content through tools like regedit), it is actually stored as a hierarchy of files. Modifications to the registry should always be made cautiously, as improper registry settings can keep a system from booting. Fortunately, it is possible to both create backup copies of the registry and replace the damaged original as needed. It is important to note that, in spite of its centrally important role on NT systems, the registry is not the central repository of *all* application parameters. Some important NT services, such as IIS, store some of their configuration information in their own binary files and some in the registry.

Unlike Unix file systems, the NT file system does not have a single root. There is a root (i.e., \ directory) on each disk, and you switch from one disk to the other by entering the drive tag *D:*. This does not imply, however, that there isn't a strong analogy between the system directory on NT systems and the root and /usr directories under Unix. Most of the directories within the WINNT directory structure are protected against modification by the general user. New (postinstallation) files are generally *not*. You should be cautious, therefore, when you install application software that important files cannot be modified or removed by users. You cannot depend on third-party providers—especially if they build for both the (security weak) Windows 95/98 and the Windows NT platforms—to do this for you.

Windows NT developers seem to lack a general consensus about where and how application software makes updates within the WINNT and WINNT\system32 directories. Solaris applications primarily arrive as packages, expecting to be installed in /opt. The only impact the installation will have on our root file systems is to add, as required, start and stop scripts in the /etc/rc?.d and /etc/init.d directories. In addition, proper permissions are established during the installation. Windows applications aren't as well behaved. You will find an assortment of application files in the /WINNT/system32 directory of any well-used NT system. Considerable attention should be paid to securing Windows NT if it is to be made as secure as you expect your Solaris systems to be out of the box.

The Command Line versus the GUI

Those of us who are longtime Unix sysadmins have a decided preference for the command line. It's not because we're old dogs unwilling to learn new tricks. It's not because we're technodweebs. We *know* that, in spite of the ease with which many things can be done using modern GUI tools (such as admintool), most of the things we need to do are more easily done in scripts in which we can also incorporate related tasks or with which we can accomplish the same task for an entire group of systems or users. Adding a user or two through admintool is easy; adding 100 is painful. A simple script and a single foreach command can be done with the job in less time than it would take us to add the first user with admintool. We also know that we don't always have a GUI available. If Sandra wants to add a user while logged in from the laptop on her sailboat and anchored off Angel Island, she's going to use the command line. If Evan wants to check the temperature of his CPUs while on a business trip to New York, he's going to use the command line.

Every version of Microsoft Windows *has* a command line, of course. The problem is that Windows (even Windows NT) does not provide the same control options on the command line that are available using the GUI. Take, for example, the issue of links. Whereas Unix systems have hard links and symbolic (soft) links and the *ln* command to create either, Windows has shortcuts. Similar in function to symbolic links, shortcuts can be created only using the Windows GUI. This is one of many things that one must consider when trying to remotely manage a Windows system or manage a group of Windows systems. If you want a shortcut, you need to visit the system in person, coax the user to create one, or use a tool like pcANYWHERE or the free VNC from AT&T Research UK.

This issue isn't a small one. The more Windows systems you support, the more you will wish that you could telnet into these clients and issue commands as easily as you can in Solaris. Tools like pcANYWHERE provide for remote control of the Windows interface, but what can you do if pcANYWHERE isn't running? Ironically, you can't start pcANYWHERE and put it into "be a host" (i.e., allow another system to remotely control me) mode from the command line. One of the authors recently drove more than 100 miles to click on a button and set up this remote control feature.

Fortunately, the situation is not as dire as we, being longtime Sun users, first imagined. Given some features available, though not obviously so, with Windows NT plus the Windows NT Resource Kit NTResKit) and some third-party tools, it is possible to approach the level of control that we have with our Unix systems.

One of the first things you need to do is equip every Windows NT system—or, at least, every Windows NT server—with a telnet service. A telnet daemon is available with the NTResKit or, inexpensively, from a number of vendors. Once you have a telnet daemon installed on the NT servers you need to administer, the need for making the rounds is dramatically reduced.

There are some commands that are available from the command line in NT natively—and we are grateful for each and every one of them. Table 18.1 shows some of them and their nearest matches in Solaris.

As you can see from Table 18.1, this set of commands—and any we might have missed—is extremely limited compared to what you can do in Solaris. In addition, the list is missing some very notable entries—such as reboot. This situation is much improved with a copy of the NT Resource Kit (4.0 or later) installed. The resource kit includes a lot of tools and commands that would have made Windows NT a more complete and usable OS. In addition, you will find collections of tools on the Web that allow you to use what appear to be Unix commands, though don't be surprised if they don't work quite like their counterparts.

Table 18.1 Solaris Commands and Windows NT Native Equivalents

SOLARIS	WINDOWS NT
share /usr/local	net share newshare=D:\apps
mount remhost: /usr/local /usr/local	net use h:\\remhost\apps
cat /etc/passwd	net users
passwd sandra	net user sandra *
adduser evan	net user evan password /ADD
ypcat group	net localgroup
/etc/init.d/httpd start	net start "World Wide Web Publishing Service"
kill PID	net stop "Service Name"
chmod and chgrp	cacls
fsck /apps	chkdsk D:
diff file1 file2	fc file1 file2
grep	find
vi file	edit file.txt

Some of the commands available for remotely managing NT systems may not work as expected. In the following excerpt, one of the authors was trying to restart IIS without success. After a hearty try, a call was made, and one of the urchins at the remote facility kindly went and recycled the box for us. How much more productive the morning would have been if the initial commands had done the trick. We've been told by folks who live with NT servers more intimately than we do that the servers like to be rebooted now and then. The system in question had been up for about three months.

```
C:\INETPUB\www;>net stop "IIS Admin Service"
The following services are dependent on the IIS Admin Service service.
Stopping the IIS Admin Service service will also stop these services.

   FTP Publishing Service
   World Wide Web Publishing Service

Do you want to continue this operation? (Y/N) [N]: Y
The requested pause or stop is not valid for this service.

More help is available by typing NET HELPMSG 2191.
C:\INETPUB\www>net helpmsg 2191

The requested pause or stop is not valid for this service.

EXPLANATION

This command is invalid for this service, or the service cannot accept the
command right now.
```

Some important network troubleshooting commands are available for Windows—some through the Resource Kit. These include ping, traceroute (tracert), ftp, netstat, route, rsh, rcp, rexec, rcp, and the at command. Though most Windows users don't know or care about many of these commands, you very well might. Most, if not all, zip programs can run from the command line, making installation of software or files easier. In addition, you should consider acquiring some great scripting tools—such as Perl, Expect and Tcl-available free from the Web. Adding these tools might help you take control of these clients in a manner that is more consistent with your typical system management style.

TIP

Run Windows NT, not Windows 95/98, on all the Windows systems you are responsible for managing and add the WinNT 4.0 Resource Kit.

You should set up *rsh*, preferably on your primary domain controller (PDC), though any domain controller will do. If you configure it to accept connections as root from a particular Unix machine, you can use rsh to change passwords on your NT clients. The Windows version of the rhosts file should be installed as \winnt\system32\drivers\etc\.rhosts.

NOTE

Your rsh should be running as Administrator or a user with account creation privileges and granted the "log on as a service" right. A useful account-synchronizing script, written in Perl and using Expect, is available from www.cis.ksu.edu/~mikhail/Passwd/passwd.tar.

The syntax for the rsh and rexec commands is as follows:

```
rsh host [-l username] [-n] command
```

and

```
rexec host [-l username] [-n] command
```

where the username argument is the login ID of the user.

Remote Management Options

At first blush, Unix systems can be remotely managed and Windows systems cannot. Tools such as telnet, rdist, and NIS/NIS+ provide us with options to determine how we want to reduce the task of managing hundreds, maybe even thousands, of systems to issuing changes that should be applied to groups of systems. We also have scripting languages and cron facilities for automating routine work. The ideal administration console allows you to perform all administrative tasks from one location and most administrative tasks with little or no duplication of effort. We'd like to say "for all users . . ." or "for each client . . ." and have our tools be adequately sensitive to the underlying differences between user environments and hardware/software platforms to do the right thing.

After spending some time exploring the options for remote management of Windows NT systems, we were encouraged. For one thing, we discovered that NT is not as badly constructed as we had imagined. In fact, Windows NT has many remote access primitives that can be used effectively—if you're willing to code in C or C++ and use system calls. For those of us less inclined toward systems programming, there are still options well worth considering.

Since automation is the crux of systems administration, we consider it next to essential that you equip your NT systems with Perl. By doing so, you will have a modern, powerful scripting language on both your Unix and NT systems (we *assume* you have and use Perl on your Solaris boxes). We've already stressed the value of the NTResKit in turning Windows NT into a complete operating system. With the NTResKit, Perl, and a reliable telnet daemon, your NT boxes will be ready to be managed. You will be able to manage accounts and services, distribute software, make changes to the registry, and reboot your NT systems from afar. You will also be able to start and stop services and determine what services are running.

Networking Issues

Most Ethernet connections today are 10-baseT and 100-baseT. Newer Suns and PCs will often be equipped with the capability to run at 10 or 100 megabits per second. Yet, even while they can easily share the same wire, there are some vastly differing technologies available when it comes to Windows NT systems. Windows NT systems have multiple network stacks available. These include NetBEUI, IPX, and TCP/IP. When an NT system is set up, a decision must be made about which of the protocol stacks to use. Some stacks, for example, NetBEUI and TCP/IP, can be used simultaneously (i.e., they don't compete, they respond to different network traffic). Our advice, however, is to forget NetBEUI, IPX, and any other Microsoft networking option and use TCP/IP. In the days when Windows clients were gathered into small networks by themselves, it made sense to run whatever network protocol seemed most natural. In today's networks, this isn't the case, and compatibility with the rest of your network is a far more worthy goal. Network settings on NT systems are made through the control panel, using the Control Panel → Network → Adapters sequence of menu choices.

In managing Windows systems, you need to decide whether to use fixed IP addresses or to assign addresses using DHCP or bootp. Either service can be provided on a Sun server and will work reliably. Avoid mixing these two strategies (fixed and assigned addresses) if you can. You don't want to run into situations where a DHCP host acquires an IP address and then finds itself conflicting with a system that claims the same address as its permanent address. If you must mix strategies, be very careful to identify the range of addresses that will be assigned dynamically and another range to be used for hosts whose addresses are assigned on a permanent basis.

We suggest using DHCP for all of your Windows clients. It's simple to set up and could be especially helpful if some of your users bring laptops into the office—their network settings will not have to change as they change locations; they will always acquire a local IP address.

Name Services

NIS+ is available on Linux, but not on Macintosh and Windows clients (as far as we know, anyway). Similarly, Linux systems will happily run ypbind and talk to your NIS servers. Macintosh and Windows systems probably won't. We suggest that you set up your Linux clients to use NIS or NIS+, and specify DNS for your Macs and PCs. This strategy won't help with usernames and passwords, of course, but users of these systems are not likely to play musical computers, and if they do, they may limit themselves to working on similar systems. In this case, you can take advantage of the User Manager for Domains tool in Windows NT to centrally manage your Windows users.

The Windows Internet Naming Service (WINS) will neither recognize Unix systems nor interoperate with DNS. The option of providing a WINS/DNS gateway is possible, but probably less effective than simply using DNS. Windows NT Internet Information Server version 4.0 includes a DNS setting, but it is not configurable through the Network Control Panel. Perhaps, in time, this service will make the integration of Unix and Windows systems easier. If you can't easily provide information to your Windows clients using DNS, you can put essential hosts in the LMHOSTS file. This file is roughly the equivalent of the /etc/hosts file on Unix systems.

File Serving

Solaris and Windows systems use incompatible technologies for sharing files across systems. Solaris uses NFS, of course. Windows systems (both NT and 95/98) use the Server Message Block (SMB) protocol. To circumvent this incompatibility, you can install NFS on your Windows clients or you can install SMB on your Solaris servers.

There probably aren't many platforms in existence on which you *cannot* run NFS. PC-NFS may have come and gone, but other products are available and more than fill the void:

- *DiskAccess*, an NFS client product from Intergraph, is included in Microsoft's Windows NT Option Pack for Solaris. Intergraph also provides NFS server software with the (purchasable) DiskShare software. Setting up Windows systems as NFS *servers* will allow you to access their file systems remotely.

- NetManage offers *Chameleon NFS*.

- Another product, called *open-NT* (nee Interix), provides a full Unix subsystem within NT.

- Network Appliance and other black-box manufacturers provide *nFS* and *CIFS*-network based storage that is accessible by both platforms.

- *Cascade* is a Sun product that will provide native SMB services and NetBIOS over IP services for Windows clients on a Sun Server. This derives from the NT server code that was licensed to AT&T from Microsoft. Cascade is described more fully in the next section.

- *Samba* is server software for Unix (e.g., Solaris and Linux) that provides network file and print services for clients using some variants of SMB protocol. SMB is a native networking protocol used by MS-DOS-based (in a very broad sense, including derivatives) clients. Samba is described in more detail in a following section.

- Hummingbird and other manufacturers provide NFS gateway services (e.g., *Maestro* from Hummingbird) that allows access to NFS resources via native NT service.

There are probably many other products, as well. We suggest that you refer to the PC-Mac TCP/IP & NFS FAQ List managed by Rawn Shah for additional possibilities and details. The URL is www.rtd.com/pcnfsfaq/faq.html.

Cascade

PC Netlink, from Sun Microsystems, Inc., provides native NT 4.0 network services on a Solaris system. Originally code named Project Cascade, PC Netlink is based on the AT&T Advanced Server for Unix product. PC Netlink offers NT file, print, directory, and security services to Windows 3.11, 95/98, and NT clients. In fact, there are no modifications required on the clients; from their perspective the PC Netlink server appears as just another NT server. Installation is simplified with InstallShield wizards. Once installed, management of PC Netlink is accomplished via the command line or with a client/server GUI-based Admintool. Administration of the NT network services is accomplished with the native NT server management tools from a Windows client.

In operation, the PC Netlink server works as a primary domain controller (PDC) or backup domain controller (BDC). The NT domain trust model is supported with full, bidirectional trusts, one-way trusts, or multidomain trust relationships. As of this writing, Sun is promising the ability to operate as a member server— that is, to provide file and print services without the need to be a domain controller. In addition to the Solaris-based directory services (NIS, NIS+, DNS, and LDAP), PC Netlink implements NetBIOS and WINS naming services.

The NT security model is implemented with support of the NT Security Account Manager (SAM), Security Identifiers (SIDs) and NT-style ACLs. Users in an NT domain do not get automatic access to native Solaris resources. For example, an NT user cannot log in to the Solaris side unless this functionality is specifically configured.

There is no automatic mapping of NT and Solaris user accounts; tools to migrate accounts (SID and Unix ID) are provided, however, and must be run as root.

The Windows clients perceive the shares on the PC Netlink server as NT File Systems (NTFSs), with the NT file security automatically maintained. Printers can be Solaris or network attached and shared between the Solaris and NT environments.

PC Netlink is bundled with many of the Sun servers (Ultra2 through E3500) and is included in the Solaris Easy Access Server 3.0. Sun provides a Sizing Guide on its Web site:

www.sun.com/interoperability/netlink/whitepaper/sizing-guide/

Samba

An alternative to installing NFS services on your clients is to provide SMB services on your Solaris server. The free software Samba centralizes the installation and administration of your file sharing by supporting SMB. Samba installation and setup is trivial; Samba is configured as a Solaris package. Figure 18.1 depicts an excerpt from a Samba configuration file (smb.conf) specifying the equivalent of an /etc/dfs/dfstab entry for a file system being made available via Samba.

NOTE
Unlike SMB on Windows clients, Samba provides unidirectional (i.e., server-side) file sharing. Samba does not provide access to the clients' file systems.

In a mixed Windows NT/95 network, an NT server defines the network domain and serves as the PDC.

Users on that system and others are authenticated by the PDC while logins are authenticated by the PDC's Security Account Manager (SAM)—username, password, and domain—database.

Another service provided by WinNT is *browsing*. An NT server can be configured as a domain master browser. In this role, it allows clients to search for available resources and printers. On the user's desktop, these resources are viewed through the network neighborhood or the Windows Explorer shell.

It is possible to use Samba as a replacement for an NT server. It can act as the primary domain controller and as the master browser. Instead of authenticating your Windows users via a Windows NT server, you can allow Samba to provide this service using your /etc/passwd file or passwd map.

Samba uses two daemon processes to support its services: *smbd* and *nmbd*. The smbd process provides file and printer support using the SMB protocol (as its name suggests). The nmbd process provides NetBIOS support to the clients. These services are generally started with a startup script, as shown here. This particular file is installed as */etc/rc2.d/S99samba* and */etc/init.d/samba*.

```
#!/bin/sh
#
# Default SAMBA initialization/shutdown script.
#

ECHO=echo
SAMBADIR=/opt/samba

case $1 in
    start)
      $ECHO "samba: \c"
        $SAMBADIR/bin/nmbd
  $ECHO "nmbd \c"
#        $SAMBADIR/bin/smbd -p 177 -s /etc/samba/smb.conf
        $SAMBADIR/bin/smbd -s /etc/samba/smb.conf
      $ECHO smbd
  ;;

    stop)
    kill 'ps -e | grep smbd | awk '{print $1}''
    kill 'ps -e | grep nmbd | awk '{print $1}''
    ;;

    restart)
    kill -HUP 'ps -e | grep smbd | awk '{print $1}''
    kill -HUP 'ps -e | grep nmbd | awk '{print $1}''
        ;;
esac
```

Two things that you need to watch out for in using Samba are how it participates with other domain controllers in the master browser election and whether you want it to serve as PDC. Pay careful attention to the lines in the configuration file (smb.conf) that determine whether Samba should attempt to play these roles. A sample smb.conf file is shown in Figure 18.1.

You can get Samba from http://samba.anu.edu.au/samba.

Managing File Types

One of the problems that you'll encounter in sharing files in a mixed client environment is the differing line-termination conventions that each of the three client populations uses. Unix systems (including Linux) use only a new-line (or linefeed) character: octal 12. Windows-based systems use both a new line and a carriage return: octal 12 and octal 15. Macintosh systems use only the carriage return: octal 15. If your systems share files, you need to do something about these conventions.

One technique is to use FTP or some version thereof, such as fetch, to transfer files from server to client and back as needed. The reason that FTP has different modes, such as text and binary, is that it handles the data differently. When

```
; Configuration file for smbd.
; ========================================================
; For format of this file, please refer to man page for
; smb.conf(5).
;
[global]
   security = user
   workgroup = FOO
   os level = 34
   preferred master = yes
   domain master = yes
   domain logons = yes
   logon script = %U.bat
   guest account = nobody

;  Global Printer settings
   printing = bsd
   printcap name = /usr/local/lib/samba/lib/printcap
   load printers = yes

;  This option sets a separate log file for each client
;  Remove it if you want a combined log file.
   log file = /spool/samba/log.%m

[netlogon]
   path = /spool/samba/netlogon
   public = yes
   writeable = no
   guest ok = yes

;  You will need a world readable lock directory and "share modes=yes"
;  if you want to support the file sharing modes for multiple users
;  of the same files
;  lock directory = /usr/local/samba/var/locks
;  share modes = yes

[homes]
   comment = Home Directories
   browseable = no
   read only = no
   create mode = 002

[printers]
   comment = All Printers
   path=/spool/samba/lp/
   print command=/usr/bin/dos2unix -ascii %s | /bin/lp -d %p -s |
rm %s
   browseable = no
```

continues

Figure 18.1   Sample smb.conf file.

```
    printable = yes
    public = yes
    writable = no
    create mode = 0700
;
; File system for PC applications
;
[apps]
    comment = PC Applications
    path = /apps
    read only = no
    valid users = mac pcleddy
```

Figure 18.1 *(Continued)*

you specify *binary*, FTP transfers a file byte by byte with no translation what-soever. The copy on the client, therefore, is an exact copy of the file on the server. When you specify *text* (this is usually the default), FTP *translates* the line endings. This means that the file is proper for the architecture of the receiving client.

Conversely, if you use NFS (or Samba) to mount server file systems on clients, all clients use the files *in place*; that is, they work on the file as it exists on the server. This can lead to some interesting results. Barber-pole output occurs when a file with only new-line characters (i.e., a Unix file) is displayed on a system expecting new-line and carriage-return characters (i.e., a Windows or DOS system):

```
Oh, ye tak the high road and I'll tak the low road,
                                                  And I'll be
in Scotland afore ye,
                         For me and my true love will
                                                  never meet a
gain on the bonnie, bonnie banks of Loch Lomond.
```

The ^{M} syndrome occurs when a file with both new-line and carriage-return characters (i.e., a Windows-based system) is displayed on a system that expects only new lines (i.e., Unix):

```
Oh, ye tak the high road and I'll tak the low road,^M
And I'll be in Scotland afore ye,^M
For me and my true love will never meet again^M
on the bonnie, bonnie banks of Loch Lomond.^M
```

One of the consequences of managing a mixed environment is this annoying problem. The solutions:

1. Use FTP (or a derivative tool).
2. Provide translation tools.

Solaris provides two commands for translating text files from Unix to DOS and back again—unix2dos and dos2unix. The *dos2unix* function could also be accomplished with a command of this nature, which removes the carriage returns:

```
cat file | tr -d "\015"
```

A *mac2unix* filter would look something like this:

```
cat file | tr "\015" "\012".
```

Binaries are, of course, a completely different issue. The best advice we can offer about binaries is to clearly differentiate them. Any Windows or Macintosh binaries that you keep on your servers should be in directories that are clearly named. Most sites don't maintain these binaries on their Sun servers. Disk space on clients is large enough to accommodate all the applications that these clients are likely to need. Of course, this means that updating these clients is a big deal. You might use server partitions to provide the means to easily update clients. Installing clients from a single mounted CD-ROM is probably the best of all possible worlds.

Printing

Sharing printers between Solaris and Windows systems can be accomplished in one of two ways. You can set up your Windows clients to print to TCP/IP printers. This is probably the easiest and most flexible way to share printers. You can also use Samba to print via the SMB protocol. If you have printers that do not have IP stacks, this may be the only option available. The *smb.conf* excerpt shown in Source 18.1 includes a printer-sharing specification.

Generally, you can set up a Solaris system or an NT server to act as a spooler for a specific printer. Whatever system you choose, consider the space required for spooling large files along with the number of people sharing the printer.

Directory Services

Where and how you manage user accounts—in your Windows NT domains or your NIS domains—is an important decision. Your users can exist in both domains and might need to work in both. If they do, you'll have to set them up twice—the same username and password in each environment will make this easier on them, but less desirable from a security point of view.

Windows NT systems have PDCs and BDCs that function in roughly the same way as master and slave NIS servers. In both systems, changes should be made only on the primary or master server and then propagated to backups or slaves.

In Windows, a system must first be registered on the PDC to become a member of the domain. This is not true on Solaris, of course, where a client can bind to an NIS domain without being included in the hosts map.

E-mail

One of the universally important services on any network is e-mail. A cornerstone of today's business model, prompt and proper delivery of e-mail is essential to a healthy network. There are a number of approaches with respect to your non-Unix clients :

1. POP clients

2. IMAP clients

3. Web-based e-mail solutions

4. Unix character-based tools

If you're using the X Window system on clients, you can, presumably, also run X-based tools to read and send e-mail from client systems. Of the other options, POP and IMAP are probably the most common choices. Most client mail tools (Eudora, Outlook, Outlook Express, et al.) allow either protocol to be used. As mentioned in the previous chapter, the option of whether to leave mail on the server is critical. For users who only use mail from a single system, the download option (i.e., *not* to leave mail on the server) is probably the best. The client software will fetch mail from the server, erasing it. For users who read e-mail from work, from home, and while on the road, this option potentially leaves different sets of e-mail messages on each of three different systems. This could make this option extremely difficult to manage and frustrating to the user, as well.

Web-based solutions, such as using the Netscape Mail tool to read mail, work well for some users. Others are not satisfied with the lack of flexibility that they have for managing their mail. The Netscape mail approach expects a single user, and doesn't work well when people share a system.

Users can log in to your Unix servers and run a mail tool through their telnet or SSH session—such as elm or pine. On the other hand, users accustomed to more user-friendly front ends might find this approach less than desirable.

Other Approaches to Compatibility

Other approaches to providing interoperability in the heterogeneous network involve using tools that don't care about the differences in the underlying hardware and operating systems.

The X Window System

One of the earliest and most effective solutions to the compatibility problems between Unix, Windows, and Macintosh incompatibilities is the X Window system. What X allows you to do is run an application on the host for which it was written (say, a Sun Enterprise file server) while controlling it (via the X server) on the client. Keep in mind here that the X terminology reverses what one normally thinks of a server and client in these arrangements. In the X vernacular, the server is the system in front of a user that is displaying windows, while the client is the software running in any particular window.

The Web

A newer and nearly ubiquitous platform for providing tools across a diverse population of clients is the Web. Any tool built to run in a browser, from a mail tool to a database, is instantly available on any system that has one. Many wise corporations are realizing that their porting days are nearly over. True, there are still compatibility problems. Netscape and Internet Explorer behave differently in some respects. Still, as a means of providing an intranet—and a wide collection of tools and information repositories across the organization—the Web is hard to beat.

A Web-related technology that is also providing application compatibility across different systems is Java.

Client/Server Applications

As nice as the Web is, it is not the ideal platform for just any application. Tools for dynamic and interactive content on the Web are still evolving, and any tool that runs through a browser is encumbered with some degree of overhead. Applications that run in a true client/server mode—in which heavy-duty back-end processing is handled on the server, with the front-end user-interaction portion of the work running on the client—are often built to run in today's typical heterogeneous network. The server software often requires the robustness and processing speed of a Sun, while the client end uses the resources of a Windows client and doesn't affect users on other systems when individual users shut their system down or find themselves staring at the blue screen of death.

Accessing Clients

You cannot remotely log in to most Windows clients. Unlike Unix systems, there is no telnet daemon available to provide you with remote login. This is another reason that these clients are both difficult and time-consuming to manage. You can purchase telnet software for Windows NT. Windows NT servers also provide an FTP service (i.e., you can ftp *to* them, not just *from* them). There is very little difference from a functional standpoint between a Windows NT server and a Windows NT host. You might insist that more critical Windows systems provide you with the means to log in and install files from your desk.

Porting Your Expertise

One of the biggest compatibility issues that many of us have to face when it comes to the Windows and Macintosh clients making their way into our offices and server rooms is not a technology issue at all, but our own readiness to deal with these systems. Many organizations have different staffs to support Unix systems and PC/Mac clients. Even so, you will find yourself in many frustrating situations if you don't know enough about the way the non-Unix systems work to be able to blame them or rule them out when some element of your interoperational network doesn't work properly.

If users come to you and say they can no longer retrieve mail from your mail server, what should you do? You can suggest that they double-check the settings in their mail tool (e.g., their POP server, username, and password), but they may just look at you and claim they haven't changed a thing. Another test is to telnet to the POP port on the server (i.e., telnet mailserver 110) and have them try their name and password right then and there. If they log in successfully, you'll know that your mail server as well as their login information is OK. This is just one situation. There will be many. The problem with separate staffs managing separate problem areas is that there is often no one bridging the gap enough to determine which domain a particular problem lies in.

We suggest that you know enough about the non-Unix platforms to be conversant in the tools. You should understand the operations of and the way to make changes to the registry on Windows systems. You should understand the system folder on a Macintosh. You should know where basic networking information is configured. This include the following information:

- The host name
- The IP address
- The network mask and router
- The name server
- The domain

You should also understand how to configure mail servers (and, hopefully, you won't have to deal with more than one or two of these since they're all different) and print services, as well as take a look at disk usage and availability.

Summary

Today's networks are heterogeneous. There seems to be a steady migration of resources. Big (and even bigger) Sun servers are moving into our computer rooms, and a mix of clients is moving into our offices and cubes. This chapter attempts to describes some strategies for managing this mixed environment, especially for making decisions with regard to Windows NT systems to make them more amenable to being managed.

What we probably need most are integrated tools that make it possible to manage Windows PCs, along with other non-Unix systems, from a central system. Network management tools with agents that run on these clients may provide some of this control, but at a hefty price tag. In the interim, a careful sharing of resources may start the evolution toward a manageable coexistence.

We discovered, in our struggles with taming out-of-the-box Windows NT systems, that the only hope of making them manageable is to add a collection of tools. The Windows NT Resource Kit is a must. Besides this, we strongly recommend that you install Perl; many versions of Perl5 are available for NT systems. We also recommend that you look into using pcANYWHERE or VNC to allow you to remotely take over control of the GUI when remote options don't cut it.

Learning to manage NT systems as well as you can your Solaris systems is going to be a learning experience. In time, we expect tools will emerge that will take advantage of Windows NT's primitives and hand us the steering wheel. In the interim, beef up your toolkit and be prepared for some hard work.

Index of Useful Web Sites

One of the nice things about being systems administrators today (as opposed to the "good old days") is the number of extremely helpful Web sites available to us. Here are some that we have visited and found useful. We are constantly discovering new ones, so this list cannot possibly be complete.

Useful Web Sites

http://ciac.llnl.gov   Computer Incident Advisory Capability (CIAC)

http://darkwing.uoregon.edu/~hak/unix.html   Hans Kuhn, University of Oregon—very nice Unix sysadmin site

http://dir.yahoo.com/Computers_and_Internet/Software/Operating_ Systems/Unix/Solaris/

http://fishbutt.fiver.net/   Solaris X86 corner—where Intel sees the Sun

http://ftp.informatik.rwth-aachen.de/Mirror/SolarisFAQ/solaris2.html   Solaris FAQ

http://home.netvigator.com/~bigbert/c sa/index.html   The Certified Solaris (@.X) Administrator Exam Guide—SunEd

http://oak.ece.ul.ie/~griffini/solaris.html   Web resources

http://smc.vnet.net/solaris_2.6.html   Freeware

www.cert.org   CERT

www.cisco.com/techtools/ip_addr.html   Handy-dandy network calculator—calculate your subnets

www.cs.ut.ee/cgi-bin/man-cgi   Unix man pages online

www.eng.auburn.edu/users/rayh/solaris/NIS+_FAQ.html   Ray Hildbrandt's NIS+ FAQ

www.geocities.com/Athens/1802/pgpcard.html   PGP reference card

www.isi.edu/in-notes/iana/assignments/port-numbers   This site lists the known port numbers—extremely useful

www.nthelp.com   NT help

www.squirrel.com/squirrel/sun-nvram-hostid.faq.html   Mark Henderson's NVRAM FAQ

www.squirrel.com/squirrel/sun-stuff.html   Useful tools for Sun workstations and Solaris collection of info and links

www.stokely.com   Real help for Unix system administration

www.sun.com/software/whitepapers.html

www.sun.com/sun-on-net/performance/se3   SymbEL release 3—Rich Pettit and Adrian Cockcroft, version 3.1, pre-FCS now available

www.sunfreeware.com   All Sun—all freeware—all the time

www.sunworld.com   E-zine covering Sun technology, geared toward sysadmins and developers

www.sunworld.com   Monthly *SunWorld* sysadmin and security columns

www.sunworld.com/common/security-faq.html   Solaris security FAQ—Peter Galvin

www.sunworld.com/sunwhere.html   SunWhere index—topical index

www.usenix.org

www.usenix.org/sage

www.webring.org/cgi-bin/webring?ring=solarisunix;list   The Solaris Web-Ring—all Solaris-related sites in one big loop

www.wildheart.org/wu-ftpd/   Online guide to wuftp

www.wins.uva.nl/pub/solaris/solaris2/   Solaris FAQ

Classes

Solaris 2.X System Administration I (SA-235)

Solaris 2.X System Administration II (SA-286)

www.cs.brown.edu/people/pbg/tutorial.html—Advanced Solaris System Administration. Instructors: Peter Galvin and Dinah McNutt.

Organizations

In the preceding references, we've included URLs for some organizations that you should become familiar with if you are not already. Two of these—CERT and CIAC—provide extremely important security information. Two others—USENIX and SAGE—are related organizations (SAGE is part of USENIX) that provide a meeting ground for people working with Unix systems. SAGE is devoted specifically to systems administration, as are the Large Scale Systems Administration (LISA) conferences.

NIS+ Resources and Notes

This appendix contains information on patches as well as other sources of information on NIS+. There are no known open issues or RFCs on NIS+.

Patches

The following is the list of all of the NIS+ patches for 5.3 through 5.7. If you are having NIS+ problems, installing these patches is a good place to start, especially if you recognize the general symptoms noted.

In order for a machine to be stable, all of the recommended patches should be installed, as well. The list of recommended patches for your operating system is available from sunsolve1.sun.com.

Solaris 2.3 NIS+ Patches

101318 SunOS 5.3	Jumbo patch for kernel (includes libc, lockd)
101384 SunOS 5.3	Admintool Jumbo patch
101582 SunOS 5.3	POINT PATCH: Password aging and NIS+ don't work together
101736 SunOS 5.3	nisplus patch
102447 OpenWindows 3.3	xdm cannot be used on NIS+ networks
103269 SunOS 5.3	nissetup default permissions not secure enough

Solaris 2.4 NIS+ Patches

101945 SunOS 5.4		Jumbo patch for kernel
102294 OpenWindows 3.4		xdm cannot be used on NIS+ networks
102336 SunOS 5.4		POINT PATCH 1091205: Password aging and NIS+ don't work together
103270 SunOS 5.4		nissetup default permissions not secure enough
101974 SunOS 5.4_x86		libnsl, nistbladm, and ypbind fixes

Solaris 2.5(.1) NIS+ Patches

103066 SunOS 5.5		rpc.nisd hangs in write(2)
103187 SunOS 5.5		libc, libnsl, libucb, nis_cachemgr, and rpc.nisd
103188 SunOS 5.5_x86		libc, libnsl, libucb, nis_cachemgr, and rpc.nisd patch
103266 SunOS 5.5		nissetup default permissions for password table not secure
104968 SunOS 5.5.1		chkey and newkey patch
103612 SunOS 5.5.1		libc, libnsl, libucb nis_cachemgr, and rpc.nisd patch
103613 SunOS 5.5.1_x86		libc, libnsl, libucb, nis_cachemgr, and rpc.nisd patch
104969 SunOS 5.5.1_x86		chkey and newkey patch

Solaris 2.6 NIS+ Patches

105562 SunOS 5.6		chkey and keylogin patch
105563 SunOS 5.6_x86		chkey and keylogin patch
105564 SunOS 5.6		/kernel/misc/rpcsec patch
105565 SunOS 5.6_x86		/kernel/misc/rpcsec patch
105401 SunOS 5.6		libnsl and NIS+ commands patch
105402 SunOS 5.6_x86		libnsl and NIS+ commands patch

Solaris 7 Patches

None at this time.

Important Man Pages

We recommend that you read, at your leisure, all of the man pages listed here. Though we cover a lot of ground in Chapter 8, we have not explained all of the commands and command options as thoroughly as these man pages do.

chkey	Change user's secure RPC key pair.
keylogin	Decrypt and store secret key with keyserv.
newkey	Create a new Diffie-Hellman key pair in the publickey database.
nis, nis+	A new version of the network information name service.
nis_cachemgr	NIS+ utility to cache location information about NIS+ servers.
nisaddcred	Create NIS+ credentials.
niscat	Display NIS+ tables and objects.
nisaddent	Create NIS+ tables from corresponding /etc files or NIS maps.
nischgrp	Change the group owner of a NIS+ object.
nischown	Change the owner of a NIS+ object.
nischmod	Change access rights on a NIS+ object.
nischttl	Change the time-to-live value of a NIS+ object.
nisclient	Initialize NIS+ credentials for NIS+ principals.
nisdefaults	Display NIS+ defaults.
niserror	Display NIS+ error messages.
nisgrep	Utility for searching NIS+ tables.
nisgrpadm	NIS+ group administration command.
nisinit	NIS+ client and server initialization utility.
nislog	Display the contents of the NIS+ transaction log.
nisln	Symbolically link NIS+ objects.
nisls	List the contents of a NIS+ directory.
nismatch	Utility for searching NIS+ tables.
nismkdir	Create NIS+ directories.
nispasswd	Change NIS+ password information.
nisping	Send ping to NIS+ servers
nispopulate	Populate the NIS+ tables in a NIS+ domain.
nisrm	Remove NIS+ objects from the namespace.

nisrmdir	Remove NIS+ directories.
nisserver	Set up NIS+ servers.
nistbladm	Administer NIS+ tables.
nistest	Return the state of the NIS+.
nisudpkeys	Update the public keys in a NIS+ directory object.
rpc.nisd	NIS+ service daemon.

Sunsolve Documents

There are a number of Sunsolve documents concerning NIS+. Those listed here either contain some additional information not included in this document, or reference rare problems and solutions to unusual problems.

FAQs

1012	NIS+ questions.

Infodocs

2216	NIS+ questions.
11742	How to convert an NIS+ root replica server to a root master.

SRDBs (Systems Resolution Database Documents)

5816	Fully qualified hostnames with NIS+.
5874	NIS+ database recovery.
6285	Change of root passwd on NIS+ server breaks authenticat.
6487	Differences between NIS and NIS+.
6640	Why does NIS+ require passwords?
6616	Is it possible to revert to NIS?
7202	Cannot change NIS passwords served by NIS+ servers.
10448	Changing the NIS+ master server.
10941	NIS+ error messages.
10951	NIS+ servers unreachable.

11728   Changing an NIS+ server's IP address.

11742   How to convert an NIS+ root replica server to a root master server.

14994   Changed root master's IP address in AdminSuite, NIS+ credentials are now bad.

Sun Educational Services

NIS+ concepts and administration offered by SunEd (contact 1-800 422-8020 to get more information)

*Solaris 2.X NIS+ Administration with Workshop

Solaris Documentation

Name Services Administration Guide, part #801-6633-10

Name Services Configuration Guide, part #801-6635-10

Online docs for NIS+ are available via docs.sun.com.

Books

Ramsey, Rick. *All About Administering NIS+*. Prentice Hall, ISBN 0-13-309576-2. 1996.

abort   To terminate a process abruptly and forcefully.

absolute pathname   A complete path to a file starting from the root (/) level (e.g., /home/nici/data/file1). Contrast with **relative pathname.**

access   To read, modify, or otherwise use a resource—for example, a file.

access control list (ACL)   A structure and related mechanism for controlling who has access and what kind of access to a resource—for example, a file or a display.

account   The ability to log in and use system resources, generally through the use of a username and password, and in conjunction with a dedicated directory and established environment. The directory and files belonging to the user.

address   A number used by systems or resources to locate other systems or resources. Important addresses include fully qualified host names, IP addresses, hardware (also called *MAC, Ethernet,* or *network*) addresses, and e-mail addresses.

address mask   A string of bits used to deselect (or hide) certain bits in an address so that the remaining bits select a particular portion of the available address space. In particular, subnet masks.

address resolution   The method by which addresses of one type are mapped to addresses of another type. For example, fully qualified host names are mapped to IP addresses by DNS servers.

address resolution protocol (ARP)   Together with its counterpart, **reverse address resolution protocol (RARP),** manages the mapping between hardware and IP addresses and maintains a cache of recent information (i.e., the arp table) to makes this process more efficient.

address space   In general, the range of addresses possible in any addressing scheme. In particular, the range of memory locations which a CPU can refer to—limited by the size of the address register(s) and/or addressing method used.

administration   The management of computing resources—in particular, systems and network administration.

Advanced Research Projects Agency (ARPA) The U.S. government agency that funded the original Internet, initially called the **ARPANET.** Now called *Defense Research Projects Agency (DARPA)*.

agent A process that collects or transfers information as part of a larger system (e.g., a message transfer agent or an SNMP agent).

alarm A reporting tool that is triggered when specific things happen on a network or system (e.g., a critical process dies). A warning message or other signal from a process, generally alerting a systems administrator to a fault or impending problem.

alert A warning message or other signal from a process, generally less severe than an alarm.

alias Another (hopefully, easier to remember) name for something. Aliases can be created for hosts, users (e.g., e-mail aliases), or commonly used commands.

American Standard Code for Information Interchange (ASCII) This set of codes enables systems to exchange information by requiring a common interpretation of byte codes. For example, the octal value 100 (binary 01000000 and hex 40) represents the character @ while the octal value 012 (binary 00001010 and hex 0A) is a line feed.

analyzer A traffic monitor that breaks out and interprets the content of packets (frames).

AnswerBook Sun's online documentation, used with OpenWindows or within a Web browser.

applet A small program written in Java and meant to run within a Web browser.

application A software program that is meant to serve a particular need. Applications provide functions that are not provided as part of Solaris (e.g., database or mapping applications).

architecture The specific features or components of a computer or the layout of a system or network.

archive A collection of files stored so as to preserve their state at a particular point in time.

A record With respect to DNS, an address record. An A record is the most straightforward of DNS records. It simply ties a name to an IP address.

argument A parameter, passed to a Solaris command or program, which modifies the command's or program's behavior. For example, -l as an argument to the ls command produces considerably more output.

ARP   See **address resolution protocol.**

ARPA   See **Advanced Research Projects Agency.**

ARPANET   A packet-switched network developed by ARPA (now DARPA) in the 1970s and used for roughly 20 years. ARPANET can be thought of as the first Internet.

ASCII   See **American Standard Code for Information Interchange** **.ASET** See **Automated Security Enhancement Tool.**

asymmetric encryption   An encryption system that uses a pair of complementary keys (one public, one private) for encrypting and decrypting files.

asymmetric multiprocessing   A form of multiprocessing in which one processor plays the role of master while all others are slaves. Contrast this with **symmetric multiprocessing,** in which all processors have an equal role.

asynchronous   At irregular intervals. Asynchronous data transfer occurs one character at a time without clocking signals.

authentication   The process by which a user's identity is verified. Authentication can involve usernames, passwords, special keys and physical devices (e.g., SecurID cards).

autofs   File system type used for automatic mounting via NFS. See **automounter.**

Automated Security Enhancement Tool (ASET)   Sun's tool for assessing the security posture of a system. The user specifies the level (low, medium, or high) of checking to be performed.

automating   Preparing scripts or programs to automatically do what would otherwise be done manually.

automounter   Sun's software that automatically mounts a directory when a user requests it (e.g., with a cd command).

availability   The condition of a system that is running and usable.

back file system   With respect to caching, the source file system. Contrast with **front file system.**

background process   A command or process that runs without restricting the user's control of the session. A user can put a process into the background by putting a & at the end of the command line or by entering ^Z and then *bg* after starting the process. Contrast with **foreground process.**

backup   A copy of a file system or particular directories stored on tape or other media, meant to be used to restore entire file systems or specific files as needed. Backups serve as protection against data loss.

backup copy   A quick copy made of a file before it is modified to safeguard against fat fingering and other problems.

backup device   A hardware device used to back up file systems, often a tape drive.

backup domain controller   A replica of the primary domain controller, often used for local (as opposed to wide-area) validation and publication of shared resources.

baud rate   The rate at which information moves between devices, usually used to refer to the speed of modems and other "slow" devices. The term itself refers to the number of signal changes in 1 second.

Berkeley Internet Name Daemon (BIND)   The implementation of DNS that ships with Solaris.

Berkeley Software Distribution (BSD)   Unix versions developed at the University of California, Berkeley. Solaris 1.x (sometimes referred to as *SunOS*) systems were based on the Berkeley distribution. Contrast with **System V** and **SVR4.**

big-endian   A way of storing binary data such that the more significant bits are stored first. Contrast with **little-endian.**

binary   A numbering system based on the number 2. Used extensively on computer systems because of its natural fit with two-state electronics. Each digit in a binary number is 0 (off) or 1 (on).

BIND   See **Berkeley Internet Name Daemon.**

binding   The process by which a client determines which server it is to use for specific information or support (e.g., DNS). In general, binding is in effect until the client terminates the relationship (e.g., kills or restarts ypbind).

bit   Stands for *binary digit*. This is the smallest addressable amount of information on a computer system. It can take on a value of 1 (on) or 0 (off). See **binary.**

block   A unit of data, as stored on a disk, that can be transferred—usually 512 bytes.

block based   The characteristic of a file system that allocates a block at a time. Contrast with **extent based.**

block (special) device   A device that transfer data in blocks.

block map   A structure that keeps track of the locations of data blocks on a disk.

boot   The process of bringing a computer from the turned-off or halted state to full operation. Short for *bootstrap.*

boot block An 8K disk block containing information essential to the boot process (e.g., the location of the boot program on the disk).

boot file With respect to DNS, the file that details the zones and the servers that are authoritative for these zones. Specifically, /etc/named.boot or /etc/named.conf.

boot PROM On Sun workstations, contains a command interpreter used for booting. See also **ID PROM, EEPROM,** and **NVRAM.**

boot server A server system used to boot client systems.

bootp A network service that provides boot information (e.g., IP addresses) to clients. Contrast with **DHCP.** Bootp is an alternative to **RARP** for booting diskless workstations.

Bourne shell (/bin/sh) The standard (and oldest) of the shells available on Solaris. Available on most, if not all, Unix systems. The Bourne shell's descendents include the Korn shell and bash.

bridge A device that connects two or more physical networks, reducing traffic on the attached networks by forwarding only packets that need to get from one network to the other. Bridges generally require no setup other than physical attachment; after that they learn when to forward packets based on observed network activity.

broadcast A packet addressing/delivery scheme by which packets are delivered to all of the hosts in a particular network or subnet.

BSD See **Berkeley Software Distribution.**

buffer A temporary work area in which data are stored, often to speed up delivery to or access by a client.

bug An unintended action by hardware or software, usually caused by oversights in the design or building stages.

bundled Hardware or software included in the original purchase. Contrast with **unbundled.**

cache A high-speed memory buffer intended to increase access times.

cachefs Local disk-based file system used to speed up NFS performance.

caching-only server A DNS server that is not authoritative for any domain, but caches data that it receives from other servers and answers queries from this cache.

call To transfer control to another program in such a way that control is returned when the called program is finished.

canonical name (CNAME)　Another name for a host as defined within DNS. CNAME records are for aliasing hostnames and always points to a name that is defined in an A record.

card cage　The racklike enclosure into which system boards are installed on some Sun servers. When properly inserted, cards connect to the system backplane.

card slot　A slot on a system board into which interface cards can be inserted.

CDE　See **Common Desktop Environment.**

CD-ROM　Compact-disc, read-only memory. High capacity read-only media. Solaris uses the High Sierra (ISO 9660) format with Rock Ridge extensions for CD-ROM file systems.

central processing unit (CPU)　The processing hardware on a computer.

cfsadmin　A tool used to build and manage cache.

change mode　Changing the permissions associated with a file in order to change access rights.

character special device　A device that transfer data character by character.

child process　A process started by another process and, to some degree, under its control.

Cipher Suite　An encryption method that includes the key exchange algorithm, symmetric encryption, and hash algorithm. It is based on **SSL.**

classing engine　A mechanism that allows an application to query a database in order to determine how a desktop object should be handled. For example, the classing engine determines the icon used to display a file and what happens when a user double-clicks on it.

client　A system that uses the resources of another (i.e., the server).

client/server model　A common way of organizing services and applications so that some part of the processing burden (often referred to as the *back end*) runs on a server while another part (the *front end* or **interface**) runs on the client.

cluster　A group of computers connected in such as way that they act as if they were a single machine with multiple CPUs. Clusters provide one approach to high availability.

CNAME　See **canonical name.**

coax　A particular cable type in which cable layers share the same axis. Used in older Ethernets.

command   An instruction a user types on a computer.

command line   The space into which commands are typed in a terminal window. Contrast with **GUI.**

command syntax   A description of the options available with a particular command. Proper syntax describes which elements are optional and which can be repeated, and so forth.

comment   Text inserted into source code, scripts, or configuration files that does not affect the way the files are used. Comments are generally intended as notes to remind anyone maintaining the files what the files are used for and why they are coded or configured in particular ways.

Common Desktop Environment (CDE)   A windowing system available on Solaris, developed jointly with HP and other vendors.

compiler   A software tool that converts high-level language (i.e., source code) into executable code. Contrast with **interpreter.**

connectionless   The communications model in which there is no setup and breakdown of a connection prior to and subsequent to the transfer of data. Contrast with **connection-oriented.**

connection-oriented   A communications model in which data transfer occurs in three stages: setup, data transfer, and breakdown.

contention   An attempt by systems or processes to use resources at the same time.

context switching   An inherent part of multiprocessing in which one process and its *context* (access to data, files, and parameters) must be stored in order for another process and its context to be loaded.

control character   A character that has a special meaning when the control key is held down simultaneously.

core dump   The residue of a crashed program-the contents of memory (sometimes referred to as *core*) dumped into a file.

crash   A system failure because of a hardware or software malfunction.

cron   The Unix scheduler. Cron uses crontab files (any user may have one) to detail what tasks are to be run when.

crontab files   Cron's configuration files. Each line has the format $m\ H\ d\ M\ D$ *task*, where m is the minutes after the hour, H is the hour (0–23), d is the date, M is the month, and D is the day of the week.

C shell   A shell with Berkeley roots, available in Solaris.

cylinder   A set of tracks on a disk that line up horizontally.

cylinder group   Consecutive cylinders grouped together into a logical unit.

daemon   A process that runs in the background, listening for requests. Daemon processes generally start up at boot time. Contrast with processes that are started by **inetd.**

data encryption   A process by which data is made inaccessible to unauthorized persons by running it through a complex, mathematically rigorous obfuscation.

Data Encryption Standard (DES)   A symmetric encryption algorithm using a 56-bit key.

dataless client   A client that uses its local disk only for root and swap and depends on file servers for everything else.

debug   To search for bugs in a particular program or process, either formally or informally.

debugger   A special program that assists in the debugging process by giving the tester the ability to step through programs, examine data structures, and so forth.

decryption   The process of returning a file to its original form from an encrypted one. Requires that the user has access to the original key (symmetric systems) or private key (asymmetric systems).

default   The value that an argument or variable will have if none is specifically assigned.

delimiter   A character used to separate fields in a configuration or data file.

DES   See **Data Encryption Standard.**

device driver   Software used to control a physical device (e.g., a disk drive or printer).

DHCP   See **Dynamic Host Configuration Protocol.**

Diffie-Hellman   An asymmetric algorithm, named after its creators, Whitfield Diffie and M. E. Hellman.

dig   An extremely valuable tool for debugging DNS. Compare with **nslookup.**

Digital Signature Algorithm (DSA)   A secure algorithm for creating digital signatures.

Digital Signature Standard (DSS)   A federal standard for signing data.

disk array   One or more physical disks organized as a single logical drive.

disk-based file system   A traditional file system, comprised of files on a hard disk.

diskfull client   A client with a disk—can be **dateless** or **standalone.**

diskless client   A client that has no disk and, therefore, relies on remote file servers to provide root, swap, and other file systems.

disk partition   A portion of a disk separated from the rest to provide space for a particular file system or raw data.

disk quotas   A system in which users are limited in how much disk space they are allowed to use. Disk quotas involve hard and soft limits along with a grace period in which, having reached a soft quota, the user is warned that file holdings must be reduced.

distributed file system   A file system that is spread across multiple systems.

DNS   See **domain name system.**

domain   In DNS, a portion of a name space that corresponds to a particular organization of division of an organization. With respect to the E10000, a virtual system using a portion of the E10000's resources.

domain name system (DNS)   The distributed naming system that defines systems on the Internet. DNS is organized into root domains, subdomains, and organizational domains, all of which communicate so that any system binding to a DNS server can determine the address of any other system (provided it has a DNS record).

dot file   File used to define user environments (e.g., .cshrc and .profile). Also called *hidden files.*

dotted decimal notation   The numbering scheme used to represent IP addresses. Four 8-bit numbers (or **octets**) are separated by dots. Each octet can assume a value between 0 and 255, though 0 and 255 are reserved in certain positions to designate network and broadcast addresses.

DSA   See **Digital Signature Algorithm.**

DSS   See **Digital Signature Standard.**

dump   A backup of a file system created in a particular format. Dump files can be *full* (including all files) or *incremental* (including only those files modified or created since the last backup at that level). Contrast with **tar files.**

Dynamic Host Configuration Protocol (DHCP)   A framework for passing configuration information to clients on a TCP/IP network. DHCP is based on **bootp,** but has the additional capability of automatically allocating reusable network addresses.

EEPROM   Electrically erasable programmable read-only memory. On Sun systems, the EEPROM is used to hold information about the system used in the boot process.

encapsulation   The technique used by layered protocols (such as TCP/IP) in which each layer's **packet** (data and addressing) is stored as the data portion of the next higher layer. For example, a portion of the data associated with a telnet login on an Ethernet would be encapsulated within a TCP packet, and subsequently encapsulated in an Ethernet frame. The process of encapsulation is reversed at the receiving end as each layer of addressing is peeled off and the data makes it way to the process awaiting it.

encryption   The process of protecting information by obfuscating its content using a difficult-to-reverse algorithm. In symmetric encryption systems, the same key is used for both encryption and decryption. In asymmetric (also known as *public/private key*) systems, a complementary set of keys is used—the public key for encryption and the private key for decryption.

end of file (EOF)   A particular marker, often ^D, that marks the end of a file.

end of line (EOL)   A particular character or set of characters used to mark the end of a line in a file. In Unix systems, a line feed marks the end of a line. In DOS, both a line feed and carriage return are used.

environment   The parameters—including search paths, aliases, and others—defined by dot files when a user logs in.

environment variables   Shell variables that are passed to child shells. Typically, environment variables are used for such things as directories (e.g., LD;usLIBRARY;usPATH and MAN;usPATH). The C shell setenv command is used to assign values.

EOF   See **End of file.**

EOL   See **End of line.**

escape   A character that removes the special meaning of the following character, allowing it to be treated simply as a character. For example, to remove the special meaning sometimes associated with $, you might use \$ instead.

Ethernet   A network topology that uses particular network cabling (e.g., coax or UTP) and uses carrier-sense multiple access (CSMA) to determine if packets (frames) have collided and, therefore, need to be resent

executable file   A file that can be executed. Requires both execute permission and executable contents to work properly.

expire   With respect to DNS, how long a secondary will hold information about a zone without successfully updating it or confirming that the data is up to date.

exporting The process by which a file server advertises and shares file systems. Also known as *sharing*.

extent-based A disk-space allocation scheme in which multiple blocks are allocated at once to make the process more efficient.

FAT With respect to Unix systems, fat is a designator applied to file systems (e.g., the fat fast Berkeley file system). With respect to Windows systems, FAT is a file system implemented for DOS; contrast with **NTFS**.

field In configuration files, a portion of a line that has a distinct meaning from the rest of the line. Fields are separated by delimiters.

field-replaceable unit (FRU) Any piece of hardware that is easily replaced in the field in minimal time without disruption to the rest of the network.

FIFOFS See **first in, first out file system.**

file handle A data structure used in NFS to uniquely identify a file. A *stale file handle* is one that is out of sync with the actual file.

file manager The GUI-based tool that allows users to manipulate files with drag-and-drop operators.

filename The name associated with a file. It is stored in the directory corresponding to its location in the file system.

filename expansion The process by which filenames are expanded from wild-card characters to full file names (e.g., data* might expand to data1, data123, and data.dmp).

file permissions The permission matrix associated with a file and stored in the inode. File permissions determine who can read, write, or execute the contents of the file. For directories, file permissions determine who can list the directory's contents and cd into the directory.

file system In Unix, the tree-structured organization of files starting from root and including local file systems as well as those mounted from remote systems.

file transfer protocol (FTP) The most common program for moving files between systems.

filter In general, a program that reads from standard input and writes to standard output, using pipes. For example, the *tr* command in *cat file / tr "A-Z" "a-z"* is a simple filter. Also, a program that processes input and selects whether to pass it on or reject it—as used in filtering routers.

firewall A system (hardware, software or both) designed to prevent unauthorized access to or from a private network.

first in, first out file system (FIFOFS)   File system that gives processes common access to data.

floppy drive   Diskette.

floptical disk drive   Electrooptical read/write technology.

footprint   A general description of the amount of space a system occupies on a surface.

foreground process   A term describing a process that has control of the current terminal. No other commands can be run until the process terminates or is put into the background.

fork   The method by which a process creates a new process.

format   The initial preparation through which a raw disk is prepared with a basic layout allowing it to be used with a particular type of system. After formatting, disks can be partitioned and file systems can be built.

forwarders   A list of addresses to which a machine should send forward requests for sites it cannot resolve.

frame   With respect to Ethernet, the data transmission unit commonly referred to as a **packet** is more properly termed a *frame*. The Ethernet frame contains two or more levels of addressing.

free space   The unused space on a disk.

front file system   With respect to caching, the local copy of a file system. Contrast with **back file system.**

FRU   See **field-replacable unit.**

fsck   A utility used to check and repair file systems.

FTP   See **file transfer protocol.**

fully qualified domain name   A domain name or host name that contains every element in the name (e.g., spoon.spatulacity.com).

gateway   Network equipment connecting dissimilar cabling or protocols.

GID   See **group ID.**

GNU   Gnu's Not Unix. A tremendously useful set of utilities available for Unix systems. The GNU C compiler, for example, is one of the most popular C compilers available. Other tools include gawk, gnuplot, gmake, and others.

graphical user interface (GUI)   A method of interacting with a computer using graphical elements and mouse control. Contrast with **command line.**

group A collection of users associated with each other by virtue of being members of the group. Group membership allows file sharing.

group ID (GID) The numeric identifier for a Unix group.

GUI See **graphical user interface.**

halt To stop the system abruptly.

hard limit With respect to disk quotas, the limit at which the user is prevented from creating or modifying files.

hard link A file that shares its data and its inode with another file.

header With respect to e-mail, the addressing information at the top of a message that identifies the sender, recipient, dates, subject line, and hosts involved in the transfer.

heterogeneous network A network composed of different types of servers and clients (in other words, a typical network).

hexadecimal A numbering system based on the value 16. Hex is used on computer systems because it is easily converted to (and tightly related to) the binary numbering system and because it is terse. For example, the hex value FFFF is equal to the number 65,535 and the binary value 1111111111111111.

high-water mark A value marking the high range of acceptable values. For example, if you set a high water mark of 90 percent for a file system, you might set off an alarm if the file system becomes more full than that.

High Sierra file system (hsfs) See **CD-ROM.**

HINFO With respect to DNS, a record (which is hardly ever used) put in place to detail system types.

hint zone With respect to DNS, a zone used solely to find a root name server to repopulate the root cache file.

hme Hundred-megabyte Ethernet. Compare with **Lance Ethernet** (le).

home directory The directory assigned to a user when an account is established. Generally, this will be /home/username and will be set up with a basic set of dot files.

homogeneous network A network composed of systems of a single basic type—for example, all Suns or all Intel-based systems.

hostid A string of characters that identifies a system. For Sun systems, this is related to the hardware address.

hot-plugging   Replacing hardware boards while a system is running. Also called *hot-swapping*.

hot-swappable   A feature of hardware that allows boards to be replaced while the system is running.

hsfs   High Sierra file system. See **CD-ROM.**

HTML   See **Hypertext Markup Language.**

HTTP   See **Hypertext Transfer Protocol.**

hundred-megabyte Ethernet (hme)   Compare with **Lance Ethernet** (le).

Hypertext Markup Language (HTML)   A special language (based on SGML) used for creating Web pages and their components.

Hypertext Transfer Protocol (HTTP)   Based on TCP/IP, this protocol allows retrieval of Web pages.

IAB   See **Internet Activities Board.**

ICMP   See **Internet Control Message Protocol.**

icon   A graphical representation of a file type or program as displayed in the File Manager.

ID PROM: In certain Sun systems, the PROM that contains such information as the serial number and Ethernet address.

IESG   See **Internet Engineering Steering Group.**

IETF   See **Internet Engineering Task Force.**

industry standard   Commonly agreed upon procedures or interfaces adopted to encourage interoperability.

inetd   The Internet daemon. The process that listens for requests and starts many network services in response. Inetd's configuration file is /etc/inetd.conf.

init   The process (procid 1) that starts at boot time and, essentially, starts all the other processes for the target run states. See **run states.**

initialization files   Another name for **dot files,** which, set in a user's home directory, establish paths, environment variables, and other operational characteristics.

integrity   The characteristic of data or files that remain intact.

inode   A data structure containing the critical parameters (i.e., metadata) describing a file (e.g., its size, location on disk, file permissions matrix, and access/update times).

input/output (I/O)   Data fed to or produced by software.

interface   Generally, the access provided to any process or program. A **GUI** is one type of interface.

Integrated services digital network (ISDN)   Combines voice and data on a single wire.

internationalization   The process of modifying a program so that it is usable in many geographical locations.

International Organization for Standardization (ISO)   An international organization that reviews products for conformance with standards for information exchange.

internet   A collection of networks used as a large network. Contrast this with the more popular term, **Internet.**

Internet   The loose connection of networks around the globe that makes international e-mail and World Wide Web browsing possible. Based on TCP/IP, the Internet works primarily because the protocols involved are rugged enough to survive data loss, disconnects, and nearly random routing.

Internet Activities Board (IAB)   Oversees development of protocols used on the Internet.

Internet address   A 32-bit address, using dotted decimal notation, that identifies a single host.

Internet Control Message Protocol (ICMP)   The control protocol of TCP/IP that manages errors and control messages. The ping command is the most prominent example of this protocol.

Internet Engineering Steering Group (IESG)   The executive committee of the Internet Engineering Task Force (IETF).

Internet Engineering Task Force (IETF)   One of the task forces of the Internet Activities Board (IAB). The IEFT has more than 40 working groups focusing on different aspects of the Internet.

Internet Packet Exchange/Sequenced Packet Exchange (IPX/SPX)   A Netware-4 specific protocol.

Internet Protocol (IP)   Relates to the networking layer of the TCP/IP protocol.

Internet Research Task Force (IRTF)   Task force responsible for research and development of Internet protocols.

interpreter   A program that translates high-level language into executable code one line at a time. Contrast with **compiler.**

interprocess control (IPC) A method for sharing data between processes.

interrupt: A signal that breaks (i.e., halts) a command or process.

interrupt request (IRQ) A signal requesting CPU attention.

I/O See **input/output.**

I/O bound The situation in which the use of input or production of output uses most of the resources of a system or process.

I/O control (ioct1) Relates to device control.

IP See **Internet Protocol.**

IP address See **Internet address.**

IPC See **interprocess control.**

IP datagram The basic unit of transmission on TCP/IP networks.

IP network number An IP address that identifies a network. For example, the address 222.12.34.0 represents a class C network composed of hosts 222.12.34.1 through 222.12.34.254.

IP Security (IPsec) A set of protocols being defined by the IETF to support secure packet exchange at the IP layer of TCP/IP communications.

IPX/SPX See **Internet Packet Exchange/Sequenced Packet Exchange.**

IRTF See **Internet Research Task Force.**

IRQ See **interrupt request.**

ISDN See **Integrated services digital network.**

ISO See **International Organization for Standardization.**

ISO 9660 An international standard for the format of CD-ROM drives. See **hsfs.**

Java An object-oriented language developed by Sun. Java is especially useful in Web applications through programs called *applets*.

JPEG A common format for color and grayscale image files, frequently used on the Web. The term derives from *Joint Photographic Experts Group*—the group that developed the standard.

JumpStart A Solaris installation method that uses profiles to facilitate installations of a large number of similar systems.

kernel The core of the Solaris operating system. The kernel manages the hardware and provides fundamental services (e.g., keeping track of running processes).

kernel architecture   The type of kernel on a given Solaris system.

kill   To stop a process by sending it a signal. The kill command sends signals of many types, most of which do not terminate the processes. See **signal.**

label   With respect to disks, the information written on a disk by the format program. It describes the disk geometry, including how the partitions are laid out. With respect to DNS, one element of a domain name. Labels need only be unique at a specific point in the tree.

Lance Ethernet (usually le0)   A 10Mb-per-second Ethernet interface used on many Sun systems.

LDAP   See **Lightweight Directory Access Protocol.**

library routines   Functions which can be called by user programs, generally those written in C.

Lightweight Directory Access Protocol (LDAP)   A method of simplifying access to a directory service modeled after X.500.

lightweight process (LWP)   Process that shares resources, thereby being less of a processing burden.

line editor   An editor that allows the user to work on the current line. Contrast with visual editor.

link   In general, a file that points to another file. **Symbolic links** (also called *soft links*) contain the names of the files they point to. **Hard links** are identical to files they are linked to.

Linux   A public-domain Unix operating system, primarily used on Intel systems as an alternative to Windows. Originally developed by Linus Torvalds.

little-endian   A way of storing binary data such that the less significant bits are stored first. Contrast with **big-endian.**

loadable kernel module   Software that can be thought of as part of the kernel, but is loaded only as needed, keeping the kernel small and efficient.

loading   The process of moving a process into memory.

local   Located on the system in front of the user, as opposed to somewhere else on the network.

Local file system   A file system on the particular host. Contrast with network-based file systems.

localization   The process of modifying a program so that it works properly in the location in which it is used.

locking   The process of making a file inaccessible to most users while it is being used by one user (or a process). Locking prevents users or processes from overwriting each other's changes.

LOFS   The loopback file system. Allows a file system to be used with an alternate path.

log   A file into which messages are stored (e.g., errors and messages about mail transfers).

login directory   The directory that a user enters when first logging in. This is almost always the user's home directory.

login shell   The shell assigned to a user in the passwd file or map.

logging   The behavior of a file system that keeps track of changes in a separate file. Logging simplifies and speeds up recovery from file system damage because the log file can be used to remake the changes.

low-water mark   A lower threshold. Compare with **high-water mark.**

lpd   Line printer daemon, a print manager in BSD. Contrast with **lpsched.**

lpq   A command to display the contents of a print queue in BSD. See also **lpstat.**

lpsched   A command that starts the print service.

lpstat   A command to view the contents of a print queue.

LWP   See **lightweight process.**

MAC   See **Message Authentication Code.**

MAC address   Another name for a hardware or Ethernet address.

magic number   A number or string stored in a file (usually at the very beginning) that identifies its type. The strings and file types are stored in the file /etc/magic.

mail client   A system that uses another (the mail server) to provide mail files and mail services.

mailing list   A list of e-mail addresses used for mailing to many users at once. See **alias.**

mail server   A system that receives mail on behalf of users, generally logged in on other systems.

major/minor device numbers   Numbers that identify devices attached to a system and allow the system to interact with these devices.

make   A command used to direct the compilation process for a program.

makefile A file used by the make command. Contains instructions about the compilation process.

management information base (MIB) A data structure on a managed device that determines what information can be collected from it by a management station.

manager A component in a distributed network management system that receives data from monitored systems.

man pages The standard Unix online documentation. Man pages are divided into sections (e.g., user commands, administrative commands, etc.) and are usually stored in nroff format.

mapping The process of relating information of one source or type with information of another source or type (e.g., mapping jost names to addresses).

master With respect to DNS and NIS/NIS+, the system from which changes are made and then propagated to slaves or replicas.

master browser An NT server that maintains a list of computers and resources available to clients. The master browser is contacted when a user attempts to use a network resource.

maximum transmission unit (MTU) The largest transmission that can be sent over a network. Most Internet routers communicate this information so that the smallest MTU of the network segments is used for the transmission.

MCP See **Microsoft Certified Professional.**

MCSE See **Microsoft Certified System Engineer.**

MD5 A secure hash algorithm developed by Ron Rivest.

mean time between failures (MTBF) The average amount of time before failures occur with respect to given hardware, determined by testing or extensive reporting.

Message Authentication Code (MAC) An algorithm that uses a secure key to ensure the integrity of a message.

metacharacter A character that has a special meaning to Unix or particular shells, generally used for pattern matching (e.g., $ or ?).

metadata Data that describes other data. For example, the attributes of a data file are metadata.

MIB See **management information base.**

Microsoft Certified Professional (MCP) An individual who has passed a series of tests on Microsoft technology.

Microsoft Certified System Engineer (MCSE)   An individual who has passed a different series of tests on Microsoft technology.

mkfs   Command used to create a new file system.

monitor   A video display or a simple program that runs before a system is booted.

monitoring   Watching or looking for problems or tracking the status of a system.

motherboard   The main circuit board in most computers.

mounting   The process of making a system available on a system. Contrast with **exporting** (sharing). See **unmounting.**

mount point   A directory on which a file system is to be mounted.

MTU   See **maximum transmission unit.**

multicast   A limited form of broadcast in which packets are sent to a subset of the possible hosts.

multihomed host   A system that is attached to more than one network (has more than one physical network interface).

multiprocessor   A system with more than one CPU.

multitasking   The process of running more than one task at a time. Unless a system has more than one CPU, multitasking actually involves running tasks so that they take turns on the CPU and *appear* to be running at the same time.

multithreading   The process by which a program can have more than one thread of control.

multiuser system   Any system that can be used by more than one person at a time.

MX   With respect to DNS, a mail exchange record. An MX record points to an SMTP mail server.

name   A string associated with an entity (user, file, device, etc.) generally known by the system by a number or address.

named pipe   A first in, first out (FIFO) file used for interprocess communication.

name space   The collection of names stored in a particular system.

National Institute of Standards and Technology (NIST)   Formerly the National Bureau of Standards.

NDS See **Novell Directory Services.**

NetBIOS With respect to Windows NT, an application program interface (API) allowing network resources to be called by name.

netgroup A collection of systems or users grouped together to facilitate their sharing of some network resource.

network The hardware, cabling, and other components and devices that connect systems together. The term generally refers to the equipment within organizational boundaries.

network-based file system A file system that is not stored and used on a single system. Contrast with **local file system.**

Network Information Service (NIS) A distributed network information service, originally called *Yellow Pages* (*yp*).

Network Information Service Plus (NIS+) The hierarchical and more secure network information service that was designed to replace NIS.

network news transfer protocol (NNTP) The protocol used with Usenet news groups.

network time protocol (NTP) A protocol for synchronizing time across systems.

newfs A command for creating a new file system.

newsgroups Electronic message groups (e.g., alt.doglovers) distributed worldwide.

new-line character The character that marks the end of a line in Unix ASCII files, octal 12.

NFS The distributed network file system developer by Sun and available for almost every operating system.

niceness value The priority value given to a Unix process. It is called *niceness* because users can lower the priority of their own processes, allowing other processes to run more quickly.

NIS See **Network Information Service.**

NIS domain The collection of information available from a NIS server.

NIS maps Collections of network information available for use on a network.

NIS+ See **Network Information Service Plus.**

NIS+ tables Collections of network information available for use on a network.

NIST   See **National Institute of Standards and Technology.**

NNTP   See **network news transfer protocol.**

node   A general term, usually synonymous with host.

nonvolatile memory   A memory device that does not lose its contents when power is lost.

Novell Directory Services (NDS)   A distributed computing infrastructure that maintains information about network resources.

nslookup   A tool used to make DNS queries, usually used for debugging. Contrast with **dig.**

NTFS   Windows NT file system. Includes a high-performance indexed directory structure. NTFS is not compatible with Windows 95 or DOS.

NTP   See **network time protocol.**

NVRAM   Nonvolatile random-access memory.

NVSIMM   A nonvolatile single in-line memory module (SIMM).

octal   The number system based on the number 8. Contrast with **hexadecimal** and **binary.**

octet   A byte—8 binary elements (bits).

ordinary file   A nonexecutable file.

output   Information or data produced by a command or process.

owner   The person associated with a file or directory. Contrast with **group.**

package   A Solaris-specific software format to facilitate installation and deinstallation.

packet   Data packaged for transmission over a network, including data and host addresses.

paging   The process of moving pages (chunks of data comprising processes and their data) in memory as needed to give all running processes opportunities to execute.

parameter   An argument to a command or program.

parent process   A process that has started another (child) process.

parity   A simple method used to ensure that data is not corrupted during transmission.

parity error   An indication that a transmission error has occurred.

partition A portion of the space on a disk, usually set up by the format program. Also called a **slice.**

password aging The process by which passwords eventually expire and must be replaced.

patch Generally, a replacement executable that repairs a bug in the original. Less frequently, a file insert for the same purpose.

patching Applying patches.

pathname The location of a file.

PC file system (pcfs) The file system type used to read and write DOS floppies.

PCT See **Private Communications Technology.**

PDC See **primary domain controller.**

peer A device, usually a computer, in the same general role as another.

peer-to-peer communication Interaction between devices working at the same level.

peripheral An external device (e.g., a printer or modem).

Perl The Practical Extraction and Report Language (or, as some prefer, the Pathologically Eclectic Rubbish Lister). Perl is an interpreted programming language that is especially adept at handling regular expressions and has many features missing from the standard shells.

permissions The set of bits that determines who can access a file and in what way.

PGP Pretty Good Privacy. An asymmetric encryption system developed by Phil Zimmermann. PGP is available as an insert for many client mail programs (e.g., Microsoft Outlook).

ping A small ICMP packet generally used to test connectivity. Ping is an *echo request* command. If the receiving system responds, the message "<hostname> is alive" is printed. The name *ping* stands for Packet Internet Groper, but this is a woeful description of what the command does. More likely, the command was named because of its similarity to the sonar echo.

pipe A Unix command element that makes the output of one process the input of the next.

PKCS See **Public Key Cryptography Standard.**

pointer See **link.**

point-to-point protocol (PPP)   A protocol for running TCP/IP on a serial line. A successor to SLIP, it provides network (IP) connections over dial-up lines. Contrast with **SLIP.**

poll   To periodically request status information from a device.

port   A communications end point used by network services.

portability   The feature of software that allows it to be moved and recompiled on systems different from the one it was developed on.

portmapper   A network service that keeps track of communications channels.

port monitor   A program that continuously watches for requests.

port numbers   The numeric port identifiers used by TCP/IP. Most are stored in the file /et/services.

POST   See **power-on self test.**

postmaster   The person who manages e-mail. The alias that directs messages about bounced mail and such to this person.

power-on self test (POST)   A set of tests run at boot time to check the hardware.

PPP   See **point-to-point protocol.**

primary domain controller (PDC)   A Windows NT service that authenticates logins and maintains the security policy for the domain. The PDC is also the default master browser. See **backup domain controller** and **master browser.**

primary server   With respect to DNS, a server that is authoritative and whose information is locally configured.

print client   A system that uses a print server to print.

print queue   A directory used to hold files waiting to be printed.

print server   A system that queues print requests and sends them to the printer when the printer is ready.

Private Communications Technology (PCT)   A secure protocol developed by Microsoft, intended as a successor to SSL 2.0.

private key   In an asymmetric encryption system, the key that is known only to the owner of the key pair. Contrast with **public key.**

process   A program and command while it is running or waiting for resources so that it can be run.

process file system (procfs)   A file system type used to provide interfaces to running processes and kernel structures.

process ID   The numeric identifier of a running process.

process status   The state of a process. Includes: running, stopped, and waiting, etc.

procfs   See **process file system.**

profile   Configuration information for a user on an NT system.

program   A file containing executable code, compiled or interpreted.

PROM   Programmable read-only memory.

PROM monitor   A simple program stored in the bootPROM, used for booting, system diagnostics, and configuration.

protocol   A formal set of exchanges, and the rules that govern them, allowing computers to work together.

proxy   A system that fronts for another in one way or another.

pseudo file system   A file system that does not correspond to files on a disk, but to some other structure or interface (e.g., swap space or running processes).

pseudouser   A username that is not associated with an actual individual, but with a function or process.

public key   In an asymmetric encryption system, the key that is publicly available. Contrast with **private key.**

Public Key Cryptography Standard (PKCS)   A cryptographic specification suite created by RSA.

query   A request for information on the part of a client system.

queue   A holding space for requests (e.g., print requests).

quota   A limit placed on users with respect to how much disk space they are allowed to use. For each user, there is a soft and hard limit determining when the user is warned about space and when the user can no longer create or edit files.

Radius   Remote access dial-in user service. A service that authenticates dial-in users. Radius is commonly run on remote access service (RAS) devices such as Cisco routers and Ascend RAS devices.

RAID   Redundant array of inexpensive disks. RAIDsystems operate as a single large drive and, usually, incorporate some level of file redundancy—for example, mirroring or striping with parity—to ensure that file systems survive the loss of a single disk.

RAM   Random-access memory. Sometimes referred to as *core* because early memory looked like tiny donuts with wires running through their cores. Contrast with **ROM.**

RARP   See **reverse address resolution protocol.**

RC4   A symmetric algorithm that uses keys of variable length (usually 40-bit or 128-bit), designed by Ron Rivest.

RSA   An asymmetric encryption algorithm used to create and verify digital signatures.

readme file   A file containing information that the user should read before configuring or installing software.

recursive   A computer program or procedure that calls itself.

redirection   The process by which the output of a command or program is directed into a file, diverting it from its normal display.

refresh   With respect to DNS, the time interval (in seconds) within which the secondaries should contact the primaries to compare the serial number in the SOA.

registry   A database of configuration information on Windows systems. Includes information about hardware, software, and settings.

regular expression   A pattern that selects a group of strings that have some component or substring in common. For example, the regular expression \d matches a single digit in Perl.

relative pathname   A pathname that is incomplete, relative to a particular directory (e.g., bin/myproc).

reliability   The characteristic of a system in which it produces consistent accurate answers.

remote procedure call (RPC)   A method for building client/server software.

remote shell (rsh)   A command that allows the user to run commands on a remote system.

remote system   A system other than the one the user is sitting at.

resolver   With respect to DNS, a client that seeks information using DNS.

reverse address resolution procotol (RARP)   The protocol on TCP/IP networks used to map physical to IP (network) addresses.

request for comments (RFC).   RFCs describe Internet protocols. The specification document, defined by the IETF and its steering group, the IESG, are available over the Internet from the Information Sciences Institute (ISI), University of Southern California.

rlogin   A telnetlike service that uses ~/.rhosts files and the file /etc/hosts.equiv in the authentication process.

robust   Reliable.

Rock Ridge file system   Extension on the High Sierra format that allows contents of a CD-ROM to look and act like a Unix file system.

root file system   The file system that contains files that describe the system.

root name servers   With respect to DNS, the servers responsible for the root-level domain (.).

root user   The superuser on Unix systems. Root is the privileged account and can, generally, do anything.

router   A system that makes routing decisions.

routing   The process of determining how to get packets from source to destination on a network or internet and getting them there.

RTU   Right to use.

run   To execute a program or command.

run level   The state in which a system is running, corresponding to the running processes and determined by the contents of the /etc/rc?.d directories. Also called run state.

runnable process   A process that is ready to run. In other words, it is not waiting for any resources other than the CPU.

SAC   See **Service Access Control.**

SAM   With respect to Windows NT, the Security Accounts Manager.

SCSI   See **small computer systems interface.**

sbus   The bus available on most Sun systems.

screen lock   A utility that locks a screen, requiring entry of the locking user's password to unlock.

screen saver   A utility that keeps a moving image on a screen or darkens it to prevent image burn in.

secondary server   With respect to DNS, an authoritative server which obtains its information from a primary using zone transfers.

Secure Shell (SSH)   The de facto standard for encrypted terminal connections. Replaces telnet in security-conscious organizations.

Secure Sockets Layer (SSL)   A protocol providing an encrypted and authenticated communications stream.

seek   A disk read operation that positions the read head at a certain location within a file.

segmentation fault   An error that occurs when a process tries to access some portion of memory that is restricted or does not exist.

sendmail   The primary mail exchange program on Unix systems.

serial number   With respect to DNS, a special (magic) number that is used strictly to determine whether secondaries are up to date.

server   A system that supplies services to other systems. A server can be a file server, print server, mail server, boot server, and so forth.

Service Access Control (SAC)   The Service Access Facility (SAF) master program.

SGML   Standardized Generalized Markup Language. See **HTML.**

shadow file   The file that holds the encrypted passwords in Solaris and other SVR4-based Unix systems.

sharing   Making file systems resources available to other clients on the net. See **exporting.**

shell   A command interpreter that interacts with a user and passes commands on to the kernel.

shell script   A file with shell commands that is made executable.

shell variable   A variable that determines how a shell operates.

signal   Any of a number of codes that can be sent to a process to tell it to do something. Typical signals tell a process to shut down (SIGKILL) or to reread its configuration file (SIGHUP). Signals are listed in the header file /usr/include /sys/signal.h.

SIMM   Single in-line memory module.

Simple Network Management Protocol (SNMP).   The most popularly used network management protocols.

slave server   A system that answers queries for the service in question (e.g., NIS), but on which changes are *not* made. Contrast with **master server** and **replica server.**

slice   Another word for **partition.**

SLIP   Serial-line Internet protocol. Contrast with **PPP.**

small computer systems interface (SCSI)   An industry standard bus used for connecting devices (e.g., disks and CD-ROMs) to a system.

SMS   Microsoft's System Management Service. A distributed management tool used to configure clients and servers.

SMTP   Simple Mail Transfer Protocol.

SNMP   See **Simple Network Management Protocol.**

SOA   See **start of authority.**

socket   A communications end point used by network communications—in particular, client/server applications.

sockfs   A file system type that provides access to network sockets.

soft limit   The lower limit, in disk quotas, at which the user is warned about the use of disk space, but still has time to react. Contrast with **hard limit.**

software distribution   Software as delivered by the manufacturer.

solution   An overused word describing hardware or software that answers a particular need.

source code   Programming commands in a language (e.g., C) that requires compilation.

source file   A file containing source code.

SPARC   Scalable Processor Architecture from Sun. SPARC is a reduced instruction set (RISC) processor.

spawn   A method by which a process creates another instance of itself.

specfs   A file system that provides access to device drivers. Contrast with **fork.**

spooling   Use of a special directory to hold files awaiting printing or some other processing.

spooling directory   A directory where files or messages are stored until they are printed or delivered.

SSH   See **Secure Shell.**

SSL   See **Secure Sockets Layer.**

stale NFS file handle   A file handle that is out of date with respect to the corresponding file on the server.

standalone   A system that does not require support from a server to run. Generally, standalone systems *are* connected to networks; the term is somewhat misleading.

standard error   The device to which Unix commands send error messages—by default, the monitor or terminal.

standard input   The device from which Unix commands receive input—by default, the keyboard.

standard output The device to which Unix commands send output—by default, the display or terminal.

start of authority (SOA) With respect to DNS, a record that contains the information that other name servers querying this one will require, and will determine how the data is handled by those name servers.

static RAM (SRAM) A RAM device that holds its contents as long as it receives power.

static distributed database A database that is distributed across numerous systems or sites, but remains relatively stable.

stealth server An authoritative server that is not listed.

stopped job A process that has been halted, but can be restarted.

striping Combining multiple disks into a single logical disk in such a way that the data is "striped" across all drives.

stub zone A zone that only replicates the NS records of a master zone.

subdirectory A directory located within another directory. Any directory, other than /, can be called a subdirectory.

subdomain With respect to DNS, a portion of a domain for which an authoritative name server exists.

subnet mask A mask that breaks a network address space into separate subnets.

subnetwork (subnet) A portion of a network separated off, generally by a router, to reduce traffic.

superblock A block on a disk that contains information about file systems.

SuperSPARC Module A card containing the SuperSPARC processor, memory, and cache controller.

superuser The privileged root user.

suspend To halt a process temporarily.

SVR4 AT&T System V, Release 4 operating system. SVR4 represents a merger between the Berkeley (BSD) and System V versions of Unix.

swap file A file used in addition to the swap partition.

SWAPFS A pseudo file system used for swapping.

swapping The process by which, when the demand for memory is excessive and the system is having difficulty maintaining the free memory list, entire processes (rather than just pages), are replaced in memory. Contrast with **paging.**

swap space   The memory/disk area used to transfer programs between disk and memory.

symbolic link   A special file that points to a file or directory. The contents of a symbolic link is the pathname to the file pointed to.

symmetric encryption   An encryption scheme that uses the same key for encryption and decryption.

symmetric multiprocessing   A form of multiprocessing in which multiple processors can run kernel-level code and run with equivalent status.

synchronous   Under the control of a timing signal.

syntax   A description of a command that shows how a command can be constructed, including arguments and options.

syslog   A general-purpose logging service available in Unix systems. Syslog maintains logs on behalf of many services. Its configuration file is /etc/syslog.conf.

system administrator   The person responsible for configuring and managing systems, especially servers.

system board   On Sun systems, a circuit board with CPUs installed.

system call   A request by a program for kernel support.

System V   A version of Unix produced by AT&T. See **SVR4.**

T1   A leased-line network connection providing 1,554,000 bits per second on twisted copper wire.

tar file   A file, usually for archiving, created by the tar command.

TCP   See **Transport Control Protocol.**

TCP/IP   See **Transmission Control Protocol/Internet Protocol.**

telnet   The virtual terminal tool used most frequently to login to remote systems. Contrast with rlogin and ssh.

temporary file system (TMPFS)   A file system that uses memory and swap space. See **swapping.**

terminal   A physical device or pseudo device for logging in and interacting with a computer.

terminal type   The name that identifies a physical terminal or emulation.

TFTP   See **trivial file transfer protocol.**

third party   A general term used to describe a product that is not associated with your system manufacturer or your own development efforts: not you and not Sun; therefore, third party.

time to live (TTL)   With respect to DNS, the length of time that an address is valid before an authoritative name server needs to be asked again.

TLI   Transport Level Interface.

TMPFS   See **temporary file system.**

TODC   Time-of-day clock.

token   (1) An indivisible unit of a programming language; (2) A succession of bits sent from one system to another to pass control (as in a token-ring network); (3) A hand-held device used in certain three-factor security systems (e.g., SecurID).

top   A utility for looking at processes—especially useful in determining which processes are using most of the CPU resources. Developed by Bill LeFebvre.

traceroute   A tool that traces the route that a packet takes over the Internet. Uses TTL and ICMP time-exceeded messages to report successive nodes in the route and timing.

traffic   The collection of packets (frames) on a network

traffic generator   A tool that creates arbitrary packets for network testing or traffic simulation

Transport Control Protocol (TCP)   The major transport protocol in TCP/IP. TCP provides a reliable connection-oriented stream delivery service and is one of the core internet protocols. TCP provides a full-duplex connection between two machines on an internet and provides for efficient data transfer across networks across different communications protocols.

Transport Control Protocol/Internet Protocol (TCP/IP)   A suite of protocols that forms the primary protocol on the Internet and most heterogeneous networks.

Transport Layer Security (TLS)   A protocol (and the IETF group working on it) for encrypted and authenticated communications. TLS is based on SSL.

tree   With respect to DNS, the entire structure starting from the root and descending to each and every host.

trivial file transfer protocol (TFTP)   A simple file transfer tool.

trust   The process by which one system extends privilege to another (e.g., accepting a remote system's authentication of a user). On Unix systems, trust involves the /etc/hosts.equiv and ~/.rhosts files.

UDP See **user datagram protocol.**

UFS UNIX file system.

UID User ID.

UID number The numeric ID associated with a user.

Unix An operating system descending from the original Unix developed at Bell Labs in 1969. The key features of Unix are that it is an interactive, multi-user, time-sharing system with a very modular design. Few of us today can remember who exactly it is that owns the term or whether the name, in fact, can be validly used when talking about Solaris or Linux. At the same time, we call ourselves Unix systems administrators and everyone knows exactly what we mean.

unbundled Not included as part of the original purpose. For Solaris, not part of the operating system, but purchased separately.

unmount The process of removing a mount, removing access to a remote file system.

user datagram protocol (UDP) Part of the TCP/IP protocol suite. A connectionless protocol above IP in the protocol stack, it includes a protocol port number for the source and the target, allowing it to distinguish between different application programs on the source and target systems.

user name The string of characters used to identify a user. The user name is associated with the UID in the passwd file.

UTP Unshielded twisted pair. A particular cabling used for network. Categories (e.g., cat 3 or cat 5 determine the network speeds possible. The twisting rate of the cable is an extremely important factor in transmission.

value-added reseller (VAR) Generally, a company that promises added value if you purchase from them rather than from the manufacturer.

variable A parameter that changes value.

virtual memory The extension of physical memory to a larger space.

visual editor An editor that allows a user to move through a file with cursor commands. Contrast with **line editor.**

volatile memory Memory that loses its data when there is no power. Compare with **nonvolatile memory.**

wide-area network (WAN) A network that covers a large geographic area and is generally composed of a number of distinct local-area networks (LANs).

wildcard A character, or metacharacter, that matches one or a number of characters. For example, *?* in a shell represents a single character.

Windows NT server   A 32-bit operating environment intended to support network services.

Windows NT workstation   A client version of Windows NT.

WINS   Windows Internet Name Service. A Windows implementation of DNS. See **domain network system** and **BIND.**

word   A unit of data storage, the length of which depends on the system type. The word length on a Sun SPARCstation is 32 bits.

WWW   World Wide Web.

X.509   A standard that specifies the format of certificates.

X11   The X Window System, Version 11, developed at MIT.

X Display Manager (XDM)   An OpenWindows program that manages X displays.

xdmcp   X display management console protocol.

X server   In the X protocol, the server is the system that serves windows to a user (i.e., the user's local system).

zone   With respect to DNS, a boundary for a name server's authoritativeness. A zone relates to the way the DNS database is partitioned and distributed.

Special credits: Much of the material in Chapter 12 was first presented as a column in *SunWorld* magazine, August 1997. Some of the material in Chapter 5 was first presented as a column in *SunExpert*, August 1998.

Birdsall, James W., *Sun Hardware Reference. http://www.si.unix-ag.org/faqs/ SUN-HW-FAQ.html*, 1994.

Budlong, Mo. Command line psychology 101. *SunWorld*, February 1999.

Budlong, Mo. Getting started with Perl, Part 1: An introduction to the language that "can do anything." *SunWorld*, May 1999.

Budlong, Mo. Getting started with Perl, Part 2: Tricks for calling Perl functions by reference. *SunWorld*, June 1999.

Budlong, Mo. Tips on good shell programming practices: What #! really does. *SunWorld*, September 1999.

Cockcroft, Adrian. Adrian Cockroft's frequently asked (performance) questions. *SunWorld*, ongoing.

Cockcroft, Adrian. Disk error detection: What tools can warn you about disk failure automatically—and efficiently—before your disks fail? *SunWorld*, July 1999.

Cockcroft, Adrian. How to optimize caching file accesses. *SunWorld*, March 1997.

Cockcroft, Adrian. Performance Q&A compendium. *SunWorld*, December 1995.

Cockcroft, Adrian. Prying into processes and workloads. *SunWorld*, April 1998.

Cockcroft, Adrian, "Sun Performance and Tuning: Java and the Internet," Second Edition. Sun Microsystems, 1998

Cockcroft, Adrian. Upgrades for SyMON and SE: What's changed in these helpful utilities? Find out here. *SunWorld*, February 1999.

Cockcroft, Adrian. What does 100 percent busy mean? *SunWorld*, August 1999.

Cockcroft, Adrian. What's the best way to probe processes? *SunWorld*, August 1996.

Cook, Rick. Solaris and Windows NT: The odd couple gets cozy. *SunWorld*, January 1999.

Costales, Bryan, with Eric Allman. *sendmail*, Second Edition. Sebastopol, CA: O'Reilly & Associates, 1997.

Galvin, Peter. Enter the Secure Shell. *SunWorld*, February 1999.

Galvin, Peter. More on mastering the Secure Shell. *SunWorld*, March 1999.

Galvin, Peter. The power of /proc: Using proc tools to solve your system problems. *SunWorld*, April 1999.

Galvin, Peter. Stop your fire-fighting. *SunWorld*, September 1999.

Henry, S. Lee. Pitching Patches. *SunExpert*, August 1998.

Henry, S. Lee, and John R. Graham. *Solaris 2.x: A System Administrator's Guide*. New York: McGraw-Hill, 1995.

Jones, Sharis L. Which server is best when mixing Windows NT into a Solaris network? *SunWorld*, August 1999.

Kasper, Paul Anthony, and Alan L. McClellan. *Automating Solaris Installations: A Custom JumpStart Guide*. Englewood Cliffs, N.J.: Sun Microsystems/Prentice Hall, 1996.

Laird, Cameron, and Kathryn Soraiz. POP goes the server: What considerations should you take into account when choosing a POP service for your Unix e-mail server? *SunWorld*, May 1999.

Marks, Evan. Create a highly available environment for your mission-critical applications. *SunWorld*, August 1997.

McDougall, Richard. Getting to know the Solaris filesystem, Part 1: Learn all about the inner workings of your on-disk filesystem, including allocation management, storage capacity and access control list support, and metadata logging. *SunWorld*, May 1999.

McDougall, Richard. Getting to know the Solaris filesystem, Part 2: What factors influence filesystem performance? *SunWorld*, May 1999.

McDougall, Richard. Getting to know the Solaris filesystem, Part 3: How is file data cached? Interactions between the filesystem cache and the virtual memory system explained *SunWorld*, July 1999.

Musciano, Chuck. How to manage and implement change in your Unix environment: When are changes necessary—and when should they be avoided? *SunWorld*, March 1999.

Musciano, Chuck. RAID basics, Part 3: Understanding the implementation of hardware- and software-based solutions: What are the benefits and drawbacks of each? *SunWorld*, August 1999.

Musciano, Chuck. RAID basics, Part 4: Uniting systems and storage: Learn how to connect your new RAID system to your servers. *SunWorld*, September 1999.

Pérez, Juan Carlos. Samba Windows-Unix tool is updated—Web-based admin capabilities added. IDG News Service, January 15, 1999.

Ramsey, Rick, *All About Administering NIS+*, Second Edition. Englewood Cliffs: N.J. Sun Microsystems, 1996.

Shah, Rawn. Building a reliable NT server, Part 1. *SunWorld*, January 1999.

Shah, Rawn. Building a reliable NT server, Part 2. *SunWorld*, February 1999.

Shah, Rawn. Building a reliable NT server, Part 3. *SunWorld*, March 1999.

Shah, Rawn. Building a reliable NT server, Part 4. *SunWorld*, April 1999.

Shah, Rawn. Building a reliable NT server, Part 5. *SunWorld*, May 1999.

Shah, Rawn. Microsoft steps further into NT-Unix integration. *SunWorld*, December 1998.

Shah, Rawn. Storage beyond RAID. *SunWorld*, July 1999.

Shah, Rawn. What is RAID? And what can it do for your network? *SunWorld*, June 1999.

Stern, Hal. ARP networking tricks. *SunWorld*, May 1997.

Stern, Hal. An automounter and NFS potpourri. *SunWorld*, July 1996.

Stern, Hal. Here's how you too can understand device numbers and mapping in Solaris. *SunWorld*, December 1996.

Stern, Hal. How can you make the network yente work for you. *SunWorld*, March 1997.

Stern, Hal. *Managing NFS and NIS*. Sebastopol, CA: O'Reilly & Associates, 1991.

Stern, Hal. Twisty little passages all autmounted alike. *SunWorld*, June 1996.

Stern, Hal. The Unix Automounter. *SunWorld*, May 1996.

Sutton, Steve. *An Intro to Windows NT Security. www.trustedsystems.com*, October 24, 1997.

Wong, Brian L. *Configuration and Capacity Planning for Solaris Servers*, Upper Saddle River, N.J.: Sun Microsystems/Prentice Hall, 1997.

Zajac, Blair. Watching your systems in realtime: What tools can you use and how do they work? *SunWorld*, July 1999.